THE CONVERSATIONS OF DR. JOHNSON

THE GOSPEL ACCORDING TO DR. JOHNSON

The Conversations of
DR. JOHNSON

Extracted from the *Life* by James Boswell

and Edited with a Preface by
RAYMOND POSTGATE

TAPLINGER PUBLISHING COMPANY

NEW YORK

This edition first published in the United States in 1970 by
TAPLINGER PUBLISHING CO., INC.
New York, New York

© this edition Raymond Postgate 1930

ISBN 0 8008 4735 0
Library of Congress Catalog Card Number 70-121337

Printed in Great Britain
by Latimer Trend & Co. Ltd., Whitstable

CONTENTS

Preface

. . . I at first intended to resent his meddling with my writings, but,
when I considered how mean an adversary he was, and at that probably
in indigent circumstances, why, sir, I forbore. . . .

SOME TWENTY years ago, when I first made the selection republished here, I printed the sentence above as a sort of plea for
indulgence of my audacity. I cannot find where it came from; it
may be Johnson's, or it may be Johnsonese. But there is some
excuse for "meddling", not indeed with his writings but with what
was written about him. Arnold Bennett described "the first forty
years of Boswell" as an almost impassable obstacle. The first forty
years are not the only obstacle. Boswell, with comprehensible piety,
inserted throughout his *Life* matter that has long ago become
tedious. Few now read the many letters of Dr. Johnson. None at
all, it is fairly safe to say, read the analyses of his books and the lists
of variant readings. Such matter has been cut away in this edition.
What has been retained is that for which every reader turns to
Boswell—the conversations of Dr. Johnson. Even here it seemed
permissible to cut something in order to reduce the gigantic *Life*
to dimensions that the ordinary man can comfortably read. There
are in particular recommendations of devotional and other books no
longer obtainable, and criticisms or praise of authors no longer read.
With these exceptions, it will be found that no important conversations and discussions have been omitted. Nothing, of course,
has been added, except a few connecting words in square brackets.
But I have translated Latin quotations in footnotes, and under the
date of October 10th 1779 I have restored Boswell's original
account of Johnson's remarks on fornication. These, as was
pointed out in *Life and Letters* for September 1930 just after my
original edition appeared, were printed in a few copies of the
first edition but were hastily suppressed by Boswell as likely to
give offence; "it is, however, mighty good stuff" he said.

It is only by his conversations that Johnson is now remembered.
Macaulay many years ago commented upon his "singular destiny

7

—to be regarded in his own age as a classic, and in ours as a companion." His *Dictionary* has long ago been superseded, his *Shakespeare* is never consulted, very few people open the files of *The Rambler* or *The Idler*, his verse is neglected, *Rasselas* unread, and it is chiefly students who still turn to his *Lives of the Poets*. But there is scarcely a reading man who does not delight in his conversation. On the face of it this is surprising. As soon as one analyses Dr. Johnson's conversation, enormous faults appear. Dr. Johnson's mind was limited. He was not only a Tory, he was that peculiarly immovable and disastrous Tory who really believes that all forms of government are almost equally bad. His prejudices were violent, his temper was short, and his conversational manners were atrocious. For reformers of all kinds, English or American, he had an intense dislike and if in his conversation his scepticism was not enough to silence them, a plain and fairly gross insult would follow. "Sir, I perceive you are a vile Whig" may have been said gaily, but there are many similar remarks recorded which were certainly not said in a gentle tone. Except in religion, he did not often express, or even praise in others, an elevated sentiment. And even in the sphere of religion, his conversation can bring but little consolation to those of his readers who look for that form of solace. Johnson's religion was a thing of horror and melancholy; he passed most of his life, if we are to believe his biographer, in a condition of misery and apprehension which did not give way to calm, if at all, until the last few days of his life. Yet there has been nobody, except perhaps the fantastic Lord Monboddo, who disliked to read the record of his talk. Even reformers and radicals have attempted to claim some portion of it for their own; they persist, despite repeated correction, in reading their own meaning into his saying "Patriotism is the last refuge of a scoundrel." For Johnson's conversation possesses two qualities, which, assumed to be common, are in fact extremely rare: wit and commonsense. His wit gives him the victory over his antagonists and his commonsense in at least eight cases out of ten adds our approval to our admiration. Other speakers attack him, or they bring forward fallacious theories, or they fall into casual inaccuracies. Johnson's wit routs his antagonists, his clear commonsense brings order into thoughtless confusion, his keenness of mind exposes conventional errors, and if his manner is rough, his good nature is obvious. We watch him with the same admiration that we give to the boxer at a fair who offers to take on all comers, and fulfils his boast by knocking down

8

one after another the corner boys of the village. There is yet another cause for Johnson's popularity, which will last for so long as there are men with an inferiority complex to release. The ordinary man, especially the ordinary man of the middle-class whose verdict has great weight in conferring immortality, knows or suspects that he cannot write plays like Shakespeare, speak like Lloyd George, or compose like Beethoven. But he sees in Johnson the figure of the man he might be and hopes he is. He sees himself too striking the table with his fist, and crushing opposition with a remark beginning "No, Sir!" Perhaps in fact he finds it difficult to carry the sentence any further, perhaps his son and daughter are not awed into silence, perhaps his intervention is even drowned by the wireless. But always in his mind is a radiant figure of himself the admired centre of the room, humiliating cranks and silencing radicals by his jovial wit and hard commonsense.

Early Life of Dr. Johnson

Samuel Johnson was born at Lichfield in Staffordshire on September 18th, 1709. He was the son of Michael Johnson, a bookseller and high Tory and sentimental Jacobite. The child was strong, and indeed was always powerful. But very early on he was disfigured and nearly blinded by the "King's evil", scrofula. Every remedy was tried in vain, even that of taking the child to London where he was touched by Queen Anne in accordance with the old superstition; he remained shortsighted to the end of his life. He was taught at a dame's school and then at Lichfield school, where discipline was as brutal as was usual in the eighteenth century. Johnson himself defended this brutality later in life, telling how Hunter, the headmaster, while flogging the boys unmercifully used to say, "And this I do to save you from the gallows." In recounting this Johnson advocated the same treatment for the opposite sex; but in a less truculent mood he admitted that Hunter "would ask a boy a question and if he did not answer it, he would beat him, without considering whether he had an opportunity of knowing how to answer it. For instance, he would call up a boy and ask him the Latin for a candlestick, which the boy could not expect to be asked." Johnson proved a clever boy, with an admirable memory and an immoderate appetite for reading. At fifteen he was sent to Stourbridge school where he remained a year; for two years after he remained at home, reading enormously but without plan or order. In 1728, his father having received some assistance to that end from a friend, he was sent up to Oxford, and took up residence at Pembroke College. His learning was already great, if irregular: he was given a tutor more for form's sake than anything else. He was active and turbulent, witty and at first merry, and often the centre of an insubordinate group of students. But he was now first attacked by a "morbid melancholy" which pursued him throughout his life and which, after his indolence, was the greatest enemy of his mental activity. Moreover, his father was poor and was growing poorer; Johnson was soon ill-clad and perhaps even hungry.

Before long the promised aid failed and in 1731 he had to leave the University without a degree and almost destitute. He forthwith took a place as usher (assistant-master) in a school at Market Bosworth. He was ill-paid, and ill-suited to the work. He soon left this post and made an effort to support himself by writing and translating, but earned very little, and lived as best he could in the house of a Birmingham friend named Hector.

It was at this time (1736) that he married. A marriage in such conditions was strange; the choice that he made was stranger still. Mrs. Porter was a widow double his age, she was affected, florid and vulgar in her behaviour, she was fat, redfaced, plain and not even wealthy. Macaulay in calling her a "raddled grandmother" merely translated into coarser phrase the descriptions which all who knew her have left. All but one, for Johnson never wavered in his devotion to his beloved "Tetty," which was his loving but provincial abbreviation of her name Elizabeth. For a year and a half this ludicrous pair attempted to run an academy near Lichfield, but secured no more than three pupils, one of whom was David Garrick, afterwards the famous actor.

In 1737, despairing of success in the provinces, Johnson accompanied his late pupil Garrick to London. Here he endured the worst sufferings of his career, and acquired those habits which marked him so strongly in later life. His method of eating, or rather tearing, his food greedily till he was gorged and the veins stood out on his forehead, his uncleanly linen, his grunts, blowings and gurgitations, his rollings and other uncontrolled motions of his face and limbs, his abruptness and even rudeness of manner, all date from this time when he lived in filth and misery, rarely certain where his next meal would come from. He had come to London at a most unfortunate time. A previous generation of writers had often been rewarded by political patronage and even gifts of important posts. A later generation had the opportunity of securing comfort by the sales of its work to the public. But at this time Sir Robert Walpole and his colleagues regarded money spent upon authors as little more than an embezzlement of funds which should have been devoted to bribing the House of Commons, while the sales of books to the general world was such that the publisher-booksellers could offer only the smallest rewards.

Johnson had written a tragedy, *Irene*, but nobody would produce it. Nor did he secure profitable employment until Edward Cave, the publisher of the *Gentleman's Magazine*, engaged him as a regular writer. He contributed articles of every kind, of which the most interesting were the reports of the "Senate of Lilliput," disguised accounts of the debates in Parliament, which it was forbidden to publish openly. Watchers brought Johnson brief notes of what the chief speakers had said and from these he reconstructed the debate, taking care (as he was frank enough to admit later) that "the Whig dogs" should have the worst of it. In 1738 he published *London, A Poem* an imitation of the third satire of Juvenal, which was the first of his works to gain public attention. It was praised by the great Pope himself. Indeed, Johnson, who was now living an almost disorderly life under the influence of the wild and ill-fated poet Richard Savage, did not suffer from exceptional neglect and obscurity. He was early distinguished among the crowd of Grub street writers: the root of the evil was that it was impossible for all but the most fortunate to earn a living by writing at all. Most of his writing continued to be done for Cave, but he wrote the introduction and part of the descriptions in the Catalogue of the Harleian Library for another publisher, Osborne. Osborne was unwise enough to be discourteous to his unkempt but robust client; Johnson knocked him down and beat him.

Johnson's next separate publication of any importance was his *Life* of his friend Richard Savage, published in 1744, shortly after Savage's death. Three years later he undertook the work which was to make him famous, the publication of his *Dictionary of the English Language*. Seven publisher-booksellers (the two trades were not separated) representing five firms contracted with him for the work. The price was £1,575, and the prospectus was inscribed to Lord Chesterfield. Johnson threw himself into the work, whose magnitude nobody had fully apprehended, with great but spasmodic energy. He did not indeed abstain wholly from other writings—in 1749 he published a much-admired poem on *The Vanity of Human Wishes*, an imitation of Juvenal's tenth satire— but for some period of time his chief attention and that of six clerks was given to the Dictionary. But the difficulty and length of the work continually adjourned the date of publication, and Johnson's attention gradually wandered to other things. Garrick's loyal presentation of his tragedy *Irene* upon the stage, which occurred in 1749, was a failure. But the next year Johnson began an enterprise which rapidly increased his reputation. He started a magazine called *The Rambler*. It was issued twice a week for two years and contained essays and sketches which were intended to recall the *Spectator* and the *Tatler*. As a periodical it was merely admired, but when it was reissued in volume form, it gained a popularity whose immensity astounds us. The style is " Johnsonese," weighted with Latin words and slow-moving. There is neither imagination nor sprightliness in its columns, and a comparison with Addison results wholly in the earlier writer's favour. Nevertheless, its publication secured for Johnson an eminence among English writers which was the first step to the dominance he was soon to achieve.

Immediately after he had ceased to write the *Rambler*—in March 1752—his mind received a severe shock, and his depression was greatly increased, by the death of his strange old wife, for whom he grieved long and sincerely.

At last, in 1755, it became clear that the dictionary was approaching completion, and even the least alert were aware that its author's increased reputation would make it a work of far greater authority than might have appeared probable when it was first proposed. Lord Chesterfield, nominally the author's patron, had "dropped" him entirely in the intervening period, practically excluding him from his house. He now made a belated attempt to recover his position, by writing two fulsome "puffs" of the forthcoming work in a magazine called *The World*. For sole reward he received a letter which is one of the few of Johnson's which have become immortal:

"To the Right Honourable the Earl of Chesterfield.

"My Lord,

February 7, 1755.

" I have been lately informed, by the proprietor of *The World*, that two papers, in which my Dictionary is recommended to the publick, were written by your Lordship. To be so distinguished is an honour, which, being very little accustomed to favours from the great, I know not well how to receive, or in what terms to acknowledge.

"When, upon some slight encouragement, I first visited your Lordship, I was overpowered, like the rest of mankind, by the enchantment of your address, and could not forbear to wish that I might boast myself *Le vainqueur du vainqueur de la terre*;—that I might obtain that regard for which I saw the world contending; but I found my attendance so little encouraged, that neither pride nor modesty would suffer me to continue it. When I had once addressed your Lordship in publick, I had exhausted all the art of pleasing which a retired and uncourtly scholar can possess. I had done all that I could; and no man is well pleased to have his all neglected, be it ever so little.

"Seven years, my Lord, have now passed, since I waited in your outward rooms, or was repulsed from your door; during which time I have been pushing on my work through difficulties, of which it is useless to complain, and have brought it, at last, to the verge of publication, without one act of assistance, one word of encouragement, or one smile of favour. Such treatment I did not expect, for I never had a Patron before.

"The shepherd in Virgil grew at last acquainted with Love, and found him a native of the rocks.

"Is not a Patron, my Lord, one who looks with unconcern on a man struggling for life in the water, and when he has reached ground, encumbers him with help? The notice which you have been pleased to take of my labours, had it been early, had been kind; but it has been delayed till I am indifferent, and cannot enjoy it; till I am solitary, and cannot impart it; till I am known, and do not want it. I hope it is no very cynical asperity, not to confess obligations where no benefit has been received, or to be unwilling that the Publick should consider me as owing that to a Patron, which Providence has enabled me to do for myself.

"Having carried on my work thus far with so little obligation to any favourer of learning, I shall not be disappointed though I should conclude it, if less be possible, with less; for I have been long wakened from that dream of hope, on which I once boasted myself with so much exultation,
"My Lord,
"Your Lordship's most humble
"Most obedient servant,
"SAM. JOHNSON."

The *Dictionary*, when it appeared, achieved a success which after ages have fully confirmed. It has proved the foundation of English lexicography. Its merits were fully appreciated at the time, and the esteem with which it was received gave Johnson a peculiarly pleasing prominence, for he was now not only an eminent writer, but one believed to be particularly qualified to lay down what was or was not good English.

But if his reputation was assured, his livelihood was not. He was even twice arrested for debt. To support himself he took in subscriptions for an edition of Shakespeare which he did not commence, and in 1758 he began the publication of a continuation of the *Rambler*, called *The Idler*, which he continued till 1760, with considerable profit. Nevertheless when his mother died in 1759 he was still so straitened for money that he had to provide, in part at least, for her funeral expenses by hastily writing a short novel called *Rasselas, Prince of Abyssinia*, a most peculiar production, which still retains considerable fame. Though cast in the form of a novel, it consists much more of a philosophical discussion, without the liveliness of *Candide*, to prove the same thesis—that this present life is on the whole evil. For this novel, though it became immediately popular, Johnson only received £100. His circumstances were not permanently eased until 1762, when Lord Bute, on behalf of the newly-crowned George III, offered him a pension of £300 a year. The offer somewhat embarrassed him. He had been in the habit of parading to his friends a sentimental and superficial Jacobitism, and in his dictionary he had defined a pensioner as a slave of state hired by a stipend to obey a master. But he consulted his friends, who advised him that these were no reasons to make him refuse. He accepted, and Lord Bute at their interview said to him expressly, "This is not given you for anything that you are to do, but for what you have done."

Now Johnson was at last enabled to rest, and his natural indolence saw to it that he did. For some years he seems to have done scarcely any work at all. The Shakespeare that he promised, and for which he had drawn subscriptions, did not appear. Eventually, Charles Churchill, a political enemy, publicly accused him of cheating. Macaulay, once again, has summed up the result as fairly as may be. "This terrible word proved effectual; and in October 1765, appeared, after a delay of nine years, the new edition of Shakespeare. This publication saved Johnson's character for honesty but added nothing to the fame of his abilities and learning."

It was shortly before this, in 1763, that Johnson met Boswell, in the circumstances which are described in this book. James Boswell was a young Scotsman whose passion it was to hunt down celebrities and interview them—Paoli, Rousseau, Wilkes or Johnson, no matter whom. He was the heir to the laird of Auchinleck in Scotland, he had money and conceit, and an absolute imperviousness to snubs. Vain, drunken, and rather silly, he was nevertheless the ideal attendant for Johnson and he wrote what is still perhaps the best biography ever written. Whenever he visited London he attached himself to Johnson and made elaborate notes of his conversations. He gained Johnson's affection and in 1773 even induced him to journey with him to the Western Hebrides, despite his dislike for the Scotch. Johnson published an *Account* of this journey in 1775, and this, with the exception of a couple of unimportant and inferior pamphlets, was his sole publication until 1779. In that year and in 1781 he published a series of *Lives of the Poets*, in ten small volumes, the last of his works and the only one which is now commonly consulted from motives other than curiosity.

It was thus at a fortunate time that Boswell made Johnson's acquaintance. The amount of writing that Johnson did in the rest of his life was barely sufficient to keep him occupied. The treasures of his mind he henceforth spilt into his conversation. He had dignity as well as leisure. He had received from Oxford university the doctor's degree which gave him the title by which he is universally known. He was surrounded by the esteem and admiration of those whose good opinion he most desired. From 1764 onwards he was the chief and most revered member of a club which allowed itself no title but that of "The Club" and whose verdicts rapidly acquired a half autocratic power over London thought. Among its members were Oliver Goldsmith the poet, David Garrick the actor, Sir Joshua Reynolds the painter, Edward Gibbon the historian, and Edmund Burke the politician. Less-known, but as dear or dearer to Johnson were Bennet Langton, a pious Greek scholar, and Topham Beauclerk, a rake and a wit. Outside this literary circle his closest friends were Mr. and Mrs. Thrale. Thrale, a wealthy brewer, received Johnson regularly at his house at Streatham, and at certain periods it seems that nearly half of Johnson's life was spent under the Thrales' roof. The close affection which united them diminished after Thrale's death, and was wholly severed when Mrs. Thrale married again in 1784. Her choice was an Italian music-master, named Piozzi, and for her decision she was pursued with a derision and contempt which to this generation seems wholly unreasonable and ungenerous.

In Johnson's own house, a dark and small building off Fleet Street, was quartered a strange assembly of the ugly, old, blind or diseased who were in receipt of his bounty, and rewarded it by continual quarrelling and complaining. At the head of the household was an elderly, blind and peevish lady named Williams. There was also another poor and old woman, Mrs. Desmoulins, and her daughter, and another destitute female, Polly Carmichael, whom her benefactor described briefly as "a stupid slut." "I had some hopes of her at first," he told Mrs. Thrale, "but when I talked to her closely and tightly, I could make nothing of her; she was wiggle-waggle, and I could never persuade her to be categorical." On the male side there were Levett, an old and incompetent quack doctor, and Frank, a negro servant.

Such then, was the condition of Dr. Johnson when Boswell became his friend. From thence till his death on December 13th, 1784, his life is best recorded in the pages that follow.

CHAPTER I

Boswell's Meeting with Dr. Johnson. Conversations in Seventeen Sixty-three

ON MONDAY the 16th of May, 1763, when I was sitting in the back parlour of Mr. Thomas Davies, the bookseller, in London, after having drunk tea with him and Mrs. Davies, Johnson unexpectedly came into the shop; and Mr. Davies having perceived him through the glass-door in the room in which we were sitting, advancing towards us,—he announced his awful approach to me, somewhat in the manner of an actor in the part of Horatio, when he addresses Hamlet on the appearance of his father's ghost, "Look, my Lord, it comes." I found that I had a very perfect idea of Johnson's figure, from the portrait of him painted by Sir Joshua Reynolds soon after he had published his Dictionary, in the attitude of sitting in his easy chair in deep meditation; which was the first picture his friend did for him, which Sir Joshua very kindly presented to me. Mr. Davies mentioned my name, and respectfully introduced me to him. I was much agitated; and recollecting his prejudice against the Scotch, of which I had heard much, I said to Davies, "Don't tell where I come from."—"From Scotland," cried Davies, roguishly. "Mr. Johnson, (said I) I do indeed come from Scotland, but I cannot help it." I am willing to flatter myself that I meant this as light pleasantry to soothe and conciliate him, and not as an humiliating abasement at the expense of my country. But however that might be, this speech was somewhat unlucky; for with that quickness of wit for which he was so remarkable, he seized the expression "come from Scotland," which I used in the sense of being of that country; and, as if I had said that I had come away from it, or left it, retorted, "That, Sir, I find, is what a very great many of your countrymen cannot help." This stroke stunned me a good deal; and when we had sat down, I felt myself not a little embarrassed, and apprehensive of what might come next. He then addressed himself to Davies: "What do you think of Garrick? He has refused me an order for the play for Miss Williams, because he knows the house will be full, and that an order would be worth three shillings." Eager to take any opening to get into conversation with him, I ventured to say, "O, Sir, I cannot think Mr. Garrick would grudge such a trifle to you." "Sir, (said he, with a stern look,) I have known David Garrick longer than you have done: and I know no right you have to talk to me on the subject." Perhaps I deserved this check; for it was rather presumptuous in me, an entire stranger, to express any doubts of the justice of his animadversion upon his old acquaintance and pupil. I now felt myself much mortified, and began to think, that the hope which I had long indulged of obtaining his acquaintance was blasted. And, in truth, had not my ardour been uncommonly strong, and my resolution uncommonly persevering, so rough a reception might have deterred me for ever from making any further attempts. Fortunately, however, I remained upon the field not wholly discomfited.

I was highly pleased with the extraordinary vigour of his conversation, and regretted that I was drawn away from it by an engagement at another place. I had, for a part of the evening, been left alone with him, and had ventured to make an observation now and then, which he received very civilly; so that I was satisfied that though there was a roughness in his manner, there was no ill-nature in his disposition. Davies followed me to the door, and when I complained to him a little of the hard blows which the great man had given me, he kindly took upon him to console me by saying, "Don't be uneasy. I can see he likes you very well."

A few days afterwards I called on Davies, and asked him if he thought I might take the liberty of waiting on Mr. Johnson at his chambers in the Temple. He said I certainly might, and that Mr. Johnson would take it as a compliment. So on Tuesday the 24th day of May, after having been enlivened by the witty sallies of Messieurs Thornton, Wilkes, Churchill, and Lloyd, with whom I had passed the morning, I boldly repaired to Johnson. His Chambers were on the first floor of No. 1, Inner-Temple-lane, and I entered them with an impression given me by the Reverend Dr. Blair, of Edinburgh, who had been introduced to him not long before, and described his having "found the Giant in his den"; an expression which, when I came to be pretty well acquainted with Johnson, I repeated to him, and he was diverted at this picturesque account of himself. Dr. Blair had been presented to him by Dr. James Fordyce. At this time the controversy concerning the pieces published by Mr. James Macpherson, as translations of Ossian, was at its height. Johnson had all along denied their authenticity; and, what was still more provoking to their admirers, maintained that they had no merit. The subject having been introduced by Dr. Fordyce, Dr. Blair, relying on the internal evidence of their antiquity, asked Dr. Johnson whether he thought any man of a modern age could have written such poems? Johnson replied, "Yes, Sir, many men, many women, and many children." Johnson at this time, did not know that Dr. Blair had just published a Dissertation, not only defending their authenticity, but seriously ranking them with the poems of Homer and Virgil; and when he was afterwards informed of this circumstance, he expressed some displeasure at Dr. Fordyce's having suggested the topick, and said, "I am not sorry that they got thus much for their pains. Sir, it was like leading one to talk of a book, when the authour is concealed behind the door."

He received me very courteously: but, it must be confessed, that his apartment, and furniture, and morning dress, were sufficiently uncouth. His brown suit of cloaths looked very rusty: he had on a little old shrivelled unpowdered wig, which was too small for his head; his shirt-neck and knees of his breeches were loose; his black worsted stockings ill drawn up; and he had a pair of unbuckled shoes by way of slippers. But all these slovenly particularities were forgotten the moment that he began to talk. Some gentlemen, whom I do not recollect, were sitting with him; and when they went away, I also rose; but he said to me, "Nay, don't go."—"Sir, (said I,) I am afraid that I intrude upon you. It is benevolent to allow me to sit and hear you." He seemed pleased with this compliment, which I sincerely paid him, and answered "Sir, I am obliged to any man who visits me."—I have preserved the following short minute of what passed this day.

"Madness frequently discovers itself merely by unnecessary deviation from the usual modes of the world. My poor friend Smart showed the disturbance of his mind, by falling upon his knees, and saying his prayers in the street, or in any other unusual place. Now although rationally speaking, it is greater madness not to pray at all, than to pray as Smart did, I am afraid there are so many who do not pray, that their understanding is not called in question."

Concerning this unfortunate poet, Christopher Smart, who was confined in a mad-house, he had, at another time, the following conversation with Dr. Burney.—BURNEY: "How does poor Smart do, Sir; is he likely to recover?" JOHNSON: "It seems as if his mind had ceased to struggle with the disease; for he grows fat upon it." BURNEY: "Perhaps, Sir, that may be from want of exercise." JOHNSON: "No, Sir; he has partly as much exercise as he used to have, for he digs in the garden. Indeed, before his confinement, he used for exercise to walk to the alehouse; but he was *carried* back again. I did not think he ought to be shut up. His infirmities were not noxious to society. He insisted on people praying with him; and I'd as lief pray with Kit Smart as any one else. Another charge was, that he did not love clean linen; and I have no passion for it."

Johnson continued. "Mankind have a great aversion to intellectual labour; but even supposing knowledge to be easily attainable, more people would be content to be ignorant than would take even a little trouble to acquire it.

"The morality of an action depends on the motive from which we act. If I fling half a crown to a beggar with intention to break his head, and he picks it up and buys victuals with it, the physical effect is good; but, with respect to me, the action is very wrong. So, religious exercises, if not performed with an intention to please God, avail us nothing. As our Saviour says of those who perform them from other motives, 'Verily they have their reward.'"

Before we parted, he was so good as to promise to favour me with his company one evening at my lodging: and, as I took my leave, shook me cordially by the hand. It is almost needless to add, that I felt no little elation at having now so happily established an acquaintance of which I had been so long ambitious.

I did not visit him again till Monday, June 13, at which time I recollect no part of his conversation, except that when I told him I had been to see Johnson ride upon three horses, he said, "Such a man, Sir, should be encouraged; for his performances shew the extent of the human power in one instance, and thus tend to raise our opinion of the faculties of man. He shews what may be attained by persevering application; so that every man may hope, that by giving as much application, although perhaps he may never ride three horses at a time, or dance upon a wire, yet he may be equally expert in whatever profession he has chosen to pursue."

He again shook me by the hand at parting, and asked me why I did not come oftener to him. Trusting that I was now in his good graces, I answered, that he had not given me much encouragement, and reminded him of the check I had received from him at our first interview. "Poh, poh! (said he, with a complacent smile,) never mind these things. Come to me as often as you can. I shall be glad to see you."

On June 25 I met him in the evening at the Mitre. We had a good supper, and port wine, of which he then sometimes drank a bottle. I find in my Journal the following minute of our conversation, which, though it will give but a very faint notion of what passed, is, in some degree a valuable record; and it will be curious in this view, as showing how habitual to his mind were some opinions which appear in his works.

"Colley Cibber, Sir, was by no means a blockhead; but by arrogating to himself too much, he was in danger of losing that degree of estimation to which he was entitled. His friends gave out that he *intended* his birth-day Odes should be bad; but that was not the case, Sir; for he kept them many months by him, and a few years before he died he shewed me one of them, with great solicitude to render it as perfect as might be, and I made some corrections, to which he was not very willing to submit. I remember the following couplet in allusion to the King and himself:

' Perch'd on the eagle's soaring wing,
The lowly linnet loves to sing.'

Sir, he had heard something of the fabulous tale of the wren sitting upon the eagle's wing, and he had applied it to a linnet. Cibber's familiar style, however, was better than that which Whitehead has assumed. *Grand* nonsense is insupportable. Whitehead is but a little man to inscribe verses to players."

I did not presume to controvert this censure, which was tinctured with his prejudice against players, but I could not help thinking that a dramatick poet might with propriety pay a compliment to an eminent performer, as Whitehead has very happily done in his verses to Mr. Garrick.

"Sir, I do not think Gray a first-rate poet. He has not a bold imagination, nor much command of words. The obscurity in which he has involved himself will not persuade us that he is sublime. His Elegy in a church-yard has a happy selection of images, but I don't like what are called his great things. His ode which begins

' Ruin seize thee, ruthless King
Confusion on thy banners wait! '

has been celebrated for its abruptness, and plunging into the subject all at once. But such arts as these have no merit, unless when they are original. We admire them only once; and this abruptness has nothing new in it. We have had it often before. Nay, we have it in the old song of Johnny Armstrong:

> ' Is there ever a man in all Scotland,
> From the highest estate to the lowest degree, &c.'

And then, Sir,

> ' Yes, there is a man in Westmoreland
> And Johnny Armstrong they do him call.'

There, now, you plunge at once into the subject. You have no previous narration to lead you to it.—The two next lines in that Ode are, I think, very good:

> ' Though fann'd by conquest's crimson wing,
> They mock the air with idle state ' ."

Finding him in a placid humour, and wishing to avail myself of the opportunity which I fortunately had of consulting a sage, to hear whose wisdom, I conceived, in the ardour of youthful imagination, that men filled with a noble enthusiasm for intellectual improvement would gladly have resorted from distant lands;— I opened my mind to him ingenuously, and gave him a little sketch of my life, to which he was pleased to listen with great attention.

I acknowledged, that though educated very strictly in the principles of religion, I had for some time been misled into a certain degree of infidelity; but that I was come now to a better way of thinking, and was fully satisfied of the truth of the Christian revelation, though I was not clear as to every point considered to be orthodox. Being at all times a curious examiner of the human mind, and pleased with an undisguised display of what had passed in it, he called to me with warmth, "Give me your hand; I have taken a liking to you." He then began to descant upon the force of testimony, and the little we could know of final causes; so that the objections of, why was it so? or why was it not so? ought not to disturb us: adding, that he himself had at one period been guilty of a temporary neglect of religion, but that it was not the result of argument, but mere absence of thought.

After having given credit to reports of his bigotry, I was agreeably surprized when he expressed the following very liberal sentiment, which has the additional value of obviating an objection to our holy religion, founded upon the discordant tenets of Christians themselves: "For my part, Sir, I think all Christians, whether Papists or Protestants, agree in the essential articles, and that their differences are trivial, and rather political than religious."

We talked of belief in ghosts. He said, "Sir, I make a distinction between what a man may experience by the mere strength of his imagination, and what imagination cannot possibly produce. Thus, suppose I should think that I saw a form, and heard a voice cry, 'Johnson, you are a very wicked fellow, and unless you repent you will certainly be punished;' my own unworthiness is so deeply impressed upon my mind, that I might *imagine* I thus saw and heard, and therefore I should not believe that an external communication had been made to me. But if a form should appear, and a voice should tell me that a particular man had died at a particular place, and a particular hour, a fact which I had no apprehension of, nor any means of knowing, and this fact, with all its circumstances, should afterwards be unquestionably proved, I should, in that case, be persuaded that I had supernatural intelligence imparted to me."

Our conversation proceeded. "Sir, (said he,) I am a friend to subordination, as most conducive to the happiness of society. There is a reciprocal pleasure in governing and being governed."

I mentioned Mallet's tragedy of "ELVIRA," which had been acted the preceding winter at Drury-lane, and that the Honourable Andrew Erskine, Mr. Dempster, and myself, had joined in writing a pamphlet, entitled "Critical Strictures" against it. That the mildness of Dempster's disposition had, however, relented; and he had candidly said, "We have hardly a right to abuse this tragedy; for bad as it is, how vain should either of us be to write one not near so good." JOHNSON: "Why no, Sir; this is not just reasoning. You *may* abuse a tragedy, though you cannot write one. You may scold a carpenter who has made you a bad table, though you cannot make a table. It is not your trade to make tables."

When I talked to him of the paternal estate to which I was heir, he said, "Sir, let me tell you, that to be a Scotch landlord, where you have a number of families dependent upon you, and attached to you, is perhaps as high a situation as humanity can arrive at. A merchant upon the 'Change of London, with a hundred thousand pounds, is nothing; an English Duke, with an immense fortune, is nothing: he has no tenants who consider themselves as under his patriarchal care, and who will follow him to the field upon an emergency."

My next meeting with Johnson was on Friday the 1st of July, when he and I and Dr. Goldsmith supped at the Mitre.

Goldsmith attempting this evening to maintain, I suppose from an affectation of paradox, "that knowledge was not desirable on its own account, for it often was a source of unhappiness." JOHNSON: "Why, Sir, that knowledge may in some cases produce unhappiness, I allow. But, upon the whole, knowledge, *per se*, is certainly an object which every man would wish to attain, although, perhaps, he may not take the trouble necessary for attaining it."

Dr. John Campbell, the celebrated political and biographical writer, being mentioned, Johnson said, "Campbell is a man of much knowledge, and has a good share of imagination. His 'Hermippus Redivivus' is very entertaining, as an account of the Hermetick philosophy, and as furnishing a curious history of the extravagances of the human mind. If it were merely imaginary, it would be nothing at all. Campbell is not always rigidly careful of truth in his conversation; but I do not believe there is any thing of this carelessness in his books. Campbell is a good man, a pious man. I am afraid he has not been in the inside of a church for many years; but he never passes a church without pulling off his hat. This shews that he has good principles. I used to go pretty often to Campbell's on a Sunday evening till I began to consider that the shoals of Scotchmen who flocked about him might probably say, when any thing of mine was well done, 'Ay, ay, he has learnt this of CAWMELL!'"

He talked very contemptuously of Churchill's poetry, observing, that "it had a temporary currency, only from its audacity of abuse, and being filled with living names, that it would sink into oblivion." I ventured to hint that he was not quite a fair judge, as Churchill had attacked him violently. JOHNSON: "Nay, Sir, I am a very fair judge. He did not attack me violently till he found I did not like his poetry; and his attack on me shall not prevent me from continuing to say what I think of him, from an apprehension that it may be ascribed to resentment. No, Sir, I called the fellow a blockhead at first, and I will call him a blockhead still. However, I will acknowledge that I have a better opinion of him now, than I once had; for he has shewn more fertility than I expected. To be sure, he is a tree that cannot produce good fruit: he only bears

26

crabs. But, Sir, a tree that produces a great many crabs is better than a tree which produces only a few."

On Tuesday, the 5th of July, I again visited Johnson. He told me he had looked into the poems of a pretty voluminous writer, Mr. (now Dr.) John Ogilvie, one of the Presbyterian ministers of Scotland, which had lately come out, but could find no thinking in them. BOSWELL: "Is there no imagination in them, Sir?" JOHNSON: "Why, Sir, there is in them what *was* imagination, but it is no more imagination in *him*, than sound is sound in the echo. And his diction too is not his own. We have long ago seen *white-robed innocence*, and *flower-bespangled meads.*"

Talking of London, he observed, "Sir, if you wish to have a just notion of the magnitude of this city, you must not be satisfied with seeing its great streets and squares, but must survey the innumerable little lanes and courts. It is not in the showy evolutions of buildings, but in the multiplicity of human habitations which are crowded together, that the wonderful immensity of London consists."

On Wednesday, July 6, he was engaged to sup with me at my lodgings in Downing-street, Westminster. But on the preceding night my landlord having behaved very rudely to me and some company who were with me, I had resolved not to remain another night in his house. I was exceedingly uneasy at the awkward appearance I supposed I should make to Johnson and the other gentleman whom I had invited, not being able to receive them at home, and being obliged to order supper at the Mitre. I went to Johnson in the morning, and talked of it as of a serious distress. He laughed, and said, "Consider, Sir, how insignificant this will appear a twelvemonth hence. There is nothing in this mighty misfortune; nay, we shall be better at the Mitre." I told him that I had been at Sir John Fielding's office, complaining of my landlord, and had been informed, that though I had taken my lodgings for a year, I might, upon proof of his bad behaviour, quit them when I pleased, without being under an obligation to pay rent for any longer time than while I possessed them. The fertility of Johnson's mind could shew itself even upon so small a matter as this. "Why, Sir, (said he,) I suppose this must be the law, since you have been told so in Bow-street. But, if your landlord could hold you to your bargain, and the lodgings should be yours for a year, you may certainly use them as you think fit. So, Sir, you may quarter two life-guardsmen upon him; or you may send the greatest scoundrel you can find into your apartments; or you may say that you want to make some experiments in natural philosophy, and may burn a large quantity of assafœtida in his house."

I had as my guests this evening at the Mitre tavern, Dr. Johnson, Dr. Goldsmith, Mr. Thomas Davies, Mr. Eccles, an Irish gentleman, for whose agreeable company I was obliged to Mr. Davies, and the Reverend Mr. John Ogilvie, who was desirous of being in company with my illustrious friend, while I in my turn, was proud to have the honour of shewing one of my countrymen upon what easy terms Johnson permitted me to live with him.

Goldsmith, as usual, endeavoured, with too much eagerness, to *shine*, and disputed very warmly, with Johnson against the well known maxim of the British constitution, "the King can do no wrong;" affirming, that, "what was morally false could not be politically true; and as the King might, in the exercise of his regal power, command and cause the doing of what was wrong, it certainly might be said, in sense and in reason, that he could do wrong." JOHNSON: "Sir, you are to consider, that in our constitution, according to its true principles, the King is the head, he is supreme: he is above every thing, and there is no power by which he can be tried. Therefore, it is, Sir, that we hold the King can do no wrong; that whatever may happen to be wrong in government may not be above our reach, by being ascribed to Majesty. Redress is always to be had against oppression, by punishing the immediate agents. The King, though he should command, cannot force a Judge to condemn a man unjustly; therefore it is the Judge whom we prosecute and punish. Political institutions are formed upon the consideration of what will most frequently tend to the good of the whole, although now and then exceptions may occur. Thus it is better in general that a nation should have a supreme legislative power, although it may at times be abused. And then, Sir, there is this consideration, *that if the abuse be enormous, Nature will rise up, and claiming her original rights, overturn a corrupt political system.*"

"Great abilities (said he) are not requisite for an Historian; for in historical composition, all the greatest powers of the human mind are quiescent. He has facts ready to his hand, so there is no exercise of invention. Imagination is not required in any high degree; only about as much as is used in the lower kinds of poetry. Some penetration, accuracy, and colouring, will fit a man for the task, if he can give the application which is necessary."

Mr. Ogilvie was unlucky enough to choose for the topick of his conversation the praises of his native country. He began with saying, that there was very rich land around Edinburgh. Goldsmith, who had studied physick there, contradicted this, very untruly, with a sneering laugh. Disconcerted a little by this, Mr. Ogilvie then took a new ground, where, I suppose, he thought himself perfectly safe; for he observed, that Scotland had a great many noble wild prospects. JOHNSON: "I believe, Sir, you have a great many. Norway, too, has noble wild prospects; and Lapland is remarkable for prodigious noble wild prospects. But, Sir, let me tell you, the noblest prospect which a Scotchman ever sees, is the high road that leads him to England!" This unexpected and pointed sally produced a roar of applause.

On the 14th we had another evening by ourselves at the Mitre. It happening to be a very rainy night, I made some common-place observations on the relaxation of nerves and depression of spirits which such weather occasioned; adding however, that it was good for the vegetable creation. Johnson, who, as we have already seen, denied that the temperature of the air had any influence on the human frame, answered, with a smile of ridicule, "Why, yes, Sir, it is good for vegetables, and for the animals who eat those vegetables, and for the animals who eat those animals." This observation of his aptly enough introduced a good supper; and I soon forgot, in Johnson's company, the influence of a moist atmosphere.

Feeling myself now quite at ease as his companion, though I had all possible reverence for him, I expressed a regret that I could not be so easy with my father, though he was not much older than Johnson, and certainly however respectable had not more learning and greater abilities to depress me. I asked him the reason of this. JOHNSON: "Why, Sir, I am a man of the world. I live in the world, and I take, in some degree, the colour of the world as it moves along. Your father is a Judge in a remote part of the island, and all his notions are taken from the old world. Besides, Sir, there must always be a struggle between a father and son, while one aims at power and the other at independence." I said, I was afraid my father would force me to be a lawyer. JOHNSON: "Sir, you need not be afraid of his forcing you to be a laborious practising lawyer; that is not in his power. For as the proverb says, 'One man may lead a horse to the water, but twenty cannot make him drink.' He may be displeased that you are not what he wishes you to be; but that displeasure will not go far. If he insists only on your having as much law as is necessary for a man of property, and then endeavours to get you into Parliament, he is quite in the right."

He enlarged very convincingly upon the excellence of rhyme over blank verse in English poetry. I mentioned to him that Dr. Adam Smith, in his lectures upon composition, when I studied under him in the College of Glasgow, had maintained the same opinion strenuously, and I repeated some of his arguments. JOHNSON: "Sir, I was once in company with Smith, and we did not take to each other; but had I known that he loved rhyme as much as you tell me he does, I should have HUGGED him."

Talking of those who denied the truth of Christianity, he said, "It is always easy to be on the negative side. If a man were now to deny that there is salt upon the table, you could not reduce him to an absurdity. Come, let us try this a little further. I deny that Canada is taken, and I can support my denial by pretty good arguments. The French are a much more numerous people than we; and it is not likely that they would allow us to take it. 'But the ministry have assured us, in all the formality of the Gazette, that it is taken.'—Very true. But the ministry have put us to an enormous expence by the war in America, and it is their interest to persuade us that we have got something for our money.—'But the fact is confirmed by thousands of men who were at the taking of it.'—Ay, but these men have still more interest in deceiving us. They don't want that you should think the French have beat them, but that they have beat the French. Now suppose you should go over and find that it really is taken, that would only satisfy yourself; for when you come home we will not believe you. We will say you have been bribed.—Yet, Sir, notwithstanding all these plausible objections, we have no doubt that Canada is really ours. Such is the weight of common testimony. How much stronger are the evidences of the Christian religion?"

"Idleness is a disease which must be combated; but I would not advise a rigid adherence to a particular plan of study. I myself have never persisted in any plan for two days together. A man ought to read just as inclination leads him; for what he reads as a task will do him little good. A young man should read five hours in a day, and so may acquire a great deal of knowledge."

To such a degree of unrestrained frankness had he now accustomed me, that in the course of this evening I talked of the numerous reflections which had been thrown out against him on account of his having accepted a pension from his present Majesty.

"Why, Sir, (said he, with a hearty laugh,) it is a mighty foolish noise that they make. I have accepted of a pension as a reward which has been thought due to my literary merit; and now that I have this pension, I am the same man in every respect that I have ever been; I retain the same principles. It is true, that I cannot now curse (smiling) the House of Hanover; nor would it be decent for me to drink King James's health in the wine that King George gives me money to pay for. But, Sir, I think that the pleasure of cursing the House of Hanover, and drinking King James's health, are amply overbalanced by three hundred pounds a year."

I described to him an impudent fellow from Scotland, who affected to be a savage, and railed at all established systems. JOHNSON: "There is nothing surprizing in this, Sir. He wants to make himself conspicuous. He would tumble in a hogstye, as long as you looked at him and called to him to come out. But let him alone, never mind him, and he'll soon give it over."

I added that the same person maintained that there was no distinction between virtue and vice. JOHNSON: "Why, Sir, if the fellow does not think as he speaks, he is lying; and I see not what honour he can propose to himself from having the character of a lyar. But if he does really think that there is no distinction between virtue and vice, why, Sir, when he leaves our houses let us count our spoons."

On Tuesday, July 18, I found tall Sir Thomas Robinson sitting with Johnson. Sir Thomas said, that the King of Prussia valued himself upon three things;—upon being a hero, a musician, and an author. JOHNSON: "Pretty well, Sir, for one man. As to his being an author, I have not looked at his poetry; but his prose is poor stuff. He writes just as you may suppose Voltaire's foot-boy to do, who has been his amanuensis. He has such parts as the valet might have, and about as much of the colouring of the style as might be got by transcribing his works."

On Wednesday, July 20, Dr. Johnson, Mr. Dempster, and my uncle Dr. Boswell, who happened to be now in London, supped with me. JOHNSON: "Pity is not natural to man. Children are always cruel. Savages are always cruel. Pity is acquired and improved by the cultivation of reason. We may have uneasy sensations for seeing a creature in distress, without pity; for we have not pity unless we wish to relieve them. When I am on my way to dine with a friend, and finding it late, have bid the coachman make haste, if I happen to attend when he whips his horses, I may feel unpleasantly that the animals are put to pain, but I do not wish him to desist. No, Sir, I wish him to drive on."

Mr. Alexander Donaldson, bookseller, of Edinburgh, had for some time opened a shop in London, and sold his cheap editions of the most popular English books, in defiance of the supposed common-law right of *Literary Property*. Johnson, though he concurred in the opinion which was afterwards sanctioned by a judgement of the House of Lords, that there was no such right, was at this time very angry that the Booksellers of London, for whom he uniformly professed much regard, should suffer from an invasion of what they had ever considered to be secure; and he was loud and violent against Mr. Donaldson. "He is a fellow who takes advantage of the law to injure his brethren; for notwithstanding that the statute secures only fourteen years of exclusive right, it has always been understood by the *trade*, that he, who buys the copyright of a book from the authour, obtains a perpetual property; and upon that belief, numberless bargains are made to transfer that property after the expiration of the statutory term. Now Donaldson, I say, takes advantage here, of people who have really an equitable title from usage; and if we consider how few of the books, of which they buy the property, succeed so well as to bring profit, we should be of opinion that the term of fourteen years is too short; it should be sixty years." DEMPSTER: "Donaldson, Sir, is anxious for the encouragement of literature. He reduces the price of books, so that poor students may buy them." JOHNSON: (laughing): "Well, Sir, allowing that to be his motive, he is no better than Robin Hood, who robbed the rich in order to give to the poor."

Rousseau's treatise on the inequality of mankind was at this time a fashionable topick. It gave rise to an observation by Mr. Dempster, that the advantages of fortune and rank were nothing to a wise man, who ought to value only merit. JOHNSON: "If a man were a savage, living in the woods by himself, this might be true; but in civilized society we all depend upon each other, and our happiness is very much owing to the good opinion of mankind. Now, Sir, in civilized society, external advantages make us more respected. A man with a good coat upon his back meets with a better reception than he who has a bad one. Sir, you may analyse this, and say what is there in it? But that will avail you nothing, for it is a part of a general system. Pound St. Paul's church into atoms, and consider any single atom; it is, to be sure, good for

32

nothing: but, put all these atoms together, and you have St. Paul's church. So it is with human felicity, which is made up of many ingredients, each of which may be shewn to be very insignificant. In civilized society, personal merit will not serve you so much as money will. Sir, you may make the experiment. Go into the street, and give one man a lecture on morality, and another a shilling, and see which will respect you most. If you wish only to support nature, Sir William Petty fixes your allowance at three pounds a year; but as times are much altered, let us call it six pounds. This sum will fill your belly, shelter you from the weather, and even get you a strong lasting coat, supposing it to be made of good bull's hide. Now, Sir, all beyond this is artificial, and is desired in order to obtain a greater degree of respect from our fellow-creatures. And, Sir, if six hundred pounds a year procure a man more consequence, and, of course, more happiness than six pounds a year, the same proportion will hold as to six thousand, and so on, as far as opulence can be carried. Perhaps he who has a large fortune may not be so happy as he who has a small one; but that must proceed from other causes than from his having the large fortune: for, *cœteris paribus*, he who is rich in a civilized society, must be happier than he who is poor; as riches, if properly used, (and it is a man's own fault if they are not,) must be productive of the highest advantages. Money, to be sure, of itself is of no use; for its only use is to part with it. Rousseau, and all those who deal in paradoxes, are led away by a childish desire of novelty. When I was a boy, I used always to choose the wrong side of a debate, because most ingenious things, that is to say, most new things, could be said upon it. Sir, there is nothing for which you may not muster up more plausible arguments, than those which are urged against wealth and other external advantages. Why, now, there is stealing; why should it be thought a crime? When we consider by what unjust methods property has been often acquired, and that what was unjustly got it must be unjust to keep, where is the harm in one man's taking the property of another from him? Besides, Sir, when we consider the bad use that many people make of their property, and how much better use the thief may make of it, it may be defended as a very allowable practice. Yet, Sir, the experience of mankind has discovered stealing to be so very bad a thing, that they make no scruple to hang a man for it. When I was running about this town a very poor fellow, I was a great arguer for the advantages of poverty; but I was, at the same time, very sorry to be poor. Sir, all the arguments which are brought to represent poverty as no evil, shew it to be evidently a great evil. You never find people labouring to convince you that you may live very happily upon a plentiful fortune.— So you hear people talking how miserable a King must be; and yet they all wish to be in his place."

It was suggested that Kings must be unhappy, because they are deprived of the greatest of all satisfactions, easy and unreserved society. JOHNSON: "That is an ill-founded notion. Being a King does not exclude a man from such society. Great Kings have always been social. The King of Prussia, the only great King at present, is very social. Charles the Second, the last King of England who was a man of parts, was social; and our Henrys and Edwards were all social."

Mr. Dempster having endeavoured to maintain that intrinsick merit *ought* to make the only distinction amongst mankind. JOHNSON: "Why, Sir, mankind have found that this cannot be. How shall we determine the proportion of intrinsick merit? Were that to be the only distinction amongst mankind, we should soon quarrel about the degrees of it. Were all distinctions abolished, the strongest would not long acquiesce, but would endeavour to obtain a superiority by their bodily strength. But, Sir, as subordination is very necessary for society, and contentions for superiority very dangerous, mankind, that is to say, all civilized nations, have settled it upon a plain invariable principle. A man is born to hereditary rank or his being appointed to certain offices, gives him a certain rank. Subordination tends greatly to human happiness. Were we all upon an equality, we should have no other enjoyment than mere animal pleasure."

I said, I considered distinction of rank to be of so much importance in civilized society, that if I were asked on the same day to dine with the first Duke in England, and with the first man in Britain for genius, I should hesitate which to prefer. JOHNSON: "To be sure, Sir, if you were to dine only once, and it were never to be known where you dined, you would choose rather to dine with the first man for genius; but to gain most respect, you should dine with the first Duke in England. For nine people in ten that you meet with, would have a higher opinion of you for having dined with a Duke; and the great genius himself would receive you better, because you had been with the great Duke."

He took care to guard himself against any possible suspicion that his settled principles of reverence for rank and respect for wealth were at all owing to mean or interested motives; for he asserted his own independence as a literary man. "No man (said he) who ever lived by literature, has lived more independently than I have done." He said he had taken longer time than he needed to have done in composing his Dictionary. He received our compliments upon that great work with complacency, and told us that the Academy *della Crusca* could scarcely believe that it was done by one man.

Next morning I found him alone, and have preserved the following fragments of his conversation. Of a gentleman who was mentioned, he said, "I have not met with any man for a long time who has given me such general displeasure. He is totally unfixed in his principles, and wants to puzzle other people." I said his principles had been poisoned by a noted infidel writer, but that he was, nevertheless, a benevolent good man. JOHNSON: "We can have no dependance upon that instinctive, that constitutional goodness which is not founded upon principle. I grant you that such a man may be a very amiable member of society. I can conceive him placed in such a situation that he is not much tempted to deviate from what is right; and as every man prefers virtue, when there is not some strong incitement to transgress its precepts, I can conceive him doing nothing wrong. But if such a man stood in need of money, I should not like to trust him; and I should certainly not trust him with young ladies, for *there* there is always temptation. Hume, and other sceptical innovators, are vain men, and will gratify themselves at any expence. Truth will not afford sufficient food to their vanity; so they have betaken themselves to errour. Truth, Sir, is a cow which will yield such people no more milk, and so they are gone to milk the bull. If I could have allowed myself to gratify my vanity at the expence of truth, what fame might I have acquired! Every thing which Hume has advanced against Christianity had passed through my mind long before he wrote. Always remember this, that after a system is well settled upon positive evidence, a few partial objections ought not to shake it. The human mind is so limited, that it cannot take in all the parts of a subject, so that there may be objections raised against any thing. There are objections against a *plenum*, and objections against a *vacuum*; yet one of them must certainly be true."

I mentioned Hume's argument against the belief of miracles, that it is more probable that the witnesses to the truth of them are mistaken, or speak falsely, than that the miracles should be true. JOHNSON: "Why, Sir, the great difficulty of proving miracles should make us very cautious in believing them. But let us consider; although God has made Nature to operate by certain fixed laws, yet it is not unreasonable to think that he may suspend those laws, in order to establish a system highly advantageous to mankind. Now the Christian Religion is a most beneficial system, as it gives us light and certainty where we were before in darkness and doubt. The miracles which prove it are attested by men who had no interest in deceiving us; but who, on the contrary, were told that they should suffer persecution, and did actually lay down their lives in confirmation of the truth of the facts which they asserted. Indeed, for some centuries the heathens did not pretend to deny the miracles; but said they were performed by the aid of evil spirits. This is a circumstance of great weight. Then, Sir, when we take the proofs derived from prophecies which have been so exactly fulfilled, we have most satisfactory evidence. Supposing a miracle possible, as to which, in my opinion, there can be no doubt, we have as strong evidence for the miracles in support of Christianity, as the nature of the thing admits."

At night, Mr. Johnson and I supped in a private room at the Turk's head coffee-house, in the Strand. "I encourage this house (said he,) for the mistress of it is a good civil woman, and has not much business."

"Sir, I love the acquaintance of young people; because, in the first place, I don't like to think myself growing old. In the next place, young acquaintances must last longest, if they do last; and then, Sir, young men have more virtue than old men; they have more generous sentiment in every respect. I love the young dogs of this age, they have more wit and humour and knowledge of life than we had; but then the dogs are not so good scholars. Sir, in my early years I read very hard. It is a sad reflection but a true one, that I knew almost as much at eighteen as I do now. My judgement, to be sure, was not so good; but, I had all the facts. I remember very well, when I was at Oxford, an old gentleman said to me, 'Young man, ply your books diligently now, and acquire a stock of knowledge; for when years come upon you, you will find that poring upon books will be but an irksome task.'"

He again insisted on the duty of maintaining subordination of rank. "Sir, I would no more deprive a nobleman of his respect, than of his money. I consider myself as acting a part in the great system of society, and I do to others as I would have them to do to me. I would behave to a nobleman as I should expect he would behave to me, were I a nobleman and he Sam. Johnson. Sir, there is one Mrs. Macaulay in this town, a great republican. One day when I was at her house, I put on a very grave countenance, and said to her, 'Madam, I am now become a convert to your way of thinking. I am convinced that all mankind are upon an equal footing; and to give you an unquestionable proof, Madam, that I am in earnest, here is a very sensible, civil, well-behaved fellow-citizen, your footman; I desire that he may be allowed to sit down and dine with us.' I thus, Sir, shewed her the absurdity of the levelling doctrine. She has never liked me since. Sir, your levellers wish to level *down* as far as themselves; but they cannot bear levelling *up* to themselves. They would all have some people under them; why not then have some people above them?" I mentioned a certain authour who disgusted me by his forwardness, and by shewing no deference to noblemen into whose company he was admitted. JOHNSON: "Suppose a shoemaker should claim an equality with him, as he does with a Lord: how he would stare. 'Why, Sir, do you stare? (says the shoemaker,) I do great service to society. 'Tis true, I am paid for doing it; but so are you, Sir: and I am sorry to say it, better paid than I am, for doing something not so necessary. For mankind could do better without your books, than without my shoes.' Thus, Sir, there would be a perpetual struggle for precedence, were there no fixed invariable rules for the distinction of rank, which creates no jealousy, as it is allowed to be accidental."

A writer of deserved eminence being mentioned, Johnson said, 'Why, Sir, he is a man of good parts, but being originally poor, he has got a love of mean company and low jocularity; a very bad thing, Sir. To laugh is good, and to talk is good. But you ought no more to think it enough if you laugh, than you are to think it enough if you talk. You may laugh in as many ways as you talk; and surely *every* way of talking that is practised cannot be esteemed."

He maintained that a boy at school was the happiest of human beings. I supported a different opinion, from which I have never yet varied, that a man is happier: and I enlarged upon the anxiety and sufferings which are endured at school. JOHNSON: "Ah! Sir, a boy's being flogged is not so severe as a man's having the hiss of the world against him. Men have a solicitude about fame; and the greater share they have of it, the more afraid they are of losing it."

On Tuesday, July 26, I found Mr. Johnson alone. It was a very wet day, and I again complained of the disagreeable effects of such weather. JOHNSON: "Sir, this is all imagination, which physicians encourage; for man lives in air, as a fish lives in water, so that if the atmosphere press heavy from above, there is an equal resistance from below. To be sure, bad weather is hard upon people who are obliged to be abroad; and men cannot labour so well in the open air in bad weather, as in good: but, Sir, a smith or a taylor, whose work is within doors, will surely do as much in rainy weather, as in fair. Some very delicate frames, indeed, may be affected by wet weather; but not common constitutions."

We talked of the education of children; and I asked him what he thought was best to teach them first. JOHNSON: "Sir, it is no matter what you teach them first, any more than what leg you shall put into your breeches first. Sir, you may stand disputing which is best to put in first, but in the mean time your breech is bare. Sir, while you are considering which of two things you should teach your child first, another boy has learnt them both."

On Thursday, July 28, we again supped in private at the Turk's Head coffee-house. JOHNSON: "Swift has a higher reputation than he deserves. His excellence is strong sense; for his humour, though very well, is not remarkably good. I doubt whether the *Tale of a Tub* be his; for he never owned it, and it is much above his usual manner."

"Has not —— a great deal of wit, Sir?" JOHNSON: "I do not think so, Sir. He is, indeed, continually attempting wit, but he fails. And I have no more pleasure in hearing a man attempting wit and failing, than in seeing a man trying to leap over a ditch and tumbling into it."

He laughed heartily when I mentioned to him a saying of his concerning Mr. Thomas Sheridan, which Foote took a wicked pleasure to circulate. "Why, Sir, Sherry is dull, naturally dull; but it must have taken him a great deal of pains to become what we now see him. Such an excess of stupidity, Sir, is not in Nature." —"So (said he,) I allowed him all his own merit."

He now added, "Sheridan cannot bear me. I bring his declamation to a point. I ask him a plain question, 'What do you mean to teach?' Besides, Sir, what influence can Mr. Sheridan have upon the language of this great country, by his narrow exertions? Sir, it is burning a farthing candle at Dover, to shew light at Calais."

Talking of a young man who was uneasy from thinking that he was very deficient in learning and knowledge, he said, "A man has no reason to complain who holds a middle place, and has many below him; and perhaps he has not six of his years above him;—perhaps not one. Though he may not know any thing perfectly, the general mass of knowledge that he has acquired is considerable. Time will do for him all that is wanting."

The conversation then took a philosophical turn. JOHNSON: "Human experience, which is constantly contradicting theory, is the great test of truth. A system, built upon the discoveries of a great many minds, is always of more strength, than what is produced by the mere workings of any one mind, which, of itself, can do little. There is not so poor a book in the world that would not be a prodigious effort were it wrought out entirely by a single mind, without the aid of prior investigators. The French writers are superficial, because they are not scholars, and so proceed upon the mere power of their own minds; and we see how very little power they have.

"As to the Christian Religion, Sir, besides the strong evidence which we have for it, there is a balance in its favour from the number of great men who have been convinced of its truth, after a serious consideration of the question. Grotius was an acute man, a lawyer, a man accustomed to examine evidence, and he was convinced. Grotius was not a recluse, but a man of the world, who certainly had no bias to the side of religion. Sir Isaac Newton set out an infidel, and came to be a very firm believer."

He this evening again recommended to me to perambulate Spain. I said it would amuse him to get a letter from me dated at Salamancha. JOHNSON: "I love the University of Salamancha; for when the Spaniards were in doubt as to the lawfulness of their conquering America, the University of Salamancha gave it as their opinion that it was not lawful."

I again begged his advice as to my method of study at Utrecht. "Come, (said he) let us make a day of it. Let us go down to Greenwich and dine, and talk of it there." The following Saturday was fixed for this excursion.

As we walked along the Strand to-night, arm in arm, a woman of the town accosted us, in the usual enticing manner. "No, no, my girl, (said Johnson) it won't do." He, however, did not treat her with harshness; and we talked of the wretched life of such women, and agreed, that much more misery than happiness, upon the whole, is produced by illicit commerce between the sexes.

On Saturday, July 30, Dr. Johnson and I took a sculler at the Temple-stairs, and set out for Greenwich. I asked him if he really thought a knowledge of the Greek and Latin languages an essential requisite to a good education. JOHNSON: "Most certainly, Sir; for those who know them have a very great advantage over those who do not. Nay, Sir, it is wonderful what a difference learning makes upon people even in the common intercourse of life, which does not appear to be much connected with it." "And yet, (said I) people go through the world very well, and carry on the business of life to good advantage, without learning." JOHNSON: "Why, Sir, that may be true in cases where learning cannot possibly be of any use; for instance, this boy rows us as well without learning, as if he could sing the song of Orpheus to the Argonauts, who were the first sailors." He then called to the boy, "What would you give, my lad, to know about the Argonauts?" "Sir, (said the boy) I would give what I have." Johnson was much pleased with his answer, and we gave him a double fare. Dr. Johnson then turning to me, "Sir, (said he) a desire of knowledge is the natural feeling of mankind; and every human being, whose mind is not debauched, will be willing to give all that he has, to get knowledge."

We landed at the Old Swan, and walked to Billingsgate, where we took oars and moved smoothly along the silver Thames. It was a very fine day. We were entertained with the immense number and variety of ships that were lying at anchor, and with the beautiful country on each side of the river.

I talked of preaching, and of the great success which those called methodists have. JOHNSON: "Sir, it is owing to their expressing themselves in a plain and familiar manner, which is the only way to do good to the common people, and which clergymen of genius and learning ought to do from a principle of duty, when it is suited to their congregations; a practice, for which they will be praised by men of sense. To insist against drunkenness as a crime, because it debases reason, the noblest faculty of man, would be of no service to the common people; but to tell them that they may die in a fit of drunkenness, and shew them how dreadful that would be, cannot fail to make a deep impression. Sir, when your Scotch clergy give up their homely manner, religion will soon decay in that country."

We walked in the evening in Greenwich Park. He asked me I suppose, by way of trying my disposition, "Is not this very fine?" Having no exquisite relish of the beauties of Nature, and being more delighted with "the busy hum of men," I answered, "Yes, Sir; but not equal to Fleet-street." JOHNSON: "You are right, Sir."

Next day, Sunday, July 31, I told him I had been that morning at a meeting of the people called Quakers, where I had heard a woman preach. JOHNSON: "Sir, a woman's preaching is like dog's walking on his hind legs. It is not done well; but you are surprized to find it done at all."

On Wednesday, August 3, we had our last social evening at the Turk's Head coffee-house, before my setting out for foreign parts, I had the misfortune, before we parted, to irritate him unintentionally. I mentioned to him how common it was in the world to tell absurd stories of him, and to ascribe to him very strange sayings. JOHNSON: "What do they make me say, Sir?" BOSWELL: "Why, Sir, as an instance very strange indeed, (laughing heartily as I spoke,) David Hume told me, you said that you would stand before a battery of cannon to restore the Convocation to its full powers."— Little did I apprehend that he had actually said this: but I was soon convinced of my errour; for, with a determined look, he thundered out, "And would I not, Sir? Shall the Presbyterian *Kirk* of Scotland have its General Assembly, and the Church of England be denied its Convocation?" He was walking up and down the room, while I told him the anecdote; but when he uttered this explosion of high-church zeal, he had come close to my chair, and his eye flashed with indignation. I bowed to the storm, and diverted the force of it, by leading him to expatiate on the influence which religion derived from maintaining the church with great external respectability.

On Friday, August 5, we set out early in the morning in the Harwich stage-coach. A fat elderly gentlewoman, and a young Dutchman, seemed the most inclined among us to conversation. At the inn where we dined, the gentlewoman said that she had done her best to educate her children; and, particularly, that she had never suffered them to be a moment idle. JOHNSON: "I wish, Madam, you would educate me too; for I have been an idle fellow all my life." "I am sure, Sir, (said she) you have not been idle." JOHNSON: "Nay, Madam, it is very true; and that gentleman there, (pointing to me,) has been idle. He was idle at Edinburgh. His father sent him to Glasgow, where he continued to be idle. He then came to London, where he has been very idle; and now he is going to Utrecht, where he will be as idle as ever." I asked him privately how he could expose me so. JOHNSON: "Poh, poh! (said he) they knew nothing about you, and will think of it no more." In the afternoon the gentlewoman talked violently against the Roman Catholicks, and of the horrours of the Inquisition. To the utter astonishment of all the passengers but myself, who knew that he could talk upon any side of a question, he defended the Inquisition, and maintained, that "false doctrine should be checked on its first appearance; that the civil power should unite with the church in punishing those who dare to attack the established religion, and that such only were punished by the Inquisition." He had in his pocket "*Pomponius Mela de Situ Orbis,*" in which he read occasionally, and seemed very intent upon ancient geography. Though by no means niggardly, his attention to what was generally right was so minute, that having observed at one of the stages that I ostentatiously gave a shilling to the coachman, when the custom was for each passenger to give only six-pence, he took me aside and scolded me, saying that what I had done would make the coachman dissatisfied with all the rest of the passengers who gave him no more than his due. This was a just reprimand; for in whatever way a man may indulge his generosity or his vanity in spending his money, for the sake of others he ought not to raise the price of any article for which there is a constant demand.

He talked of Mr. Blacklock's poetry, so far as it was descriptive of visible objects; and observed, that "as its authour had the misfortune to be blind, we may be absolutely sure that such passages are combinations of what he has remembered of the works of other writers who could see. That foolish fellow, Spence, has laboured to explain philosophically how Blacklock may have done, by means of his own faculties, what it is impossible he should do. The solution, as I have given it, is plain. Suppose, I know a man to be so lame that he is absolutely incapable to move himself, and I find him in a different room from that in which I left him; shall I puzzle myself with idle conjectures, that, perhaps, his nerves have by some unknown change all at once become effective? No, Sir, it is clear how he got into a different room: he was *carried.*"

Having stopped a night at Colchester, Johnson talked of that town with veneration, for having stood a siege for Charles the First. The Dutchman alone now remained with us. He spoke English tolerably well; and thinking to recommend himself to us by expatiating on the superiority of the criminal jurisprudence of this country over that of Holland, he inveighed against the barbarity of putting an accused person to the torture, in order to force a confession. But Johnson was as ready for this, as for the Inquisition. "Why, Sir, you do not, I find, understand the law of your own country. To torture in Holland is considered as a favour to an accused person; for no man is put to the torture there, unless there is as much evidence against him as would amount to conviction in England. An accused person among you, therefore, has one chance more to escape punishment, than those who are tried among us."

At supper this night he talked of good eating with uncommon satisfaction. "Some people (said he,) have a foolish way of not minding, or pretending not to mind, what they eat. For my part, I mind my belly very studiously, and very carefully; for I look upon it, that he who does not mind his belly, will hardly mind any thing else."

While we were left by ourselves, after the Dutchman had gone to bed, Dr. Johnson talked of that studied behaviour which many have recommended and practised. He disapproved of it; and said, "I never consider whether I should be a grave man, or a merry man, but just let inclination, for the time, have its course."

I teased him with fanciful apprehensions of unhappiness. A moth having fluttered round the candle, and burnt itself, he laid hold of this little incident to admonish me; saying, with a sly look, and in a solemn but a quiet tone, "That creature was its own tormentor, and I believe its name was BOSWELL."

Next day we got to Harwich, to dinner; and my passage in the packet-boat to Helvoetsluys being secured, and my baggage put on board, we dined at our inn by ourselves. I happened to say, it would be terrible if he should not find a speedy opportunity of returning to London, and be confined in so dull a place. JOHNSON: "Don't, Sir, accustom yourself to use big words for little matters. It would *not* be *terrible*, though I *were* to be detained some time here."

We went and looked at the church, and having gone into it, and walked up to the altar, Johnson, whose piety was constant and fervent, sent me to my knees, saying, "Now that you are going to leave your native country, recommend yourself to the protection of your CREATOR and REDEEMER."

After we came out of the church, we stood talking for some time together of Bishop Berkeley's ingenious sophistry to prove the

43

non-existence of matter, and that every thing in the universe is merely ideal. I observed, that though we are satisfied his doctrine is not true, it is impossible to refute it. I never shall forget the alacrity with which Johnson answered, striking his foot with mighty force against a large stone, till he rebounded from it,— "I refute it *thus*."

My revered friend walked down with me to the beach, where we embraced and parted with tenderness, and engaged to correspond by letters. I said, "I hope, Sir, you will not forget me in my absence." JOHNSON: "Nay, Sir, it is more likely you should forget me, than that I should forget you." As the vessel put out to sea, I kept my eyes upon him for a considerable time, while he remained rolling his majestic frame in his usual manner; and at last I perceived him walk back into the town, and he disappeared.

CHAPTER II

Dr. Johnson's Conversations in Seventeen Sixty-six

I RETURNED to London in February 1766, and found Dr. Johnson in a good house in Johnson's court, Fleet-street, in which he had accommodated Miss Williams with an apartment on the ground floor, while Mr. Levett occupied his post in the garret: his faithful Francis was still attending upon him. He received me with much kindness. The fragments of our first conversation, which I have preserved, are these: I told him that Voltaire, in a conversation with me, had distinguished Pope and Dryden thus:—"Pope drives a handsome chariot, with a couple of neat trim nags; Dryden a coach, and six stately horses." JOHNSON: "Why, Sir, the truth is, they both drive coaches and six; but Dryden's horses are either galloping or stumbling: Pope's go at a steady even trot." He said of Goldsmith's *Traveller*, which had been published in my absence, "There has not been so fine a poem since Pope's time."

Talking of education, "People have now-a-days, (said he,) got a strange opinion that every thing should be taught by lectures. Now, I cannot see that lectures can do so much good as reading the books from which the lectures are taken. I know nothing that can be best taught by lectures, except where experiments are to be shewn. You may teach chymistry by lectures:—You might teach making of shoes by lectures!"

At night I supped with him at the Mitre Tavern, that we might renew our social intimacy at the original place of meeting. But there was now a considerable difference in his way of living. Having had an illness, in which he was advised to leave off wine, he had, from that period, continued to abstain from it, and drank only water, or lemonade.

I told him that a foreign friend of his, whom I had met with abroad, was so wretchedly perverted to infidelity, that he treated the hopes of immortality with brutal levity; and said, "As man dies like a dog, let him lie like a dog." JOHNSON: "*If* he dies like a dog, *let* him lie like a dog." I added, that this man said to me, "I hate mankind, for I think myself one of the best of them, and I know how bad I am." JOHNSON: "Sir, he must be very singular in his opinion, if he thinks himself one of the best of men; for none of his friends think him so."—He said, "No honest man could be a Deist; for no man could be so after a fair examination of the proofs of Christianity." I named Hume. JOHNSON: "No, Sir; Hume owned to a clergyman in the bishoprick of Durham, that he had never read the New Testament with attention."—I mentioned Hume's notion, that all who are happy are equally happy; a little Miss with a new gown at a dancing-school ball, a General at the head of a victorious army, and an orator, after having made an eloquent speech in a great assembly. JOHNSON: "Sir, that all who are happy, are equally happy, is not true. A peasant and a philosopher may be equally *satisfied*, but not equally *happy*. Happiness consists in the multiplicity of agreeable consciousness. A peasant has not capacity for having equal happiness with a philosopher."

Dr. Johnson was very kind this evening, and said to me, "You have now lived five-and-twenty years, and you have employed them well." "Alas, Sir, (said I,) I fear not. Do I know history? Do I know mathematicks? Do I know law?" JOHNSON: "Why, Sir, though you may know no science so well as to be able to teach it, and no profession so well as to be able to follow it, your general mass of knowledge of books and men renders you very capable to make yourself master of any science, or fit yourself for any profession." I mentioned that a gay friend had advised me against being a lawyer, because I should be excelled by plodding block-heads. JOHNSON: "Why, Sir, in the formulary and statutory part of law, a plodding blockhead may excel; but in the ingenious and rational part of it a plodding blockhead can never excel."

I talked of the mode adopted by some to rise in the world, by courting great men, and asked him whether he had ever submitted to it. JOHNSON: "Why, Sir, I never was near enough to great men, to court them. You may be prudently attached to great men, and yet independent. You are not to do what you think wrong; and, Sir, you are to calculate, and not pay too dear for what you get. You must not give a shilling's worth of court for sixpence worth of good. But if you can get a shilling's worth of good for sixpence worth of court, you are a fool if you do not pay court."

He said, "If convents should be allowed at all, they should only be retreats for persons unable to serve the publick, or who have served it. It is our first duty to serve society; and, after we have done that, we may attend wholly to the salvation of our own souls. A youthful passion for abstracted devotion should not be encouraged."

Our next meeting at the Mitre was on Saturday the 15th of February, when I presented to him my old and most intimate friend, the Reverend Mr. Temple, then of Cambridge. I having mentioned that I had passed some time with Rousseau in his wild retreat, and having quoted some remark made by Mr. Wilkes, with whom I had spent many pleasant hours in Italy, Johnson said, (sarcastically,) "It seems, Sir, you have kept very good company abroad, Rousseau and Wilkes!" Thinking it enough to defend one at a time, I said nothing as to my gay friend, but answered with a smile, "My dear Sir, you don't call Rousseau bad company. Do you really think *him* a bad man?" JOHNSON: "Sir, if you are talking jestingly of this, I don't talk with you. If you mean to be serious, I think him one of the worst of men; a rascal, who ought to be hunted out of society, as he has been. Three or four nations have expelled him: and it is a shame that he is protected in this country." BOSWELL: "I don't deny, Sir, but that his novel may, perhaps, do harm; but I cannot think his intention was bad." JOHNSON: "Sir, that will not do. We cannot prove any man's intention to be bad. You may shoot a man through the head, and say you intended to miss him; but the Judge will order you to be hanged. An alleged want of intention, when evil is committed, will not be allowed in a court of justice. Rousseau, Sir, is a very bad man. I would sooner sign a sentence for his transportation, than that of any felon who has gone from the Old Bailey these many years. Yes, I should like to have him work in the plantations." BOSWELL: "Sir, do you think him as bad a man as Voltaire?" JOHNSON: "Why, Sir, it is difficult to settle the proportion of iniquity between them."

On his favourite subject of subordination, Johnson said, "So far is it from being true that men are naturally equal, that no two people can be half an hour together but one shall acquire an evident superiority over the other."

I mentioned the advice given us by philosophers, to console ourselves, when distressed or embarrassed, by thinking of those who are in a worse situation than ourselves. This, I observed, could not apply to all, for there must be some who have nobody worse than they are. JOHNSON: "Why, to be sure, Sir, there are; but they don't know it. There is no being so poor and so contemptible, who does not think there is somebody still poorer, and still more contemptible."

One evening, when a young gentleman teased him with an account of the infidelity of his servant, who, he said, would not believe the scriptures, because he could not read them in the original tongues, and be sure that they were not invented; "Why, foolish fellow, (said Johnson,) has he any better authority for almost everything that he believes?" BOSWELL: "Then the vulgar, Sir, never can know they are right, but must submit themselves to the learned." JOHNSON: "To be sure, Sir. The vulgar are the children of the State, and must be taught like children." BOSWELL: "Then, Sir, a poor Turk must be a Mahometan, just as a poor Englishman must be a Christian?" JOHNSON: "Why, yes, Sir; and what then? This now is such stuff as I used to talk to my mother, when I first began to think myself a clever fellow; and she ought to have whipt me for it."

Another evening Dr. Goldsmith and I called on him, with the hope of prevailing on him to sup with us at the Mitre. We found him indisposed, and resolved not to go abroad. "Come then, (said Goldsmith,) we will not go to the Mitre to-night, since we cannot have the big man with us." Johnson then called for a bottle of port, of which Goldsmith and I partook, while our friend, now a water-drinker, sat by us. GOLDSMITH: "I think, Mr. Johnson, you don't go near the theatres now. You give yourself no more concern about a new play, than if you had never had any thing to do with the stage." JOHNSON: "Why, Sir, our tastes greatly alter. The lad does not care for the child's rattle, and the old man does not care for the young man's whore." GOLDSMITH: "Nay, Sir; but your Muse was not a whore." JOHNSON: "Sir, I do not think she was. But as we advance in the journey of life we drop some of the things which have pleased us; whether it be that we are fatigued and don't choose to carry so many things any farther, or that we find other things which we like better." BOSWELL: "But, Sir, why don't you give us something in some other way?" GOLDSMITH: "Ay, Sir, we have a claim upon you." JOHNSON: "No, Sir, I am not obliged to do any more. No man is obliged to do as much as he can do. A man is to have part of his life to himself. If a soldier has fought a good many campaigns, he is not to be blamed, if he retires to ease and tranquillity. A physician, who has practised long in a great city, may be excused, if he retires to a small town, and takes less practice. Now, Sir, the good I can do by my conversation bears the same proportion to the good I can do by my writings, that the practice of a physician, retired to a small town, does to his practice in a great city." BOSWELL: "But I wonder, Sir, you have not more pleasure in writing than in not writing." JOHNSON: "Sir, you *may* wonder."

He talked of making verses, and observed, "The great difficulty is, to know when you have made good ones. When composing, I have generally had them in my mind, perhaps fifty at a time, walking up and down in my room; and then I have written them down, and often, from laziness, have written only half lines. I have written a hundred lines in a day. I remember, I wrote a hundred lines of *The Vanity of Human Wishes* in a day. Doctor, (turning to Goldsmith,) I am not quite idle; I made one line t'other day; but I made no more." GOLDSMITH: "Let us hear it; we'll put a bad one to it." JOHNSON: "No, Sir; I have forgot it."

CHAPTER III

In Seventeen Sixty-eight and Seventeen Sixty-nine

In the spring of 1768, having published my *Account of Corsica, with the Journal of a Tour to that Island*, I returned to London, very desirous to see Dr. Johnson, and hear him upon the subject. I found he was at Oxford, where I followed him. Instead of giving, with the circumstances of time and place, such fragments of his conversation as I preserved during this visit to Oxford, I shall throw them together in continuation.

I asked him whether, as a moralist, he did not think that the practice of the law, in some degree, hurt the nice feeling of honesty. JOHNSON: "Why, no, Sir, if you act properly. You are not to deceive your clients with false representations of your opinion: you are not to tell lies to a judge." BOSWELL: "But what do you think of supporting a cause which you know to be bad?" JOHNSON: "Sir, you do not know it to be good or bad till the judge determines it. I have said that you are to state facts fairly; so that your thinking, or what you call knowing, a cause to be bad, must be from reasoning, must be from your supposing your arguments to be weak and inconclusive. But, Sir, that is not enough. An argument which does not convince yourself, may convince the Judge to whom you urge it; and if it does convince him, why, then, Sir, you are wrong, and he is right. It is his business to judge; and you are not to be confident in your own opinion that a cause is bad, but to say all you can for your client, and then hear the Judge's opinion." BOSWELL: "But, Sir, does not affecting a warmth when you have no warmth, and appearing to be clearly of one opinion, when you are in reality of another opinion, does not such dissimulation impair one's honesty? Is there not some danger that a lawyer may put on the same mask in common life, in the intercourse with his friends?" JOHNSON: "Why no, Sir. Every body knows you are paid for affecting warmth for your client; and it is, therefore, properly no dissimulation: the moment you come from the bar you resume your usual behaviour. Sir, a man will no more carry the artifice of the bar into the common intercourse of society, than a man who is paid for tumbling upon his hands will continue to tumble upon his hands when he should walk on his feet."

"I have not been troubled for a long time with authours desiring my opinion of their works. I used once to be sadly plagued with a man who wrote verses, but who literally had no other notion of a verse, but that it consisted of ten syllables. *Lay your knife and your fork, across your plate*, was to him a verse:

Lay yōur knife ānd your fŏrk, acrŏss your plāte

As he wrote a great number of verses, he sometimes by chance made good ones, though he did not know it."

Johnson expatiated on the advantages of Oxford for learning. "There is here, Sir, (said he), such a progressive emulation. The students are anxious to appear well to their tutors; the tutors are anxious to have their pupils appear well in the college; the colleges are anxious to have their students appear well in the University; and there are excellent rules of discipline in every college. That the rules are sometimes ill observed, may be true; but is nothing against the system. The members of an University may, for a season, be unmindful of their duty. I am arguing for the excellency of the institution."

His prejudice against Scotland appeared remarkably strong at this time. When I talked of our advancement in literature, "Sir, (said he,) you have learnt a little from us, and you think yourselves very great men. Hume would never have written History, had not Voltaire written it before him. He is an echo of Voltaire." BOSWELL: "But, Sir, we have Lord Kames." JOHNSON: "You *have* Lord Kames. Keep him; ha, ha, ha! We don't envy you him. Do you ever see Dr. Robertson?" BOSWELL: "Yes, Sir." JOHNSON: "Does the dog talk of me?" BOSWELL: "Indeed, Sir, he does, and loves you." Thinking that I now had him in a corner, and being solicitous for the literary fame of my country, I pressed him for his opinion on the merit of Dr. Robertson's *History of Scotland*. But, to my surprize, he escaped.—"Sir, I love Robertson, and I won't talk of his book."

An essay, written by Mr. Deane, a Divine of the Church of England, maintaining the future life of brutes, by an explication of certain parts of the scriptures, was mentioned, and the doctrine insisted on by a gentleman who seemed fond of curious speculation. Johnson, who did not like to hear of any thing concerning a future state which was not authorized by the regular canons of orthodoxy,

51

discouraged this talk; and being offended at its continuation, he watched an opportunity to give the gentleman a blow of reprehension. So, when the poor speculatist, with a serious metaphysical pensive face, addressed him, "But really, Sir, when we see a very sensible dog, we don't know what to think of him," Johnson, rolling with joy at the thought which beamed in his eye, turned quickly round, and replied, "True, Sir: and when we see a very foolish *fellow*, we don't know what to think of *him*." He then rose up, strided to the fire, and stood for some time laughing and exulting.

I told him that I had several times when in Italy, seen the experiment of placing a scorpion within a circle of burning coals; that it ran round and round in extreme pain; and finding no way to escape, retired to the centre, and like a true Stoick philosopher, darted its sting into its head, and thus at once, freed itself from its woes. "*This must end 'em.*" I said, this was a curious fact, as it shewed deliberate suicide in a reptile. Johnson would not admit the fact. He said, Maupertuis was of opinion that it does not kill itself, but dies of the heat, that it gets to the centre of the circle, as the coolest place; that its turning its tail in upon its head is merely a convulsion and that it does not sting itself. He said he would be satisfied if the great anatomist Morgagni, after dissecting a scorpion on which the experiment had been tried, should certify that its sting had penetrated into its head.

He seemed pleased to talk of natural philosophy. "That woodcocks, (said he,) fly over the northern countries, is proved, because they have been observed at sea. Swallows certainly sleep all the winter. A number of them conglobulate together, by flying round and round, and then all in a heap throw themselves under water, and lye in the bed of a river." He told us, one of his first essays was a Latin poem upon the glow-worm. I am sorry I did not ask where it was to be found.

He talked of the heinousness of the crime of adultery, by which the peace of families was destroyed. He said, "Confusion of progeny constitutes the essence of the crime; and therefore a woman who breaks her marriage vows is much more criminal than a man who does it. A man, to be sure, is criminal in the sight of God; but he does not do his wife a very material injury, if he does not insult her; if, for instance, from mere wantonness of appetite, he steals privately to her chambermaid. Sir, a wife ought not greatly to resent this. I would not receive home a daughter who had run away from her husband on that account. A wife should study to reclaim her husband by more attention to please him. Sir, a man will not, once in a hundred instances, leave his wife and go to a harlot, if his wife has not been negligent of pleasing."

I asked him if it was not hard that one deviation from chastity should so absolutely ruin a young woman. JOHNSON: "Why no, Sir; it is the great principle which she is taught. When she has given up that principle she has given up every notion of female honour and virtue, which are all included in chastity."

At this time I observed upon the dial-plate of his watch a short Greek inscription, taken from the New Testament, Νύξ γὰρ ἔρχεται, being the first words of our Saviour's solemn admonition to the improvement of that time which is allowed us to prepare for eternity; "the night cometh when no man can work." He sometimes afterwards laid aside this dial-plate; and when I asked him the reason, he said, "It might do very well upon a clock which a man keeps in his closet; but to have it upon his watch which he carries about with him, and which is often looked at by others, might be censured as ostentatious."

Upon his arrival in London in May, he surprized me one morning with a visit at my lodging in Half-Moon-street, and was in the kindest and most agreeable frame of mind. As he had objected to a part of one of his letters being published, I thought it right to take this opportunity of asking him explicitly whether it would be improper to publish his letters after his death. His answer was "Nay, Sir, when I am dead, you may do as you will."

He talked in his usual style with a rough contempt of popular liberty. "They make a rout about *universal* liberty, without considering that all that is to be valued, or indeed can be enjoyed by individuals, is *private* liberty. Political liberty is good only so far as it produces private liberty. Now, Sir, there is the liberty of the press, which you know is a constant topick. Suppose you and I and two hundred more were restrained from printing our thoughts: what then? What proportion would that restraint upon us bear to the private happiness of the nation?"

Soon afterwards, he supped at the Crown and Anchor tavern, in the Strand, with a company whom I collected to meet him. They were Dr. Percy, now Bishop of Dromore, Dr. Douglas, now Bishop of Salisbury, Mr. Langton, Dr. Robertson the Historian, Dr. Hugh Blair, and Mr. Thomas Davies, who wished much to be introduced to these eminent Scotch literati; but on the present occasion, he had very little opportunity of hearing them talk, for with an excess of prudence, for which Johnson afterwards found fault with them, they hardly opened their lips, and only to say something which they were certain would not expose them to the sword of Goliath; such was their anxiety for their fame when in the presence of Johnson. He was this evening in remarkable vigour of mind, and eager to exert himself in conversation, which he did with great readiness and fluency; but I am sorry to find that I have preserved but a small part of what passed.

He was vehement against old Dr. Mounsey, of Chelsea College, as "a fellow who swore and talked bawdy." "I have often been in his company, (said Dr. Percy,) and never heard him swear or talk bawdy." Mr. Davies who sat next to Dr. Percy, having after this had some conversation aside with him, made a discovery which, in his zeal to pay court to Dr. Johnson, he eagerly proclaimed aloud from the foot of the table: "O, Sir, I have found out a very good reason why Dr. Percy never heard Mounsey swear or talk bawdy, for he tells me he never saw him but at the Duke of Northumberland's table." "And so, Sir, (said Dr. Johnson loudly to Dr. Percy) you would shield this man from the charge of swearing and talking bawdy, because he did not do so at the Duke of Northumberland's table. Sir, you might as well tell us that you had seen him hold up his hand at the Old Bailey, and he neither swore nor talked bawdy; or that you had seen him in the cart at Tyburn, and he neither swore nor talked bawdy. And is it thus, Sir, that you presume to controvert what I have related?" Dr. Johnson's animadversion was uttered in such a manner, that Dr. Percy seemed to be displeased, and soon afterwards left the company, of which Johnson did not at that time take any notice.

Swift having been mentioned, Johnson, as usual, treated him with little respect as an author. Some of us endeavoured to support the Dean of St. Patrick's, by various arguments. One in particular praised his "Conduct of the Allies." JOHNSON: "Sir, his 'Conduct of the Allies' is a performance of very little ability." "Surely, Sir, (said Dr. Douglas,) you must allow it has strong facts." JOHNSON: "Why, yes, Sir; but what is that to the merit of the composition? In the Sessions-paper of the Old Bailey there are strong facts. House-breaking is a strong fact; robbery is a strong fact; and murder is a *mighty* strong fact: but is great praise due to the historian of those strong facts? No, Sir, Swift has told what he had to tell distinctly enough, but that is all. He had to count ten, and he has counted it right."—Then recollecting that Mr. Davies, by acting as an *informer*, had been the occasion of his talking somewhat too harshly to his friend Dr. Percy, for which, probably, when the first ebullition was over, he felt some compunction, he took an opportunity to give him a hit: so added, with a preparatory laugh, "Why, Sir, Tom Davies might have written 'the Conduct of the Allies.'" Poor Tom being thus suddenly dragged into ludicrous notice in presence of the Scottish Doctors, to whom he was ambitious of appearing to advantage, was grievously mortified. Nor did his punishment rest here; for upon subsequent occasions, whenever he, "statesman all o'er," assumed a strutting importance, I used to hail him—"*the Authour of the Conduct of the Allies.*"

When I called upon Dr. Johnson next morning, I found him highly satisfied with his colloquial prowess the preceding evening. "Well, (said he,) we had good talks." BOSWELL: "Yes, Sir, you tossed and gored several persons."

Such particulars of Johnson's conversation in 1769 as I have committed to writing, I shall here introduce, without any strict attention to methodical arrangement. Sometimes short notes of different days shall be blended together, and sometimes a day may seem important enough to be separately distinguished.

He said, "The duration of Parliament, whether for seven years or the life of the King, appears to me so immaterial, that I would not give half a crown to turn the scale one way or the other. The *habeas corpus* is the single advantage which our government has over that of other countries."

On the 30th of September we dined together at the Mitre. I attempted to argue for the superior happiness of the savage life, upon the usual fanciful topicks. JOHNSON: "Sir, there can be nothing more false. The savages have no bodily advantages beyond those of civilized men. They have not better health; and as to care or mental uneasiness, they are not above it, but below it, like bears. No, Sir; you are not to talk such paradox: let me have no more on't. It cannot entertain, far less can it instruct. Lord Monboddo, one of your Scotch Judges, talked a great deal of such nonsense. I suffered *him*; but I will not suffer *you*." BOSWELL: "But, Sir, does not Rousseau talk such nonsense?" JOHNSON: "True, Sir, but Rousseau *knows* he is talking nonsense, and laughs at the world for staring at him." BOSWELL: "How so, Sir?" JOHNSON: "Why, Sir, a man who talks nonsense so well, must know that he is talking

55

nonsense. But I am *afraid*, (chuckling and laughing,) Monboddo does *not* know that he is talking nonsense." BOSWELL: "Is it wrong then, Sir, to affect singularity, in order to make people stare?" JOHNSON: "Yes, if you do it by propagating errour; and, indeed, it is wrong in any way. There is in human nature a general inclination to make people stare; and every wise man has himself to cure of it, and does cure himself. If you wish to make people stare by doing better than others, why make them stare till they stare their eyes out. But consider how easy it is to make people stare, by being absurd. I may do it by going into a drawing-room without my shoes. You remember the gentleman in 'The Spectator,' who had a commission of lunacy taken out against him for his extreme singularity, such as never wearing a wig, but a night-cap. Now, Sir, abstractedly, the night-cap was best: but, relatively, the advantage was overbalanced by his making the boys run after him."

Talking of a London life, he said, "The happiness of London is not to be conceived but by those who have been in it. I will venture to say, there is more learning and science within the circumference of ten miles from where we now sit, than in all the rest of the kingdom." BOSWELL: "The only disadvantage is the great distance at which people live from one another." JOHNSON: "Yes, Sir; but that is occasioned by the largeness of it, which is the cause of all the other advantages." BOSWELL: "Sometimes I have been in the humour of wishing to retire to a desart." JOHNSON: "Sir, you have desart enough in Scotland."

When I censured a gentleman of my acquaintance for marrying a second time, as it shewed a disregard of his first wife, he said "Not at all, Sir. On the contrary, were he not to marry again, it might be concluded that his first wife had given him a disgust to marriage; but by taking a second wife he pays the highest compliment to the first, by shewing that she made him so happy as a married man, that he wishes to be so a second time."

On the 6th of October I complied with this obliging invitation, [from Mr. and Mrs. Thrale, to visit them at Streatham], and found, at an elegant villa, six miles from town, every circumstance that can make society pleasing. Johnson, though quite at home, was yet looked up to with an awe, tempered by affection, and seemed to be equally the care of his host and hostess. I rejoiced at seeing him so happy.

He played off his wit against Scotland with a good humoured pleasantry, which gave me, though no bigot to national prejudices, an opportunity for a little contest with him. I having said that England was obliged to us for gardeners, almost all their good gardeners being, Scotchmen;—JOHNSON: "Why, Sir, that is because gardening is much more necessary amongst you than with us, which makes so many of your people learn it. It is *all* gardening with you. Things which grow wild here, must be cultivated with great care in Scotland. Pray now (throwing himself back in his chair, and laughing,) are you ever able to bring the *sloe* to perfection?"

I boasted that we had the honour of being the first to abolish the unhospitable, troublesome, and ungracious custom of giving vails to servants. JOHNSON: "Sir, you abolished vails, because you were too poor to be able to give them."

Mrs. Thrale then praised Garrick's talents for light, gay poetry; and, as a specimen, repeated his song in "Florizel and Perdita," and dwelt with peculiar pleasure on this line:

"I'd smile with the simple, and feed with the poor."

JOHNSON: "Nay, my dear Lady, this will never do. Poor David! Smile with the simple;—What folly is that? And who would feed with the poor that can help it? No, no; let me smile with the wise, and feed with the rich." I repeated this sally to Garrick, and wondered to find his sensibility as a writer not a little irritated by it. To soothe him I observed, that Johnson spared none of us; and I quoted the passage in Horace, in which he compares one who attacks his friends for the sake of a laugh, to a pushing ox, that is marked by a bunch of hay put upon his horns: "*fœnum habet in cornu.*"[1] "Ay, (said Garrick, vehemently,) he has a whole *mow* of it."

Talking of history, Johnson said "We may know historical facts to be true, as we may know facts in common life to be true. Motives are generally unknown. We cannot trust to the characters we find in history, unless when they are drawn by those who knew the persons; as those, for instance, by Sallust and by Lord Clarendon."

He would not allow much merit to Whitfield's oratory. "His popularity, Sir, (said he,) is chiefly owing to the peculiarity of his manner. He would be followed by crowds were he to wear a night-cap in the pulpit, or were he to preach from a tree."

I know not from what spirit of contradiction he burst out into a violent declamation against the Corsicans, of whose heroism I talked in high terms. "Sir, (said he,) what is all this rout about the

[1] He has hay on his horns.

Corsicans? They have been at war with the Genoese for upwards of twenty years, and have never yet taken their fortified towns. They might have battered down their walls, and reduced them to powder in twenty years. They might have pulled the walls in pieces, and cracked the stones with their teeth in twenty years." It was in vain to argue with him upon the want of artillery: he was not to be resisted for the moment.

On the evening of October 10, I presented Dr. Johnson to General Paoli. I had greatly wished that two men, for whom I had the highest esteem, should meet. They met with a manly ease, mutually conscious of their own abilities and of the abilities of each other. The General spoke Italian, and Dr. Johnson English, and understood one another very well, with a little aid of interpretation from me, in which I compared myself to an isthmus which joins two great continents. Upon Johnson's approach, the General said, "From what I have read of your works, Sir, and from what Mr. Boswell has told me of you, I have long held you in great veneration." The General talked of languages being formed on the particular notions and manners of a people, without knowing which, we cannot know the language. We may know the direct signification of single words; but by these no beauty of expression, no sally of genius, no wit is conveyed to the mind. All this must be by allusion to other ideas. "Sir, (said Johnson,) you talk of language, as if you had never done any thing else but study it, instead of governing a nation." The General said, "*Questo e un troppo gran complimento;*" this is too great a compliment. Johnson answered, "I should have thought so, Sir, if I had not heard you talk." The General asked him what he thought of the spirit of infidelity which was so prevalent. JOHNSON: "Sir, this gloom of infidelity, I hope, is only a transient cloud passing through the hemisphere, which will soon be dissipated, and the sun break forth with his usual splendour." "You think then, (said the General,) that they will change their principles like their clothes." JOHNSON: "Why, Sir, if they bestow no more thought on principles than on dress, it must be so." The General said, that "a great part of the fashionable infidelity was owing to a desire of shewing courage. Men who have no opportunities of shewing it as to things in this life, take death and futurity as objects on which to display it." JOHNSON: "That is mighty foolish affection. Fear is one of the passions of human nature, of which it is impossible to divest it. You remember that the Emperour Charles V. when he read upon the tomb-stone of a

Spanish nobleman, 'Here lies one who never knew fear,' wittily said, 'Then he never snuffed a candle with his fingers.'"

Dr. Johnson went home with me, and drank tea till late in the night. He said, "General Paoli had the loftiest port of any man he had ever seen." He denied that military men were always the best bred men. "Perfect good breeding, he observed, consists in having no particular mark of any profession, but a general elegance of manners; whereas, in a military man, you can commonly distinguish the *brand* of a soldier, *l'homme d'épée*."

Dr. Johnson shunned to-night any discussion of the perplexed question of fate and free will, which I attempted to agitate: "Sir, (said he,) we *know* our will is free, and *there's* an end on't."

He honoured me with his company at dinner on the 16th of October, at my lodgings in Old Bond-street, with Sir Joshua Reynolds, Mr. Garrick, Dr. Goldsmith, Mr. Murphy, Mr. Bickerstaff, and Mr. Thomas Davies. Garrick played round him with a fond vivacity, taking hold of the breasts of his coat, and, looking up in his face with a lively archness, complimented him on the good health which he seemed then to enjoy; while the sage, shaking his head, beheld him with a gentle complacency. One of the company not being come at the appointed hour. I proposed, as usual upon such occasions, to order dinner to be served; adding, "Ought six people to be kept waiting for one?" "Why, yes (answered Johnson, with a delicate humanity,) if the one will suffer more by your sitting down, than the six will do by waiting." Goldsmith, to divert the tedious minutes, strutted about, bragging of his dress, and I believe was seriously vain of it, for his mind was wonderfully prone to such impressions. "Come, come, (said Garrick,) talk no more of that. You are perhaps, the worst—eh, eh!"—Goldsmith was eagerly attempting to interrupt him, when Garrick went on, laughing ironically, "Nay, you will always *look* like a gentleman; but I am talking of being well or *ill drest*." "Well, let me tell you, (said Goldsmith), when my taylor brought home my bloom-coloured coat, he said, 'Sir, I have a favour to beg of you. When any body asks you who made your clothes, be pleased to mention John Filby, at the Harrow, in Water-lane.'" JOHNSON: "Why, Sir, that was because he knew the strange colour would attract crowds to gaze at it, and thus they might hear of him, and see how well he could make a coat even of so absurd a colour."

After dinner our conversation first turned upon Pope. Johnson said, his characters of men were admirably drawn, those of women not so well. He repeated to us, in his forcible melodious manner, the concluding lines of the Dunciad. While he was talking loudly in praise of those lines one of the company ventured to say, "Too fine for such a poem:—a poem on what?" JOHNSON: (with a disdainful look,): "Why, on *dunces*. It was worth while being a dunce then. Ah, Sir, hadst *thou* lived in those days! It is not worth while being a dunce now, when there are no wits." Goldsmith said, that Pope's character of Addison shewed a deep knowledge of the human heart. Johnson said, that the description of the temple, in "The Mourning Bride," was the finest poetical passage he had ever read; he recollected none in Shakespeare equal to it.—"But, (said Garrick, all alarmed for 'The God of his idolatry,') we know not the extent and variety of his powers. We are to suppose there are such passages in his works. Shakespeare must not suffer from the badness of our memories." Johnson diverted by this enthusiastick jealousy went on with great ardour. "No, Sir, Congreve has *nature*;" (smiling on the tragick eagerness of Garrick;) but composing himself, he added, "Sir, this is not comparing Congreve on the whole with Shakespeare on the whole; but only maintaining that Congreve has one finer passage than any that can be found in Shakespeare. Sir, a man may have no more than ten guineas in the world, but he may have those ten guineas in one piece; and so may have a finer piece than a man who has ten thousand pounds: but then he has only one ten-guinea piece. What I mean is, that you can shew me no passage where there is simply a description of material objects, without any intermixture of moral notions, which produces such an effect." Mr. Murphy mentioned Shakespeare's description of the night before the battle of Agincourt; but it was observed it had *men* in it. Mr. Davies suggested the speech of Juliet, in which she figures herself awaking in the mob of her ancestors. Some one mentioned the description of Dover Cliff. JOHNSON: "No, Sir; it should be all precipice,—all vacuum. The crows impede your fall. The diminished appearance of the boats, and other circumstances, are all very good description; but do not impress the mind at once with the horrible idea of immense height. The impression is divided; you pass on by computation, from one stage of the tremendous space to another. Had the girl in 'The Mourning Bride,' said she could not.cast her shoe to the top of one of the pillars in the temple, it would not have aided the idea, but weakened it."

Talking of a Barrister who had a bad utterance, some one, (to rouse Johnson,) wickedly said, that he was unfortunate in not having been taught oratory by Sheridan. JOHNSON: "Nay, Sir, if he had been taught by Sheridan, he would have cleared the room." GARRICK: "Sheridan has too much vanity to be a good man."—We shall now see Johnson's mode of *defending* a man; taking him into his own hands, and discriminating. JOHNSON: "No, Sir. There is, to be sure, in Sheridan, something to reprehend, and every thing to laugh at; but, Sir, he is not a bad man. No, Sir, were mankind to be divided into good and bad, he would stand considerably within the ranks of good. And, Sir, it must be allowed that Sheridan excels in plain declamation, though he can exhibit no character."

Mrs. Montague, a lady distinguished for having written an Essay on Shakespeare, being mentioned;—REYNOLDS: "I think that essay does her honour." JOHNSON: "Yes, Sir, it does *her* honour, but it would do nobody else honour. I have, indeed, not read it all. But when I take up the end of a web, and find it pack-thread, I do not expect, by looking further, to find embroidery. Sir, I will venture to say, there is not one sentence of true criticism in her book." GARRICK: "But, Sir, surely it shews how much Voltaire has mistaken Shakespeare, which nobody else has done." JOHNSON: "Sir, nobody else has thought it worth while. And what merit is there in that? You may as well praise a schoolmaster for whipping a boy who has construed ill. No, Sir, there is no real criticism in it: none shewing the beauty of thought, as formed on the workings of the human heart."

Johnson proceeded: "The Scotchman has taken the right method in his 'Elements of Criticism.' I do not mean that he has taught us any thing; but he has told us old things in a new way." MURPHY: "He seems to have read a great deal of French criticism and wants to make it his own; as if he had been for years anatomising the heart of man, and peeping into every cranny of it." GOLDSMITH: "It is easier to write that book, than to read it." JOHNSON: "We have an example of true criticism in Burke's 'Essay on the Sublime and Beautiful;' and, if I recollect, there is also Du Bos; and Bouhours, who shews all beauty to depend on truth. There is no great merit in telling how many plays have ghosts in them, and how this ghost is better than that. You must shew how terrour is impressed on the human heart.—In the description of night in Macbeth, the beetle and the bat detract from the general idea of darkness,—inspissated gloom."

Politicks being mentioned, he said, "This petitioning is a new mode of distressing government, and a mighty easy one. I will undertake to get petitions either against quarter guineas or half guineas, with the help of a little hot wine. There must be no yielding to encourage this. The object is not important enough. We are not to blow up half a dozen palaces, because one cottage is burning."

The conversation then took another turn. JOHNSON: "It is amazing what ignorance of certain points one sometimes finds in men of eminence. A wit about town, who wrote Latin bawdy verses, asked me, how it happened that England and Scotland, which were once two kingdoms, were now one:—and Sir Fletcher Norton did not seem to know that there were such publications as the Reviews."

On Thursday, October 19, I passed the evening with him at his house. He advised me to complete a Dictionary of words peculiar to Scotland, of which I shewed him a specimen. "Sir, (said he,) Ray has made a collection of north-country words. By collecting those of your country, you will do a useful thing towards the history of the language." He bade me also go on with collections which I was making upon the antiquities of Scotland. "Make a large book; a folio." BOSWELL: "But of what use will it be, Sir?' JOHNSON: "Never mind the use; do it."

I complained that he had not mentioned Garrick in his Preface to Shakespeare; and asked him if he did not admire him. JOHNSON: "Yes, as 'a poor player, who frets and struts his hour upon the stage;'—as a shadow." BOSWELL: "But has he not brought Shakespeare into notice?" JOHNSON: "Sir, to allow that, would be to lampoon the age. Many of Shakespeare's plays are the worse for being acted: Macbeth, for instance." BOSWELL: "What, Sir, is nothing gained by decoration and action? Indeed, I do wish that you had mentioned Garrick.". JOHNSON: "My dear Sir, had I mentioned him, I must have mentioned many more; Mrs. Pritchard, Mrs. Cibber,—Nay, and Mr. Cibber too; he too altered Shakespeare." BOSWELL: "You have read his apology, Sir?" JOHNSON: "Yes, it is very entertaining. But as for Cibber himself, taking from his conversation all that he ought not to have said, he was a poor creature. I remember when he brought me one of his Odes to have my opinion of it, I could not bear such nonsense, and would not let him read it to the end; so little respect had I for *that great man*! (laughing.) Yet I remember Richardson wondering that I could treat him with familiarity."

I mentioned to him that I had seen the execution of several convicts at Tyburn, two days before, and that none of them seemed to be under any concern. JOHNSON: "Most of them, Sir, have never thought at all." BOSWELL: "But is not the fear of death natural to man?" JOHNSON: "So much so, Sir, that the whole of life is but keeping away the thoughts of it." He then, in a low and earnest tone, talked of his meditating upon the awful hour of his own dissolution, and in what manner he should conduct himself upon that occasion: "I know not (said he,) whether I should wish to have a friend by me, or have it all between God and myself."

Talking of our feeling for the distresses of others;—JOHNSON: "Why, Sir, there is much noise made about it, but it is greatly exaggerated. No, Sir, we have a certain degree of feeling to prompt us to do good; more than that, Providence does not intend. It would be misery to no purpose." BOSWELL: "But suppose now, Sir, that one of your intimate friends were apprehended for an offence for which he might be hanged." JOHNSON: "I should do what I could to bail him, and give him any other assistance; but if he were once fairly hanged, I should not suffer." BOSWELL: "Would you eat your dinner that day, Sir?" JOHNSON: "Yes, Sir; and eat it as if he were eating it with me. Why, there's Baretti, who is to be tried for his life to-morrow, friends have risen up for him on every side; yet if he should be hanged, none of them will eat a slice of plum-pudding the less. Sir, that sympathetick feeling goes a very little way in depressing the mind."

I told him that I had dined lately at Foote's, who shewed me a letter which he had received from Tom Davies, telling him that he had not been able to sleep from the concern he felt on account of "*This sad affair of Baretti,*" begging of him to try if he could suggest any thing that might be of service; and, at the same time, recommending to him an industrious young man who kept a pickle-shop. JOHNSON: "Ay, Sir, here you have a specimen of human sympathy; a friend hanged, and a cucumber pickled. We know not whether Baretti or the pickle-man has kept Davies from sleep: nor does he know himself. And as to his not sleeping, Sir; Tom Davies is a very great man; Tom has been upon the stage and knows how to do those things: I have not been upon the stage, and cannot do those things." BOSWELL: "I have often blamed myself, Sir, for not feeling for others, as sensibly as many say they do." JOHNSON: "Sir, don't be duped by them any more. You will find these very feeling people are not very ready to do you good. They *pay* you by *feeling.*"

BOSWELL: "Foote has a great deal of humour." JOHNSON: "Yes, Sir." BOSWELL: "He has a singular talent of exhibiting character." JOHNSON: "Sir, it is not a talent it is a vice; it is what others abstain from. It is not comedy, which exhibits the character of a species, as that of a miser gathered from many misers: it is a farce which exhibits individuals." BOSWELL: "Did not he think of exhibiting you, Sir?" JOHNSON: "Sir, fear restrained him; he knew I would have broken his bones. I would have saved him the trouble of cutting off a leg; I would not have left him a leg to cut off." BOSWELL: "Pray, Sir, is not Foote an infidel?" JOHNSON: "I do not know, Sir, that the fellow is an infidel; but if he be an infidel, he is an infidel as a dog is an infidel; that is to say, he has never thought upon the subject." BOSWELL: "I suppose, Sir, he has thought superficially, and seized the first notions which occurred to his mind." JOHNSON: "Why then, Sir, still he is like a dog, that snatches the piece next him. Did you never observe that dogs have not the power of comparing? A dog will take a small bit of meat as readily as a large, when both are before him."

He again talked of the passage in Congreve with high commendation, and said, "Shakespeare never has six lines together without a fault. Perhaps you may find seven: but this does not refute my general assertion. If I come to an orchard, and say there's no fruit here, and then comes a poring man, who finds two apples and three pears, and tells me, 'Sir, you are mistaken, I have found both apples and pears,' I should laugh at him; what would that be to the purpose?"

BOSWELL: "What do you think of Dr. Young's 'Night Thoughts,' Sir?" JOHNSON: "Why, Sir, there are very fine things in them." BOSWELL: "Is there not less religion in the nation now, Sir, than there was formerly?" JOHNSON: "I don't know, Sir, that there is." BOSWELL: "For instance, there used to be a chaplain in every great family, which we do not find now." JOHNSON: "Neither do you find any of the state servants which great families used formerly to have. There is a change of modes in the whole department of life."

On the 26th of October, we dined together at the Mitre tavern. I found fault with Foote for indulging his talent of ridicule at the expence of his visitors, which I colloquially termed making fools of his company. JOHNSON: "Why, Sir, when you go to see Foote, you do not go to see a saint: you go to see a man who will be entertained at your house, and then bring you on a publick stage; who will entertain you at his house, for the very purpose of bringing you on a publick stage. Sir, he does not make fools of his company; they whom he exposes are fools already: he only brings them into action."

Talking of trade, he observed, "It is a mistaken notion that a vast deal of money is brought into a nation by trade. It is not so. Commodities come from commodities; but trade produces no capital accession of wealth. However, though there should be little profit in money, there is a considerable profit in pleasure, as it gives to one nation the productions of another; as we have wines and fruits, and many other foreign articles, brought to us." BOSWELL: "Yes, Sir, and there is a profit in pleasure, by its furnishing occupation to such numbers of mankind." JOHNSON: "Why, Sir, you cannot call that pleasure to which all are averse, and which none begin but with the hope of leaving off; a thing which men dislike before they have tried it, and when they have tried it." BOSWELL: "But, Sir, the mind must be employed, and we grow weary when idle." JOHNSON: "That is, Sir, because others being busy, we want company; but if we are all idle, there would be no growing weary; we should all entertain one another. There is, indeed, this in trade:—it gives men an opportunity of improving their situation. If there were no trade, many who are poor would always remain poor. But no man loves labour for itself." BOSWELL: "Yes, Sir, I know a person who does. He is a very laborious Judge, and he loves the labour." JOHNSON: "Sir, that is because he loves respect and distinction. Could he have them without labour, he would like it less." BOSWELL: "He tells me he likes it for itself." —"Why, Sir, he fancies so, because he is not accustomed to abstract."

There was a pretty large circle this evening. Dr. Johnson was in very good humour, lively, and ready to talk upon all subjects. Mr. Fergusson, the self-taught philosopher, told him of a new invented machine which went without horses: a man who sat in it turned a handle, which worked a spring that drove it forward. "Then, Sir, (said Johnson,) what is gained is, the man has his choice whether he will move himself alone, or himself and the machine too." Dominicetti being mentioned, he would not allow him any merit. "There is nothing in all this boasted system. No, Sir; medicated baths can be no better than warm water: their only effect can be that of tepid moisture." One of the company took the other side, maintaining that medicines of various sorts, and some too of most powerful effect, are introduced into the human frame by the medium of the pores; and, therefore, when warm water is impregnated with salutiferous substances, it may produce great effects as a bath. This appeared to me very satisfactory. Johnson did not answer it; but talking for victory, and determined to be master of the field, he had recourse to the device which Goldsmith imputed to him in the witty words of one of Cibber's comedies: "There is no arguing with Johnson; for when his pistol misses fire, he knocks you down with the butt end of it." He turned to the gentleman, "Well, Sir, go to Dominicetti, and get thyself fumigated; but be sure that the steam be directed to thy *head*, for *that* is the *peccant part*." This produced a triumphant roar of laughter from the motley assembly of philosophers, printers, and dependents, male and female.

I know not how so whimsical a thought came into my mind, but I asked, "If, Sir, you were shut up in a castle, and a new-born child with you, what would you do?" JOHNSON: "Why, Sir, I should not much like my company." BOSWELL: "But would you take the trouble of rearing it?" He seemed, as may well be supposed, unwilling to pursue the subject: but upon my persevering in my question, replied, "Why yes, Sir, I would; but I must have all conveniences. If I had no garden, I would make a shed on the roof, and take it there for fresh air. I should feed it, and wash it much, and with warm water to please it, not with cold water to give it pain." BOSWELL: "But, Sir, does not heat relax." JOHNSON: "Sir, you are not to imagine the water is to be very hot. I would not *coddle* the child. No, Sir, the hardy method of treating children does no good. I'll take you five children from London, who shall cuff five Highland children. Sir, a man bred in London will carry a burthen, or run, or wrestle, as well as a man brought up in the hardest manner in the country." BOSWELL: "Good living, I suppose, makes the Londoners strong." JOHNSON: "Why, Sir, I don't know that it does. Our chairmen from Ireland, who are as strong men as any, have been brought up upon potatoes. Quantity makes up for quality." BOSWELL: "Would you teach this child that I have furnished you with, anything?" JOHNSON: "No, I should not be apt to teach it." BOSWELL: "Would not you have a pleasure in teaching it?" JOHNSON: "No, Sir, I should *not* have a pleasure in teaching it." BOSWELL: "Have you not a pleasure in teaching men!— *There* I have you. You have the same pleasure in teaching men, that I should have in teaching children." JOHNSON: "Why, some thing about that."

BOSWELL: "Do you think, Sir, that what is called natural affection is born with us? It seems to me to be the effect of habit, or of gratitude for kindness. No child has it for a parent whom it has

66

not seen." JOHNSON: "Why, Sir, I think there is an instinctive natural affection in parents towards their children."

Russia being mentioned as likely to become a great empire, by the rapid increase of population:—JOHNSON: "Why, Sir, I see no prospect of their propagating more. They can have no more children than they can get. I know of no way to make them breed more than they do. It is not from reason and prudence that people marry, but from inclination. A man is poor; he thinks, 'I cannot be worse, and so I'll e'en take Peggy.'" BOSWELL: "But have not nations been more populous at one period than another?" JOHNSON: "Yes, Sir; but that has been owing to the people being less thinned at one period than another, whether by emigrations, war, or pestilence, not by their being more or less prolifick. Births at all times bear the same proportion to the same number of people." BOSWELL: "But, to consider the state of our own country;—does not throwing a number of farms into one hand hurt population?" JOHNSON: "Why no, Sir; the same quantity of food being produced, will be consumed by the same number of mouths, though the people may be disposed of in different ways. We see, if corn be dear, and butchers' meat cheap, the farmers all apply themselves to the raising of corn, till it becomes plentiful and cheap, and then butchers' meat becomes dear; so that an equality is always preserved. No, Sir, let fanciful men do as they will, depend upon it, it is difficult to disturb the system of life." BOSWELL: "But, Sir, is it not a very bad thing for landlords to oppress their tenants, by raising their rents?" JOHNSON: "Very bad. But, Sir, it never can have any general influence: it may distress some individuals. For, consider this: landlords cannot do without tenants. Now tenants will not give more for land, than land is worth. If they can make more of their money by keeping a shop, or any other way, they do it, and so oblige landlords to let land come back to a reasonable rent in order that they may get tenants. Land in England, is an article of commerce. A tenant who pays his landlord his rent, thinks himself no more obliged to him than you think yourself obliged to a man in whose shop you buy a piece of goods. He knows the landlord does not let him have his land for less than he can get from others, in the same manner as the shopkeeper sells his goods. No shopkeeper sells a yard of ribband for six-pence when seven-pence is the current price." BOSWELL: "But, Sir, is it not better that tenants should be dependent on landlords?" JOHNSON: "Why, Sir, as there are many more tenants than landlords, perhaps strictly speaking, we should wish not. But if you please you may let your lands cheap, and so get the value, part in money and part in homage. I should agree with you in that." BOSWELL: "So, Sir, you laugh at schemes of political improvement." JOHNSON: "Why, Sir, most schemes of political improvement are very laughable things."

He observed, "Providence has wisely ordered that the more numerous men are, the more difficult it is for them to agree in any thing, and so they are governed. There is no doubt, that if the poor should reason, 'We'll be the poor no longer, we'll make the rich take their turn,' they could easily do it, were it not that they can't agree. So the common soldiers, though so much more numerous than their officers, are governed by them for the same reason."

He said, "Mankind have a strong attachment to the habitations to which they have been accustomed. You see the inhabitants of Norway do not with one consent quit it, and go to some part of America, where there is a mild climate, and where they may have the same produce from land, with the tenth part of the labour. No, Sir; their affection for their old dwellings, and the terrour of a general change, keep them at home. Thus, we see many of the finest spots in the world thinly inhabited, and many rugged spots well inhabited."

I had hired a Bohemian as my servant while I remained in London, and being much pleased with him, I asked Dr. Johnson whether his being a Roman Catholick should prevent my taking him with me to Scotland. JOHNSON: "Why no, Sir. If *he* has no objection, you can have none." BOSWELL: "So, Sir, you are no great enemy to the Roman Catholick religion." JOHNSON: "No more, Sir, than to the Presbyterian religion." BOSWELL: "You are joking." JOHNSON: "No, Sir, I really think so. Nay, Sir, of the two, I prefer the Popish." BOSWELL: "How so, Sir?" JOHNSON: "Why, Sir, the Presbyterians have no church, no apostolical ordination." BOSWELL: "And do you think that absolutely essential, Sir?" JOHNSON: "Why, Sir, as it was an apostolical institution, I think it is dangerous to be without it. And Sir, the Presbyterians have no publick worship: they have no form of prayer in which they know they are to join. They go to hear a man pray, and are to judge whether they will join with him." BOSWELL: "But, Sir, their doctrine is the same with that of the Church of England. Their confession of faith, and the thirty-nine articles contain the same points, even the doctrine of predestination." JOHNSON: "Why, yes, Sir; predestination was a part of the clamour of the times, so it is mentioned in our articles, but with as little positiveness as could be." BOSWELL: "Is it necessary, Sir, to believe all the thirty-nine articles?" JOHNSON: "Why, Sir, that is a question which has been much agitated. Some have thought it necessary that they should all be believed; others have considered them to be only articles of peace, that is to say, you are not to preach against them." BOSWELL: "It appears to me, Sir, that predestination, or what is equivalent to it, cannot be avoided, if we hold an universal prescience in the Deity." JOHNSON: "Why, Sir, does not God every day see things going on without preventing them?" BOSWELL: "True, Sir, but if a thing be *certainly* foreseen, it must be fixed, and cannot happen otherwise; and if we apply this consideration to the human mind, there is no free will, nor do I see how prayer can be of any avail." He mentioned Dr. Clarke, and Bishop Bramhall on Liberty and Necessity, and bid me read South's Sermons on Prayer; but avoided the question which has ex-cruciated philosophers and divines, beyond any other.

I proceeded: "What do you think, Sir, of Purgatory, as believed by the Roman Catholicks?" JOHNSON: "Why, Sir, it is a very harmless doctrine. They are of opinion that the generality of mankind are neither so obstinately wicked as to deserve ever-lasting punishment, nor so good as to merit being admitted into the society of blessed spirits; and therefore that God is graciously pleased to allow of a middle state, where they may be purified by certain degrees of suffering. You see, Sir, there is nothing un-reasonable in this." BOSWELL: "But then, Sir, their Masses for the dead?" JOHNSON: "Why, Sir, if it be once established that there are souls in purgatory, it is as proper to pray for *them*, as for our brethren of mankind who are yet in this life." BOSWELL: "The idolatry of the Mass?" JOHNSON: "Sir, there is no idolatry in the Mass. They believe God to be there, and they adore him." BOSWELL: "The worship of saints?" JOHNSON: "Sir, they do not worship saints; they invoke them; they only ask their prayers. I am talking all this time of the *doctrines* of the Church of Rome. I grant you that in *practice*, Purgatory is made a lucrative imposition, and that the people do become idolatrous as they recommend themselves to the tutelary protection of particular saints. I think their giving the sacrament only in one kind is criminal, because it is contrary to the express institution of CHRIST, and I wonder how the Council of Trent admitted it." BOSWELL: "Confession?" JOHNSON: "Why, I don't know but that is a good thing. The scripture says, 'Confess

69

your faults one to another,' and the priests confess as well as the laity. Then it must be considered that their absolution is only upon repentance, and often upon penance also. You think your sins may be forgiven without penance, upon repentance alone."

When we were alone, I introduced the subject of death, and endeavoured to maintain that the fear of it might be got over. I told him that David Hume said to me, he was no more uneasy to think he should *not be* after his life, than that he *had not been* before he began to exist. JOHNSON: "Sir, if he really thinks so, his perceptions are disturbed; he is mad; if he does not think so, he lies. He may tell you, he holds his finger in the flame of a candle, without feeling pain; would you believe him? When he dies, he at least gives up all he has." BOSWELL: "Foote, Sir, told me, that when he was very ill he was not afraid to die." JOHNSON: "It is not true, Sir. Hold a pistol to Foote's breast, or to Hume's breast, and threaten to kill them, and you'll see how they behave." BOSWELL: "But may we not fortify our minds for the approach of death?"—Here I am sensible I was in the wrong, to bring before his view what he ever looked upon with horrour; for although when in a celestial frame of mind in his *Vanity of Human Wishes*, he had supposed death to be "kind Nature's signal for retreat," from this state of being to "a happier seat," his thoughts upon this awful change were in general full of dismal apprehensions. His mind resembled the vast amphitheatre, the Colisæum at Rome. In the centre stood his judgement, which like a mighty gladiator, combated those apprehensions that, like the wild beasts of the *Arena*, were all around in cells, ready to be let out upon him. After a conflict, he drives them back into their dens; but not killing them, they were still assailing him. To my question, whether we might not fortify our minds for the approach of death, he answered, in a passion, "No, Sir, let it alone. It matters not how a man dies, but how he lives. The act of dying is not of importance, it lasts so short a time." He added, (with an earnest look,) "A man knows it must be so, and submits. It will do him no good to whine."

I attempted to continue the conversation. He was so provoked, that he said: "Give us no more of this;" and was thrown into such a state of agitation, that he expressed himself in a way that alarmed and distressed me; shewed an impatience that I should leave him, and when I was going away, called to me sternly, "Don't let us meet to-morrow."

I went home exceedingly uneasy. All the harsh observations which

I had ever heard made upon his character, crowded into my mind; and I seemed to myself like the man who had put his head into the lion's mouth a great many times with perfect safety, but at last had it bit off.

Next morning I sent him a note, stating that I might have been in the wrong, but it was not intentionally; he was therefore, I could not help thinking, too severe upon me. That notwithstanding our agreement not to meet that day, I would call on him in my way to the city, and stay five minutes by my watch. "You are, (said I) in my mind, since last night, surrounded with cloud and storm. Let me have a glimpse of sunshine, and go about my affairs in serenity and cheerfulness."

Upon entering his study, I was glad that he was not alone, which would have made our meeting more awkward. There were with him Mr. Steevens and Mr. Tyers, both of whom I now saw for the first time. My note had, on his now reflection, softened him, for he received me very complacently; so that I unexpectedly found myself at ease; and joined in the conversation.

Johnson spoke unfavourably of a certain pretty voluminous authour, saying, "He used to write anonymous books, and then other books commending those books, in which there was something of rascality."

I whispered him, "Well, Sir, you are now in good humour." JOHNSON: "Yes, Sir." I was going to leave him, and had got as far as the staircase. He stopped me, and smiling, said, "Get you gone *in*;" a curious mode of inviting me to stay, which I accordingly did for some time longer.

I went to him early in the morning of the tenth of November. "Now (said he,) that you are going to marry, do not expect more from life, than life will afford. You may often find yourself out of humour, and you may often think your wife not studious enough to please you; and yet you may have reason to consider yourself as upon the whole very happily married."

Talking of marriage in general, he observed, "Our marriage service is too refined. It is calculated only for the best kind of marriages; whereas, we should have a form for matches of convenience, of which there are many." He agreed with me that there was no absolute necessity for having the marriage ceremony performed by a regular clergyman, for this was not commanded in scripture.

CHAPTER IV

In Seventeen Seventy-two

ON THE 21st of March, 1772, I was happy to find myself again in my friend's study, and was glad to see my old acquaintance, Mr. Francis Barber, who was now returned home. Dr. Johnson received me with a hearty welcome.

A gentleman having come in who was to go as a Mate in the ship along with Mr. Banks and Dr. Solander, Dr. Johnson asked what were the names of the ships destined for the expedition. The gentleman answered, they were once to be called the *Drake* and the *Ralegh*, but now they were to be called the *Resolution* and the *Adventure*. JOHNSON: "Much better; for had the *Ralegh* returned without going round the world, it would have been ridiculous. To give them the names of the *Drake* and the *Ralegh* was laying a trap for satire." BOSWELL: "Had not you some desire to go upon this expedition, Sir?" JOHNSON: "Why yes, but I soon laid it aside. Sir, there is very little of intellectual, in the course. Besides, I see but at a small distance. So it was not worth my while to go to see birds fly, which I should not have seen fly; and fishes swim, which I should not have seen swim."

He spoke of St. Kilda, the most remote of the Hebrides. I told him, I thought of buying it. JOHNSON: "Pray do, Sir. We will go and pass a winter amid the blasts there. We shall have fine fish, and we will take some dried tongues with us, and some books. We will have a strong built vessel, and some Orkney men to navigate her. We must build a tolerable house: but we may carry with us a wooden house ready made, and requiring nothing but to be put up. Consider, Sir, by buying St. Kilda, you may keep the people from falling into worse hands. We must give them a clergyman, and he shall be one of Beattie's choosing. He shall be educated at Marischal College. I'll be your Lord Chancellor, or what you please." BOSWELL: "Are you serious, Sir, in advising me to buy St. Kilda? for if you should advise me to go to Japan, I believe I should do it." JOHNSON: "Why yes, Sir, I am serious." BOSWELL: "Why then I'll see what can be done."

I gave him an account of the two parties in the church of Scotland, those for supporting the rights of patrons, independent of the people, and those against it. JOHNSON: "It should be settled one way or other. I cannot wish well to a popular election of the clergy, when I consider that it occasions such animosities, such unworthy courting of the people, such slanders between the contending parties, and other disadvantages. It is enough to allow the people to remonstrate against the nomination of a minister for solid reasons." (I suppose he meant heresy or immorality.)

He was engaged to dine abroad, and asked me to return to him in the evening, at nine, which I accordingly did.

We drank tea with Mrs. Williams, who told us a story of second sight, which happened in Wales where she was born. He listened to it very attentively, and said he should be glad to have some instances of that faculty well authenticated. His elevated wish for more and more evidence for spirit, in opposition to the grovelling belief of materialism, led him to a love of such mysterious disquisitions. He again justly observed, that we could have no certainty of the truth of supernatural appearances, unless something was told us which we could not know by ordinary means, or something done which could not be done but by supernatural power; that Pharaoh in reason and justice required such evidence from Moses; nay, that our Saviour said, "If I had not done among them the works which none other man did, they had not had sin." He had said in the morning, that Macaulay's *History of St. Kilda* was very well written, except some foppery about liberty and slavery. I mentioned to him that Macaulay told me, he was advised to leave out of his book the wonderful story that upon the approach of a stranger all the inhabitants catch cold; but that it had been so well authenticated, he determined to retain it. JOHNSON: "Sir, to leave things out of a book, merely because people tell you they will not be believed, is meanness. Macaulay acted with more magnanimity."

We talked of the Roman Catholick religion, and how little difference there was in essential matters between ours and it. JOHNSON: "True, Sir; all denominations of Christians have really little difference in point of doctrine, though they may differ widely in external forms. There is a prodigious difference between the external form of one of your Presbyterian churches in Scotland, and a church in Italy; yet the doctrine taught is essentially the same."

I mentioned the petition to Parliament for removing the subscription to the Thirty-nine Articles. JOHNSON: "It was soon thrown out. Sir, they talk of not making boys at the University subscribe to what they do not understand; but they ought to consider, that our Universities were founded to bring up members for the Church of England, and we must not supply our enemies with arms from our arsenal. No, Sir, the meaning of subscribing is, not that they fully understand all the articles, but that they will adhere to the Church of England. Now take it in this way, and suppose that they should only subscribe their adherence to the Church of England, there would be still the same difficulty; for still the young men would be subscribing to what they do not understand. For if you should ask them, what do you mean by the Church of England? Do you know in what it differs from the Presbyterian Church? from the Romish Church? from the Greek Church? from the Coptick Church? they could not tell you. So, Sir, it comes to the same thing." BOSWELL: "But, would it not be sufficient to subscribe the Bible?" JOHNSON: "Why no, Sir; for all sects will subscribe the Bible; nay, the Mahometans will subscribe the Bible; for the Mahometans acknowledge JESUS CHRIST, as well as Moses, but maintain that God sent Mahomet as a still greater prophet than either."

In the morning we had talked of old families, and the respect due to them. JOHNSON: "Sir, you have a right to that kind of respect, and are arguing for yourself. I am for supporting the principle, and am disinterested in doing it, as I have no such right." BOSWELL: "Why, Sir, it is one more incitement to a man to do well." JOHNSON: "Yes, Sir, and it is a matter of opinion very necessary to keep society together. What is it but opinion, by which we have a respect for authority, that prevents us, who are the rabble, from rising up and pulling down you who are gentlemen from your places, and saying, 'We will be gentlemen in our turn?' Now, Sir, that respect for authority is much more easily granted to a man whose father has had it, than to an upstart, and so Society is more easily supported." BOSWELL: "Perhaps, Sir, it might be done by the respect belonging to office, as among the Romans, where the dress, the *toga*, inspired reverence." JOHNSON: "Why, we know very little about the Romans. But, surely, it is much easier to respect a man who has always had respect, than to respect a man who we know was last year no better than ourselves, and will be no better next year. In republicks there is no respect for authority, but a fear of power." BOSWELL: "At present, Sir, I think riches seem to gain most respect." JOHNSON: "No, Sir, riches do not gain hearty respect; they only procure external attention. A very rich man, from low beginnings, may buy his election in a borough; but, *cæteris paribus*, a man of family will be preferred. People will prefer a man for whose father their fathers have voted, though they should get no more money, or even less. That shows that the respect for family is not merely fanciful, but has an actual operation. If gentlemen of family would allow the rich upstarts to spend their money profusely, which they are ready enough to do, and not vie with them in expence, the upstarts would soon be at an end, and the gentlemen would remain; but if the gentlemen will vie in expence with the upstarts, which is very foolish, they must be ruined."

I gave him an account of the excellent mimickry of a friend of mine in Scotland; observing, at the same time, that some people thought it a very mean thing. JOHNSON: "Why, Sir, it is making a very mean use of man's powers. But to be a good mimick, requires great powers; great acuteness of observation, great retention of what is observed, and great pliancy of organs to represent what is observed. I remember a lady of quality in this town, Lady —— who was a wonderful mimick, and used to make me laugh immoderately. I have heard she is now gone mad." BOSWELL: "It is amazing how a mimick can not only give you the gestures and voice of a person whom he represents; but even what a person would say on any particular subject." JOHNSON: "Why, Sir, you are to consider that the manner and some particular phrases of a person do much to impress you with an idea of him, and you are not sure that he would say what the mimick says in his character." BOSWELL: "I don't think Foote a good mimick, Sir." JOHNSON: "No, Sir, his imitations are not like. He gives you something different from himself, but not the character which he means to assume. He goes out of himself, without going into other people. He cannot take off any person unless he is strongly marked, such as George Faulkner. He is like a painter who can draw the portrait of a man who has a wen upon his face, and who therefore is easily known. If a man hops upon one leg, Foote can hop upon one leg. But he has not that nice discrimination which your friend seems to possess. Foote is, however, very entertaining with a kind of conversation between wit and buffoonery."

On Saturday, March 27, I introduced to him Sir Alexander Macdonald, with whom he had expressed a wish to be acquainted. He received him very courteously.

Sir Alexander observed, that the Chancellors in England are

chosen from views much inferiour to the office, being chosen from temporary political views. JOHNSON: "Why, Sir, in such a government as ours, no man is appointed to an office because he is the fittest for it, nor hardly in any other government; because there are so many connections and dependencies to be studied. A despotick prince may choose a man to an office, merely because he is the fittest for it. The King of Prussia may do it." SIR A.: "I think, Sir, almost all great lawyers, such at least as have written upon law, have known only law, and nothing else." JOHNSON: "Why no, Sir; Judge Hale was a great lawyer, and wrote upon law; and yet he knew a great many other things, and has written upon other things. Selden, too." SIR A.: "Very true, Sir; and Lord Bacon. But was not Lord Coke a mere lawyer?" JOHNSON: "Why, I am afraid he was; but he would have taken it very ill if you had told him so. He would have prosecuted you for scandal." BOSWELL: "Lord Mansfield is not a mere lawyer." JOHNSON: "No, Sir, I never was in Lord Mansfield's company; but Lord Mansfield was distinguished at the University. Lord Mansfield, when he first came to town, 'drank champagne with the wits,' as Prior says. He was the friend of Pope." SIR A.: "Barristers, I believe, are not so abusive now as they were formerly. I fancy they had less law long ago, and so were obliged to take to abuse, to fill up the time. Now they have such a number of precedents, they have no occasion for abuse." JOHNSON: "Nay, Sir, they had more law long ago than they have now. As to precedents, to be sure they will increase in course of time; but the more precedents there are, the less occasion is there for law; that is to say, the less occasion is there for investigating principles." SIR A.: "I have been correcting several Scotch accents in my friend Boswell. I doubt, Sir, if any Scotchman ever attains to a perfect English pronunciation." JOHNSON: "Why, Sir, few of them do, because they do not persevere after acquiring a certain degree of it. But, Sir, there can be no doubt that they may attain to a perfect English pronunciation, if they will. We find how near they come to it; and certainly, a man who conquers nineteen parts of the Scottish accent, may conquer the twentieth. But, Sir, when a man has got the better of nine tenths he grows weary, he relaxes his diligence, he finds he has corrected his accent so far as not to be disagreeable, and he no longer desires his friends to tell him when he is wrong; nor does he choose to be told. Sir, when people watch me narrowly, and I do not watch myself, they will find me out to be of a particular county. In the same manner, Dunning may be found out to be a

Devonshire man. So most Scotchmen may be found out. But, Sir, little aberrations are of no disadvantage. I never catched Mallet in a Scotch accent; and yet Mallet, I suppose, was past five-and-twenty before he came to London."

BOSWELL: "It may be of use, Sir, to have a Dictionary to ascertain the pronunciation." JOHNSON: "Why, Sir, my Dictionary shows you the accent of words, if you can but remember them." BOSWELL: "But, Sir, we want marks to ascertain the pronunciation of the vowels. Sheridan, I believe, has finished such a work." JOHNSON: "Why, Sir, consider how much easier it is to learn a language by the ear, than by any marks. Sheridan's Dictionary may do very well; but you cannot always carry it about with you; and, when you want the word, you have not the Dictionary. It is like a man who has a sword that will not draw. It is an admirable sword, to be sure: but while your enemy is cutting your throat, you are unable to use it. Besides, Sir, what entitles Sheridan to fix the pronunciation of English? He has, in the first place, the disadvantage of being an Irishman: and if he says he will fix it after the example of the best company, why they differ among themselves. I remember an instance: when I published the Plan for my Dictionary, Lord Chesterfield told me that the word *great* should be pronounced so as to rhyme to *state*; and Sir William Yonge sent me word that it should be pronounced so as to rhyme to *seat*, and that none but an Irishman would pronounce it *grait*. Now here were two men of the highest rank, the one, the best speaker in the House of Lords, the other, the best speaker in the House of Commons, differing entirely."

I again visited him at night. Finding him in a very good humour, I ventured to lead him to the subject of our situation in a future state, having much curiosity to know his notions on that point. JOHNSON: "Why, Sir, the happiness of an unembodied spirit will consist in a consciousness of the favour of God, in the contemplation of truth, and in the possession of felicitating ideas." BOSWELL: "But, Sir, is there any harm in our forming to ourselves conjectures as to the particulars of our happiness, though the scripture has said but very little on the subject? 'We know not what we shall be'." JOHNSON: "Sir, there is no harm. What philosophy suggests to us on this topick is probable: what scripture tells us is certain. Dr. Henry More has carried it as far as philosophy can. You may buy both his theological and philosophical works in two volumes folio, for about eight shillings." BOSWELL: "One of the most pleasing thoughts is, that we shall see our friends again." JOHNSON: "Yes, Sir; but you must consider, that when we are become purely rational, many of our friendships will be cut off. Many friendships are formed by a community of sensual pleasures: all these will be cut off. We form many friendships with bad men, because they have agreeable qualities, and they can be useful to us; but, after death, they can no longer be of use to us. We form many friendships by mistake, imagining people to be different from what they really are. After death, we shall see every one in a true light. Then, Sir, they talk of our meeting our relations: but then all relationship is dissolved: and we shall have no regard for one person more than another, but for their real value. However, we shall either have the satisfaction of meeting our friends, or be satisfied without meeting them." BOSWELL: "Yet, Sir, we see in scripture, that Dives still retained an anxious concern about his brethren." JOHNSON: "Why, Sir, we must either suppose that passage to be metaphorical, or hold with many divines, and all the Purgatorians, that departed souls do not all at once arrive at the utmost perfection of which they are capable." BOSWELL: "I think, Sir, that is a very rational supposition." JOHNSON: "Why, yes, Sir; but we do not know it is a true one. There is no harm in believing it: but you must not compel others to make it an article of faith; for it is not revealed." BOSWELL: "Do you think, Sir, it is wrong in a man who holds the doctrine of Purgatory, to pray for the souls of his deceased friends?" JOHNSON: "Why no, Sir." BOSWELL: "I have been told, that in the Liturgy of the Episcopal Church of Scotland, there was a form of prayer for the dead." JOHNSON: "Sir, it is not in the Liturgy which Laud framed for the Episcopal Church of Scotland: if there is a Liturgy older than that, I should be glad to see it." BOSWELL: "As to our employment in a future state, the sacred writings say little. The Revelation, however, of St. John gives us many ideas, and particularly mentions musick." JOHNSON: "Why, Sir, ideas must be given you by means of something which you know: and as to musick there are some philosophers and divines who have maintained that we shall not be spiritualized to such a degree, but that something of matter very much refined, will remain. In that case, musick may make a part of our future felicity."

BOSWELL: "This objection is made against the truth of ghosts appearing: that if they are in a state of happiness, it would be a punishment to them to return to this world; and if they are in a state of misery, it would be giving them a respite." JOHNSON: "Why, Sir, as the happiness or misery of embodied spirits does not depend upon place, but is intellectual, we cannot say that they are less happy or less miserable by appearing upon earth."

We went down between twelve and one to Mrs. Williams's room, and drank tea.

I mentioned Elwal, the heretick, whose trial Sir John Pringle had given me to read. JOHNSON: "Sir, Mr. Elwal was, I think, an ironmonger at Wolverhampton; and he had a mind to make himself famous, by being the founder of a new sect, which he wished much should be called *Elwallians*. He held, that every thing in the Old Testament that was not typical, was to be of perpetual observance: and so he wore a ribband in the plaits of his coat, and he also wore a beard. I remember I had the honour of dining in company with Mr. Elwal. There was one Barter, a miller, who wrote against him; and you had the controversy between MR. ELWAL and MR. BARTER. To try to make himself distinguished he wrote a letter to King George the Second, challenging him to dispute with him, in which he said, 'George, if you be afraid to come by yourself, to dispute with a poor old man, you may bring a thousand of your *black*-guards with you; and if you should still be afraid, you may bring a thousand of your *red*-guards.' The letter had something of the impudence of Junius to our present King. But the men of Wolverhampton were not so inflammable as the Common-Council of London; so Mr. Elwal failed in his scheme of making himself a man of great consequence."

On Tuesday, March 31, he and I dined at General Paoli's. A question was started whether the state of marriage was natural to man. JOHNSON: "Sir, it is so far from being natural for a man and woman to live in a state of marriage, that we find all the motives which they have for remaining in that connection, and the restraints which civilized society imposes to prevent separation, are hardly sufficient to keep them together." The General said, that in a state of nature a man and woman uniting together, would form a strong and constant affection, by the mutual pleasure each would receive; and that the same causes of dissention would not arise between them, as occur between husband and wife in a civilized state. JOHNSON: "Sir, they would have dissentions enough though of another kind. One would choose to go a hunting in this wood, the other in that; one would choose to go a fishing in this lake, the other in that; or, perhaps, one would choose to go a hunting, when the other would choose to go a fishing; and so they would part. Besides, Sir, a savage man and a savage woman meet by chance; and when the man sees another woman that pleases him better, he will leave the first."

We then fell into a disquisition whether there is any beauty independent of utility. The General maintained there was not. Dr. Johnson maintained that there was; and he instanced a coffee cup which he held in his hand, the painting of which was of no real use, as the cup could hold the coffee equally well if plain; yet the painting was beautiful.

Dr. Johnson went home with me to my lodgings in Conduit-street and drank tea, previous to our going to the Pantheon, which neither of us had seen before.

I asked him, how far he thought wealth should be employed in hospitality. JOHNSON: "You are to consider that ancient hospitality, of which we hear so much, was in an uncommercial country, when men being idle, were glad to be entertained at rich men's tables. But in a commercial country, a busy country, time becomes precious, and therefore hospitality is not so much valued. No doubt there is still room for a certain degree of it; and a man has a satisfaction in seeing his friends eating and drinking around him. But promiscuous hospitality is not the way to gain real influence. You must help some people at table before others; you must ask some people how they like their wine oftener than others. You therefore offend more people than you please. You are like the French statesman who said, when he granted a favour, '*J'ai fait dix mécontents et un ingrat.*' Besides, Sir, being entertained ever so well at a man's table, impresses no lasting regard or esteem. No, Sir, the way to make sure of power and influence is, by lending money confidentially to your neighbours at a small interest, or perhaps at no interest at all, and having their bonds in your possession." BOSWELL: "May not a man, Sir, employ his riches to advantage, in educating young men of merit?" JOHNSON: "Yes, Sir, if they fall in your way; but if it be understood that you patronize young men of merit, you will be harassed with solicitations. You will have numbers forced upon you, you will have no merit; some will force them upon you from mistaken partiality; and some from downright interested motives, without scruple; and you will be disgraced."

"Were I a rich man, I would propagate all kinds of trees that will grow in the open air. A green-house is childish. I would intro-duce foreign animals into the country; for instance, the reindeer."

We then walked to the Pantheon. The first view of it did not strike us so much as Ranelagh, of which he said, the "*coup d'œil* was the finest thing he had ever seen." The truth is, Ranelagh is of a more beautiful form; more of it, or rather indeed the whole *rotunda*, appears at once, and it is better lighted. However, as Johnson observed, we saw the Pantheon in time of mourning, when there was a dull uniformity; whereas we had seen Ranelagh, when the view was enlivened with a gay profusion of colours.

I said there was not half a guinea's worth of pleasure in seeing this place. JOHNSON: "But, Sir, there is half a guinea's worth of inferiority to other people in not having seen it." BOSWELL: "I doubt, Sir, whether there are many happy people here." JOHNSON: "Yes, Sir, there are many happy people here. There are many people here who are watching hundreds, and who think hundreds are watching them."

Happening to meet Sir Adam Ferguson, I presented him to Dr. Johnson. Sir Adam expressed some apprehension that the Pantheon would encourage luxury. "Sir, (said Johnson,) I am a great friend to publick amusements; for they keep people from vice. You now (addressing himself to me,) would have been with a wench, had you not been here.—O! I forgot you were married."

Sir Adam suggested, that luxury corrupts a people, and destroys the spirit of liberty. JOHNSON: "Sir, that is all visionary. I would not give half a guinea to live under one form of Government rather than another. It is of no moment to the happiness of an individual. Sir, the danger of the abuse of power is nothing to a private man. What Frenchman is prevented from passing his life as he pleases?" SIR ADAM: "But, Sir, in the British constitution it is surely of importance to keep up a spirit in the people, so as to preserve a balance against the crown." JOHNSON: "Sir, I perceive you are a vile Whig. —Why all this childish jealousy of the power of the crown? The crown has not power enough. When I say that all governments are alike, I consider that in no government power can be abused long. Mankind will not bear it. If a sovereign oppresses his people to a great degree, they will rise and cut off his head. There is a remedy in human nature against tyranny, that will keep us safe under every form of government. Had not the people of France thought themselves honoured in sharing in the brilliant actions of Louis XIV. they would not have endured him; and we may say the same of the King of Prussia's people." Sir Adam introduced the ancient Greeks and Romans. JOHNSON: "Sir, the mass of both of them were barbarians. The mass of every people must be barbarous where there is no printing, and consequently knowledge is not generally diffused. Knowledge is diffused among our people by the newspapers." Sir Adam mentioning the orators, poets and artists of Greece. JOHNSON: "Sir, I am talking of the mass of the people. We see even what the boasted Athenians were. The little effect which Demosthenes's orations had upon them, shews that they were barbarians."

Sir Adam was unlucky in his topicks; for he suggested a doubt of the propriety of Bishops having seats in the House of Lords. JOHNSON: "How so, Sir? Who is more proper for having the dignity of a peer, than a bishop, provided a Bishop be what he ought to be; and if improper Bishops be made, that is not the fault of the Bishops, but of those who make them."

On Sunday, April 5, after attending divine service at St. Paul's church, I found him alone. Of a schoolmaster of his acquaintance, a native of Scotland, he said, "He has a great deal of good about him; but he is also very defective in some respects. His inner part is good, but his outer part is mighty awkward. You in Scotland do not attain that nice critical skill in languages, which we get in our schools in England. I would not put a boy to him, whom I intended for a man of learning. But for the sons of citizens, who are to learn a little, get good morals, and then go to trade, he may do very well."

I mentioned a cause in which I had appeared as counsel at the bar of the General Assembly of the Church of Scotland, where a *Probationer*, (as one licensed to preach, but not yet ordained, is called,) was opposed in his application to be inducted, because it was alledged that he had been guilty of fornication five years before. JOHNSON: "Why, Sir, if he has repented, it is not a sufficient objection. A man who is good enough to go to heaven, is good enough to be a clergyman." I told him, that by the rules of the Church of Scotland, in their "Book of Discipline," if a *scandal* as it is called, is not prosecuted for five years, it cannot afterwards be proceeded upon, " unless it be *of a heinous nature*, or again become flagrant; " and that hence a question arose, whether fornication was a sin of a heinous nature; and that I had maintained, that it did not deserve that epithet, in as much as it was not one of those sins which argue very great depravity of heart: in short, was not, in the general acceptation of mankind a heinous sin. JOHNSON: "No, Sir, it is not a heinous sin. A heinous sin is that for which a man is punished with death or banishment." BOSWELL: "But, Sir, after I had argued that it was not a heinous sin, an old clergyman rose up, and repeating the text of scripture denouncing judgment against whoremongers, asked, whether, considering this, there could be any doubt of fornication being a heinous sin." JOHNSON: "Why, Sir, observe the word *whoremonger*. Every sin, if persisted in, will become heinous. Whoremonger is a dealer in whores, as ironmonger is a dealer in iron. But as you don't call a man an ironmonger for buying and selling a penknife; so you don't call a man a whore-monger for getting one wench with child."

I spoke of the inequality of the livings of the clergy in England, and the scanty provisions of some of the Curates. JOHNSON: "Why, yes, Sir; but it cannot be helped. You must consider, that the revenues of the clergy are not at the disposal of the state, like the pay of the army. Different men have founded different churches; and some are better endowed, some worse. The state cannot interfere and make an equal division of what has been particularly appropriated. Now when a clergyman has but a small living, or even two small livings, he can afford very little to the Curate."

On Monday, April 6, I dined with him at Sir Alexander Macdonald's, where was a young officer in the regimentals of the Scots Royal, who talked with a vivacity, fluency, and precision so uncommon, that he attracted particular attention. He proved to be the Honourable Thomas Erskine, youngest brother to the Earl of Buchan, who has since risen into such brilliant reputation at the bar in Westminster-hall.

Fielding being mentioned, Johnson exclaimed, "he was a blockhead;" and upon my expressing my astonishment at so strange an assertion, he said, "What I mean by his being a blockhead is, that he was a barren rascal." BOSWELL: "Will you not allow, Sir, that he draws very natural pictures of human life?" JOHNSON: "Why, Sir, it is of very low life. Richardson used to say, that had he not known who Fielding was, he should have believed he was an ostler. Sir, there is more knowledge of the heart in one letter of Richardson's, than in all 'Tom Jones.' I, indeed, never read 'Joseph Andrews.'" ERSKINE: "Surely, Sir, Richardson is very tedious." JOHNSON: "Why, Sir, if you were to read Richardson for the story, your impatience would be so much fretted that you would hang yourself. But you must read him for the sentiment, and consider the story as only giving occasion to the sentiment."

We talked of gaming, and animadverted on it with severity.

JOHNSON: "Nay, gentlemen, let us not aggravate the matter. It is not roguery to play with a man who is ignorant of the game, while you are master of it, and so win his money; for he thinks he can play better than you, as you think you can play better than he; and the superior skill carries it." ERSKINE: "He is a fool, but you are not a rogue." JOHNSON: "That's much about the truth, Sir. It must be considered, that a man who only does what every one of the society to which he belongs would do, is not a dishonest man. In the republick of Sparta, it was agreed, that stealing was not dishonourable, if not discovered. I do not commend a society where there is an agreement that what would not otherwise be fair, shall be fair; but I maintain, that an individual of any society, who practises what is allowed, is not a dishonest man." BOSWELL: "So then, Sir, you do not think ill of a man who wins perhaps forty thousand pounds in a winter?" JOHNSON: "Sir, I do not call a gamester a dishonest man; but I call him an unsocial man, an unprofitable man. Gaming is a mode of transferring property without producing any intermediate good. Trades gives employment to numbers, and so produces intermediate good."

Mr. Erskine told us, that when he was in the island of Minorca, he not only read prayers, but preached two sermons to the regiment. He seemed to object to the passage in scripture, where we are told that the angel of the Lord smote in one night forty thousand Assyrians. "Sir, (said Johnson,) you should recollect that there was a supernatural interposition; they were destroyed by pestilence. You are not to suppose that the angel of the LORD went about and stabbed each of them with a dagger, or knocked them on the head, man by man."

After Mr. Erskine was gone, a discussion took place, whether the present Earl of Buchan, when Lord Cardross, did right to refuse to go Secretary of the Embassy to Spain, when Sir James Gray, a man of inferiour rank, went Ambassadour. Dr. Johnson said, that perhaps in point of interest he did wrong; but in point of dignity he did well. Sir Alexander insisted that he was wrong; and said that Mr. Pitt intended it as an advantageous thing for him. "Why, Sir, (said Johnson,) Mr. Pitt might think it an advantageous thing for him to make him a vintner, and get him all the Portugal trade: but he would have demeaned himself strangely had he accepted of such a situation. Sir, had he gone Secretary while his inferiour was Ambassadour, he would have been a traitor to his rank and family."

I talked of the little attachment which subsisted between near relations in London. "Sir, (said Johnson,) in a country so commercial as ours, where every man can do for himself, there is not so much occasion for that attachment. No man is thought the worse of here, whose brother was hanged. In uncommercial countries, many of the branches of a family must depend on the stock; so, in order to make the head of the family take care of them, they are represented as connected with his reputation, that, self-love being interested, he may exert himself to promote their interest. You have first large circles, or clans; as commerce increases, the connection is confined to families; by degrees, that too goes off, as having become unnecessary, and there being few opportunities of intercourse. One brother is a merchant in the city, and another is an officer in the guards; how little intercourse can these two have."

I argued warmly for the old feudal system. Sir Alexander opposed it, and talked of the pleasure of seeing all men free and independent. JOHNSON: "I agree with Mr. Boswell, that there must be a high satisfaction in being a feudal Lord; but we are to consider that we ought not to wish to have a number of men unhappy for the satisfaction of one."—I maintained that numbers, namely, the vassals or followers, were not unhappy; for that there was a reciprocal· satisfaction between the Lord and them; he being kind in his authority over them; they being respectful and faithful to him.

On Thursday, April 9, I called on him to beg he would go and dine with me at the Mitre tavern. He had resolved not to dine at all this day, I know not for what reason; and I was so unwilling to be deprived of his company, that I was content to submit to suffer a want, which was at first somewhat painful, but he soon made me forget it; and a man is always pleased with himself, when he finds his intellectual inclinations predominate.

He observed, that to reason philosophically on the nature of prayer, was very unprofitable.

Talking of ghosts, he said, he knew one friend, who was an honest man and a sensible man, who told him he had seen a ghost; old Mr. Edward Cave, the printer at St. John's Gate. He said, Mr. Cave did not like to talk of it, and seemed to be in great horrour whenever it was mentioned. BOSWELL: "Pray, Sir, what did he say was the appearance?" JOHNSON: "Why, Sir, something of a shadowy being."

85

I mentioned witches, and asked him what they properly meant. JOHNSON: "Why, Sir, they properly mean those who make use of the aid of evil spirits." BOSWELL: "There is no doubt, Sir, a general report and belief of their having existed." JOHNSON: "You have not only the general report and belief, but you have many voluntary solemn confessions." He did not affirm anything positively upon a subject which it is the fashion of the times to laugh at as a matter of absurd credulity. He only seemed willing, as a candid enquirer after truth, however strange and inexplicable, to shew that he understood what might be urged for it.

On Friday, April 10, I dined with him at General Oglethorpe's, where we found Dr. Goldsmith.

I started the question, whether duelling was consistent with moral duty. The brave old General fired at this, and said, with a lofty air, "Undoubtedly a man has a right to defend his honour." GOLDSMITH: (turning to me,) "I ask you first, Sir, what would you do if you were affronted?" I answered, I should think it necessary to fight. "Why then, (replied Goldsmith,) that solves the question." JOHNSON: "No, Sir, it does not solve the question. It does not follow, that what a man would do is therefore right." I said, I wished to have it settled, whether duelling was contrary to the laws of Christianity. Johnson immediately entered on the subject, and treated it in a masterly manner; and so far as I have been able to recollect, his thoughts were these: "Sir, as men become in a high degree refined, various causes of offence arise; which are considered to be of such importance, that life must be staked to atone for them, though in reality they are not so. A body that has received a very fine polish may be easily hurt. Before men arrive at this artificial refinement, if one tells his neighbour—he lies, his neighbour tells him—he lies; if one gives his neighbour a blow, his neighbour gives him a blow: but in a state of highly polished society, an affront is held to be a serious injury. It must, therefore, be resented, or rather a duel must be fought upon it; as men have agreed to banish from their society one who puts up with an affront without fighting a duel. Now, Sir, it is never unlawful to fight in self-defence. He, then, who fights a duel, does not fight from passion against his antagonist, but out of self-defence; to avert the stigma of the world, and to prevent himself from being driven out of society. I could wish there was not that superfluity of refinement; but while such notions prevail, no doubt a man may lawfully fight a duel."

86

The General told us, that when he was a very young man, I think only fifteen, serving under Prince Eugene of Savoy, he was sitting in a company at table with a Prince of Wirtemberg. The Prince took up a glass of wine, and, by a fillip, made some of it fly in Oglethorpe's face. Here was a nice dilemma. To have challenged him instantly, might have fixed a quarrelsome character upon the young soldier: to have taken no notice of it, might have been considered as cowardice. Oglethorpe, therefore, keeping his eye upon the Prince, and smiling at the time, as if he took what his Highness had done in jest, said "*Mon Prince*——," (I forget the French words he used, the purport however was,) "That's a good joke: but we do it much better in England;" and threw a whole glass of wine in the Prince's face. An old General who sat by, said, "*Il a bien fait, mon Prince, vous l'avez commencé:*" and thus all ended in good humour.

A question was started, how far people who disagree in a capital point can live in friendship together. Johnson said they might. Goldsmith said they could not, as they had not the *idem velle atque idem nolle*—the same likings and the same aversions. JOHNSON: "Why, Sir, you must shun the subject as to which you disagree. For instance, I can live very well with Burke: I love his knowledge, his genius, his diffusion, and affluence of conversation; but I would not talk to him of the Rockingham party." GOLDSMITH: "But, Sir, when people live together who have something as to which they disagree, and which they want to shun, they will be in the situation mentioned in the story of Bluebeard: 'You may look into all the chambers but one.' But we should have the greatest inclination to look into that chamber, to talk of that subject." JOHNSON: (with a loud voice): "Sir, I am not saying that *you* could live in friendship with a man from whom you differ as to some point: I am only saying that I could do it. You put me in mind of Sappho in Ovid."

Of our friend Goldsmith he said, "Sir, he is so much afraid of being unnoticed, that he often talks merely lest you should forget that he is in the company." BOSWELL: "Yes, he stands forward." JOHNSON: "True, Sir; but if a man is to stand forward, he should wish to do it not in an aukward posture, not in rags, not so as that he shall only be exposed to ridicule." BOSWELL: "For my part, I like very well to hear honest Goldsmith talk away carelessly." JOHNSON: "Why, yes, Sir; but he should not like to hear himself."

On Tuesday April 14, I talked of the recent expulsion of six students from the University of Oxford, who were methodists, and would not desist from publickly praying and exhorting. JOHNSON: "Sir, that expulsion was extremely just and proper. What have they to do at an University, who are not willing to be taught, but will presume to teach? Where is religion to be learnt, but at an University? Sir, they were examined, and found to be mighty ignorant fellows." BOSWELL: "But, was it not hard, Sir, to expel them, for I am told they were good beings?" JOHNSON: "I believe they might be good beings; but they were not fit to be in the University of Oxford. A cow is a very good animal in the field, but we turn her out of a garden." Lord Elibank used to repeat this as an illustration uncommonly happy.

Desirous of calling Johnson forth to talk, and exercise his wit, though I should myself be the object of it, I resolutely ventured to undertake the defence of convivial indulgence in wine, though he was not to-night in the most genial humour. After urging the common plausible topicks, I at last had recourse to the maxim, *in vino veritas*, a man who is well warmed with wine will speak truth. JOHNSON: "Why, Sir; that may be an argument for drinking, if you suppose men in general to be liars. But, Sir, I would not keep company with a fellow, who lyes as long as he is sober, and whom you must make drunk before you can get a word of truth out of him."

Mr. Langton told us, he was about to establish a school upon his estate, but it had been suggested to him, that it might have a tendency to make the people less industrious. JOHNSON: "No, Sir. While learning to read and write is a distinction, the few who have that distinction may be the less inclined to work; but when every body learns to read and write, it is no longer a distinction. A man who has a laced waistcoat is too fine a man to work; but if every body had laced waistcoats, we should have people working in laced waistcoats. There are no people whatever more industrious, none who work more, than our manufacturers; yet they have all learned to read and write. Sir, you must not neglect doing a thing immediately good, from fear of remote evil;—from fear of its being abused. A man who has candles may sit up too late, which he would not do if he had not candles; but nobody will deny that the art of making candles, by which light is continued to us beyond the time that the sun gives us light, is a valuable art, and ought to be preserved." BOSWELL: "But, Sir, would it not be better to follow

Nature; and go to bed and rise just as nature gives us light or withholds it?" JOHNSON: "No, Sir; for then we should have no kind of equality in the partition of our time between sleeping and waking. It would be very different in different seasons and in different places. In some of the northern parts of Scotland how little light is there in the depth of winter!"

On Sunday, April 19, being Easter-day, General Paoli and I paid him a visit before dinner. We talked of the notion that blind persons can distinguish colours by the touch. Johnson said, that Professor Sanderson mentions his having attempted to do it, but that he found he was aiming at an impossibility; that to be sure a difference in the surface makes the difference of colours; but that difference is so fine, that it is not sensible to the touch. The General mentioned jugglers and fraudulent gamesters, who could know cards by the touch. Dr. Johnson said, "the cards used by such persons must be less polished than ours commonly are."

We talked of sounds. The General said, there was no beauty in a simple sound, but only in an harmonious composition of sounds. I presumed to differ from this opinion, and mentioned the soft and sweet sound of a fine woman's voice. JOHNSON: "No, Sir, if a serpent or a toad uttered it, you would think it ugly." BOSWELL: "So you would think, Sir, were a beautiful tune to be uttered by one of those animals." JOHNSON: "No, Sir, it would be admired. We have seen fine fiddlers whom we liked as little as toads" (laughing).

Talking on the subject of taste in the arts, he said, that difference of taste was, in truth, difference of skill. BOSWELL: "But, Sir, is there not a quality called taste, which consists merely in perception or in liking; for instance, we find people differ much as to what is the best style of English composition. Some think Swift's the best; others prefer a fuller and grander way of writing." JOHNSON: "Sir, you must first define what you mean by style, before you can judge who has a good taste in style, and who has a bad. The two classes of persons whom you have mentioned, don't differ as to good and bad. They both agree that Swift has a good neat style; but one loves a neat style, another loves a style of more splendour. In like manner, one loves a plain coat, another loves a laced coat; but neither will deny that each is good in its kind."

While I remained in London this spring, I was with him at several other times, both by himself and in company. Without specifying each particular day, I have preserved the following memorable things.

A gentleman having to some of the usual arguments for drinking added this: "You know, Sir, drinking drives away care, and makes us forget whatever is disagreeable. Would not you allow a man to drink for that reason?" JOHNSON: "Yes, Sir, if he sat next *you*."

He said, "there is no permanent national character: it varies according to circumstances. Alexander the Great swept India: now the Turks sweep Greece."

A learned gentleman, who in the course of conversation wished to inform us of this simple fact, that the Counsel upon the circuit at Shrewsbury were much bitten by fleas, took, I suppose, seven or eight minutes in relating it circumstantially. He in a plentitude of phrase told us, that large bales of woollen cloth were lodged in the town-hall;—that by reason of this, fleas nestled there in prodigious numbers; that the lodgings of the counsel were near the town-hall: —and that those little animals moved from place to place with wonderful agility. Johnson sat in great impatience till the gentleman had finished his tedious narrative, and then burst out (playfully however), "It is a pity, Sir, that you have not seen a lion; for a flea has taken you such a time, that a lion must have served you a twelve-month."

He would not allow Scotland to derive any credit from Lord Mansfield; for he was educated in England. "Much (said he,) may be made of a Scotchman, if he be *caught* young."

Talking of a modern historian and a modern moralist, he said, "There is more thought in the moralist than in the historian. There is but a shallow stream of thought in history." BOSWELL: "But surely, Sir, an historian has reflection." JOHNSON: "Why yes, Sir; and so has a cat when she catches a mouse for her kitten. But she cannot write like *******; neither can *********."

He said, "I am very unwilling to read the manuscripts of authours, and give them my opinion. If the authours who apply to me have money, I bid them boldly print without a name; if they have written in order to get money, I tell them to go to the booksellers and make the best bargain they can." BOSWELL: "But, Sir, if a bookseller should bring you a manuscript to look at?" JOHNSON: "Why, Sir, I would desire the bookseller to take it away."

I mentioned a friend of mine who had resided long in Spain, and was unwilling to return to Britain. JOHNSON: "Sir, he is attached to some woman." BOSWELL: "I rather believe, Sir, it is the fine climate which keeps him there." JOHNSON: "Nay Sir, how can you talk so? What is *climate* to happiness? Place me in the heart of Asia

90

should I not be exiled? What proportion does climate bear to the complex system of human life? You may advise me to live at Bologna to eat sausages. The sausages there are the best in the world; they lose much by being carried."

On Saturday, May 9, Mr. Dempster and I had agreed to dine by ourselves at the British Coffee-house. Johnson, on whom I happened to call in the morning, said he would join us, which he did, and we spent a very agreeable day, though I recollect but little of what passed.

He said, "Walpole was a minister given by the King to the people: Pitt was a minister given by the people to the King,—as an adjunct."

"The misfortune of Goldsmith in conversation is this: he goes on without knowing how he is to get off. His genius is great, but his knowledge is small. As they say of a generous man, it is a pity he is not rich, we may say of Goldsmith, it is a pity he is not knowing. He would not keep his knowledge to himself."

CHAPTER V

In Seventeen Seventy-three

On Saturday, April 3, the day after my arrival in London in 1773, I went to his house late in the evening, and sat with Mrs. Williams till he came home. I found in the London *Chronicle*, Dr. Goldsmith's apology to the publick for beating Evans, a bookseller, on account of a paragraph in a newspaper published by him, which Goldsmith thought impertinent to him and to a lady of his acquaintance. The apology was written so much in Dr. Johnson's manner, that both Mrs. Williams and I supposed it to be his; but when he came home, he soon undeceived us. When he said to Mrs. Williams, "Well, Dr. Goldsmith's *manifesto* has got into your paper;" I asked him if Dr. Goldsmith had written it, with an air that made him see I suspected it was his, though subscribed by Goldsmith. JOHNSON: "Sir, Dr. Goldsmith would no more have asked me to write such a thing as that for him, than he would have asked me to feed him with a spoon, or to do any thing else that denoted his imbecility. I as much believe that he wrote it, as if I had seen him do it. Sir, had he shown it to any one friend, he would not have been allowed to publish it. He has, indeed, done it very well; but it is a foolish thing well done. I suppose he has been so much elated with the success of his new comedy, that he has thought every thing that concerned him must be of importance to the publick." BOSWELL: "I fancy, Sir, this is the first time that he has been engaged in such an adventure." JOHNSON: "Why, Sir, I believe it is the first time he has *beat*; he may have *been beaten* before. This, Sir, is a new plume to him."

I mentioned Sir John Dalrymple's *Memoirs of Great-Britain and Ireland*, and his discoveries to the prejudice of Lord Russel and Algernon Sydney. JOHNSON: "Why, Sir, every body who had just notions of Government thought them rascals before. It is well that all mankind now see them to be rascals." BOSWELL: "But, Sir, may not those discoveries be true without their being rascals?" JOHNSON: "Consider, Sir, would any of them have been willing to have had it known that they intrigued with France? Depend upon it, Sir, he who does what he is afraid should be known, has something rotten about him. This Dalrymple seems to be an honest fellow; for he tells equally what makes against both sides. But nothing can be poorer than his mode of writing, it is the mere bouncing of a school-boy. Great He! but greater She! and such stuff."

At Mr. Thrale's, in the evening, he repeated his usual paradoxical declamation against action in publick speaking. "Action, can have no effect upon reasonable minds. It may augment noise, but it never can enforce argument. If you speak to a dog, you use action; you hold up your hand thus, because he is a brute; and in proportion as men are removed from brutes, action will have the less influence upon them." MRS. THRALE: "What then, Sir, becomes of Demosthenes's saying? 'Action, action action!'" JOHNSON: "Demosthenes, Madam, spoke to an assembly of brutes; to a barbarous people."

Lord Chesterfield being mentioned, Johnson remarked, that almost all of that celebrated nobleman's witty sayings were puns. He, however, allowed the merit of good wit to his Lordship's saying of Lord Tyrawley and himself, when both very old and infirm: "Tyrawley and I have been dead these two years; but we don't choose to have it known."

On Tuesday, April 13, he and Dr. Goldsmith and I dined at General Oglethorpe's. Goldsmith expatiated on the common topick, that the race of our people was degenerated, and that this was owing to luxury. JOHNSON: "Sir, in the first place, I doubt the fact. I believe there are as many tall men in England now, as ever there were. But, secondly, supposing the stature of our people to be diminished, that is not owing to luxury; for, Sir, consider to how very small a proportion of our people luxury can reach. Our soldiery, surely, are not luxurious, who live on six-pence a day; and the same remark will apply to almost all the other classes. Luxury, so far as it reaches the poor, will do good to the race of people; it will strengthen and multiply them. Sir, no nation was ever hurt by luxury; for, as I said before, it can reach but to a very few. I admit that the great increase of commerce and manufactures hurts the military spirit of a people; because it produces a competition for something else than martial honours,—a competition for riches. It also hurts the bodies of the peoples; for you will observe, there is no man who works at any particular trade, but you may know him from his appearance to do so. One part or the other of his body being more used than the rest, he is in some degree deformed: but, Sir, that is not luxury. A tailor sits cross-legged; but that is not luxury." GOLDSMITH: "Come, you're just going to the same place by another road." JOHNSON: "Nay, Sir, I say that is not *luxury*. Let us take a walk from Charing-Cross to Whitechapel, through, I suppose, the greatest series of shops in the world, what is there in any of these shops, (if you except gin-shops,) that can do any human being any harm?" GOLDSMITH: "Well, Sir, I'll accept your challenge. The very next shop to Northumberland house is a pickle-shop." JOHNSON: "Well, Sir: do we not know that a maid can in one afternoon make pickles sufficient to serve a whole family for a year? nay, that five pickle-shops can serve all the kingdom? Besides, Sir, there is no harm done to any body by the making of pickles, or the eating of pickles."

We drank tea with the ladies; and Goldsmith sung Tony Lumpkin's song in his comedy, "She Stoops to Conquer," and a very pretty one, to an Irish tune, which he had designed for Miss Hardcastle: but as Mrs. Bulkeley, who played the part, could not sing, it was left out. He afterwards wrote it down for me, by which means it was preserved, and now appears amongst his poems. Dr. Johnson, on his way home, stopped at my lodgings in Piccadilly, and sat with me, drinking tea a second time, till a late hour.

I told him that Mrs. Macaulay said, she wondered how he could reconcile his political principles with his moral: his notions of inequality and subordination with wishing well to the happiness of all mankind who might live so agreeably, had they all their portions of land, and none to domineer over another. JOHNSON: "Why, Sir, I reconcile my principles very well, because mankind are happier in a state of inequality and subordination. Were they to be in this pretty state of equality, they would soon degenerate into brutes;— they would become Monboddo's nation;—their tails would grow. Sir, all would be losers, were all to work for all:—they would have no intellectual improvement. All intellectual improvement arises from leisure; all leisure arises from one working for another."

Talking of the family of Stuart, he said, "It should seem that the family at present on the throne has now established as good a right as the former family, by the long consent of the people; and that to disturb this right might be considered as culpable. At the same time I own, that it is a very difficult question, when considered with respect to the house of Stuart. To oblige people to take oaths as to the disputed right, is wrong. I know not whether I could take them: but I do not blame those who do."

On Thursday, April 15, I dined with him and Dr. Goldsmith at General Paoli's. We found here Signor Martinelli, of Florence, authour of a History of England, in Italian, printed at London.

An animated debate took place whether Martinelli should continue his History of England to the present day. GOLDSMITH: "To be sure he should." JOHNSON: "No, Sir; he would give great offence. He would have to tell of almost all the living great what they do not wish told." GOLDSMITH: "It may, perhaps, be necessary for a native to be more cautious; but a foreigner who comes among us without prejudice, may be considered as holding the place of a Judge, and may speak his mind freely." JOHNSON: "Sir, a foreigner when he sends a work from the press, ought to be on his guard against catching the errour and mistaken enthusiasm of the people among whom he happens to be." GOLDSMITH: "Sir, he wants only to sell his history, and to tell truth; one an honest, the other a laudable motive." JOHNSON: "Sir, they are both laudable motives. It is laudable in a man to wish to live by his labours; but he should write so as he may *live* by them, not as so he may be knocked on the head. I would advise him to be at Calais before he publishes his history of the present age. A foreigner who attaches himself to a political party in this country, is in the worst state that can be imagined: he is looked upon as a mere intermeddler. A native may do it from interest." BOSWELL: "Or principle." GOLDSMITH: "There are people who tell a hundred political lies every day, and are not hurt by it. Surely, then, one may tell truth with safety." JOHNSON: "Why, Sir, in the first place, he who tells a hundred lies has disarmed the force of his lies. But besides; a man had rather have a hundred lies told of him, than one truth which he does not wish should be told." GOLDSMITH: "For my part, I'd tell truth, and shame the devil." JOHNSON: "Yes, Sir; but the devil will be angry. I wish to shame the devil as much as you do, but I should choose to be out of the reach of his claws." GOLDSMITH: "His claws can do you no harm, when you have the shield of truth."

It having been observed that there was little hospitality in London; JOHNSON: "Nay, Sir, any man who has a name, or who has the power of pleasing, will be very generally invited in London. The man Sterne, I have been told, has had engagements for three months." GOLDSMITH: "And a very dull fellow." JOHNSON: "Why, no, Sir."

Martinelli told us, that for several years he lived much with Charles Townshend, and that he ventured to tell him he was a bad joker. JOHNSON: "Why, Sir, this much I can say upon the subject. One day he and a few more agreed to go and dine in the country, and each of them was to bring a friend in his carriage with him. Charles Townshend asked Fitzherbert to go with him, but told him, 'You must find somebody to bring you back: I can only carry you there.' Fitzherbert did not much like this arrangement. He however consented, observing sarcastically, 'It will do very well; for then the same jokes will serve you in returning as in going.'"

An eminent publick character being mentioned;—JOHNSON: "I remember being present when he shewed himself to be so corrupted, or at least something so different from what I think right, as to maintain, that a member of parliament should go along with his party right or wrong. Now, Sir, this is so remote from native virtue, from scholastick virtue, that a good man must have undergone a great change before he can reconcile himself to such a doctrine. It is maintaining that you may lie to the publick; for you lie when you call that right which you think wrong, or the reverse. A friend of ours who is too much an echo of that gentleman, observed, that a man who does not stick uniformly to a party, is only waiting to be bought. Why then, said I, he is only waiting to be what that gentleman is already."

I spoke of Mr. Harris, of Salisbury, as being a very learned man, and in particular an eminent Grecian. JOHNSON: "I am not sure of that. His friends give him out as such, but I know not who of his friends are able to judge of it." GOLDSMITH: "He is what is much better: he is a worthy humane man." JOHNSON: "Nay, Sir, that is not to the purpose of our argument: that will as much prove that he can play upon the fiddle as well as Giardini, as that he is an eminent Grecian." GOLDSMITH: "The greatest musical performers have but small emoluments. Giardini, I am told, does not get above seven hundred a year." JOHNSON: "That is indeed but little for a man to get, who does best that which so many endeavour to do. There is nothing, I think, in which the power of art is shown so much as in playing on the fiddle. In all other things we can do something at first. Any man will forge a bar of iron, if you give him a hammer; not so well as a smith, but tolerably. A man will saw a piece of wood, and make a box, though a clumsy one; but give him a fiddle and a fiddle-stick, and he can do nothing."

On Wednesday, April 21, I dined with him at Mr. Thrale's. A gentleman attacked Garrick for being vain. JOHNSON: "No wonder, Sir, that he is vain; a man who is perpetually flattered in every mode that can be conceived. So many bellows have blown the fire, that one wonders he is not by this time become a cinder." BOSWELL: "And such bellows too. Lord Mansfield with his cheeks like to burst: Lord Chatham like an Æolus. I have read such notes from them to him, as were enough to turn his head." JOHNSON: "True. When he whom every body else flatters, flatters me, I then am truly happy."

The modes of living in different countries, and the various views with which men travel in quest of new scenes, having been talked of, a learned gentleman who holds a considerable office in the law expatiated on the happiness of a savage life, and mentioned an instance of an officer who had actually lived for some time in the wilds of America, of whom, when in that state, he quoted this reflection with an air of admiration, as if it had been deeply philosophical: "Here am I, free and unrestrained, amidst the rude magnificence of Nature, with this Indian woman by my side, and this gun, with which I can procure food when I want it: what more can be desired for human happiness?" It did not require much sagacity to foresee that such a sentiment would not be permitted to pass without due animadversion. JOHNSON: "Do not allow yourself, Sir, to be imposed upon by such gross absurdity. It is sad stuff; it is brutish. If a bull could speak, he might as well exclaim,—Here am I with this cow and this grass; what being can enjoy better felicity?"

We talked of the melancholy end of a gentleman who had destroyed himself. JOHNSON: "It was owing to imaginary difficulties in his affairs, which, had he talked with any friend, would soon have vanished." BOSWELL: "Do you think, Sir, that all who commit suicide are mad?" JOHNSON: "Sir, they are often not universally disordered in their intellects, but one passion presses so upon them, that they yield to it, and commit suicide, as a passionate man will stab another." He added, "I have often thought, that after a man has taken the resolution to kill himself, it is not courage in him to do any thing, however desperate, because he has nothing to fear." GOLDSMITH: "I don't see that." JOHNSON: "Nay, but my dear Sir, why should not you see what every one else sees?" GOLDSMITH: "It is for fear of something that he has resolved to kill himself: and will not that timid disposition restrain him?" JOHNSON: "It does not signify that the fear of something made him resolve; it is upon the state of his mind, after the resolution is taken, that I argue. Suppose a man, either from fear, or pride, or conscience, or whatever motive, has resolved to kill himself; when once the resolution is taken, he has nothing to fear. He may then go and take the King of Prussia by the nose, at the head of his army. He cannot fear the rack, who is resolved to kill himself. When Eustace Budgel was walking down to the Thames, determined to drown himself, he might, if he pleased, without any apprehension of danger, have turned aside, and first set fire to St. James's palace."

On Tuesday, April 27, Mr. Beauclerk and I called on him in the morning.

He said, "Goldsmith should not be for ever attempting to shine in conversation: he has not temper for it, he is so much mortified when he fails. Sir, a game of jokes is composed partly of skill, partly of chance, a man may be beat at times by one who has not the tenth part of his wit. Now Goldsmith's putting himself against another, is like a man laying a hundred to one who cannot spare the hundred. It is not worth a man's while. A man should not lay a hundred to one, unless he can easily spare it, though he has a hundred chances for him: he can get but a guinea, and he may lose a hundred. Goldsmith is in this state. When he contends, if he gets the better, it is a very little addition to a man of his literary reputation: if he does not get the better, he is miserably vexed."

Goldsmith, however, was often very fortunate in his witty contests, even when he entered the lists with Johnson himself. Sir Joshua Reynolds was in company with them one day, when Goldsmith said, that he thought he could write a good fable, mentioned the simplicity which that kind of composition requires, and observed, that in most fables the animals introduced seldom talk in character. "For instance, (said he,) the fable of the little fishes, who saw birds fly over their heads, and envying them, petitioned Jupiter to be changed into birds. The skill (continued he,) consists in making them talk like little fishes." While he indulged himself in this fanciful reverie, he observed Johnson shaking his sides, and laughing. Upon which he smartly proceeded, "Why, Dr. Johnson, this is not so easy as you seem to think; for if you were to make little fishes talk, they would talk like WHALES."

On Thursday, April 29, I dined with him at General Oglethorpe's, where were Sir Joshua Reynolds, Mr. Langton, Dr. Goldsmith, and Mr. Thrale.

The custom of eating dogs at Otaheite being mentioned, Goldsmith observed, that this was also a custom in China: that a dog-butcher is as common there as any other butcher; and that when he walks abroad all the dogs fall on him. JOHNSON: "That is not owing to his killing dogs, Sir. I remember a butcher at Lichfield, whom a dog that was in the house where I lived, always attacked. It is the smell of carnage which provokes this, let the animals he has killed be what they may." GOLDSMITH: "Yes, there is a general abhorrence in animals at the signs of massacre. If you put a tub full of blood into a stable, the horses are like to go mad." JOHNSON: "I doubt that." GOLDSMITH: "Nay, Sir, it is a fact well authenticated." THRALE: "You had better prove it before you put it into your book on natural history. You may do it in my stable if you will." JOHNSON: "Nay, Sir, I would not have him prove it. If he is content to take his information from others, he may get through his book with little trouble, and without much endangering his reputation. But if he makes experiments for so comprehensive a book as his, there would be no end to them; his erroneous assertions would then fall upon himself; and he might be blamed for not having made experiments as to every particular."

The character of Mallet having been introduced, and spoken of slightingly by Goldsmith; JOHNSON: "Why, Sir, Mallet had talents enough to keep his literary reputation alive as long as he himself lived; and that, let me tell you, is a good deal." GOLDSMITH: "But I cannot agree that it was so. His literary reputation was dead long before his natural death. I consider an authour's literary reputation to be alive only while his name will insure a good price for his copy from the booksellers. I will get you (to Johnson,) a hundred guineas for any thing whatever that you shall write, if you put your name to it."

Goldsmith having said, that Garrick's compliment to the Queen, which he introduced into the play of *The Chances*, which he had altered and revised this year, was mean and gross flattery; JOHNSON: "Why, Sir, I would not *write*, I would not give solemnly under my hand, a character beyond what I thought really true; but a speech on the stage, let it flatter ever so extravagantly, is formular. It has always been formular to flatter Kings and Queens; so much so, that even in our church-service we have 'our most religious King,' used indiscriminately, whoever is King. Nay, they even flatter themselves;—'we have been graciously pleased to grant.'—No modern flattery, however, is so gross as that of the Augustan age where the Emperour was deified. '*Præsens Divus habebitur Augustus.*' And as to meanness, (rising into warmth) how is it mean

99

in a player,—a showman,—a fellow who exhibits himself for a shilling, to flatter his Queen? The attempt, indeed, was dangerous; for if it had missed, what became of Garrick, and what became of the Queen? As Sir William Temple says of a great General, it is necessary not only that his designs be formed in a masterly manner, but that they should be attended with success. Sir, it is right, at a time when the Royal Family is not generally liked, to let it be seen that the people like at least one of them." SIR JOSHUA REYNOLDS: "I do not perceive why the profession of a player should be despised; for the great and ultimate end of all the employments of mankind is to produce amusement. Garrick produces more amusement than any body." BOSWELL: "You say, Dr. Johnson, that Garrick exhibits himself for a shilling. In this respect he is only on a footing with a lawyer who exhibits himself for his fee, and even will maintain any nonsense or absurdity, if the case require it. Garrick refuses a play or a part which he does not like: a lawyer never refuses." JOHNSON: "Why, Sir, what does this prove? only that a lawyer is worse. Boswell is now like Jack in *The Tale of a Tub*, who, when he is puzzled by an argument, hangs himself. He thinks I shall cut him down, but I'll let him hang" (laughing vociferously.) SIR JOSHUA REYNOLDS: "Mr. Boswell thinks that the profession of a lawyer being unquestionably honourable, if he can show the profession of a player to be more honourable, he proves his argument."

On Friday, April 30, I dined with him at Mr. Beauclerk's, where were Lord Charlemont, Sir Joshua Reynolds and some more members of the LITERARY CLUB, whom he had obligingly invited to meet me, as I was this evening to be ballotted for as candidate for admission into that distinguished society. Johnson had done me the honour to propose me, and Beauclerk was very zealous for me.

Goldsmith being mentioned; JOHNSON: "It is amazing how little Goldsmith knows. He seldom comes where he is not more ignorant than any one else." SIR JOSHUA REYNOLDS: "Yet there is no man whose company is more liked." JOHNSON: "To be sure, Sir. When people find a man of the most distinguished abilities as a writer, their inferiour while he is with them, it must be highly gratifying to them. What Goldsmith comically says of himself is very true,—he always gets the better when he argues alone; meaning, that he is master of a subject in his study, and can write well upon it; but when he comes into company, grows confused, and unable to talk. Take him as a poet, his *Traveller* is a very fine performance; ay, and so is his *Deserted Village* were it not sometimes too much the echo of his *Traveller*. Whether, indeed, we take him as a poet,—as a comick writer,—or as an historian, he stands in the first class." BOSWELL: "An historian! My dear Sir, you surely will not rank his compilation of the Roman History with the works of other historians of this age?" JOHNSON: "Why, who are before him?" BOSWELL: "Hume,—Robertson,—Lord Lyttelton." JOHNSON: (His antipathy to the Scotch beginning to rise.) "I have not read Hume; but, doubtless, Goldsmith's History is better than the *verbiage* of Robertson, or the foppery of Dalrymple." BOSWELL: "Will you not admit the superiority of Robertson, in whose history we find such penetration—such painting?" JOHNSON: "Sir, you must consider how that penetration and that painting are employed. It is not history, it is imagination. He who describes what he never saw, draws from fancy. Robertson paints minds as Sir Joshua paints faces in a history-piece: he imagines an heroick countenance. You must look upon Robertson's work as romance and try it by that standard. History it is not. Besides, Sir, it is the great excellence of a writer to put into his book as much as his book will hold. Goldsmith has done this in his History. Now Robertson might have put twice as much into his book. Robertson is like a man who has packed gold in wool; the wool takes up more room than the gold. No, Sir; I always thought Robertson would be crushed by his own weight,— would be buried under his own ornaments. Goldsmith tells you shortly all you want to know: Robertson detains you a great deal too long. No man will read Robertson's cumbrous detail a second time; but Goldsmith's plain narrative will please again and again. I would say to Robertson what an old tutor of a college said to one of his pupils: 'Read over your compositions, and wherever you meet with a passage which you think is particularly fine, strike it out.' Goldsmith's abridgement is better than that of Lucius Florus or Eutropius; and I will venture to say, that if you compare him with Vertot, in the same places of the Roman History, you will find that he excels Vertot. Sir, he has the art of compiling, and of saying every thing he has to say in a pleasing manner. He is now writing a Natural History, and will make it as entertaining as a Persian Tale."

JOHNSON: "I remember once being with Goldsmith in Westminster-abbey. While we surveyed the Poet's Corner, I said to him,

" *Forsitan et nostrum nomen miscebitur istis.*"[1]

[1] Perhaps our name too will be mingled with these.

When we got to Temple-bar, he stopped me, pointed to the heads upon it, and slily whispered me,

" *Forsitan et nostrum nomen miscebitur* ISTIS "

Johnson praised John Bunyan highly. "His *Pilgrim's Progress* has great merit, both for invention, imagination, and the conduct of the story; and it has had the best evidence of its merit, the general and continued approbation of mankind. Few books, I believe, have had a more extensive sale. It is remarkable, that it begins very much like the poem of Dante; yet there was no translation of Dante when Bunyan wrote. There is reason to think that he had read Spenser."

A proposition which had been agitated, that monuments to eminent persons should, for the time to come, be erected in St. Paul's church as well as in Westminster-abbey, was mentioned; and it was asked, who should be honoured by having his monument first erected there. Somebody suggested Pope. JOHNSON: "Why, Sir, as Pope was a Roman Catholic, I would not have his to be first. I think Milton's rather should have the precedence. I think more highly of him now than I did at twenty. There is more thinking in him and in Butler, than in any of our poets."

Some of the company expressed a wonder why the authour of so excellent a book as *The Whole Duty of Man* should conceal himself. JOHNSON: "There may be different reasons assigned for this, any one of which would be very sufficient. He may have been a clergy-man, and may have thought that his religious counsels would have less weight when known to come from a man whose profession was Theology. He may have been a man whose practice was not suitable to his principles, so that his character might injure the effect of his book, which he had written in a season of penitence. Or he may have been a man of rigid self-denial, so that he would have no reward for his pious labours while in this world, but refer it all to a future state."

The gentlemen went away to their club, and I was left at Beauclerk's till the fate of my election should be announced to me. I sat in a state of anxiety which even the charming conversation of Lady Di Beauclerk could not entirely dissipate. In a short time I received the agreeable intelligence that I was chosen. I hastened to the place of meeting, and was introduced to such a society as can seldom be found. Mr. Edmund Burke, whom I then saw for the first time, and whose splendid talents had long made me ardently wish for his acquaintance; Dr. Nugent, Mr. Garrick, Dr. Goldsmith, Mr. (afterwards Sir William) Jones, and the company with whom I had dined. Upon my entrance, Johnson placed himself behind a chair, on which he leaned as on a desk or pulpit, and with humorous formality gave me a *Charge*, pointing out the conduct expected from me as a good member of this club.

On Saturday, May 1, we dined by ourselves at our old rendezvous, the Mitre tavern. He was placid, but not much disposed to talk. He observed, that "The Irish mix better with the English than the Scotch do; their language is nearer to English; as a proof of which, they succeed very well as players, which Scotchmen do not. Then, Sir, they have not that extreme nationality which we find in the Scotch. I will do you, Boswell, the justice to say, that you are the most *unscottified* of your countrymen. You are almost the only instance of a Scotchman that I have known, who did not at every other sentence bring in some other Scotchman."

On Friday, May 7, I breakfasted with him at Mr. Thrale's in the Borough. While we were alone, I endeavoured as well as I could to apologise for a lady who had been divorced from her husband by act of Parliament. I said, that he had used her very ill, had behaved brutally to her, and that she could not continue to live with him without having her delicacy contaminated; that all affection for him was thus destroyed; that the essence of conjugal union being gone, there remained only a cold form, a mere civil obligation; that she was in the prime of life, with qualities to produce happiness; that these ought not to be lost; and, that the gentleman on whose account she was divorced had gained her heart while thus unhappily situated. Seduced, perhaps, by the charms of the lady in question, I thus attempted to palliate what I was sensible could not be justified; for when I had finished my harangue, my venerable friend gave me a proper check: "My dear Sir, never accustom your mind to mingle virtue and vice. The woman's a whore, and there's an end on't."

He described the father of one of his friends thus: "Sir, he was so exuberant a talker at publick meetings, that the gentlemen of his county were afraid of him. No business could be done for his declamation."

I dined with him this day at the house of my friends, Messieurs Edward and Charles Dilly, booksellers in the Poultry: there were present, their elder brother Mr. Dilly of Bedfordshire, Dr. Goldsmith, Mr. Langton, Mr. Claxton, Reverend Dr. Mayo, a dissenting minister, the Reverend Mr. Toplady, and my friend the Reverend Mr. Temple.

Hawkesworth's compilation of the voyages to the South Sea being mentioned:—JOHNSON: "Sir, if you talk of it as a subject of commerce, it will be gainful; if as a book that is to increase human knowledge, I believe there will not be much of that. Hawkesworth can tell only what the voyagers have told him; and they have found very little, only one new animal, I think." BOSWELL: "But many insects, Sir." JOHNSON: "Why, Sir, as to insects, Ray reckons of British insects twenty thousand species. They might have staid at home and discovered enough in that way."

Talking of birds, I mentioned Mr. Daines Barrington's ingenious Essay against the received notion of their migration. JOHNSON: "I think we have as good evidence for the migration of woodcocks as can be desired. We find they disappear at a certain time of the year, and appear again at a certain time of the year; and some of them, when weary in their flight, have been known to alight on the rigging of ships far out at sea." One of the company observed, that there had been instances of some of them found in summer in Essex. JOHNSON: "Sir, that strengthens our argument. *Exceptio probat regulam.*[1] Some being found shews, that, if all remained, many would be found. A few sick or lame ones may be found." GOLDSMITH: "There is a partial migration of the swallows; the stronger ones migrate, the others do not."

BOSWELL: "I am well assured that the people of Otaheite who have the bread tree, the fruit of which serves them for bread, laughed heartily when they were informed of the tedious process necessary with us to have bread;—plowing, sowing, harrowing, reaping, threshing, grinding, baking." JOHNSON: "Why, Sir, all ignorant savages will laugh when they are told of the advantages of civilized life. Were you to tell men who live without houses, how we pile brick upon brick, and rafter upon rafter, and that after a house is raised to a certain height, a man tumbles off a scaffold and breaks his neck; he would laugh heartily at our folly in building; but it does not follow that men are better without houses. No, Sir, (holding up a slice of a good loaf,) this is better than the bread tree."

He repeated an argument, which is to be found in his *Rambler*, against the notion that the brute creation is endowed with the faculty of reason: "birds build by instinct; they never improve; they build their first nest as well as any one they ever build." GOLDSMITH: "Yet we see if you take away a bird's nest with the

[1] The exception tests the rule.

eggs in it, she will make a slighter nest and lay again." JOHNSON: "Sir, that is because at first she has full time and makes her nest deliberately. In the case you mention she is pressed to lay, and must therefore make her nest quickly, and consequently it will be slight." GOLDSMITH: "The nidification of birds is what is least known in natural history, though one of the most curious things in it."

I introduced the subject of toleration. JOHNSON: "Every society has a right to preserve publick peace and order, and therefore has a good right to prohibit the propagation of opinions which have a dangerous tendency. To say the *magistrate* has this right, is using an inadequate word: it is the *society* for which the magistrate is agent. He may be morally or theologically wrong in restraining the propagation of opinions which he thinks dangerous, but he is politically right." MAYO: "I am of opinion, Sir, that every man is entitled to liberty of conscience in religion; and that the magistrate cannot restrain that right." JOHNSON: "Sir, I agree with you. Every man has a right to liberty of conscience, and with that the magistrate cannot interfere. People confound liberty of thinking with liberty of talking; nay, with liberty of preaching. Every man has a physical right to think as he pleases; for it cannot be discovered how he thinks. He has not a moral right, for he ought to inform himself and think justly. But, Sir, no member of a society has a right to *teach* any doctrine contrary to what the society holds to be true. The magistrate, I say, may be wrong in what he thinks; but while he thinks himself right, he may and ought to enforce what he thinks." MAYO: "Then, Sir, we are to remain always in errour, and truth never can prevail; and the magistrate was right in persecuting the first Christians." JOHNSON: "Sir, the only method by which religious truth can be established is by martyrdom. The magistrate has a right to enforce what he thinks; and he who is conscious of the truth has a right to suffer. I am afraid there is no other way of ascertaining the truth, but by persecution on the one hand and enduring it on the other." GOLDSMITH: "But how is a man to act, Sir? Though firmly convinced of the truth of his doctrine, may he not think it wrong to expose himself to persecution? Has he a right to do so? Is it not, as it were, committing voluntary suicide?" JOHNSON: "Sir, as to voluntary suicide, as you call it, there are twenty thousand men in an army who will go without scruple to be shot at, and mount a breach for five-pence a day." GOLDSMITH: "But have they a moral right to do this?" JOHNSON: "Nay, Sir, if you will not take the universal opinion of mankind, I have nothing to say. If mankind cannot defend their own way of thinking, I cannot defend it. Sir, if a man is in doubt whether it would be better for him to expose himself to martyrdom or not, he should not do it. He must be convinced that he has a delegation from heaven." GOLDSMITH: "I would consider whether there is the greater chance of good or evil upon the whole. If I see a man who has fallen into a well, I would wish to help him out; but if there is a greater probability that he shall pull me in, than that I shall pull him out, I would not attempt it. So were I to go to Turkey, I might wish to convert the grand Signor to the Christian faith; but when I considered that I should probably be put to death without effectuating my purpose in any degree, I should keep myself quiet." JOHNSON: "Sir, you must consider that we have perfect and imperfect obligations. Perfect obligations, which are generally not to do something, are clear and positive; as, 'thou shalt not kill.' But charity, for instance, is not definable by limits. It is a duty to give to the poor; but no man can say how much another should give to the poor, or when a man has given too little to save his soul. In the same manner it is a duty to instruct the ignorant, and of consequence to convert infidels to Christianity; but no man in the common course of things is obliged to carry this to such a degree as to incur the danger of martyrdom, as no man is obliged to strip himself to the shirt, in order to give charity. I have said, that a man must be persuaded that he has a particular delegation from heaven." GOLDSMITH: "How is this to be known? Our first reformers, who were burnt for not believing bread and wine to be CHRIST"—JOHNSON; (interrupting him,) "Sir, they were not burnt for not believing bread and wine to be CHRIST, but for insulting those who did believe it. And, Sir, when the first reformers began, they did not intend to be martyred: as many of them ran away as could." BOSWELL: "But, Sir, there was your countryman Elwal, who you told me challenged King George with his black-guards and his red-guards." JOHNSON: "My countryman, Elwal, Sir, should have been put in the stocks: a proper pulpit for him; and he'd have had a numerous audience. A man who preaches in the stocks will always have hearers enough." BOSWELL: "But Elwal thought himself in the right." JOHNSON: "We are not providing for mad people; there are places for them in the neighbourhood" (meaning Moorfields.) MAYO: "But, Sir, is it not very hard that I should not be allowed to teach my children what I really believe to be the truth?" JOHNSON: "Why, Sir, you might contrive to teach your children *extrà scandalum*;[1] but, Sir, the magistrate, if he knows it, has a right to restrain you. Suppose you teach your children to be thieves?" MAYO: "This is making a joke of the subject." JOHNSON: "Nay, Sir, take it thus:—that you teach them the community of goods; for which there are as many plausible arguments as for most erroneous doctrines. You teach them that all things at first were in common, and that no man had a right to anything but as he laid his hands upon it; and that this still is, or ought to be, the rule amongst mankind. Here, Sir, you sap a great principle in society,—property. And don't you think the magistrate would have a right to prevent you? Or, suppose you should teach your children the notion of the Adamites, and they should run naked into the streets, would not the magistrate have a right to flog 'em into their doublets?" MAYO: "I think the magistrate has no right to interfere till there is some overt act." BOSWELL: "So, Sir, though he sees an enemy to the state charging a blunderbuss, he is not to interfere till it is fired off!" MAYO: "He must be sure of its direction against the state." JOHNSON: "The magistrate is to judge of that.—He has no right to restrain your thinking, because the evil centers in yourself. If a man were sitting at this table, and chopping off his fingers, the magistrate, as guardian of the community, has no authority to restrain him, however he might do it from kindness as a parent.—Though, indeed, upon more consideration, I think he may; as it is probable, that he who is chopping off his own fingers, may soon proceed to chop off those of other people. If I think it right to steal Mr. Dilly's plate, I am a bad man; but he can say nothing to me. If I make an open declaration that I think so, he will keep me out of his house. If I put forth my hand, I shall be sent to Newgate. This is the gradation of thinking, preaching, and acting: if a man thinks erroneously, he may keep his thoughts to himself, and nobody will trouble him; if he preaches erroneous doctrine, society may expel him; if he acts in consequence of it, the law takes place, and he is hanged." MAYO: "But, Sir, ought not Christians to have liberty of conscience?" JOHNSON: "I have already told you so, Sir. You are coming back to where you were." BOSWELL: "Dr. Mayo is always taking a return post-chaise, and going the stage over again. He has it at half-price." JOHNSON: "Dr. Mayo, like other champions for unlimited toleration, has got a set of words. Sir, it is no matter, politically, whether the

[1] Without scandal.

magistrate be right or wrong. Suppose a club were to be formed, to drink confusion to King George the Third, and a happy restoration to Charles the Third; this would be very bad with respect to the State; but every member of that club must either conform to its rules, or be turned out of it. Old Baxter, I remember, maintains, that the magistrate should 'tolerate all things that are tolerable.' This is no good definition of toleration upon any principle; but it shews that he thought some things were not tolerable." TOPLADY: "Sir, you have untwisted this difficult subject with great dexterity."

During this argument, Goldsmith sat in restless agitation, from a wish to get in and *shine*. Finding himself excluded, he had taken his hat to go away, but remained for some time with it in his hand, like a gamester, who, at the close of a long night, lingers for a little while, to see if he can have a favourable opening to finish with success. Once when he was beginning to speak, he found himself overpowered by the loud voice of Johnson, who was at the opposite end of the table, and did not perceive Goldsmith's attempt. Thus disappointed of his wish to obtain the attention of the company, Goldsmith in a passion threw down his hat, looking angrily at Johnson, and exclaimed in a bitter tone, " *Take it.*" When Toplady was going to speak, Johnson uttered some sound, which led Goldsmith to think that he was beginning again, and taking the words from Toplady. Upon which, he seized this opportunity of venting his own envy and spleen, under the pretext of supporting another person: "Sir, (said he to Johnson,) the gentleman has heard you patiently for an hour: pray allow us now to hear him." JOHNSON: (sternly,) "Sir, I was not interrupting the gentleman. I was only giving him a signal of my attention. Sir, you are impertinent." Goldsmith made no reply, but continued in the company for some time.

A gentleman present ventured to ask Dr. Johnson if there was not a material difference as to toleration of opinions which lead to action, and opinions merely speculative; for instance, would it be wrong in the magistrate to tolerate those who preach against the doctrine of the TRINITY? Johnson was highly offended, and said, "I wonder, Sir, how a gentleman of your piety can introduce this subject in a mixed company." He told me afterwards, that the impropriety was, that perhaps some of the company might have talked on the subject in such terms as might have shocked him; or he might have been forced to appear in their eyes a narrow-minded man. The gentleman, with submissive deference, said, he had only

108

hinted at the question from a desire to hear Dr. Johnson's opinion upon it. JOHNSON: "Why, then, Sir, I think that permitting men to preach any opinion contrary to the doctrine of the established church, tends, in a certain degree, to lessen the authority of the church, and consequently, to lessen the influence of religion." "It may be considered (said the gentleman,) whether it would not be politick to tolerate in such a case." JOHNSON: "Sir, we have been talking of *right*: this is another question. I think it is *not* politick to tolerate in such a case."

BOSWELL: "Pray, Mr. Dilly, how does Dr. Leland's *History of Ireland* sell?" JOHNSON: (bursting forth with a generous indignation,) "The Irish are in a most unnatural state; for we see there the minority prevailing over the majority. There is no instance, even in the ten persecutions, of such severity as that which the protestants of Ireland have exercised against the Catholicks. Did we tell them we have conquered them, it would be above board: to punish them by confiscation and other penalties, as rebels, was monstrous injustice. King William was not their lawful sovereign: he had not been acknowledged by the Parliament of Ireland, when they appeared in arms against him."

I here suggested something favourable of the Roman Catholicks. TOPLADY: "Does not their invocation of saints suppose omnipresence in the saints?" JOHNSON: "No, Sir; it supposes only pluripresence; and when spirits are divested of matter, it seems probable that they should see with more extent than when in an embodied state. There is, therefore, no approach to an invasion of any of the divine attributes, in the invocation of saints. But I think it is will worship, and presumption. I see no command for it, and therefore think it is safer not to practise it."

He and Mr. Langton and I went together to THE CLUB, where we found Mr. Burke, Mr. Garrick, and some other members, and amongst them our friend Goldsmith, who sat silently brooding over Johnson's reprimand to him after dinner. Johnson perceived this, and said aside to some of us, "I'll make Goldsmith forgive me;" and then called to him in a loud voice, "Dr. Goldsmith,—something passed to-day where you and I dined; I ask your pardon." Goldsmith answered placidly, "It must be much from you, Sir, that I take ill." And so at once the difference was over, and they were on as easy terms as ever, and Goldsmith rattled away as usual.

On Sunday, May 8, I dined with Johnson at Mr. Langton's with Dr. Beattie and some other company. He descanted on the subject of Literary Property. "There seems (said he,) to be in authours a stronger right of property than that by occupancy; a metaphysical right, a right, as it were, of creation, which should from its nature be perpetual; but the consent of nations is against it; and indeed reason and the interest of learning are against it; for were it to be perpetual, no book, however useful, could be universally diffused amongst mankind, should the proprietor take it into his head to restrain its circulation. No book could have the advantage of being edited with notes, however necessary to its elucidation, should the proprietor perversely oppose it. For the general good of the world, therefore, whatever valuable work has once been created by an authour, and issued out by him, should be understood as no longer in his power, but as belonging to the publick; at the same time the authour is entitled to an adequate reward. This he should have by an exclusive right to his work for a considerable number of years."

He attacked Lord Monboddo's strange speculation on the primitive state of human nature; observing, "Sir, it is all conjecture about a thing useless, even were it known to be true. Knowledge of all kinds is good. Conjecture, as to things useful, is good; but conjecture as to what it would be useless to know, such as whether men went upon all four, is very idle."

On Monday, May 9, as I was to set out on my return to Scotland next morning, I was desirous to see as much of Dr. Johnson as I could.

I dined with him at General Paoli's. He was obliged by indisposition, to leave the company early; he appointed me, however, to meet him in the evening at Mr. (now Sir Robert) Chambers's in the Temple, where he accordingly came, though he continued to be very ill. Chambers, as is common on such occasions, prescribed various remedies to him. JOHNSON: (fretted by pain,) "Pr'ythee don't tease me. Stay till I am well, and then you shall tell me how to cure myself." He grew better, and talked with a noble enthusiasm of keeping up the representation of respectable families. His zeal on this subject was a circumstance in his character exceedingly remarkable, when it is considered that he himself had no pretensions to blood. I heard him once say, "I have great merit in being zealous for subordination and the honours of birth; for I can hardly tell who was my grandfather." He maintained the dignity and propriety of male succession, in opposition to the opinion of one of our friends, who had that day employed Mr. Chambers to draw his will, devising his estate to his three sisters, in preference to a remote heir male. Johnson called them "three *dowdies*," and said, with as high a spirit as the boldest Baron in the most perfect days of the feudal system, "An ancient estate should always go to males. It is mighty foolish to let a stranger have it because he marries your daughter, and takes your name. As for an estate newly acquired by trade, you may give it, if you will, to the dog *Towser*, and let him keep his *own* name."

I have known him at times exceedingly diverted at what seemed to others a very small sport. He now laughed immoderately, without any reason that we could perceive, at our friend's making his will; called him the *testator*, and added, "I dare say he thinks he has done a mighty thing. He won't stay till he gets home to his seat in the country, to produce this wonderful deed: he'll call up the landlord of the first inn on the road; and, after a suitable preface upon mortality and the uncertainty of life, will tell him that he should not delay making his will; and here, Sir, will he say, is my will, which I have just made, with the assistance of one of the ablest lawyers in the kingdom; and he will read it to him, (laughing all the time.) He believes he has made this will; but he did not make it: you, Chambers, made it for him. I trust you have had more conscience than to make him say, 'being of sound understanding;' ha, ha, ha! I hope he has left me a legacy. I'd have his will turned into verse, like a ballad."

Mr. Chambers did not by any means relish this jocularity upon a matter of which *pars magna fuit*,[1] and seemed impatient till he got rid of us. Johnson could not stop his merriment, but continued it all the way till he got without the Temple-gate. He then burst into such a fit of laughter, that he appeared to be almost in a convulsion; and, in order to support himself, laid hold of one of the posts at the side of the foot pavement, and sent forth peals so loud, that in the silence of the night his voice seemed to resound from Temple-bar to Fleet-ditch.

This most ludicrous exhibition of the awful, melancholy, and venerable Johnson, happened well to counteract the feelings of sadness which I used to experience when parting with him for a considerable time. I accompanied him to his door, where he gave me his blessing.

[1] He was a great part.

CHAPTER VI

In Seventeen Seventy-five

ON TUESDAY, March 21, 1775, I arrived in London, and on repairing to Dr. Johnson's before dinner, found him in his study, sitting with Mr. Peter Garrick, the elder brother of David, strongly resembling him in countenance and voice, but of more sedate and placid manners.

Both at this interview, and in the evening at Mr. Thrale's, where he and Mr. Peter Garrick and I met again, he was vehement on the subject of the Ossian controversy; observing, "We do not know that there are any ancient Erse manuscripts; and we have no other reason to disbelieve that there are men with three heads, but that we do not know that there are any such men." He also was outrageous, upon his supposition that my countrymen "loved Scotland better than truth," saying, "All of them,—nay not all,—but *droves* of them, would come up, and attest any thing for the honour of Scotland." He also persevered in his wild allegation, that he questioned if there was a tree between Edinburgh and the English border older than himself. I assured him he was mistaken, and suggested that the proper punishment would be that he should receive a stripe at every tree above a hundred years old, that was found within that space. He laughed, and said, "I believe I might submit to it for a *baubee*!"

On Friday, March 24, I met him at the LITERARY CLUB, where were Mr. Beauclerk, Mr. Langton, Mr. Colman, Dr. Percy, Mr. Vesey, Sir Charles Bunbury, Dr. George Fordyce, Mr. Steevens, and Mr. Charles Fox.

Johnson was in high spirits this evening at the club, and talked with great animation and success. He attacked Swift, as he used to do upon all occasions. "*The Tale of a Tub* is so much superiour to his other writings, that one can hardly believe he was the authour of it: there is in it such a vigour of mind, such a swarm of thoughts, so much of nature, and art, and life." I wondered to hear him say of *Gulliver's Travels*, "When once you have thought of big men and little men, it is very easy to do all the rest." I endeavoured to make a stand for Swift, and tried to rouse those who were much more able to defend him; but in vain. Johnson at last, of his own accord, allowed very great merit to the inventory of articles found in the pocket of "the Man Mountain," particularly the description of his watch, which it was conjectured was his God, as he consulted it upon all occasions. He observed, that "Swift put his name to but two things, (after he had a name to put,) *The Plan for the Improvement of the English language*, and the last *Drapier's Letter*."

From Swift, there was an easy transition to Mr. Thomas Sheridan.—JOHNSON: "Sheridan is a wonderful admirer of the tragedy of Douglas, and presented its authour with a gold medal. Some years ago, at a coffee-house in Oxford, I called to him, 'Mr. Sheridan, Mr. Sheridan, how came you to give a gold medal to Home, for writing that foolish play?' This, you see, was wanton and insolent; but I *meant* to be wanton and insolent. A medal has no value but as a stamp of merit. And was Sheridan to assume to himself the right of giving that stamp? If Sheridan was magnificent enough to bestow a gold medal as an honorary reward of dramatick excellence, he should have requested one of the Universities to choose the person on whom it should be conferred. Sheridan had no right to give a stamp of merit: it was counterfeiting Apollo's coin."

On Monday, March 27, I breakfasted with him at Mr. Strahan's. He told us, that he was engaged to go that evening to Mrs. Abington's benefit. "She was visiting some ladies whom I was visiting, and begged that I would come to her benefit. I told her I could not hear: but she insisted so much on my coming, that it would have been brutal to have refused her." This was a speech quite characteristical. He loved to bring forward his having been in the gay circles of life; and he was, perhaps, a little vain of the solicitations of this elegant and fashionable actress. He told us, the play was to be *The Hypocrite*, altered from Cibber's *Nonjuror*, so as to satirize the Methodists. "I do not think (said he,) the character of the Hypocrite justly applicable to the Methodists, but it was very applicable to the Nonjurors. I once said to Dr. Madan, a clergyman of Ireland, who was a great Whig, that perhaps a Nonjuror would have been less criminal in taking the oaths imposed by the ruling power, than refusing them; because refusing them, necessarily laid him under almost an irresistible temptation to be more criminal; for, a man *must* live, and if he precludes himself from the support furnished by the establishment, will probably be reduced to very wicked shifts to maintain himself." BOSWELL:

"I should think, Sir, that a man who took the oaths contrary to his principles, was a determined wicked man, because he was sure he was committing perjury, whereas a Nonjuror might be insensibly led to do what was wrong, without being so directly conscious of it." JOHNSON: "Why, Sir, a man who goes to bed to his patron's wife is pretty sure that he is committing wickedness." BOSWELL: "Did the nonjuring clergyman do so, Sir?" JOHNSON: "I am afraid many of them did."

Mr. Strahan had taken a poor boy from the country as an apprentice, upon Johnson's recommendation. Johnson having enquired after him, said, "Mr. Strahan, let me have five guineas on account, and I'll give this boy one. Nay, if a man recommends a boy, and does nothing for him, it is sad work. Call him down."

I followed him into the court-yard, behind Mr. Strahan's house; and there I had a proof of what I had heard him profess, that he talked alike to all. "Some people tell you that they let themselves down to the capacity of their hearers. I never do that. I speak uniformly, in as intelligible a manner as I can."

"Well, my boy, how do you go on?"—"Pretty well, Sir; but they are afraid I an't strong enough for some parts of the business." JOHNSON: "Why, I shall be sorry for it; for when you consider with how little mental power and corporeal labour a printer can get a guinea a week, it is a very desirable occupation for you. Do you hear,—take all the pains you can; and if this does not do, we must think of some other way of life for you. There's a guinea."

Here was one of the many, many instances of his active benevolence. At the same time, the slow and sonorous solemnity with which, while he bent himself down, he addressed a little thick short-legged boy, contrasted with the boy's aukwardness and awe, could not but excite some ludicrous emotions.

Next day I dined with Johnson at Mr. Thrale's. He attacked Gray, calling him "a dull fellow." BOSWELL: "I understand he was reserved, and might appear dull in company; but surely he was not dull in poetry." JOHNSON: "Sir, he was dull in company, dull in his closet, dull every where. He was dull in a new way, and that made many people think him GREAT. He was a mechanical poet." He then repeated some ludicrous lines, which have escaped my memory, and said, "Is not that GREAT, like his Odes?" Mrs. Thrale maintained that his Odes were melodious; upon which he exclaimed,

"'Weave the warp, and weave the woof,'"—

I added, in a solemn tone,

> " ' The winding sheet of Edward's race.'

There is a good line."—"Ay, (said he) and the next line is a good one," (pronouncing it contemptuously;)

> ' Give ample verge and room enough.'—

"No, Sir, there are but two good stanzas in Gray's poetry, which are in his *Elegy in a Country Churchyard*." He then repeated the stanza,
> ' For who to dumb forgetfulness a prey,' &c.

mistaking one word; for instead of *precincts* he said *confines*. He added, "The other stanza I forget."

A young lady who had married a man much her inferiour in rank being mentioned, a question arose how a woman's relations should behave to her in such a situation. While I contended that she ought to be treated with an inflexible steadiness of displeasure, Mrs. Thrale was all for mildness and forgiveness, and according to the vulgar phrase, "making the best of a bad bargain." JOHNSON: "Madam, we must distinguish. Were I a man of rank, I would not let a daughter starve who had made a mean marriage; but having voluntarily degraded herself from the station which she was originally entitled to hold, I would support her only in that which she herself had chosen; and would not put her on a level with my other daughters. You are to consider, Madam, that it is our duty to maintain the subordination of civilized society; and when there is a gross and shameful deviation from rank, it should be punished so as to deter others from the same perversion."

On Friday, March 31, I supped with him and some friends at a tavern. One of the company attempted, with too much forwardness, to rally him on his late appearance at the theatre; but had reason to repent of his temerity. "Why, Sir, did you go to Mrs. Abington's benefit? Did you see?" JOHNSON: "No, Sir." "Did you hear?" JOHNSON: "No, Sir." "Why then, Sir, did you go?" JOHNSON: "Because, Sir, she is a favourite of the publick, and when the publick cares the thousandth part for you that it does for her, I will go to your benefit too."

Next morning I won a small bet from Lady Diana Beauclerk, by asking him as to one of his particularities, which her Ladyship laid I durst not do. It seems he had been frequently observed at the club to put into his pocket the Seville oranges, after he had squeezed the juice of them into the drink which he made for himself. Beauclerk and Garrick talked of it to me, and seemed to think that he had a strange unwillingness to be discovered. We could not divine what he did with them; and this was the bold question to be put. I saw on his table the spoils of the preceding night, some fresh peels nicely scraped and cut into pieces. "O, Sir, (said I,) I now partly see what you do with the squeezed oranges which you put into your pocket at the Club." JOHNSON: "I have a great love for them." BOSWELL: "And pray, Sir, what do you do with them? You scrape them it seems, very neatly, and what next?" JOHNSON: "Let them dry, Sir." BOSWELL: "And what next?" JOHNSON: "Nay, Sir, you shall know their fate no further." BOSWELL: "Then the world must be left in the dark. It must be said (assuming a mock solemnity,) he scraped them and let them dry, but what he did with them next, he never could be prevailed upon to tell." JOHNSON: "Nay, Sir, you should say it more emphatically:—he could not be prevailed upon, even by his dearest friends, to tell."

I visited him by appointment in the evening, and we drank tea with Mrs. Williams. He told me that he had been in the company of a gentleman whose extraordinary travels had been much the subject of conversation. But I found he had not listened to him with that full confidence, without which there is little satisfaction in the society of travellers. I was curious to hear what opinion so able a judge as Johnson had formed of his abilities, and I asked if he was not a man of sense. JOHNSON: "Why, Sir, he is not a distinct relater; and I should say, he is neither abounding nor deficient in sense. I did not perceive any superiority of understanding." BOSWELL: "But will you not allow him a nobleness of resolution, in penetrating into distant regions?" JOHNSON: "That, Sir, is not to the present purpose. We are talking of sense. A fighting cock has a nobleness of resolution."

Next day, Sunday April 2, I dined with him at Mr. Hoole's. We talked of Pope. JOHNSON: "He wrote his *Dunciad* for fame. That was his primary motive. Had it not been for that, the dunces might have railed against him till they were weary, without his troubling himself about them. He delighted to vex them, no doubt; but he had more delight in seeing how well he could vex them."

His *Taxation no Tyranny* being mentioned, he said, "I think I have not been attacked enough for it. Attack is the re-action;

I never think I have hit hard, unless it re-bounds." BOSWELL: "I don't know, Sir, what you would be at. Five or six shots of small arms in every newspaper, and repeated cannonading in pamphlets, might, I think, satisfy you. But, Sir, you'll never make out this match, of which we have talked, with a certain political lady, since you are so severe against her principles." JOHNSON: "Nay, Sir, I have the better chance for that. She is like the Amazons of old; she must be courted by the sword. But I have not been severe upon her." BOSWELL: "Yes, Sir, you have made her ridiculous." JOHNSON: "That was already done, Sir. To endeavour to make *her* ridiculous, is like blacking the chimney."

He made the common remark on the unhappiness which men who have led a busy life experience, when they retire in expectation of enjoying themselves at ease, and that they generally languish for want of their habitual occupation, and wish to return to it. He mentioned as strong an instance of this as can well be imagined. "An eminent tallow-chandler in London, who had acquired a considerable fortune, gave up the trade in favour of his foreman, and went to live at a country-house near town. He soon grew weary, and paid frequent visits to his old shop, where he desired they might let him know their *melting days*, and he would come and assist them; which he accordingly did. Here, Sir, was a man, to whom the most disgusting circumstances in the business to which he had been used, was a relief from idleness."

On Wednesday, April 5, I dined with him at Messieurs Dillys, with Mr. John Scott of Amwell, the Quaker, Mr. Langton, Mr. Miller, (now Sir John,) and Dr. Thomas Campbell, an Irish clergyman.

We talked of publick speaking. JOHNSON: "We must not estimate a man's powers by his being able or not able to deliver his sentiments in publick. Isaac Hawkins Browne, one of the first wits of this country, got into Parliament, and never opened his mouth. For my own part, I think it is more disgraceful never to try to speak, than to try it, and fail; as it is more disgraceful not to fight, than to fight and be beaten." "Why then, (I asked,) is it thought disgraceful for a man not to fight, and not disgraceful not to speak in publick?" JOHNSON: "Because there may be other reasons for a man's not speaking in publick than want of resolution: he may have nothing to say, (laughing.) Whereas, Sir, you know courage is reckoned the greatest of all virtues; because, unless a man has that virtue, he has no security for preserving any other."

He observed, that "the statutes against bribery were intended to prevent upstarts with money from getting into Parliament:" adding, that "if he were a gentleman of landed property, he would turn out all his tenants who did not vote for the candidate whom he supported." LANGTON: "Would not that, Sir, be checking the freedom of election?" JOHNSON: "Sir, the law does not mean that the privilege of voting should be independent of old family interest; of the permanent property of the country."

On Thursday, April 6, I dined with him at Mr. Thomas Davies's, with Mr. Hicky, the painter, and my old acquaintance, Mr. Moody, the player.

Dr. Johnson, as usual, spoke contemptuously of Colley Cibber. "It is wonderful that a man who for forty years had lived with the great and the witty, should have acquired so ill the talents of conversation; and he had but half to furnish; for one half of what he said was oaths." He however, allowed considerable merit to some of his comedies, and said there was no reason to believe that the *Careless Husband* was not written by himself. Davies said, he was the first dramatick writer who introduced genteel ladies upon the stage. Johnson refuted his observation by instancing several such characters in comedies before his time. DAVIES: (trying to defend himself from a charge of ignorance,) "I mean genteel moral characters." "I think (said Hicky,) gentility and morality are inseparable." BOSWELL: "By no means, Sir. The genteelest characters are often the most immoral. Does not Lord Chesterfield give precepts for uniting wickedness and the graces? A man, indeed, is not genteel when he gets drunk; but most vices may be committed very genteely: a man .may debauch his friend's wife genteely: he may cheat at cards genteely." HICKY: "I do not think *that* is genteel." BOSWELL: "Sir, it may not be like a gentleman, but it may be genteel." JOHNSON: "You are meaning two different things. One means exteriour grace; the other honour. It is certain that a man may be very immoral with exteriour grace. Lovelace, in *Clarissa*, is a very genteel and a very wicked character. Tom Hervey, who died t'other day, though a vicious man, was one of the genteelest men that ever lived." Tom Davies instanced Charles the Second. JOHNSON: (taking fire at any attack upon that Prince, for whom he had an extraordinary partiality,) "Charles the Second was licentious in his practice; but he always had a reverence for what was good. Charles the Second knew his people, and rewarded merit. The Church was at no time better filled than in his reign.

118

He was the best King we have had from his time till the reign of his present Majesty, except James the Second, who was a very good King, but unhappily believed that it was necessary for the salvation of his subjects that they should be Roman Catholicks. *He* had the merit of endeavouring to do what he thought was for the salvation of the souls of his subjects, till he lost a great Empire. *We*, who thought that we should *not* be saved if we were Roman Catholicks, had the merit of maintaining our religion, at the expence of submitting ourselves to the government of King William, (for it could not be done otherwise,)—to the government of one of the most worthless scoundrels that ever existed. No; Charles the Second was not such a man as——, (naming another King.) He did not destroy his father's will.

"He took money, indeed, from France: but he did not betray those over whom he ruled. He did not let the French fleet pass ours. George the First knew nothing, and desired to know nothing; did nothing, and desired to do nothing; and the only good thing that is told of him is, that he wished to restore the crown to its hereditary successor." He roared with prodigious violence against George the Second. When he ceased, Moody interjected, in an Irish tone, and with a comick look, "Ah! poor George the Second."

I mentioned that Dr. Thomas Campbell had come from Ireland to London, principally to see Dr. Johnson. He seemed angry at this observation. DAVIES: "Why, you know, Sir, there came a man from Spain to see Livy; and Corelli came to England to see Purcell, and, when he heard he was dead, went directly back again to Italy." JOHNSON: "I should not have wished to be dead to disappoint Campbell, had he been so foolish as you represent him; but I should have wished to have been a hundred miles off." This was apparently perverse; and I do believe it was not his real way of thinking: he could not but like a man who came so far to see him. He laughed with some complacency, when I told him Campbell's odd expression to me concerning him: "That having seen such a man, was a thing to talk of a century hence,"—as if he could live so long.

We got into an argument whether the Judges who went to India might with propriety engage in trade. Johnson warmly maintained that they might, "For why (he urged) should not Judges get riches, as well as those who deserve them less?" I said, they should have sufficient salaries, and have nothing to take off their attention from the affairs of the publick. JOHNSON: "No

Judge, Sir, can give his whole attention to his office; and it is very proper that he should employ what time he has to himself, to his own advantage, in the most profitable manner." "Then, Sir, (said Davies, who enlivened the dispute by making it somewhat dramatick,) he may become an insurer; and, when he is going to the bench, he may be stopped,—'Your Lordship cannot go yet; here is a bunch of invoices: several ships are about to sail.'" JOHNSON: "Sir, you may as well say a Judge should not have a house; for they may come and tell him, 'Your Lordship's house is on fire;' and so, instead of minding the business of his Court, he is to be occupied in getting the engine with the greatest speed. There is no end of this. Every Judge who has land, trades to a certain extent in corn or in cattle; and in the land itself: undoubtedly his steward acts for him, and so do clerks for a great merchant. A Judge may be a farmer; but he is not to geld his own pigs. A Judge may play a little at cards for his amusement; but he is not to play at marbles, or chuck farthing in the Piazza. No, Sir, there is no profession to which a man gives a very great proportion of his time. It is wonderful when a calculation is made, how little the mind is actually employed in the discharge of any profession. No man would be a Judge, upon the condition of being totally a Judge. The best employed lawyer has his mind at work but for a small proportion of his time: a great deal of his occupation is merely mechanical.—I once wrote for a magazine: I made a calculation, that if I should write but a page a day, at the same rate, I should, in ten years, write nine volumes in folio, of an ordinary size and print." BOSWELL: "Such as Carte's History?" JOHNSON: "Yes, Sir. When a man writes from his own mind, he writes very rapidly. The greatest part of a writer's time is spent in reading, in order to write; a man will turn over half a library to make one book."

We spoke of Rolt, to whose Dictionary of Commerce, Dr. Johnson wrote the Preface. JOHNSON: "Old Gardner the bookseller employed Rolt and Smart to write a monthly miscellany, called *The Universal Visitor*. There was a formal written contract, which Allen the Printer saw. Gardner thought as you do of the Judge. They were bound to write nothing else; they were to have, I think, a third of the profits of his sixpenny pamphlet; and the contract was for ninety-nine years. I wish I had thought of giving this to Thurlow, in the cause about Literary Property. What an excellent instance would it have been of the oppression of booksellers towards poor authours!" (Smiling.) Davies, zealous for the honour of

120

the Trade, said, Gardner was not properly a bookseller. JOHNSON: "Nay, Sir; he certainly was a bookseller. He had served his time regularly, was a member of the Stationers' company, kept a shop in the face of mankind, purchased copyright, and was a *bibliopole*, Sir, in every sense. I wrote for some months in *The Universal Visitor*, for poor Smart, while he was mad, not then knowing the terms on which he was engaged to write, and thinking I was doing him good. I hoped his wits would soon return to him. Mine returned to me, and I wrote in *The Universal Visitor* no longer."

Friday, April 7, I dined with him at a Tavern, with a numerous company.

Ossian being mentioned;—JOHNSON: "Supposing the Irish and Erse languages to be the same, which I do not believe, yet as there is no reason to suppose that the inhabitants of the Highlands and Hebrides ever wrote their native language, it is not to be credited that a long poem was preserved among them. If we had no evidence of the art of writing being practised in one of the counties of England, we should not believe that a long poem was preserved *there*, though in the neighbouring counties, where the same language was spoken, the inhabitants could write." BEAUCLERK: "The ballad of Lilliburlero was once in the mouths of all the people of this country, and is said to have had a great effect in bringing about the Revolution. Yet I question whether any body can repeat it now; which shews how improbable it is that much poetry should be preserved by tradition."

One of the company suggested an internal objection to the antiquity of the poetry said to be Ossian's, that we do not find the wolf in it, which must have been the case had it been of that age.

The mention of the wolf had led Johnson to think of other wild beasts; and while Sir Joshua Reynolds and Mr. Langton were carrying on a dialogue about something which engaged them earnestly, he, in the midst of it, broke out, "Pennant tells of Bears ——" (what he added, I have forgotten.) They went on, which he being dull of hearing, did not perceive, or, if he did, was not willing to break off his talk; so he continued to vociferate his remarks and *Bear* ("like a word in a catch" as Beauclerk said,) was repeatedly heard at intervals, which coming from him who, by those who did not know him, had been so often assimilated to that ferocious animal, while we who were sitting around could hardly stifle laughter, produced a very ludicrous effect. Silence having ensued, he proceeded: "We are told, that the black bear is innocent; but I should not like to trust myself with him." Mr. Gibbon muttered in a low tone of voice, "I should not like to trust myself with *you*."

Patriotism having become one of our topicks, Johnson suddenly uttered, in a strong determined tone, an apophthegm, at which many will start: "Patriotism is the last refuge of a scoundrel." But let it be considered, that he did not mean a real and generous love of our country, but that pretended patriotism which so many, in all ages and countries, have made a cloak for self interest. I maintained, that certainly all patriots were not scoundrels. Being urged, (not by Johnson) to name one exception, I mentioned an eminent person, whom we all greatly admired. JOHNSON: "Sir, I do not say that he is *not* honest; but we have no reason to conclude from his political conduct that he *is* honest. Were he to accept a place from this ministry, he would lose that character of firmness which he has, and might be turned out of his place in a year. This ministry is neither stable, nor grateful to their friends, as Sir Robert Walpole was: so that he may think it more for his interest to take his chance of his party coming in."

Mrs. Pritchard being mentioned, he said: "Her playing was quite mechanical. It is wonderful how little mind she had. Sir, she had never read the tragedy of Macbeth all through. She no more thought of the play out of which her part was taken, than a shoemaker thinks of the skin, out of which the piece of leather, of which he is making a pair of shoes, is cut."

On Monday, April 10, I dined with him at General Oglethorpe's, with Mr. Langton and the Irish Dr. Campbell.

He this day enlarged upon Pope's melancholy remark,

" Man never *is*, but always *to be* blest."

He asserted, that *the present* was never a happy state to any human being; but that, as every part of life, of which we are conscious, was at some point of time a period yet to come, in which felicity was expected, there was some happiness produced by hope. Being pressed upon this subject, and asked if he really was of opinion, that though, in general, happiness was very rare in human life, a man was not sometimes happy in the moment that was present, he answered, "Never, but when he is drunk."

No more of his conversation for some days appears in my journal, except that when a gentleman told him he had bought a suit of lace for his lady, he said, "Well, Sir, you have done a good thing and a wise thing." "I have done a good thing, (said the gentleman,) but I do not know that I have done a wise thing." JOHNSON: "Yes, Sir; no money is better spent than what is laid out for domestick satisfaction. A man is pleased that his wife is drest as well as other people; and a wife is pleased that she is drest."

On Friday, April 14, being Good-Friday, I repaired to him in the morning, according to my usual custom on that day, and breakfasted with him. I observed that he fasted so very strictly, that he did not even taste bread, and took no milk with his tea; I suppose because it is a kind of animal food.

He entered upon the state of the nation, and thus discoursed: "Sir, the great misfortune now is, that government has too little power. All that it has to bestow must of necessity be given to support itself; so that it cannot reward merit. No man, for instance, can now be made a Bishop for his learning and piety; his only chance for promotion is his being connected with somebody who has parliamentary interest. Our several ministers in this reign have outbid each other in concessions to the people. Lord Bute, though a very honourable man,—a man who meant well,—a man who had his blood full of prerogative,—was a theoretical statesman,—a book-minister,—and thought this country could be governed by the influence of the Crown alone. Then, Sir, he gave up a great deal. He advised the King to agree that the Judges should hold their places for life, instead of losing them at the accession of a new King. Lord Bute, I suppose, thought to make the King popular by this concession; but the people never minded it; and it was a most impolitick measure. There is no reason why a Judge should hold his office for life, more than any other person in publick trust. A Judge may be partial otherwise than to the Crown: we have seen Judges partial to the populace. A Judge may become corrupt, and yet there may not be legal evidence against him. A Judge may become froward from age. A Judge may grow unfit for his office in many ways. It was desirable that there should be a possibility of being delivered from him by a new King. That is now gone by an Act of Parliament *ex gratiâ* of the Crown. Lord Bute advised the King to give up a very large sum of money, for which nobody thanked him. It was of consequence to the King, but nothing to the publick, among whom it was divided. When I say Lord Bute advised, I mean, that such acts were done when he was minister, and we are to suppose that he advised them.—Lord Bute shewed an undue partiality to Scotchmen. He turned out Dr. Nichols, a very eminent man, from being physician to the King, to make room for one of his countrymen, a man very low in his profession. He had ********* and **** to go on errands for him; but he should not have had Scotchmen; and, certainly, he should not have suffered them to have access to him before the first people in England."

I told him, that the admission of one of them before the first people in England, which had given the greatest offence, was no more than what happens at every minister's levee, where those who attend are admitted in the order that they have come, which is better than admitting them according to their rank; for if that were to be the rule, a man who has waited all the morning might have the mortification to see a peer, newly come, go in before him, and keep him waiting still. JOHNSON: "True, Sir; but **** should not have come to the levee, to be in the way of people of consequence. He saw Lord Bute at all times; and could have said what he had to say at any time, as well as at the levee. There is now no Prime Minister: there is only an agent for government in the House of Commons. We are governed by the Cabinet: but there is no one head there since Sir Robert Walpole's time." BOSWELL: "What then, Sir, is the use of Parliament?" JOHNSON: "Why, Sir, Parliament is a large council to the King; and the advantage of such a council is, having a great number of men of property concerned in the legislature, who, for their own interest, will not consent to bad laws. And you must have observed, Sir, the administration is feeble and timid, and cannot act with that authority and resolution which is necessary. Were I in power, I would turn out every man who dared to oppose me. Government has the distribution of offices, that it may be enabled to maintain its authority."

"Lord Bute (he added,) took down too fast, without building up something new." BOSWELL: "Because, Sir, he found a rotten building. The political coach was drawn by a set of bad horses; it was necessary to change them." JOHNSON: "But he should have changed them one by one."

As we walked to St. Clement's church, and saw several shops open upon this most solemn fast-day of the Christian world, I remarked, that one disadvantage arising from the immensity of London, was, that nobody was heeded by his neighbour; there was no fear of censure for not observing Good-Friday, as it ought to be kept, and as it is kept in country-towns. He said, it was, upon the whole, very well observed even in London. He however, owned that London was too large; but added, "It is nonsense to say the head is too big for the body. It would be as much too big, though the body were ever so large; that is to say, though the country were ever so extensive. It has no similiarity to a head connected with a body."

Dr. Wetherell, Master of University College, Oxford, accompanied us home from church; and after he was gone, there came two other gentlemen, one of whom uttered the common-place complaints, that by the increase of taxes, labour would be dear, other nations would undersell us, and our commerce would be ruined. JOHNSON, (smiling:) "Never fear, Sir. Our commerce is in a very good state; and suppose we had no commerce at all, we could live very well on the produce of our own country." I cannot omit to mention, that I never knew any man who was less disposed to be querulous than Johnson. Whether the subject was his own situation, or the state of the publick, or the state of human nature in general, though he saw the evils, his mind was turned to resolution, and never to whining or complaint.

After the evening service, he said, "Come, you shall go home with me, and sit just an hour." But he was better than his word; for after we had drunk tea with Mrs. Williams, he asked me to go up to his study with him, where we sat a long while together in a serene and undisturbed frame of mind, sometimes in silence, and sometimes conversing, as we felt ourselves inclined, or more properly speaking, as *he* was inclined; for during all the course of my long intimacy with him, my respected attention never abated, and my wish to hear him was such, that I constantly watched every dawning of communications from the great and illuminated mind.

He observed, "All knowledge is of itself of some value. There is nothing so minute or inconsiderable, that I would not rather know it than not. In the same manner, all power, of whatever sort, is of itself desirable. A man would not submit to learn to hem a ruffle, of his wife's, or his wife's maid: but if a mere wish could attain it, he would rather wish to be able to hem a ruffle."

I told him that our friend Goldsmith had said to me that he had come too late into the world, for that Pope and other poets had taken up the places in the Temple of Fame; so that as but a few at any period can possess poetical reputation, a man of genius can now hardly acquire it. JOHNSON: "That is one of the most sensible things I have ever heard of Goldsmith. It is difficult to get literary fame, and it is every day growing more difficult. Ah, Sir, that should make a man think of securing happiness in another world, which all who try sincerely for it may attain. In comparison of that, how little are all other things! The belief of immortality is impressed upon all men, and all men act under an impression of it, however they may talk, and though, perhaps, they may be scarcely sensible of it." I said, it appeared to me that some people had not the least notion of immortality; and I mentioned a distinguished gentleman of our acquaintance. JOHNSON: "Sir, if it were not for the notion of immortality, he would cut a throat to fill his pockets." When I quoted this to Beauclerk, who knew much more of the gentleman than we did, he said in his acid manner, "He would cut a throat to fill his pockets, if it were not for fear of being hanged."

Dr. Johnson proceeded: "Sir, there is a great cry about infidelity: but there are, in reality, very few infidels. I have heard a person, originally a Quaker, but now, I am afraid, a Deist, say, that he did not believe there were, in all England, above two hundred infidels."

On Sunday, April 16, being Easter-day, after having attended the solemn service at St. Paul's, I dined with Dr. Johnson and Mrs. Williams. I maintained that Horace was wrong in placing happiness in *Nil admirari*, for that I thought admiration one of the most agreeable of all our feelings; and I regretted that I had lost much of my disposition to admire, which people generally do as they advance in life. JOHNSON: "Sir, as a man advances in life, he gets what is better than admiration,—Judgement, to estimate things at their true value." I still insisted that admiration was more pleasing than judgement, as love is more pleasing than friendship. The feeling of friendship is like that of being comfortably filled with roast beef; love, like being enlivened with champagne. JOHNSON: "No, Sir; admiration and love are like being intoxicated with champagne; judgément and friendship like being enlivened. Waller has hit upon the same thought with you, but I don't believe you have borrowed from Waller. I wish you would enable yourself to borrow more."

He then took occasion to enlarge on the advantages of reading, and combated the idle superficial notion, that knowledge enough may be acquired in conversation. "The foundation (said he) must be laid by reading. General principles must be had from books, which, however, must be brought to the test of real life. In conversation you never get a system. What is said upon a subject is to be gathered from a hundred people. The parts of a truth, which a man gets thus, are at such a distance from each other that he never attains to a full view."

On Tuesday, April 11, he and I were engaged to go to dine with Mr. Cambridge, at his beautiful villa on the banks of the Thames, near Twickenham. Johnson was in such good spirits, that every thing seemed to please him as we drove along.

Our conversation turned on a variety of subjects. He thought portrait-painting an improper employment for a woman. "Publick practice of any art, (he observed,) and staring in men's faces, is very indelicate in a female." I happened to start a question, whether when a man knows that some of his intimate friends are invited to the house of another friend, with whom they are all equally intimate, he may join them without an invitation. JOHNSON: "No, Sir; he is not to go when he is not invited. They may be invited on purpose to abuse him" (smiling).

As a curious instance how little a man knows, or wishes to know his own character in the world, or, rather as a convincing proof that Johnson's roughness was only external, and did not proceed from his heart, I insert the following dialogue. JOHNSON: "It is wonderful, Sir, how rare a quality good humour is in life. We meet with very few good humoured men." I mentioned four of our friends, none of whom he would allow to be good humoured. One was *acid*, another was *muddy*, and to the others he had objections which have escaped me. Then, shaking his head and stretching himself at ease in the coach, and smiling with much complacency, he turned to me and said, "I look upon *myself* as a good humoured fellow." The epithet *fellow*, applied to the great lexicographer, the stately Moralist, the Masterly Critick, as if he had been *Sam* Johnson, a mere pleasant companion, was highly diverting; and this light notion of himself struck me with wonder. I answered, also smiling, "No, no, Sir; that will *not* do. You are good natured, but not good humoured: you are irascible. You have not patience with folly and absurdity. I believe you would pardon them, if there were time to deprecate your vengeance; but punishment follows so quick after sentence, that they cannot escape."

He defended his remark in his *Journey to the Western Islands* upon the general insufficiency of education in Scotland; and confirmed to me the authenticity of his witty saying on the learning of the Scotch;—"Their learning is like bread in a besieged town: every man gets a little, but no man gets a full meal." "There is (said he,) in Scotland a diffusion of learning, a certain portion of it widely and thinly spread. A merchant has as much learning as one of their clergy."

He talked of Isaac Walton's *Lives*, which was one of his most favourite books. Dr. Donne's Life, he said, was the most perfect of them. He observed, that "it was wonderful that Walton, who was in a very low situation in life, should have been familiarly received by so many great men, and that at a time when the ranks of society were kept more separate than they are now." He supposed that Walton had then given up his business as a linen-draper and sempster, and was only an authour; and added, "that he was a great panegyrist." BOSWELL: "No quality will get a man more friends than a disposition to admire the qualities of others. I do not mean flattery, but a sincere admiration." JOHNSON: "Nay, Sir, flattery pleases very generally. In the first place, the flatterer may think what he says to be true: but, in the second place, whether he thinks so or not, he certainly thinks those whom he flatters of consequence enough to be flattered."

No sooner had we made our bow to Mr. Cambridge, in his library, than Johnson ran eagerly to one side of the room intent on poring over the backs of the books. Sir Joshua Reynolds observed, (aside,) "He runs to the books as I do to the pictures: but I have the advantage. I can see much more of the pictures than he can of the books." Mr. Cambridge, upon this, politely said, "Dr. Johnson, I am going with your pardon, to accuse myself, for I have the same custom which I perceive you have. But it seems odd that one should have such a desire to look at the backs of books." Johnson, ever ready for contest, instantly started from his reverie, wheeled about and answered, "Sir, the reason is very plain. Knowledge is of two kinds. We know a subject ourselves, or we know where we can find information upon it. When we enquire into any subject the first thing we have to do is to know what books have treated of it. This leads us to look at catalogues, and the backs of books in libraries."

The common remark as to the utility of reading history being made;—JOHNSON: "We must consider how very little history there is; I mean real authentick history. That certain Kings reigned, and certain battles were fought, we can depend upon as true; but all the colouring, all the philosophy of history is conjecture."

"The Beggar's Opera," and the common question, whether it was pernicious in its effects, having been introduced;—JOHNSON:

"As to this matter, which has been very much contested, I myself am of opinion, that more influence has been ascribed to 'The Beggar's Opera,' than it in reality ever had; for I do not believe that any man was ever made a rogue by being present at its representation. At the same time I do not deny that it may have some influence, by making the character of a rogue familiar, and in some degree pleasing." Then collecting himself, as it were, to give a heavy stroke: "There is in it such a *labefactation* of all principles as may be injurious to morality."

While he pronounced this response, we sat in a comical sort of restraint, smothering a laugh, which we were afraid might burst out.

We talked of a young gentleman's marriage with an eminent singer, and his determination that she should no longer sing in publick, though his father was very earnest she should, because her talents would be liberally rewarded so as to make her a good fortune. It was questioned whether the young gentleman who had not a shilling in the world, but was blest with very uncommon talents, was not foolishly delicate, or foolishly proud, and his father truly rational without being mean. Johnson, with all the high spirit of a Roman senator, exclaimed, "He resolved wisely and nobly to be sure. He is a brave man. Would not a gentleman be disgraced by having his wife singing publickly for hire? No, Sir, there can be no doubt here. I know not if I should not *prepare* myself for a publick singer, as readily as let my wife be one."

Johnson arraigned the modern politicks of this country, as entirely devoid of all principle of whatever kind. "Politicks (said he) are now nothing more than means of rising in the world. With this sole view do men engage in politicks, and their whole conduct proceeds upon it. How different in that respect is the state of the nation now from what it was in the time of Charles the First, during the Usurpation, and after the Restoration, in the time of Charles the Second. *Hudibras* affords a strong proof how much hold political principles had then upon the minds of men. There is in *Hudibras* a great deal of bullion which will always last. But to be sure the brightest strokes of his wit owed their force to the impression of the characters, which was upon men's minds at the time; to their knowing them, at table and in the street; in short, being familiar with them; and above all, to his satire being directed against those whom a little while before they had hated and feared. The nation in general has ever been loyal, has been at all times attached to the monarch, though a few daring rebels have been wonderfully powerful for a time. The murder of Charles the First was undoubtedly not committed with the approbation or consent of the people. Had that been the case, Parliament would not have ventured to consign the regicides to their deserved punishment. And we know what exuberance of joy there was when Charles the Second was restored. If Charles the Second had bent all his mind to it, had made it his sole object, he might have been as absolute as Louis the Fourteenth." A gentleman observed he would have done no harm if he had. JOHNSON: "Why, Sir, absolute princes seldom do any harm. But they who are governed by them are governed by chance. There is no security for good government." CAMBRIDGE: "There have been many sad victims to absolute government." JOHNSON: "So, Sir, have there been to popular factions." BOSWELL: "The question is, which is worst, one wild beast or many?"

Somebody found fault with writing verses in a dead language, maintaining that they were merely arrangements of so many words, and laughed at the Universities of Oxford and Cambridge, for sending forth collections of them not only in Greek and Latin, but even in Syriack, Arabick, and other more unknown tongues. JOHNSON: "I would have as many of these as possible; I would have verses in every language that there are the means of acquiring. Nobody imagines that an University is to have at once two hundred poets; but it should be able to shew two hundred scholars. Pieresc's death was lamented, I think, in forty languages. And I would have had at every coronation, and every death of a king, every *Gaudium*, and every *Luctus*, University-verses, in as many languages as can be acquired. I would have the world to be thus told, 'Here is a school where everything may be learnt.'"

On Monday, May 8, we went together and visited the mansions of Bedlam. I accompanied him home, and dined and drank tea with him.

Talking of an acquaintance of ours, distinguished for knowing an uncommon variety of miscellaneous articles both in antiquities and polite literature, he observed, "You know, Sir, he runs about with little weight upon his mind." And talking of another very ingenious gentleman, who from warmth of his temper was at variance with many of his acquaintance, and wished to avoid them, he said, "Sir, he leads the life of an outlaw."

On Friday, May 12, as he had been so good as to assign me a room in his house, where I might sleep occasionally, when I happened to sit with him to a late hour, I took possession of it this night, found everything in excellent order, and was attended by honest Francis with a most civil assiduity. I asked Johnson whether I might go to a consultation with another lawyer upon Sunday, as that appeared to me to be doing work as much in my way, as if an artisan should work on the day appropriated for religious rest. JOHNSON: "Why, Sir, when you are of consequence enough to oppose the practice of consulting upon Sunday, you should do it: but you may go now. It is not criminal, though it is not what one should do, who is anxious for the preservation and increase of piety, to which a peculiar observance of Sunday is a great help. The distinction is clear between what is of moral and what is of ritual obligation."

On Saturday, May 13, I breakfasted with him by invitation, accompanied by Mr. Andrew Crosbie, a Scotch Advocate, whom he had seen at Edinburgh, and the Hon. Colonel (now General) Edward Stopford, brother to Lord Courtown, who was desirious of being introduced to him.

It being asked whether it was reasonable for a man to be angry at another whom a woman had preferred to him?—JOHNSON: "I do not see, Sir, that it is reasonable for a man to be angry at another, whom a woman has preferred to him: but angry he is, no doubt; and he is loath to be angry at himself."

I set out for Scotland on the 23rd.

CHAPTER VII

In Seventeen Seventy-six

WHEN I met him in London the following year, (1776), the account which he gave me of his French tour, was, "Sir, I have seen all the visibilities of Paris, and around it; but to have formed an acquaintance with the people there, would have required more time than I could stay. I was just beginning to creep into acquaintance by means of Colonel Drumgold, a very high man, Sir, head of *l'Ecole Militaire*, a most complete character, for he had first been a professor of rhetorick, and then became a soldier. And, Sir, I was very kindly treated by the English Benedictines, and have a cell appropriated to me in their convent."

He observed, "The great in France live very magnificently, but the rest very miserably. There is no happy middle state as in England. The shops of Paris are mean; the meat in the markets is such as would be sent to a gaol in England; and Mr. Thrale justly observed, that the cookery of the French was forced upon them by necessity; for they could not eat their meat, unless they added some taste to it. The French are an indelicate people; they will spit upon any place. At Madame ——'s, a literary lady of rank, the footman took the sugar in his fingers, and threw it into my coffee. I was going to put it aside; but hearing it was made on purpose for me, I e'en tasted Tom's fingers. The same lady would needs make tea *à l'Angloise*. The spout of the tea-pot did not pour freely; she bade the footman blow into it. France is worse than Scotland in every thing but climate. Nature has done more for the French; but they have done less for themselves than the Scotch have done."

It happened that Foote was at Paris at the same time with Dr. Johnson, and his descriptions of my friend while there, was abundantly ludicrous. He told me, that the French were quite astonished at his figure and manner, and at his dress, which he obstinately continued exactly as in London;—his brown clothes, black stockings, and plain shirt. He mentioned, that an Irish gentleman said to Johnson, "Sir, you have not seen the best French players." JOHNSON: "Players, Sir! I look on them as no better than creatures set upon tables and joint stools to make faces and produce laughter, like dancing dogs."—"But, Sir, you will allow that some players are better than others?" JOHNSON: "Yes, Sir, as some dogs dance better than others."

When Johnson was in France, he was generally very resolute in speaking Latin. It was a maxim with him that a man should not let himself down, by speaking a language which he speaks imperfectly. Indeed, we must have often observed, how inferiour, how much like a child a man appears, who speaks a broken tongue. When Sir Joshua Reynolds, at one of the dinners of the Royal Academy, presented him to a Frenchman of great distinction, he would not deign to speak French, but talked Latin, though his Excellency did not understand it, owing, perhaps to Johnson's English pronunciation: yet upon another occasion he was observed to speak French to a Frenchman of high rank, who spoke English; and being asked the reason, with some expression of surprise,—he answered, "because I think my French is as good as his English."

In the course of this year Dr. Burney informs me that, "he very frequently met Dr. Johnson at Mr. Thrale's, at Streatham, where they had many long conversations, often sitting up as long as the fire and candles lasted, and much longer than the patience of the servants subsisted."

A few of Johnson's sayings, which that gentleman recollects shall here be inserted.

"I never take a nap after dinner but when I have had a bad night, and then the nap takes me."

"The writer of an epitaph should not be considered as saying nothing but what is strictly true. Allowance must be made for some degree of exaggerated praise. In lapidary inscriptions a man is not upon oath."

"There is now less flogging in our great schools than formerly, but then less is learned there; so that what the boys get at one end they lose at the other."

"More is learned in publick than in private schools, from emulation; there is the collision of mind with mind, or the radiation of many minds pointing to one centre. Though few boys make their own exercises, yet if a good exercise is given up, out of a great number of boys, it is made by somebody."

"I hate by-roads in education. Education is as well known, and has long been as well known, as ever it can be. Endeavouring to make children prematurely wise is useless labour. Suppose they have more knowledge at five or six years old than other children, what use can be made of it? It will be lost before it is wanted, and the waste of so much time and labour of the teacher can never be repaid. Too much is expected from precocity, and too little performed. Miss —— was an instance of early cultivation, but in what did it terminate? In marrying a little Presbyterian parson, who keeps an infant boarding-school, so that all her employment now is,

" To suckle fools, and chronicle small-beer."

She tells the children, 'This is a cat, and that is a dog, with four legs and a tail; see there! you are much better than a cat or a dog, for you can speak.' If I had bestowed such an education on a daughter, and had discovered that she thought of marrying such a fellow, I would have sent her to the *Congress*."

"After having talked slightingly of musick, he was observed to listen very attentively while Miss Thrale played on the harpsichord, and with eagerness he called to her, 'Why don't you dash away like Burney?' Dr. Burney upon this said to him, 'I believe, Sir, we shall make a musician of you at last.' Johnson with candid complacency replied, 'Sir, I shall be glad to have a new sense given to me.'"

"He had come down one morning to the breakfast-room, and been a considerable time by himself before any body appeared. When on a subsequent day he was twitted by Mrs. Thrale for being very late, which he generally was, he defended himself by alluding to the extraordinary morning, when he had been too early. 'Madam, I do not like to come down to *vacuity*.'"

"Dr. Burney having remarked that Mr. Garrick was beginning to look old, he said, 'Why, Sir, you are not to wonder at that; no man's face has had more wear and tear.'"

Having arrived in London late on Friday, the 15th of March, I hastened next morning to wait on Dr. Johnson, at his house; but found he was removed from Johnson's-court, No. 7, to Bolt-court, No. 8, still keeping to his favourite Fleet-street. My reflection at the time upon this change as marked in my *Journal*, is as follows: "I felt a foolish regret that he had left a court which bore his name;[1] but it was not foolish to be affected with some tenderness of regard for a place in which I had seen him a great deal, from whence I had often issued a better and a happier man than when I went in, and which had often appeared to my imagination while I trod its pavement, in the solemn darkness of the

[1] He said, when in Scotland, that he was *Johnson of that Ilk*.

night, to be sacred to wisdom and piety." Being informed that he was at Mr. Thrale's in the Borough, I hastened thither, and found Mrs. Thrale and him at breakfast. I was kindly welcomed. In a moment he was in a full glow of conversation, and I felt myself elevated as if brought into another state of being. Mrs. Thrale and I looked to each other while he talked, and our looks expressed our congenial admiration and affection for him. I shall ever recollect this scene with great pleasure. I exclaimed to her, "I am now in-tellectually, *Hermippus redivivus*, I am quite restored by him, by transfusion of mind." "There are many (she replied) who admire and respect Mr. Johnson; but you and I *love* him."

I mentioned with much regret the extravagance of the re-presentative of a great family in Scotland, by which there was danger of its being ruined; and as Johnson respected it for its anti-quity, he joined with me in thinking it would be happy if this person should die. Mrs. Thrale seemed shocked at this, as feudal barbarity; and said, "I do not understand this preference of the estate to its owner; of the land to the man who walks upon that land." JOHNSON: "Nay, Madam, it is not a preference of the land to its owner; it is the preference of a family to an individual. Here is an establishment in a country, which is of importance for ages, not only to the chief but to his people; an establishment which extends upwards and downwards; that this should be destroyed by one idle fellow is a sad thing."

He said, "Entails are good, because it is good to preserve in a country serieses of men, to whom the people are accustomed to look up as to their leaders. But I am for leaving a quantity of land in commerce, to excite industry, and keep money in the country; for if no land were to be bought in the country, there would be no encouragement to acquire wealth, because a family could not be founded there; or if it were acquired, it must be carried away to another country where land may be bought. And although the land in every country will remain the same, and be as fertile where there is no money, as where there is, yet all that portion of the happiness of civil life, which is produced by money circulating in a country, would be lost." BOSWELL: "Then, Sir, would it be for the ad-vantage of a country that all its lands were sold at once?" JOHNSON: "So far, Sir, as money produces good, it would be an advantage; for, then that country would have as much money circulating in it as it is worth. But to be sure this would be counterbalanced by dis-advantages attending a total change of proprietors."

I expressed my opinion that the power of entailing should be limited thus: "That there should be one third, or perhaps one half of the land of a country kept free for commerce; that the proportion allowed to be entailed, should be parcelled out so that no family could entail above a certain quantity. Let a family, according to the abilities of its representatives be richer or poorer in different generations, or always rich if its representatives be always wise: but let its absolute permanency be moderate. In this way we should be certain of there being always a number of established roots; and as in the course of nature, there is in every age an extinction of some families, there would be continual openings for men ambitious of perpetuity, to plant a stock in the entail ground." JOHNSON: "Why, Sir, mankind will be better able to regulate the system of entails, when the evil of too much land being locked up by them is felt, than we can do at present when it is not felt."

I mentioned Dr. Adam Smith's book on *The Wealth of Nations*, which was just published, and that Sir John Pringle had observed to me, that Dr. Smith, who had never been in trade, could not be expected to write well on that subject any more than a lawyer upon physick. JOHNSON: "He is mistaken, Sir; a man who has never been engaged in trade himself may undoubtedly write well upon trade, and there is nothing which requires more to be illustrated by philosophy than trade does. As to mere wealth, that is to say, money, it is clear that one nation or one individual cannot increase its store but by making another poorer: but trade procures what is more valuable, the reciprocation of the peculiar advantages of different countries. A merchant seldom thinks but of his own particular trade. To write a good book upon it, a man must have extensive views. It is not necessary to have practised, to write well upon a subject." I mentioned law as a subject on which no man could write well without practice. JOHNSON: "Why, Sir, in England, where so much money is to be got by the practice of law, most of our writers upon it have been in practice; though Blackstone had not been much in practice when he published his *Commentaries*. But upon the Continent, the great writers on law have not all been in practice: Grotius, indeed, was; but Puffendorf was not, Burlamaqui was not."

When we had talked of the great consequence which a man acquired by being employed in his profession, I suggested a doubt of the justice of the general opinion, that it is improper in a lawyer to solicit employment; for why, I urged, should it not be equally allowable to solicit that as the means of consequence, as it is to solicit votes to be elected a member of Parliament? Mr. Strahan had told me that a countryman of his and mine, who had risen to eminence in the law, had, when first making his way, solicited him to get him employed in city causes. JOHNSON: "Sir, it is wrong to stir up law-suits; but when once it is certain that a law-suit is to go on, there is nothing wrong in a lawyer's endeavouring that he shall have the benefit, rather than another. BOSWELL: "You would not solicit employment, Sir, if you were a lawyer." JOHNSON: "No, Sir; but not because I should think it wrong, but because I should disdain it." This was a good distinction, which will be felt by men of just pride. He proceeded: "However, I would not have a lawyer to be wanting to himself in using fair means. I would have him to inject a little hint now and then, to prevent his being overlooked."

He thus discoursed upon supposed obligation in settling estates: —"Where a man gets the unlimited property of an estate, there is no obligation upon him in *justice* to leave it to one person rather than to another. There is a motive of preference from *kindness*, and this kindness is generally entertained for the nearest relation. If I *owe* a particular man a sum of money, I am obliged to let that man have the next money I get, and cannot in justice let another have it; but if I owe money to no man, I may dispose of what I get as I please. There is not a *debitum justitiæ*[1] to a man's next heir; there is only a *debitum caritatis.*[2] It is plain, then, that I have morally a choice according to my liking. If I have a brother in want, he has a claim from affection to my assistance; but if I have also a brother in want, whom I like better, he has a preferable claim. The right of an heir at law is only this, that he is to have the succession to an estate, in case no other person is appointed to it by the owner. His right is merely preferable to that of the King."

He said, "The value of every story depends on its being true. A story is a picture either of an individual or of human nature in general: if it be false, it is a picture of nothing. For instance: suppose a man should tell that Johnson, before setting out for Italy, as he had to cross the Alps, sat down to make himself wings. This many people would believe: but it would be a picture of nothing. ***** (naming a worthy friend of ours,) used to think a story a story, till I shewed him that truth was essential to it." I observed, that Foote entertained us with stories which were not true; but that, indeed it was properly not as narratives that Foote's

[1] A debt of justice.   [2] A debt of kindness.

stories pleased us, but as collections of ludicrous images. JOHNSON: "Foote is quite impartial, for he tells lies of every body."

We landed at the Temple-stairs, where we parted.

I found him in the evening in Mrs. William's room. We talked of religious orders. He said, "It is as unreasonable for a man to go into a Carthusian convent for fear of being immoral, as for a man to cut off his hands for fear he should steal. There is, indeed, great resolution in the immediate act of dismembering himself; but when that is once done, he has no longer any merit: for though it is out of his power to steal, yet he may all his life be a thief in his heart. So when a man has once become a Carthusian, he is obliged to continue so, whether he chooses it or not. Their silence, too, is absurd. We read in the Gospel of the apostles being sent to preach, but not to hold their tongues. All severity that does not tend to increase good, or prevent evil, is idle. I said to the Lady Abbess of a convent, 'Madame, you are here, not for the love of virtue, but the fear of vice,' She said, 'She should remember this as long as she lived.'"

Finding him still persevering in his abstinence from wine, I ventured to speak to him of it.—JOHNSON: "Sir, I have no objection to a man's drinking wine, if he can do it in moderation. I found myself apt to go to excess in it, and therefore, after having been for some time without it, on account of illness, I thought it better not to return to it. Every man is to judge for himself, according to the effects which he experiences. One of the fathers tells us, he found fasting made him so peevish that he did not practice it."

Though he often enlarged upon the evil of intoxication, he was by no means harsh and unforgiving to those who indulged in occasional excess in wine. One of his friends, I well remember, came to sup at a tavern with him and some other gentlemen, and too plainly discovered that he had drunk too much at dinner. When one who loved mischief, thinking to produce a severe censure, asked Johnson, a few days afterwards, "Well, Sir, what did your friend say to you, as an apology for being in such a situation?" Johnson answered, "Sir, he said all that a man *should* say: he said he was sorry for it."

I heard him once give a very judicious practical advice upon this subject: "A man who has been drinking wine at all freely, should never go into a new company. With those who have partaken of wine with him, he may be pretty well in unison; but he will probably be offensive, or appear ridiculous, to other people."

He allowed very great influence to education. "I do not deny, Sir, but there is some original difference in minds; but it is nothing in comparison of what is formed by education. We may instance the science of *numbers*, which all minds are equally capable of attaining: yet we find a prodigious difference in the powers of different men, in that respect after they are grown up, because their minds have been more or less exercised in it: and I think the same cause will explain the difference of excellence in other things, gradations admitting always some difference in the first principles."

I again visited him on Monday. He took occasion to enlarge, as he often did, upon the wretchedness of a sea-life. "A ship is worse than a gaol. There is, in a gaol, better air, better company, better conveniency of every kind; and a ship has the additional disadvantage of being in danger. When men come to like a sea-life, they are not fit to live on land."—"Then (said I) it would be cruel in a father to breed his son to the sea." JOHNSON: "It would be cruel in a father who thinks as I do. Men go to sea, before they know the unhappiness of that way of life; and when they have come to know it, they cannot escape from it, because it is then too late to choose another profession; as indeed is generally the case with men, when they have once engaged in any particular way of life."

On Tuesday, March 19, which was fixed for our proposed jaunt, (to Oxford, Birmingham, Lichfield and Ashbourne), we met in the morning at the Somerset coffee-house in the Strand, where we were taken up by the Oxford coach. He was accompanied by Mr. Gwyn, the architect; and a gentleman of Merton College, whom he did not know, had the fourth seat. We soon got into conversation; for it was very remarkable of Johnson, that the presence of a stranger had no restraint upon his talk. I observed that Garrick, who was about to quit the stage, would soon have an easier life. JOHNSON: "I doubt that, Sir." BOSWELL: "Why, Sir, he will be Atlas with the burthen off his back." JOHNSON: "But I know not, Sir, if he will be so steady without his load. However, he should never play any more, but be entirely the gentleman, and not partly the player; he should no longer subject himself to be hissed by a mob, or to be insolently treated by performers, whom he used to rule with a high hand, and who would gladly retaliate." BOSWELL: "I think he should play once a year for the benefit of decayed actors, as it has been said he means to do." JOHNSON: "Alas, Sir! he will soon be a decayed actor himself."

Johnson expressed his disapprobation of ornamental architecture, such as magnificent columns supporting a portico, or expensive pilasters supporting merely their own capitals "because it consumes labour disproportionate to its utility." For the same reason he satyrised statuary. "Painting (said he,) consumes labour not disproportionate to its effect; but a fellow will hack half a year at a block of marble to make something in stone that hardly resembles a man. The value of statuary is owing to its difficulty. You would not value the finest head cut upon a carrot."

Gwyn was a fine lively rattling fellow. Dr. Johnson kept him in subjection, but with kindly authority. The spirit of the artist however, rose against what he thought a Gothick attack, and he made a brisk defence. "What, Sir, you will allow no value to beauty in architecture or in statuary? Why should we allow it then in writing? Why do you take the trouble to give us so many fine allusions, and bright images, and elegant phrases? You might convey all your instruction without these ornaments." Johnson smiled with complacency; but said, "Why, Sir, all these ornaments are useful, because they obtain an easier reception for truth; but a building is not at all more convenient for being decorated with superfluous carved work."

Gwyn at last was lucky enough to make one reply to Dr. Johnson, which he allowed to be excellent. Johnson censured him for taking down a church which might have stood many years, and building a new one at a different place, for no other reason but that there might be a direct road to a new bridge; and his expression was, "You are taking a church out of the way, that the people may go in a straight line to the bridge."—"No, Sir, (said Gwyn,) I am putting the church *in* the way, that the people may not *go out of the way*." JOHNSON: (with a hearty loud laugh of approbation,) "Speak no more. Rest your colloquial fame upon this."

Upon our arrival at Oxford, we put up at the Angel inn, and passed the evening by ourselves in easy and familiar conversation. Talking of constitutional melancholy, he observed, "A man so afflicted, Sir, must divert distressing thoughts, and not combat with them." BOSWELL: "May not he think them down, Sir?" JOHNSON: "No, Sir. To attempt to *think them down* is madness. He should have a lamp constantly burning in his bed chamber during the night, and if wakefully disturbed, take a book, and read, and compose himself to rest. To have the management of the mind is a great art, and it may be attained in a considerable degree by experience and habitual exercise." BOSWELL: "Should

140

not he provide amusements for himself? Would it not, for instance, be right for him to take a course of chymistry?" JOHNSON: "Let him take a course of chymistry, or a course of rope-dancing, or a course of any thing to which he is inclined at the time. Let him contrive to have as many retreats for his mind as he can, as many things to which it can fly from itself. Burton's *Anatomy of Melancholy* is a valuable work. It is, perhaps, overloaded with quotation. But there is a great spirit and great power in what Burton says, when he writes from his own mind."

We next day went to Pembroke College, and waited on his old friend, Dr. Adams, the master of it, whom I found to be a most polite, pleasing, communicative man.

Dr. Adams told us, that in some of the Colleges at Oxford, the fellows had excluded the students from social intercourse with them in the common room. JOHNSON: "They are in the right, Sir: there can be no real conversation, no fair exertion of mind amongst them, if the young men are by; for a man who has a character does not choose to stake it in their presence." BOSWELL: "But, Sir, may there not be very good conversation without a contest for superiority?" JOHNSON: "No animated conversation, Sir, for it cannot be but one or other will come off superiour. I do not mean that the victor must have the better of the argument, for he may take the weak side; but his superiority of parts and knowledge will necessarily appear; and he to whom he thus shews himself superiour is lessened in the eyes of the young men. You know it was said, '*Mallem cum Scaligero errare quam cum Clavio recte sapere.*'[1] In the same manner take Bentley's and Jason de Nores' Comments upon Horace, you will admire Bentley more when wrong, than Jason when right."

We walked with Dr. Adams into the master's garden, and into the common room. JOHNSON: (after a reverie of meditation,) "Ay! Here I used to play at draughts with Phil. Jones and Fludyer. Jones loved beer, and did not get very forward in the church. Fludyer turned out a scoundrel, a Whig, and said he was ashamed of having been bred at Oxford. He had a living at Putney, and got under the eye of some retainers to the court at that time, and so became a violent Whig: but he had been a scoundrel all along to be sure." BOSWELL: "Was he a scoundrel, Sir, in any other way than that of being a political scoundrel? Did he cheat at draughts?" JOHNSON: "Sir, we never played for *money*."

We then went to Trinity College, where he introduced me to

[1] I would rather be wrong with Scaliger than be right with Clavius.

Mr. Thomas Warton, with whom we passed a part of the evening. We talked of biography.—JOHNSON: "It is rarely well executed. They only who live with a man can write his life with any genuine exactness and discrimination; and few people who have lived with a man know what to remark about him. The chaplain of a late Bishop, whom I was to assist in writing some memoirs of his Lordship, could tell me scarcely any thing."

I said, Mr. Robert Dodsley's life should be written, as he had been so much connected with the wits of his time, and by his literary merit had raised himself from the station of a footman. Mr. Warton said, he had published a little volume under the title of *The Muse in Livery*. JOHNSON: "I doubt whether Dodsley's brother would thank a man who should write his life; yet Dodsley himself was not unwilling that his original low condition should be recollected. When Lord Lyttelton's *Dialogues of the Dead* came out, one of which is between Apicius, an ancient epicure, and Dartineuf, a modern epicure, Dodsley said to me, 'I knew Dartineuf well, for I was once his footman.'"

Biography led us to speak of Dr. John Campbell, who had written a considerable part of the *Biographia Britannica*. Johnson, though he valued him highly, was of opinion that there was not so much in his great work, *A Political Survey of Great Britain*, as the world had been taught to expect; and had said to me, that he believed Campbell's disappointment on account of the bad success of that work, had killed him. He this evening observed of it, "That work was his death." Mr. Warton, not adverting to his meaning, answered, "I believe so; from the great attention he bestowed on it." JOHNSON: "Nay, Sir, he died of *want* of attention, if he died at all by that book."

We talked of a work much in vogue at that time, written in a very mellifluous style, but which, under pretext of another subject, contained much artful infidelity. I said it was not fair to attack us unexpectedly; he should have warned us of our danger, before we entered his garden of flowery eloquence, by advertising, "Spring-guns and man-traps set here." The authour had been an Oxonian, and was remembered there for having "turned Papist." I observed, that as he had changed several times—from the Church of England to the Church of Rome,—from the Church of Rome to infidelity,— I did not despair yet of seeing him a methodist preacher. JOHNSON: (laughing,) "It is said, that his range has been more extensive, and that he has once been Mahometan. However, now that he has published his infidelity, he will probably persist in it." BOSWELL: "I am not quite sure of that, Sir."

Mr. Wharton, being engaged, could not sup with us at our inn; we had therefore another evening by ourselves.

I censured some ludicrous fantastick dialogues between two coach horses and other such stuff, which Baretti had lately published. He joined with me, and said, "Nothing odd will do long. *Tristram Shandy* did not last." I expressed a desire to be acquainted with a lady who had been much talked of, and universally celebrated for extraordinary address and insinuation. JOHNSON: "Never believe extraordinary characters which you hear of people. Depend upon it, Sir, they are exaggerated. You do not see one man shoot a great deal higher than another." I mentioned Mr. Burke. JOHNSON: "Yes; Burke *is* an extraordinary man. His stream of mind is perpetual." It is very pleasing to me to record, that Johnson's high estimation of the talents of this gentleman was uniform from their early acquaintance. Sir Joshua Reynolds informs me, that when Mr. Burke was first elected a member of Parliament, and Sir John Hawkins expressed a wonder at his attaining a seat, Johnson said, "Now we who know Mr. Burke, know, that he will be one of the first men in the country." And once, when Johnson was ill, and unable to exert himself as much as usual without fatigue, Mr. Burke having been mentioned, he said, "That fellow calls forth all my powers. Were I to see Burke now it would kill me." So much was he accustomed to consider conversation as a contest, and such was his notion of Burke as an opponent.

We dined at an excellent inn at Chapel-house, where he expatiated on the felicity of England in its taverns and inns, and triumphed over the French for not having, in any perfection, the tavern life. "There is no private house, (said he,) in which people can enjoy themselves so well, as at a capital tavern. Let there be ever so great plenty of good things, ever so much grandeur, ever so much elegance, ever so much desire that every body should be easy; in the nature of things it cannot be: there must always be some degree of care and anxiety. The master of the house is anxious to entertain his guests; the guests are anxious to be agreeable to him; and no man, but a very impudent dog indeed, can as freely command what is in another man's house, as if it were his own. Whereas, at a tavern, there is a general freedom from anxiety. You are sure you are welcome: and the more noise you make, the more trouble you give, the more good things you call for, the welcomer you are. No servants will attend you with the alacrity which waiters do, who are incited by the prospect of an immediate reward in proportion as they please. No, Sir; there is nothing which has yet been contrived by man, by which so much happiness is produced as by a good tavern or inn." He then repeated, with great emotion, Shenstone's lines:

> ' Whoe'er has travell'd life's dull round,
> Where'er his stages may have been,
> May sigh to think he still has found
> The warmest welcome at an inn.'

In the afternoon, as we were driven rapidly along in the post-chaise, he said to me "Life has not many things better than this."

He spoke slightingly of Dyer's *Fleece.*—"The subject, Sir, cannot be made poetical. How can a man write poetically of serges and druggets! Yet you will hear many people talk to you gravely of that *excellent* poem, THE FLEECE." Having talked of Grainger's *Sugar-cane*, I mentioned to him Mr. Langton's having told me, that this poem, when read in manuscript at Sir Joshua Reynolds's, had made all the assembled wits burst into a laugh, when, after much blank verse pomp, the poet began a new paragraph thus:

> ' Now, Muse, let's sing of *rats.*'

And what increased the ridicule was, that one of the company, who slyly overlooked the reader, perceived that the word had been originally *mice*, and had been altered to *rats*, as more dignified.

This passage does not appear in the printed work, Dr. Grainger, or some of his friends, it should seem, having become sensible that introducing even *rats*, in a grave poem, might be liable to banter. He, however, could not bring himself to relinquish the idea; for they are thus, in a still more ludicrous manner, peri-phrastically exhibited in his poem as it now stands:

> ' Nor with less waste the whisker'd vermin race
> A countless clan despoil the lowland cane.'

Johnson said, that Dr. Grainger was an agreeable man; a man who would do any good that was in his power. His translation of Tibullus, he thought, was very well done; but *The Sugar-Cane, a Poem*, did not please him; for, he exclaimed, "What could he make of a sugar-cane? One might as well write 'The Parsley-bed, a Poem:' or 'The Cabbage-garden, a Poem.'" BOSWELL: "You must

144

then *pickle* your cabbage with the *sal atticum.*" JOHNSON: "You know there is already *The Hop-Garden, a Poem*: and, I think, one could say a great deal about cabbage. The poem might begin with the advantages of civilized society over a rude state, exemplified by the Scotch, who had no cabbages till Oliver Cromwell's soldiers introduced them; and one might thus shew how arts are propagated by conquest, as they were by the Roman arms." He seemed to be much diverted with the fertility of his own fancy.

I told him, that I heard Dr. Percy was writing the history of the wolf in Great-Britain. JOHNSON: "The wolf, Sir! why the wolf? Why does he not write of the bear, which we had formerly? Nay, it is said we had the beaver. Or why does he not write of the grey rat, the Hanover rat, as it is called, because it is said to have come into this country about the time that the family of Hanover came? I should like to see '*The History of the Grey Rat, by Thomas Percy, D.D., Chaplain in Ordinary to His Majesty,*'" (laughing immoderately). BOSWELL: "I am afraid a court chaplain could not decently write of the grey rat." JOHNSON: "Sir, he need not give it the name of the Hanover rat."

He mentioned to me the singular history of an ingenious acquaintance. "He had practised physick in various situations with no great emolument. A West-India gentleman, whom he delighted by his conversation, gave him a bond for a handsome annuity during his life, on the condition of his accompanying him to the West-Indies, and living with him there for two years. He accordingly embarked with the gentleman; but upon the voyage fell in love with a young woman who happened to be one of the passengers, and married the wench. From the imprudence of his disposition he quarrelled with the gentleman, and declared he would have no connection with him. So he forfeited the annuity. He settled as a physician in one of the Leeward Islands. A man was sent out to him merely to compound his medicines. This fellow set up as a rival to him in his practice of physick, and got so much the better of him in the opinion of the people of the island, that he carried away all the business, upon which he returned to England, and soon after died."

On Friday, March 22, having set out early from Henley, where we had lain the preceding night, we arrived at Birmingham about nine o'clock, and, after breakfast, went to call on his old schoolfellow Mr. Hector. A very stupid maid, who opened the door, told us, that, "her master was gone out; he was gone to the country;

she could not tell when he would return." In short, she gave us a miserable reception; and Johnson observed, "She would have behaved no better to people who wanted him in the way of his profession." He said to her, "My name is Johnson; tell him I called. Will you remember the name?" She answered with rustick simplicity, in the Warwickshire pronunciation, "I don't understand you, Sir."—"Blockhead, (said he,) I'll write." I never heard the word *blockhead* applied to a woman before, though I do not see why it should not, when there is evident occasion for it. He, however, made another attempt to make her understand him, and roared loud in her ear, "*Johnson*," and then she catched the sound.

We next called on Mr. Lloyd, one of the people called Quakers. He too was not at home, but Mrs. Lloyd was, and received us courteously, and asked us to dinner. Johnson said to me, "After the uncertainty of all human things at Hector's, this invitation came very well." We walked about the town and he was pleased to see it increasing.

I talked of legitimation by subsequent marriage, which obtained in the Roman Law, and still obtains in the law of Scotland. JOHNSON: "I think it a bad thing; because the chastity of women being of the utmost importance, as all property depends upon it, they who forfeit it should not have any possibility of being restored to good character, nor should the children, by an illicit connection, attain the full right of lawful children, by the posteriour consent of the offending parties."

Mr. Lloyd joined us in the street; and in a little while we met *Friend Hector*, as Mr. Lloyd called him. It gave me pleasure to observe the joy which Johnson and he expressed on seeing each other again. Mr. Lloyd and I left them together, while he obligingly shewed me some of the manufactures of this very curious assemblage of artificers. We all met at dinner at Mr. Lloyd's, where we were entertained with great hospitality. Mr. and Mrs. Lloyd had been married the same year with their Majesties and like them, had been blessed with a numerous family of fine children, their numbers being exactly the same. Johnson said, "Marriage is the best state for a man in general; and every man is a worse man, in proportion as he is unfit for the married state."

Dr. Johnson said to me in the morning, "You will see, Sir, at Mr. Hector's, his sister, Mrs. Careless, a clergyman's widow. She was the first woman with whom I was in love. It dropt out of my head imperceptibly; but she and I shall always have a kindness for each other." He laughed at the notion that a man can never be really in love but once, and considered it as a mere romantick fancy.

[On this day after a visit elsewhere,] Mr. Hector took me to his house, where we found Johnson sitting placidly at tea, with his *first love*; who though now advanced in years, was a genteel woman, very agreeable and well bred.

Johnson lamented to Mr. Hector the state of one of their school-fellows, Mr. Charles Congreve, a clergyman, which he thus described: "He obtained, I believe, considerable preferment in Ireland, but now lives in London, quite as a valetudinarian, afraid to go into any house but his own. He takes a short airing in his post-chaise every day. He has an elderly woman, whom he calls cousin, who lives with him, and jogs his elbow, when his glass has stood too long empty, and encourages him in drinking, in which he is very willing to be encouraged; not that he gets drunk, for he is a very pious man, but he is always muddy. He confesses to one bottle of port every day, and he probably drinks more. He is quite unsocial; his conversation is quite monosyllabical; and when, at my last visit, I asked him what o'clock it was? that signal of my departure had so pleasing an effect on him, that he sprung up to look at his watch, like a greyhound bounding at a hare." When Johnson took leave of Mr. Hector, he said, "Don't grow like Congreve; nor let me grow like him, when you are near me."

When he again talked of Mrs. Careless to-night, he seemed to have had his affection revived; for he said, "If I had married her, it might have been as happy for me." BOSWELL: "Pray, Sir, do you not suppose that there are fifty women in the world, with any one of whom a man may be as happy, as with any one woman in particular?" JOHNSON: "Ay, Sir, fifty thousand." BOSWELL: "Then, Sir, you are not of opinion with some who imagine that certain men and certain women are made for each other; and that they cannot be happy if they miss their counterparts." JOHNSON: "To be sure not, Sir. I believe marriages would in general be as happy, and often more so, if they were all made by the Lord Chancellor, upon a due consideration of the characters and circumstances, without the parties having any choice in the matter."

I wished to have staid at Birmingham to-night, to have talked more with Mr. Hector; but my friend was impatient to reach his native city; so we drove on that stage in the dark, and were long pensive and silent. When we came within the focus of the Lichfield lamps, "now (said he,) we are getting out of a state of death." We put up at the Three Crowns, not one of the great inns, but a good old fashioned one, which was kept by Mr. Wilkins, and was the very next house to that in which Johnson was born and brought up, and which was still his own property.

Very little business appeared to be going forward in Lichfield. I found however two strange manufactures for so inland a place, sail-cloth and streamers for ships; and I observed them making some saddle-cloths, and dressing sheepskins: but upon the whole, the busy hand of industry seemed to be quite slackened. "Surely, Sir, (said I,) you are an idle set of people." "Sir, (said Johnson,) we are a city of philosophers, we work with our heads, and make the boobies of Birmingham work for us with their hands."

A physician being mentioned who had lost his practice, because his whimsically changing his religion had made people distrustful of him, I maintained that this was unreasonable, as religion is unconnected with medical skill. JOHNSON: "Sir, it is not unreasonable; for when people see a man absurd in what they understand, they may conclude the same of him in what they do not understand. If a physician were to take to eating of horse-flesh, nobody would employ him; though one may eat horse-flesh, and be a very skilful physician. If a man were educated in an absurd religion, his continuing to profess it would not hurt him, though his changing to it would."

On Monday, March 25, we breakfasted at Mrs. Lucy Porter's. Johnson had sent an express to Dr. Taylor's, acquainting him of our being at Lichfield, and Taylor had returned an answer that his post-chaise should come for us this day. While we sat at breakfast, Dr. Johnson received a letter by the post, which seemed to agitate him very much. When he had read it, he exclaimed, "One of the most dreadful things that has happened in my time." The phrase *my time*, like the word *age*, is usually understood to refer to an event of a publick or general nature. I imagined something like an assassination of the King—like a gunpowder plot carried into execution—or like another fire of London. When asked, "What is it, Sir?" he answered, "Mr. Thrale has lost his only son!" He said, "This is a total extinction to their family, as much as if they were sold into captivity." Upon my mentioning that Mr. Thrale had daughters, who might inherit his wealth;—"Daughters, (said Johnson, warmly,) he'll no more value his daughters than——" I was going to speak.—"Sir, (said he,) don't you know how you yourself think? Sir, he wishes to propagate his name." In short, I saw male succession strong in his mind, even where there was no name, no family of any long standing. I said, it was lucky he was not present when this misfortune happened. JOHNSON: "It is lucky for *me*. People in distress never think that you feel enough." BOSWELL: "And, Sir, they will have the hope of seeing you, which will be a relief in the mean time; and when you get to them, the pain will be so far abated, that they will be capable of being consoled by you, which, in the first violence of it, I believe, would not be the case." JOHNSON: "No, Sir; violent pain of mind, like violent pain of body, *must* be severely felt." BOSWELL: "I own, Sir, I have not so much feeling for the distress of others, as some people have, or pretend to have; but I know this, that I would do all in my power to relieve them." JOHNSON: "Sir, it is affectation to pretend to feel the distress of others, as much as they do themselves. It is equally so, as if one should pretend to feel as much pain while a friend's leg is cutting off, as he does. No, Sir; you have expressed the rational and just nature of sympathy. I would have gone to the extremity of the earth to have preserved this boy."

He was soon quite calm. The letter was from Mr. Thrale's clerk, and concluded, "I need not say how much they wish to see you in London," He said, "We shall hasten back from Taylor's."

After dinner Dr. Johnson wrote a letter to Mrs. Thrale, on the death of her son. I said it would be very distressing to Thrale, but she would soon forget it, as she had so many things to think of. JOHNSON: "No, Sir, Thrale will forget it first. *She* has many things that she *may* think of. *He* has many things that he *must* think of."

In the evening we went to the Town-hall, which was converted into a temporary theatre, and saw *Theodosius*, with *The Stratford Jubilee*. I was happy to see Dr. Johnson sitting in a conspicuous part of the pit, and receiving affectionate homage from all his acquaintance. We were quite gay and merry. I afterwards mentioned to him that I condemned myself for being so, when poor Mr. and Mrs. Thrale were in such distress. JOHNSON: "You are wrong, Sir; twenty years hence Mr. and Mrs. Thrale will not suffer much pain from the death of their son. Now, Sir, you are to consider, that distance of place, as well as distance of time, operates upon the human feelings. I would not have you be gay in the presence of the distressed, because it would shock them; but you may be gay at a distance. Pain for the loss of a friend, or of a relation whom we love, is occasioned by the want which we feel. In time the vacuity is filled with something else; or sometimes the vacuity closes up of itself."

Here I shall record some fragments of my friend's conversation during this jaunt.

"Marriage, Sir, is much more necessary to a man than to a woman: for he is much less able to supply himself with domestick comforts. You will recollect my saying to some ladies the other day, that I had often wondered why young women should marry, as they have so much more freedom, and so much more attention paid to them while unmarried, than when married. I indeed did not mention the *strong* reason for their marrying—the *mechanical* reason." BOSWELL: "Why that *is* a strong one. But does not imagination make it much more important than it is in reality? Is it not, to a certain degree, a delusion in us as well as in women?" JOHNSON: "Why yes, Sir; but it is a delusion that is always beginning again." BOSWELL: "I don't know but there is upon the whole more misery than happiness produced by that passion." JOHNSON: "I don't think so, Sir."

"Never speak of a man in his own presence. It is always indelicate, and may be offensive."

"Questioning is not the mode of the conversation among gentlemen. It is assuming a superiority, and it is particularly wrong to question a man concerning himself. There may be parts of his former life which he may not wish to be made known to other persons, or even brought to his own recollection."

"A man should be careful never to tell tales of himself to his own disadvantage. People may be amused and laugh at the time, but they will be remembered and brought out against him upon some subsequent occasion."

I mentioned an acquaintance of mine, a sectary, who was a very religious man, who not only attended regularly on publick worship with those of his communion, but made a particular study of the Scriptures, and even wrote a commentary on some parts of them, yet was known to be very licentious in indulging himself with women; maintaining that men are to be saved by faith alone, and that the Christian religion had not prescribed any fixed rule for the intercourse between the sexes. JOHNSON: "Sir, there is no trusting to that crazy piety."

I observed that it was strange how well Scotchmen were known to one another in their own country, though born in very distant counties; for we do not find that the gentlemen of neighbouring counties in England are mutually known to each other. Johnson, with his usual acuteness, at once saw and explained the reason of this; "Why, Sir, you have Edinburgh, where the gentlemen from all your counties meet, and which is not so large but they are all known. There is no such common place of collection in England, except London, where from its great size and diffusion, many of those who reside in contiguous counties of England, may long remain unknown to each other."

On Tuesday, March 26, there came for us an equipage properly suited to a wealthy well-beneficed clergyman: Dr. Taylor's large, roomy post-chaise, drawn by four stout plump horses, and driven by two steady jolly postillions, which conveyed us to Ashbourne; where I found my friend's schoolfellow living upon an establishment perfectly corresponding with his substantial creditable equipage: his house, garden, pleasure grounds, table, in short every thing good, and no scantiness appearing.

Dr. Johnson and Dr. Taylor met with great cordiality.

Dr. Taylor commended a physician who was known to him and Dr. Johnson, and said, "I fight many battles for him, as many people in the country dislike him." JOHNSON: "But you should consider, Sir, that by every one of your victories he is a loser; for, every man of whom you get the better, will be very angry, and resolve not to employ him; whereas if people get the better of you in argument about him, they'll think, 'We'll send for Dr. ****** nevertheless.'"

Next day we talked of a book in which an eminent judge was arraigned before the bar of the publick, as having pronounced an unjust decision in a great cause. Dr. Johnson maintained that this publication would not give any uneasiness to the judge. "For, (said he,) either he acted honestly, or he meant to do injustice. If he acted honestly, his own consciousness will protect him; if meant to do injustice, he will be glad to see the man who attacks him, so much vexed."

Next day, as Dr. Johnson had acquainted Dr. Taylor of the reason for his returning speedily to London, it was resolved that we should set out after dinner. A few of Dr. Taylor's neighbours were his guests that day.

Dr. Johnson talked with approbation of one who had attained to the state of the philosophical wise man, that is, to have no want of any thing. "Then, Sir, (said I,) the savage is a wise man." "Sir, (said he,) I do not mean simply being without—but not having a want." I maintained, against this proposition, that it was better to have fine clothes, for instance, than not to feel the want of them. JOHNSON: "No, Sir; fine clothes are good only as they supply the want of other means of procuring respect. Was Charles the Twelfth, think you, less respected for his coarse blue coat and black stock? And you find the King of Prussia dresses plain, because the dignity of his character is sufficient." I here brought myself into a scrape, for I heedlessly said, "Would not *you*, Sir, be the better for velvet embroidery?" JOHNSON: "Sir, you put an end to all argument when you introduce your opponent himself. Have you no better manners? There is *your want*." I apologised by saying, I had mentioned him as an instance of one who wanted as little as any man in the world, and yet, perhaps, might receive some additional lustre from dress.

On Thursday, March 28, we pursued our journey. I mentioned that old Mr. Sheridan complained of the ingratitude of Mr. Wedderburne and General Fraser, who had been much obliged to him when they were young Scotchmen entering upon life in England. JOHNSON: "Why, Sir, a man is very apt to complain of the ingratitude of those who have risen far above him. A man when he gets into a higher sphere, into other habits of life, cannot keep up all his former connections. Then, Sir, those who knew him formerly upon a level with themselves, may think that they ought still to be treated as on a level, which cannot be; and an acquaintance in a former situation may bring out things which it would be very disagreeable to have mentioned before higher company, though, perhaps, every body knows of them."

He said, "It is commonly a weak man, who marries for love." We then talked of marrying women of fortune; and I mentioned a common remark, that a man may be, upon the whole, richer by marrying a woman with a very small portion, because a woman of fortune will be proportionally expensive; whereas a woman who brings none will be very moderate in expenses. JOHNSON: "Depend upon it, Sir, this is not true. A woman of fortune being used to the handling of money, spends it judiciously: but a woman who gets the command of money for the first time upon her marriage, has such a gust in spending it, that she throws it away with great profusion."

Having lain at St. Alban's, on Thursday, March 28, we breakfasted the next morning at Barnet. I expressed to him a weakness of mind which I could not help; an uneasy apprehension that my wife and children, who were at a great distance from me, might, perhaps, be ill. "Sir, (said he,) consider how foolish you would think it in *them* to be apprehensive that *you* are ill." This sudden turn relieved me for the moment; but I afterwards perceived it to be an ingenious fallacy. I might, to be sure, be satisfied that they had no reason to be apprehensive about me, because I *knew* that I myself was well: but we might have a mutual anxiety, without the charge of folly; because each was, in some degree, uncertain as to the condition of the other.

I enjoyed the luxury of our approach to London, that metropolis which we both loved so much, for the high and varied intellectual pleasure which it furnishes. I experienced immediate happiness while whirled along with such a companion, and said to him, "Sir, you observed one day at General Oglethorpe's, that a man is never happy for the present, but when he is drunk. Will you not add,— or when driving rapidly in a post-chaise?" JOHNSON: "No, Sir, you are driving rapidly *from* something, or *to* something."

Talking of melancholy, he said, "Some men, and very thinking men too, have not those vexing thoughts. Sir Joshua Reynolds is the same all the year round. Beauclerk, except when ill and in pain, is the same. But I believe most men have them in the degree in which they are capable of having them. If I were in the country, and were distressed by that malady, I would force myself to take a book; and every time I did it I should find it the easier. Melancholy, indeed, should be diverted by every means but drinking."

On Wednesday, April 3, in the morning I found him very busy putting his books in order, and as they were generally very old ones, clouds of dust were flying around him. He had on a pair of large gloves such as hedgers use. His present appearance put me in mind of my uncle, Dr. Boswell's description of him, "A robust genius, born to grapple with whole libraries."

I gave him an account of a conversation which had passed between me and Captain Cook, the day before, at dinner at Sir John Pringle's; and he was much pleased with the conscientious accuracy of that celebrated circumnavigator, who set me right as to many of the exaggerated accounts given by Dr. Hawkesworth of his Voyages. I told him that while I was with the Captain, I catched the enthusiasm of curiosity and adventure, and felt a strong inclination to go with him on his next voyage. JOHNSON: "Why, Sir, a man *does* feel so, till he considers how very little he can learn from such voyages." BOSWELL: "But one is carried away with the general

grand and indistinct notion of A VOYAGE ROUND THE WORLD."
JOHNSON: "Yes, Sir, but a man is to guard himself against taking a thing in general." I said I was certain that a great part of what we are told by the travellers to the South Sea must be conjecture, because they had not enough of the language of those countries to understand so much as they have related. Objects falling under the observation of the senses might be clearly known; but every thing intellectual, every thing abstract—politicks, morals, and religion, must be darkly guessed. Dr. Johnson was of the same opinion. He upon another occasion, when a friend mentioned to him several extraordinary facts, as communicated to him by the circumnavigators, slily observed, "Sir, I never before knew how much I was respected by these gentlemen; they told *me* none of these things."

He had been in company with Omai, a native of one of the South Sea Islands, after he had been some time in this country. He was struck by the elegance of his behaviour, and accounted for it thus: "Sir, he had passed his time, while in England, only in the best company; so that all that he had acquired of our manners was genteel. As a proof of this, Sir, Lord Mulgrave and he dined one day at Streatham; they sat with their backs to the light fronting me, so that I could not see distinctly; and there was so little of the savage in Omai, that I was afraid to speak to either, lest I should mistake one for the other."

We agreed to dine to-day at the Mitre tavern, after the rising of the House of Lords, where a branch of the litigation concerning the Douglas Estate, in which I was one of the counsel, was to come on. I brought with me Mr. Murray, Solicitor-General of Scotland, now one of the Judges of the Court of Session, with the title of Lord Henderland. I mentioned Mr. Solicitor's relation, Lord Charles Hay, with whom I knew Dr. Johnson had been acquainted. JOHNSON: "I wrote something for Lord Charles; and I thought he had nothing to fear from a court-martial. I suffered a great loss when he died; he was a mighty pleasing man in conversation, and a reading man. The character of a soldier is high. They who stand forth the foremost in danger, for the community, have the respect of mankind. An officer is much more respected than any other man who has as little money. In a commercial country, money will always purchase respect. But you find, an officer, who has, properly speaking, no money, is every where well received and treated with attention. The character of a soldier always stands him in stead."

BOSWELL: "Yet, Sir, I think that common soldiers are worse thought of than other men in the same rank in life; such as labourers." JOHNSON: "Why, Sir, a common soldier is usually a very gross man, and any quality which procures respect may be overwhelmed by grossness. A man of learning may be so vicious or so ridiculous that you cannot respect him. A common soldier too, generally eats more than he can pay for. But when a common soldier is civil in his quarters, his red coat procures him a degree of respect." The peculiar respect paid to the military character in France was mentioned. BOSWELL: "I should think that where military men were so numerous, they would be less valued as not being rare." JOHNSON: "Nay, Sir, wherever a particular character or profession is high in the estimation of a people, those who are of it will be valued above other men. We value an Englishman high in this country, and yet Englishmen are not rare in it."

Mr. Murray praised the ancient philosophers for the candour and good humour with which those of different sects disputed with each other. JOHNSON: "Sir, they disputed with good humour, because they were not in earnest as to religion. Had the ancients been serious in their belief, we should not have had their Gods exhibited in the manner we find them represented in the Poets. The people would not have suffered it. They disputed with good humour upon their fanciful theories, because they were not interested in the truth of them: when a man has nothing to lose, he may be in good humour with his opponent. Accordingly you see in Lucian, the Epicurean, who argues only negatively, keeps his temper; the Stoick, who has something positive to preserve, grows angry. Being angry with one who controverts an opinion which you value, is a necessary consequence of the uneasiness which you feel. Every man who attacks my belief, diminishes in some degree my confidence in it, and therefore makes me uneasy; and I am angry with him who makes me uneasy. Those only who believed in revelation have been angry at having their faith called in question; because they only had something upon which they could rest as matter of fact." MURRAY: "It seems to me that we are not angry at a man for controverting an opinion which we believe and value; we rather pity him." JOHNSON: "Why, Sir, to be sure when you wish a man to have that belief which you think is of infinite advantage, you wish well to him; but your primary consideration is your own quiet. If a madman were to come into this room with a stick in his hand, no doubt we should pity the state of his mind;

but our primary consideration would be to take care of ourselves. We should knock him down first, and pity him afterwards. No, Sir, every man will dispute with great good humour upon a subject in which he is not interested. I will dispute very calmly upon the probability of another man's son being hanged; but if a man zealously enforces the probability that my own son will be hanged, I shall certainly not be in a very good humour with him." I added this illustration, "If a man endeavours to convince me that my wife, whom I love very much, and in whom I place great confidence, is a disagreeable woman, and is even unfaithful to me, I shall be very angry, for he is putting me in fear of being unhappy." MURRAY: "But, Sir, truth will always bear an examination." JOHNSON: "Yes, Sir, but it is painful to be forced to defend it. Consider, Sir, how should you like, though conscious of your innocence, to be tried before a jury for a capital crime, once a week."

I introduced the topick, which is often ignorantly urged, that the Universities of England are too rich; so that learning does not flourish in them as it would do, if those who teach had smaller salaries, and depended on their assiduity for a great part of their income. JOHNSON: "Sir, the very reverse of this is the truth; the English Universities are not rich enough. Our fellowships are only sufficient to support a man during his studies to fit him for the world, and accordingly in general they are held no longer than till an opportunity offers of getting away. Now and then, perhaps, there is a fellow who grows old in his college; but this is against his will, unless he be a man very indolent indeed. A hundred a year is reckoned a good fellowship, and that is no more than is necessary to keep a man decently as a scholar. We do not allow our fellows to marry, because we consider academical institutions as pre-paratory to a settlement in the world. It is only by being employed as a tutor, that a fellow can obtain any thing more than a livelihood. To be sure a man, who has enough without teaching, will probably not teach; for we would all be idle if we could. In the same manner, a man who is to get nothing by teaching, will not exert himself. Gresham-College was intended as a place of instruction for London; able professors were to read lectures gratis, they contrived to have no scholars; whereas, if they had been allowed to receive but sixpence a lecture from each scholar, they would have been emulous to have had many scholars. Every body will agree that it should be the interest of those who teach to have scholars; and this is the case in our Universities. That they are too rich is certainly not true;

for they have nothing good enough to keep a man of eminent learning with them for his life. In the foreign Universities a professorship is a high thing. It is as much almost as a man can make by his learning; and therefore we find the most learned men abroad are in the Universities. It is not so with us. Our Universities are impoverished of learning, by the penury of their provisions. I wish there were many places of a thousand a year at Oxford, to keep first-rate men of learning from quitting the University."

I mentioned Mr. Maclaurin's uneasiness on account of a degree of ridicule carelessly thrown on his deceased father, in Goldsmith's *History of Animated Nature*, in which that celebrated mathematician is represented as being subject to fits of yawning so violent as to render him incapable of proceeding in his lecture; a story altogether unfounded, but for the publication of which the law would give no reparation. This led us to agitate the question, whether legal redress could be obtained, even when a man's deceased relation was calumniated in a publication. Mr. Murray maintained there should be reparation, unless the authour could justify himself by proving the fact. JOHNSON: "Sir, it is of so much more consequence that truth should be told, than that individuals should not be made uneasy, that it is much better that the law does not restrain writing freely concerning the characters of the dead. Damages will be given to a man who is calumniated in his life-time, because he may be hurt in his worldly interest, or at least hurt in his mind: but the law does not regard that uneasiness which a man feels on having his ancestor calumniated. That is too nice. Let him deny what is said, and let the matter have a fair chance by discussion. But if a man could say nothing against a character but what he can prove, history could not be written; for a great deal is known of men of which proof cannot be brought. A minister may be notoriously known to take bribes, and yet you may not be able to prove it." Mr. Murray suggested that the authour should be obliged to show some sort of evidence, though he would not require a strict legal proof: but Johnson firmly and resolutely opposed any restraint whatever, as adverse to a free investigation of the characters of mankind.

On Thursday, April 4, having called on Dr. Johnson, I said, it was a pity that truth was not so firm as to bid defiance to all attacks, so that it might be shot at as much as people chose to attempt, and yet remain unhurt. JOHNSON: "Then, Sir, it would not be shot at. Nobody attempts to dispute that two and two make four: but with contests concerning moral truth, human passions are generally mixed, and therefore it must ever be liable to assault and misrepresentation."

On Friday, April 5, being Good Friday, after having attended the morning service at St. Clement's church, I walked home with Johnson. We talked of the Roman Catholick religion. JOHNSON: "In the barbarous ages, Sir, priests and people were equally deceived; but afterwards there were gross corruptions introduced by the clergy, such as indulgences to priests to have concubines, and the worship of images, not, indeed, inculcated, but knowingly permitted." He strongly censured the licensed stews at Rome. BOSWELL: "So then, Sir, you would allow of no irregular intercourse whatever between the sexes?" JOHNSON: "To be sure I would not, Sir. I would punish it much more than it is done, and so restrain it. In all countries there has been fornication, as in all countries there has been theft; but there may be more or less of the one, as well as of the other, in proportion to the force of law. All men will naturally commit fornication, as all men will naturally steal. And, Sir, it is very absurd to argue, as has been often done, that prostitutes are necessary to prevent the violent effects of appetite from violating the decent order of life; nay, should be permitted in order to preserve the chastity of our wives and daughters. Depend upon it, Sir, severe laws, steadily enforced, would be sufficient against those evils, and would promote marriage."

I stated to him this case:—"Suppose a man has a daughter, who he knows has been seduced, but her misfortune is concealed from the world? should he keep her in his house? Would he not, by doing so, be accessary to imposition? And, perhaps, a worthy, unsuspecting man might come and marry this woman, unless the father inform him of the truth." JOHNSON: "Sir, he is accessary to no imposition. His daughter is in his house; and if a man courts her, he takes his chance. If a friend, or, indeed, if any man asks his opinion whether he should marry her, he ought to advise him against it, without telling why, because his real opinion is then required. Or, if he has other daughters who know of her frailty, he ought not to keep her in his house. You are to consider the state of life is this; we are to judge of one another's characters as well as we can; and a man is not bound in honesty or honour, to tell us the faults of his daughter or of himself. A man who has debauched his friend's daughter is not obliged to say to every body—Take care of me; don't let me into your house without suspicion. I once debauched a friend's daughter. I may debauch yours."

Mr. Thrale called upon him, and appeared to bear the loss of his son with a manly composure.

Dr. Johnson gave us one of the many sketches of character which were treasured in his mind, and which he was wont to produce quite unexpectedly in a very entertaining manner. "I lately, (said he,) received a letter from the East-Indies, from a gentleman whom I formerly knew very well; he had returned from that country with a handsome fortune, as it was reckoned, before means were found to acquire those immense sums which have been brought from thence of late; he was a scholar, and an agreeable man, and lived very prettily in London, till his wife died. After her death, he took to dissipation and gaming, and lost all he had. One evening he lost a thousand pounds to a gentleman whose name I am sorry I have forgotten. Next morning he sent the gentleman five hundred pounds, with an apology that it was all he had in the world. The gentleman sent the money back to him, declaring he would not accept of it; and adding, that if Mr. —— had occasion for five hundred pounds more, he would lend it to him. He resolved to go out again to the East-Indies, and make his fortune anew. He got a considerable appointment, and I had some intention of accompanying him. Had I thought then as I do now, I should have gone: but at that time, I had objections to quitting England."

I mentioned a new gaming-club, of which Mr. Beauclerk had given me an account, where the members played to a desperate extent. JOHNSON: "Depend upon it, Sir, this is mere talk. *Who* is ruined by gaming? You will not find six instances in an age. There is a strange rout made about deep play; whereas you have many more people ruined by adventurous trade, and yet we do not hear such an outcry against it." THRALE: "There may be few people absolutely ruined by deep play; but very many are much hurt in their circumstances by it." JOHNSON: "Yes, Sir, and so are very many by other kinds of expence." I had heard him talk once before in the same manner; and at Oxford he said, "he wished he had learned to play cards." The truth, however, is, that he loved to display his ingenuity in argument; and therefore would sometimes in conversation maintain opinions which he was sensible were wrong, but in supporting which, his reasoning and wit would be most conspicuous. He would begin thus: "Why, Sir, as to the good or evil of card-playing——" "Now, (said Garrick,) he is thinking which side he shall take." He appeared to have a pleasure in contradiction, especially when any opinion whatever was delivered with an air of confidence; so that there was hardly any topick if not one of the great truths of Religion and Morality, that he might not have been incited to argue, either for or against.

I repeated to him an argument of a lady of my acquaintance, who maintained, that her husband's having been guilty of numberless infidelities, released her from conjugal obligations, because they were reciprocal. JOHNSON: "This is miserable stuff, Sir. To the contract of marriage, besides the man and wife, there is a third party—Society; and if it be considered as a vow—God: and, therefore, it cannot be dissolved by their consent alone. Laws are not made for particular cases, but for men in general. A woman may be unhappy with her husband; but she cannot be freed from him without the approbation of the civil and ecclesiastical power. A man may be unhappy, because he is not so rich as another; but he is not to seize upon another's property with his own hand." BOSWELL: "But, Sir, this lady does not want that the contract should be dissolved; she only argues that she may indulge herself in gallantries with equal freedom as her husband does, provided she takes care not to introduce a spurious issue into his family. You know, Sir, what Macrobius has told of Julia." JOHNSON: "This lady of yours, Sir, I think, is very fit for a brothel."

After coffee, we went to afternoon service in St. Clement's church. Observing some beggars in the street as we walked along, I said to him, I supposed there was no civilised country in the world, where the misery of want in the lowest classes of the people was prevented. JOHNSON: "I believe, Sir, there is not; but, it is better that some should be unhappy, than that none should be happy, which would be the case in a general state of equality."

Upon the question whether a man who had been guilty of vicious actions would do well to force himself into solitude and sadness? JOHNSON: "No, Sir, unless it prevent him from being vicious again. With some people, gloomy penitence is only madness turned upside down. A man may be gloomy, till, in order to be relieved from gloom, he has recourse again to criminal indulgencies."

On Wednesday, April 10, I dined with him at Mr. Thrale's, where were Mr. Murphy and some other company.

I said, I disliked the custom which some people had of bringing their children into company, because it in a manner forced us to pay foolish compliments to please their parents. JOHNSON: "You are right, Sir. We may be excused for not caring much about other people's children, for there are many who care very little about their own children. It may be observed, that men, who from being engaged in business, or from their course of life in whatever way, seldom see their children, do not care much about them. I myself should not have had much fondness for a child of my own." MRS. THRALE: "Nay, Sir, how can you talk so?" JOHNSON: "At least, I never wished to have a child."

He talked of Lord Lyttelton's extreme anxiety as an authour; observing, that "he was thirty years in preparing his *History*, and that he employed a man to point it for him; as if (laughing) another man could point his sense better than himself." Mr. Murphy said, he understood his history was kept back several years for fear of Smollett. JOHNSON: "This seems strange to Murphy and me, who never felt that anxiety, but sent what we wrote to the press, and let it take its chance." MRS. THRALE: "The time has been, Sir, when you felt it." JOHNSON: "Why really, Madam, I do not recollect a time when that was the case."

Johnson mentioned Dr. Barry's *System of Physick*. "He was a man (said he,) who had acquired a high reputation in Dublin, came over to England, and brought his reputation with him, but had not great success. His notion was, that pulsation occasions death by attrition; and that, therefore, the way to preserve life is to retard pulsation. But we know that pulsation is strongest in infants, and that we increase in growth while it operates in its regular course; so it cannot be the cause of destruction." Soon after this, he said something very flattering to Mrs. Thrale, which I do not recollect; but it concluded with wishing her long life. "Sir (said I,) if Dr. Barry's system be true, you have now shortened Mrs. Thrale's life, perhaps, some minutes, by accelerating her pulsation."

On Thursday, April 11, I dined with him at General Paoli's, in whose house I now resided, and where I had ever afterwards the honour of being entertained with the kindest attention as his constant guest, while I was in London, till I had a house of my own there. I mentioned my having that morning introduced to Mr. Garrick, Count Neni, a Flemish Nobleman of great rank and fortune, to whom Garrick talked of Abel Drugger as a *small part*; and related, with pleasant vanity, that a Frenchman, who had seen him in one of his low characters, exclaimed, "*Comment! je ne le crois pas. Ce n'est pas Monsieur Garrick, ce Grand Homme!*" Garrick added, with an appearance of grave recollection, "If I were to begin life again, I think I should not play those low characters." Upon which I observed, "Sir, you would be in the wrong; for your great excellence is your variety of playing, your representing so well, characters so very different." JOHNSON: "Garrick, Sir, was not in earnest in what he said; for, to be sure, his peculiar excellence is his variety; and, perhaps, there is not any one character which has not been as well acted by somebody else, as he could do it." BOSWELL: "Why, then, Sir, did he talk so?" JOHNSON: "Why, Sir, to make you answer as you did." BOSWELL: "I don't know, Sir; he seemed to dip deep into his mind for the reflection." JOHNSON: "He had not far to dip, Sir; he had said the same thing, probably, twenty times before."

Of a nobleman raised at a very early period to high office, he said, "His parts, Sir, are pretty well for a Lord; but would not be distinguished in a man who had nothing else but his parts."

A journey to Italy was still in his thoughts. He said, "A man who has not been in Italy, is always conscious of an inferiority, from his not having seen what it is expected a man should see. The grand object of travelling is to see the shores of the Mediterranean. On those shores were the four great Empires of the world; the Assyrian, the Persian, the Grecian, and the Roman.—All our religion, almost all our law, almost all our arts, almost all that sets us above savages, has come to us from the shores of the Mediterranean." The General observed, that "THE MEDITERRANEAN would be a noble subject for a poem."

We talked of translation. I said, I could not define it, nor could I think of a similitude to illustrate it; but that it appeared to me the translation of poetry could be only imitation. JOHNSON: "You may translate books of science exactly. You may also translate history, in so far as it is not embellished with oratory, which is poetical. Poetry, indeed, cannot be translated; and, therefore, it is the poets that preserve languages; for we would not be at the trouble to learn a language, if we could have all that is written in it just as well in a translation. But as the beauties of poetry cannot be preserved in any language except that in which it was originally written, we learn the language."

A gentleman maintained that the art of printing had hurt real learning, by disseminating idle writings.—JOHNSON: "Sir, if it had not been for the art of printing, we should now have no learning at all; for books would have perished faster than they could have been transcribed."

The same gentleman maintained, that a general diffusion of knowledge among a people was a disadvantage; for it made the vulgar rise above their humble sphere. JOHNSON: "Sir, while knowledge is a distinction, those who are possessed of it will naturally rise above those who are not. Merely to read and write was a distinction at first; but we see when reading and writing have become general, the common people keep their stations. And so, were higher attainments to become general, the effect would be the same."

"Goldsmith (he said,) referred every thing to vanity; his virtues, and his vices too were from that motive. He was not a social man. He never exchanged mind with you."

We spent the evening at Mr. Hoole's. Mr. Mickle, the excellent translator of *The Lusiad*, was there. I have preserved little of the conversation of this evening. Dr. Johnson said, "Thomson had a true poetical genius, the power of viewing every thing in a poetical light. His fault is such a cloud of words sometimes, that the sense can hardly peep through. Shiels, who compiled *Cibber's Lives of the Poets*, was one day sitting with me. I took down Thomson, and read aloud a large portion of him, and then asked,— Is not this fine? Shiels having expressed the highest admiration, 'Well, Sir, (said I,) I have omitted every other line.'"

I related a dispute between Goldsmith and Mr. Robert Dodsley, one day when they and I were dining at Tom Davies's, in 1762. Goldsmith asserted, that there was no poetry produced in this age. Dodsley appealed to his own Collection, and maintained, that though you could not find a palace like Dryden's *Ode on St. Cecilia's Day*, you had villages composed of very pretty houses; and he mentioned particularly *The Spleen*. JOHNSON: "I think Dodsley gave up the question. He and Goldsmith said the same thing; only he said it in a softer manner than Goldsmith did; for he acknowledged that there was no poetry, nothing that towered above the common mark. You may find wit and humour in verse, and yet no poetry. *Hudibras* has a profusion of these; yet it is not to be reckoned a poem. *The Spleen*, in Dodsley's collection, on which you say he chiefly rested, is not poetry." BOSWELL: "Does not Gray's poetry, Sir, tower above the common mark?" JOHNSON: "Yes, Sir; but we must attend to the difference between what men in general cannot do if they would, and what every man may do if he would. Sixteen-string Jack towered above the common mark." BOSWELL: "Then, Sir, what is poetry?"

JOHNSON: "Why, Sir, it is much easier to say what it is not. We all *know* what light is; but it is not easy to *tell* what it is."

On Friday, April 12, I dined with him at our friend Tom Davies's, where we met Mr. Cradock, of Leicestershire, authour of *Zobeide*, a tragedy; a very pleasing gentleman, to whom my friend Dr. Farmer's very excellent *Essay on the Learning of Shakespeare* is addressed; and Dr. Harwood, who has written and published various works; particularly a fantastical translation of the New Testament, in modern phrase, and with a Socinian twist.

I introduced Aristotle's doctrine in his *Art of Poetry*, of "the κάθαρσις τῶν παθημάτων, the purging of the passions," as the purpose of tragedy. "But how are the passions to be purged by terrour and pity?" (said I, with an assumed air of ignorance, to incite him to talk, for which it was often necessary to employ some address.) JOHNSON: "Why, Sir, you are to consider what is the meaning of purging in the original sense. It is to expel impurities from the human body. The mind is subject to the same imperfection. The passions are the great movers of human actions; but they are mixed with such impurities, that it is necessary they should be purged or refined by means of terrour and pity. For instance, ambition is a noble passion; but by seeing upon the stage, that a man who is so excessively ambitious as to raise himself by injustice, is punished, we are terrified at the fatal consequences of such a passion. In the same manner a certain degree of resentment is necessary; but if we see that a man carries it too far, we pity the object of it, and are taught to moderate that passion." My record upon this occasion does great injustice to Johnson's expression, which was so forcible and brilliant, that Mr. Cradock whispered me, "O that his words were written in a book!"

I observed the great defect of the tragedy of *Othello* was, that it had not a moral; for that no man could resist the circumstances of suspicion which were artfully suggested to Othello's mind. JOHNSON: "In the first place, Sir, we learn from *Othello* this very useful moral, not to make an unequal match; in the second place, we learn not to yield too readily to suspicion. The handkerchief is merely a trick, though a very pretty trick; but there are no other circumstances of reasonable suspicion, except what is related by Iago of Cassio's warm expressions concerning Desdemona in his sleep; and that depended entirely upon the assertion of one man. No, Sir, I think *Othello* has more moral than almost any play."

Talking of a penurious gentleman of our acquaintance, Johnson said, "Sir, he is narrow, not so much from avarice, as from impotence to spend his money. He cannot find in his heart to pour out a bottle of wine; but he would not much care if it should sour."

We discussed the question, whether drinking improved conversation and benevolence. Sir Joshua maintained it did. JOHNSON: "No, Sir; before dinner men meet with great inequality of understanding; and those who are conscious of their inferiority, have the modesty not to talk. When they have drunk wine, every man feels himself happy, and loses that modesty, and grows impudent and vociferous: but he is not improved: he is only not sensible of his defects." Sir Joshua said the Doctor was talking of the effects of excess in wine; but that a moderate glass enlivened the mind, by giving a proper circulation to the blood. "I am, (said he,) in very good spirits, when I get up in the morning. By dinner-time I am exhausted; wine puts me in the same state as when I got up: and I am sure that moderate drinking makes people talk better." JOHNSON: "No, Sir; wine gives not light, gay, ideal hilarity; but tumultuous, noisy, clamorous merriment. I have heard none of those drunken,—nay, drunken is a coarse word,—none of those *vinous* flights." SIR JOSHUA: "Because you have sat by, quite sober, and felt an envy of the happiness of those who were drinking." JOHNSON: "Perhaps, contempt.—And, Sir, it is not necessary to be drunk one's self, to relish the wit of drunkenness. Do we not judge of the drunken wit of the dialogue between Iago and Cassio, the most excellent in its kind, when we are quite sober? Wit is wit, by whatever means it is produced; and, if good, will appear so at all times. I admit that the spirits are raised by drinking, as by the common participation of any pleasure: cock-fighting, or bear-baiting, will raise the spirits of a company, as drinking does, though surely they will not improve conversation. I also admit, that there are some sluggish men who are improved by drinking; as there are fruits which are not good till they are rotten. There are such men, but they are medlars. I indeed allow that there have been a very few men of talents who were improved by drinking; but I maintain that I am right as to the effects of drinking in general: and let it be considered, that there is no position, however false in its universality, which is not true of some particular man." Sir William Forbes said, "Might not a man warmed with wine be like a bottle of beer, which is made brisker by being set before the fire?"—"Nay, (said Johnson, laughing,) I cannot answer that: that is too much for me."

I observed, that wine did some people harm, by inflaming, confusing, and irritating their minds; but that the experience of mankind had declared in favour of moderate drinking. JOHNSON: "Sir, I do not say it is wrong to produce self-complacency by drinking; I only deny that it improves the mind. When I drank wine, I scorned to drink it when in company. I have drunk many a bottle by myself; in the first place, because I had need of it to raise my spirits: in the second place, because I would have nobody to witness its effects upon me."

He said, that for general improvement, a man should read whatever his immediate inclination prompts him to; though to be sure, if a man has a science to learn, he must regularly and resolutely advance. He added, "what we read with inclination makes a much stronger impression. If we read without inclination, half the mind is employed in fixing the attention; so there is but one half to be employed on what we read." He told us, he read Fielding's *Amelia* through, without stopping. He said, "if a man begins to read in the middle of a book, and feels an inclination to go on, let him not quit it, to go to the beginning. He may perhaps not feel again the inclination."

Soon after this day, he went to Bath with Mr. and Mrs. Thrale.

I shall group together such of his sayings as I preserved during the few days that I was at Bath with him.

Of a person who differed from him in politicks, he said, "In private life he is a very honest gentleman; but I will not allow him to be so in publick life. People *may* be honest, though they are doing wrong; that is, between their Maker and them. But *we*, who are suffering by their pernicious conduct, are to destroy them. We are sure that —— acts from interest. We know what his genuine principles were. They who allow their passions to confound the distinctions between right and wrong, are criminal. They may be convinced; but they have not come honestly by their conviction."

It having been mentioned, I know not with what truth, that a certain female political writer, whose doctrines he disliked, had of late become very fond of dress, sat hours together at her toilet, and even put on rouge:—JOHNSON: "She is better employed at her toilet, than using her pen. It is better she should be reddening her own cheeks, than blackening other people's characters."

Of the father of one of our friends, he observed, "He never clarified his notions, by filtrating them through other minds. He had a canal upon his estate, where at one place the bank was too low.—I dug the canal deeper," said he.

A literary lady of large fortune was mentioned, as one who did good to many, but by no means "by stealth," and instead of "blushing to find it fame," acted evidently from vanity. JOHNSON: "I have seen no beings who do as much good from benevolence, as she does from whatever motive. If there are such under the earth, or in the clouds, I wish they would come up, or come down. What Soame Jenyns says upon this subject is not to be minded; he is a wit. No, Sir; to act from pure benevolence is not possible for finite beings. Human benevolence is mingled with vanity, interest, or some other motive."

A gentleman, expressed a wish to go and live three years at Otaheite, or New Zealand, in order to obtain a full acquaintance with people, so totally different from all that we have ever known, and be satisfied what pure nature can do for man. JOHNSON: "What could you learn, Sir? What can savages tell, but what they themselves have seen? Of the past, or the invisible, they can tell nothing. The inhabitants of Otaheite and New Zealand are not in a state of pure nature; for it is plain they broke off from some other people. Had they grown out of the ground, you might have judged of a state of pure nature. Fanciful people may talk of a mythology being amongst them; but it must be invention. They have once had religion, which has been gradually debased. And what account of their religion can you suppose to be learnt from savages? Only consider, Sir, our own state: our religion is in a book; we have an order of men whose duty it is to teach it, we have one day in the week set apart for it, and this is in general pretty well observed: Yet ask the first ten gross men you meet, and hear what they can tell of their religion."

After Dr. Johnson's return to London, I was several times with him at his house, where I occasionally slept, in the room that had been assigned for me. I dined with him at Dr. Taylor's, at General Oglethorpe's, and at General Paoli's. To avoid a tedious minuteness, I shall group together what I have preserved of his conversation during this period also, without specifying each scene where it passed, except one, which will be found so remarkable as certainly to deserve a very particular relation.

"Where there is no education, (he observed,) as in savage countries, men will have the upper hand of women. Bodily strength, no doubt, contributes to this; but it would be so, exclusive of that;

•for it is mind that always governs. When it comes to dry understanding, man has the better."

"There is much talk of the misery which we cause to the brute creation; but they are recompensed by existence. If they were not useful to man, and therefore protected by him, they would not be nearly so numerous."

"That man is never happy for the present is so true, that all his relief from unhappiness is only forgetting himself for a little while. Life is a progress from want to want, not from enjoyment to enjoyment."

"Though many men are nominally entrusted with the administration of hospitals and other publick institutions, almost all the good is done by one man, by whom the rest are driven on; owing to confidence in him, and indolence in them."

A gentleman, whom I found sitting with him one morning, said, that in his opinion the character of an infidel was more detestable than that of a man notoriously guilty of an atrocious crime. I differed from him, because we are surer of the odiousness of the one, than of the errour of the other. JOHNSON: "Sir, I agree with him; for the infidel would be guilty of any crime if he were inclined to it."

"Many things which are false are transmitted from book to book, and gain credit in the world. One of these is the cry against the evil of luxury. Now the truth, is that luxury produces much good. Take the luxury of buildings in London. Does it not produce real advantage in the conveniency and elegance of accommodation, and this all from the exertion of industry? People will tell you, with a melancholy face, how many builders are in gaol. It is plain they are in gaol, not for building; for rents are not fallen.—A man gives half a guinea for a dish of green peas. How much gardening does this occasion? how many labourers must the competition to have such things early in the market keep in employment? You will hear it said, very gravely, 'Why was not the half guinea, thus spent in luxury, given to the poor? To how many might it have afforded a good meal.' Alas! has it not gone to the *industrious* poor, whom it is better to support than the *idle* poor? You are much surer that you are doing good when you *pay* money to those who work, as the recompence of their labour, than when you *give* money merely in charity. Suppose the ancient luxury of a dish of peacock's brains were to be revived, how many carcases would be left to the poor at a cheap rate: and as to the rout that is made about people

168

who are ruined by extravagance, it is no matter to the nation that some individuals suffer. When so much general productive exertion is the consequence of luxury, the nation does not care though there are debtors in gaol: nay they would not care though their creditors were there too."

When I complained of having dined at a splendid table without hearing one sentence of conversation worthy of being remembered, he said, "Sir, there seldom is any such conversation." BOSWELL: "Why then meet at table?" JOHNSON: "Why to eat and drink together, and to promote kindness; and, Sir, this is better done when there is no solid conversation: for when there is, people differ in opinion, and get into bad humour, or some of the company who are not capable of such conversation, are left out, and feel themselves uneasy. It was for this reason Sir Robert Walpole said, he always talked bawdy at his table, because in that all could join."

Being irritated by hearing a gentleman ask Mr. Levett a variety of questions concerning him, when he was sitting by, he broke out, "Sir, you have but two topicks, yourself and me. I am sick of both." "A man, (said he,) should not talk of himself, nor much of any particular person. He should take care not to be made a proverb; and, therefore, should avoid having any one topick of which people can say, 'We shall hear him upon it.' There was a Dr. Oldfield, who was always talking of the Duke of Marlborough. He came into a coffee house one day, and told that his Grace had spoken in the House of Lords for half an hour. 'Did he indeed speak for half an hour?' (said Belchier, the surgeon,)—'Yes.'—'And what did he say of Dr. Oldfield?'—'Nothing.'—'Why then, Sir, he was very ungrateful; for Dr. Oldfield could not have spoken for a quarter of an hour, without saying something of him.'"

"Every man is to take existence on the terms on which it is given to him. To some men it is given on condition of not taking liberties, which other men may take without much harm. One may drink wine, and be nothing the worse for it; on another, wine may have effects so inflammatory as to injure him both in body and mind, and perhaps, make him commit something for which he may deserve to be hanged."

I am now to record a very curious incident in Dr. Johnson's life, which fell under my own observation; of which *pars magna fui*,[1] and which I am persuaded will, with the liberal-minded, be much to his credit.

[1] I was a great part.

My desire of being acquainted with celebrated men of every description, had made me, much about the same time, obtain an introduction to Dr. Samuel Johnson and to John Wilkes, Esq. Two men more different could perhaps not be selected out of all mankind. They had even attacked one another with some asperity in their writings; yet I lived in habits of friendship with both.

But I conceived an irresistible wish, if possible, to bring Dr. Johnson and Mr. Wilkes together. How to manage it, was a nice and difficult matter.

My worthy booksellers and friends, Messieurs Dilly in the Poultry, at whose hospitable and well-covered table I have seen a greater number of literary men, than at any other, except that of Sir Joshua Reynolds, had invited me to meet Mr. Wilkes and some more gentlemen, on Wednesday, May 15. "Pray, (said I,) let us have Dr. Johnson."—"What, with Mr. Wilkes? not for the world, (said Mr. Edward Dilly;) Dr. Johnson would never forgive me." —"Come, (said I,) if you'll let me negociate for you, I will be answerable that all shall go well." DILLY: "Nay, if you will take it upon you, I am sure I shall be very happy to see them both here."

Notwithstanding the high veneration which I entertained for Dr. Johnson, I was sensible that he was sometimes a little actuated by the spirit of contradiction, and by means of that I hoped I should gain my point. I was persuaded that if I had come upon him with a direct proposal, "Sir, will you dine in company with Jack Wilkes?" he would have flown into a passion, and would probably have answered, "Dine with Jack Wilkes, Sir! I'd as soon dine with Jack Ketch." I therefore, while we were sitting quietly by ourselves at his house in an evening, took occasion to open my plan thus:— "Mr. Dilly, Sir, sends his respectful compliments to you, and would be happy if you would do him the honour to dine with him on Wednesday next along with me, as I must soon go to Scotland." JOHNSON: "Sir, I am obliged to Mr. Dilly. I will wait upon him——" BOSWELL: "Provided, Sir, I suppose, that the company which he is to have, is agreeable to you." JOHNSON: "What do you mean, Sir? What do you take me for? Do you think I am so ignorant of the world, as to imagine that I am to prescribe to a gentleman what company he is to have at his table? BOSWELL: "I beg your pardon, Sir, for wishing to prevent you from meeting people whom you might not like. Perhaps he may have some of what he calls his patriotick friends with him." JOHNSON: "Well, Sir, and what then? What care *I* for his *patriotick friends*? Poh!" BOSWELL: "I should not be surprized to find Jack Wilkes there." JOHNSON: "And if Jack Wilkes *should* be there, what is that to *me*, Sir? My dear friend, let us have no more of this. I am sorry to be angry with you; but really it is treating me strangely to talk to me as if I could not meet any company whatever, occasionally." BOSWELL: "Pray, forgive me, Sir; I meant well. But you shall meet whoever comes, for me." Thus I secured him, and told Dilly that he would find him very well pleased to be one of his guests on the day appointed.

Upon the much expected Wednesday, I called on him about half an hour before dinner, as I often did when we were to dine out together, to see that he was ready in time, and to accompany him. I found him buffeting his books, as upon a former occasion, covered with dust, and making no preparation for going abroad. "How is this, Sir? (said I). Don't you recollect that you are to dine at Mr. Dilly's?" JOHNSON: "Sir, I did not think of going to Dilly's: it went out of my head. I have ordered dinner at home with Mrs. Williams." BOSWELL: "But my dear Sir, you know you were engaged to Mr. Dilly, and I told him so. He will expect you, and will be much disappointed if you don't come." JOHNSON: "You must talk to Mrs. Williams about this."

Here was a sad dilemma. I feared that what I was so confident I had secured, would yet be frustrated. He had accustomed himself to shew Mrs. Williams such a degree of humane attention, as frequently imposed some restraint upon him; and I knew that if she should be obstinate, he would not stir. I hastened down stairs to the blind lady's room, and told her I was in great uneasiness, for Dr. Johnson had engaged to me to dine that day at Mr. Dilly's, but that he had told me he had forgotten his engagement, and had ordered dinner at home. "Yes, Sir, (said she, pretty peevishly,) Dr. Johnson is to dine at home."—"Madam, (said I,) his respect for you is such, that I know he will not leave you, unless you absolutely desire it. But as you have so much of his company, I hope you will be good enough to forgo it for a day: as Mr. Dilly is a very worthy man, has frequently had agreeable parties at his house for Dr. Johnson, and will be vexed if the Doctor neglects him to-day. And then, Madam, be pleased to consider my situation; I carried the message, and I assured Mr. Dilly that Dr. Johnson was to come; and no doubt he has made a dinner, and invited a company, and boasted of the honour he expected to have. I shall be quite disgraced if the Doctor is not there." She gradually softened to my solicitations, which were certainly as earnest as most entreaties to ladies upon any occasion, and was graciously pleased to empower me to tell Dr. Johnson, "That all things considered, she thought he should certainly go." I flew back to him, still in dust, and careless of what should be the event, "indifferent in his choice to go or stay"; but as soon as I had announced to him Mrs. William's consent, he roared, "Frank, a clean shirt," and was very soon drest. When I had him fairly seated in a hackney-coach with me, I exulted as much as a fortune-hunter who has got an heiress into a post-chaise with him to set out for Gretna-Green.

When we entered Mr. Dilly's drawing-room, he found himself in the midst of a company he did not know. I kept myself snug and silent, watching how he would conduct himself. I observed him whispering to Mr. Dilly, "Who is that gentleman, Sir?"—"Mr. Arthur Lee."—JOHNSON: "Too, too, too," (under his breath,) which was one of his habitual mutterings. Mr. Arthur Lee could not but be very obnoxious to Johnson, for he was not only a *patriot*, but an *American*. He was afterwards minister from the United States at the Court of Madrid. "And who is the gentleman in lace?"—"Mr. Wilkes, Sir." This information confounded him still more; he had some difficulty to restrain himself, and taking up a book, sat down upon a window-seat and read, or at least kept his eye upon it intently for some time, till he composed himself. His feelings, I dare say, were aukward enough. But he no doubt recollected his having rated me for supposing that he could be at all disconcerted by any company, and he, therefore, resolutely set himself to behave quite as an easy man of the world, who could adapt himself at once to the disposition and manners of those whom he might chance to meet.

The cheering sound of "Dinner is upon the table," dissolved his reverie, and we *all* sat down without any symptom of ill humour. There were present, beside Mr. Wilkes, and Mr. Arthur Lee, who was an old companion of mine when he studied physick at Edinburgh, Mr. (now Sir John) Miller, Dr. Lettsom, and Mr. Slater, the druggist. Mr. Wilkes placed himself next to Dr. Johnson, and behaved to him with so much attention and politeness, that he gained upon him insensibly. No man eat more heartily than Johnson, or loved better what was nice and delicate. Mr. Wilkes was very assiduous in helping him to some fine veal. "Pray give me leave, Sir;—It is better here—A little of the brown—Some fat,

Sir—A little of the stuffing—Some gravy—Let me have the pleasure of giving you some butter—Allow me to recommend a squeeze of this orange;—or the lemon, perhaps, may have more zest."—"Sir, Sir, I am obliged to you, Sir," cried Johnson, bowing, and turning his head to him with a look for some time of "surly virtue," but, in a short while, of complacency.

Foote being mentioned, Johnson said, "He is not a good mimick." One of the company added, "A merry Andrew, a buffoon." JOHNSON: "But he has wit too, and is not deficient in ideas, or in fertility and variety of imagery, and not empty of reading; he has knowledge enough to fill up his part. One species of wit he has in an eminent degree, that of escape. You drive him into a corner with both hands; but he's gone, Sir, when you think you have got him—like an animal that jumps over your head. Then he has a great range for wit; he never lets truth stand between him and a jest, and he is sometimes mighty coarse. Garrick is under many restraints from which Foote is free." WILKES: "Garrick's wit is more like Lord Chesterfield's." JOHNSON: "The first time I was in company with Foote was at Fitzherbert's. Having no good opinion of the fellow, I was resolved not to be pleased; and it is very difficult to please a man against his will. I went on eating my dinner pretty sullenly, affecting not to mind him. But the dog was so very comical, that I was obliged to lay down my knife and fork, throw myself back upon my chair, and fairly laugh it out. No, Sir, he was irresistible. He upon one occasion experienced, in an extraordinary degree, the efficacy of his powers of entertaining. Amongst the many and various modes which he tried of getting money, he became a partner with a small-beer brewer, and he was to have a share of the profits for procuring customers amongst his numerous acquaintance. Fitzherbert was one who took his small-beer; but it was so bad that the servants resolved not to drink it. They were at some loss how to notify their resolution, being afraid of offending their master, who they knew liked Foote much as a companion. At last they fixed upon a little black boy, who was rather a favourite, to be their deputy, and deliver their remonstrance; and having invested him with the whole authority of the kitchen, he was to inform Mr. Fitzherbert, in all their names, upon a certain day, that they would drink Foote's small-beer no longer. On that day Foote happened to dine at Fitzherbert, and this boy served at table; he was so delighted with Foote's stories, and merriment, and grimace, that when he went down stairs, he told them, "This is the finest man I have ever seen. I will not deliver your message. I will drink his small-beer."

Somebody observed that Garrick could not have done this. WILKES: "Garrick would have made the small-beer still smaller. He is now leaving the stage; but he will play *Scrub* all his life." I knew that Johnson would let nobody attack Garrick but himself, as Garrick said to me, and I had heard him praise his liberality; so to bring out his commendation of his celebrated pupil, I said, loudly, "I have heard Garrick is liberal." JOHNSON: "Yes, Sir, I know that Garrick has given away more money than any man in England that I am acquainted with, and that not from ostentatious views. Garrick was very poor when he began life; so when he came to have money, he probably was very unskilful in giving away, and saved when he should not. But Garrick began to be liberal as soon as he could; and I am of opinion, the reputation of avarice which he has had, has been very lucky for him, and prevented his having many enemies. You despise a man for avarice, but do not hate him. Garrick might have been much better attacked for living with more splendour than is suitable to a player: if they had had the wit to have assaulted him in that quarter, they might have galled him more. But they have kept clamouring about his avarice, which has rescued him from much obloquy and envy."

Mr. Wilkes remarked, that "among all the bold flights of Shakespeare's imagination, the boldest was making Birnamwood march to Dunsinane; creating a wood where there never was a shrub; a wood in Scotland! ha! ha! ha!" And he also observed, that "the clannish slavery of the Highlands of Scotland was the single exception to Milton's remark of 'The Mountain Nymph, sweet Liberty,' being worshipped in all hilly countries."—"When I was at Inverary (said he,) on a visit to my old friend, Archibald, Duke of Argyle, his dependents congratulated me on being such a favourite of his Grace. I said, 'It is then, gentlemen, truly lucky for me; for if I had displeased the Duke, and he had wished it, there is not a Campbell among you but would have been ready to bring John Wilkes's head to him in a charger. It would have been only

" Off with his head! so much for *Aylesbury*."

I was then member for Aylesbury."

WILKES: "We have no City-Poet now: that is an office which has gone into disuse. The last was Elkanah Settle. There is something

174

in *names* which one cannot help feeling. Now *Elkanah Settle* sounds so *queer*, who can expect much from that name? We should have no hesitation to give it for John Dryden, in preference to Elkanah Settle, from the names only, without knowing their different merits." JOHNSON: " I suppose Sir, Settle did as well for Aldermen in his time, as John Home could do now. Where did Beckford, and Trecothick learn English?"

Mr. Arthur Lee mentioned some Scotch who had taken possession of a barren part of America, and wondered why they should choose it. JOHNSON: "Why, Sir, all barrenness is comparative. The *Scotch* would not know it to be barren." BOSWELL: "Come, come, he is flattering the English. You have now been in Scotland, Sir, and say if you did not see meat and drink enough there." JOHNSON: "Why yes, Sir; meat and drink enough to give the inhabitants sufficient strength to run away from home." All these quick and lively sallies were said sportively, quite in jest, and with a smile, which showed that he meant only wit. Upon this topick he and Mr. Wilkes could perfectly assimilate; here was a bond of union between them, and I was conscious that as both of them had visited Caledonia, both were fully satisfied of the strange narrow ignorance of those who imagine that it is a land of famine. But they amused themselves with persevering in the old jokes. When I claimed a superiority for Scotland over England in one respect, that no man can be arrested there for a debt merely because another swears it against him; but there must first be the judgement of a court of law ascertaining its justice; and that a seizure of the person, before judgement is obtained, can take place only, if his creditor should swear that he is about to fly from the country, or, as it is technically expressed, is *in meditatione fugæ*: WILKES: "That, I should think may be safely sworn of all the Scotch nation." JOHNSON: (To Mr. Wilkes) "You must know, Sir, I lately took my friend Boswell, and shewed him genuine civilized life in an English provincial town. I turned him loose at Lichfield, my native city, that he might see for once real civility: for you know he lives among savages in Scotland, and among rakes in London." WILKES: "Except when he is with grave, sober, decent people, like you and me." JOHNSON: (smiling) "And we ashamed of him."

They were quite frank and easy. Johnson told the story of his asking Mrs. Macaulay to allow her footman to sit down with them, to prove the ridiculousness of the arguments for the equality of mankind: and he said to me afterwards, with a nod of satisfaction,

"You saw Mr. Wilkes acquiesced." Wilkes talked with all imaginable freedom of the ludicrous title given to the Attorney-General, *Diabolus Regis*; adding, "I have reason to know something about that officer; for I was prosecuted for a libel." Johnson, who many people would have supposed must have been furiously angry at hearing this talked of so lightly, said not a word. He was now, *indeed*, "a good-humoured fellow."

After dinner we had an accession of Mrs. Knowles, the Quaker lady, well known for her various talents, and of Mr. Alderman Lee. Amidst some patriotick groans, somebody (I think the Alderman) said, "Poor old England is lost." JOHNSON: "Sir, it is not so much to be lamented that old England is lost, as that the Scotch have found it." WILKES: "Had Lord Bute governed Scotland only, I should not have taken the trouble to write his eulogy, and dedicate 'MORTIMER' to him."

Mr. Wilkes held a candle to shew a fine print of a beautiful female figure which hung in the room, and pointed out the elegant contour of the bosom with the finger of an arch connoisseur. He afterwards in a conversation with me waggishly insisted, that all the time Johnson shewed visible signs of a fervent admiration of the corresponding charms of the fair Quaker.

I attended Dr. Johnson home, and had the satisfaction to hear him tell Mrs. Williams how much he had been pleased with Mr. Wilkes's company, and what an agreeable day he had passed.

I talked a good deal to him of the celebrated Margaret Caroline Rudd, whom I had visited, induced by the fame of her talents, address, and irresistible power of fascination. To a lady who disapproved of my visiting her, he said on a former occasion, "Nay, Madam, Boswell is in the right; I should have visited her myself, were it not that they have now a trick of putting every thing into the newspapers." This evening he exclaimed, "I envy him his acquaintance with Mrs. Rudd."

On the evening of the next day I took leave of him, being to set out for Scotland. I thanked him with great warmth for all his kindness. "Sir, (said he,) you are very welcome. Nobody repays it with more."

CHAPTER VIII

In Seventeen Seventy-seven

In SUNDAY evening, Sept. 14, 1777, I arrived at Ashbourne [to meet Dr. Johnson], and drove directly up to Dr. Taylor's door. Dr. Johnson and he appeared before I had got out of the post-chaise, and welcomed me cordially.

I told them that I had travelled all the preceding night, and gone to bed at Leek, in Staffordshire; and that when I rose to go to church in the afternoon, I was informed there had been an earth-quake, of which, it seems the shock had been felt in some degree at Ashbourne. JOHNSON: "Sir, it will be much exaggerated in public talk: for, in the first place, the common people do not accurately adapt their thoughts to the objects; nor, secondly, do they accurately adapt their words to their thoughts; they do not mean to lie; but, taking no pains to be exact, they give you very false accounts. A great part of their language is proverbial. If any thing rocks at all, they say *it rocks like a cradle*; and in this way they go on."

The subject of grief for the loss of relations and friends being introduced, I observed that it was strange to consider how soon it in general wears away. Dr. Taylor mentioned a gentleman of the neighbourhood as the only instance he had ever known of a person who had endeavoured to *retain* grief. He told Dr. Taylor, that after his Lady's death, which affected him deeply, he *resolved* that the grief, which he cherished with a kind of sacred fondness, should be lasting; but that he found he could not keep it long. JOHNSON: "All grief for what cannot in the course of nature be helped, soon wears away; in some sooner, indeed, in some later; but it never continues very long, unless where there is madness, such as will make a man have pride so fixed in his mind, as to imagine himself a king; or any other passion in an unreasonable way: for all un-necessary grief is unwise, and therefore will not be long retained by a sound mind. If, indeed, the cause of our grief is occasioned by our own misconduct, if grief is mingled with remorse of con-science, it should be lasting." BOSWELL: "But, Sir, we do not approve of a man who very soon forgets the loss of a wife or a friend." JOHNSON: "Sir, we disapprove of him, not because he soon forgets his grief; for the sooner it is forgotten the better, but because we suppose, that if he forgets his wife or his friend soon, he has not had much affection for them."

I was somewhat disappointed in finding that the edition of the English Poets, for which he was to write Prefaces and Lives, was not an undertaking directed by him: but that he was to furnish a Preface and Life to any poet the booksellers pleased. I asked him if he would do this to any dunce's works, if they should ask him. JOHNSON: "Yes, Sir, and *say* he was a dunce." My friend seemed now not much to relish talking of this edition.

Johnson gave us on Monday, Sept. 15, in his happy discriminative manner, a portrait of the late Mr. Fitzherbert of Derbyshire. "There was (said he) no sparkle, no brilliancy in Fitzherbert; but I never knew a man who was so generally acceptable. He made every body quite easy, overpowered nobody by the superiority of his talents, made no man think worse of himself by being his rival, seemed always to listen, did not oblige you to hear much from him, and did not oppose what you said. Every body liked him; but he had no friend, as I understand the word, nobody with whom he exchanged intimate thoughts. People were willing to think well of every thing about him. A gentleman was making an affected rant, as many people do, of great feelings about 'his dear son,' who was at school near London; how anxious he was lest he might be ill, and what he would give to see him. 'Can't you (said Fitzherbert,) take a post-chaise and go to him?' This, to be sure, *finished* the affected man, but there was not much in it. However, this was circulated as wit for a whole winter, and I believe part of a summer too; a proof that he was no very witty man. He was an instance of the truth of the observation, that a man will please more upon the whole by negative qualities than by positive; by never offending, than by giving a great deal of delight. In the first place, men hate more steadily than they love; and if I have said something to hurt a man once, I shall not get the better of this, by saying many things to please him."

Next evening the Reverend Mr. Seward, of Lichfield, who was passing through Ashbourne in his way home, drank tea with us. Johnson described him thus:—"Sir, his ambition is to be a fine talker; so he goes to Buxton, and such places, where he may find companies to listen to him. And, Sir, he is a valetudinarian, one

178

of those who are always mending themselves. I do not know a more disagreeable character than a valetudinarian, who thinks he may do any thing that is for his ease, and indulges himself in the grossest freedoms: Sir, he brings himself to the state of a hog in a stye."

Dr. Taylor's nose happening to bleed, he said, it was because he had omitted to have himself blooded four days after a quarter of a year's interval. Dr. Johnson, who was a great dabbler in physick, disapproved much of periodical bleeding. "For (said he) you accustom yourself to an evacuation which Nature cannot perform of herself, and therefore she cannot help you, should you from forgetfulness or any other cause omit it; so you may be suddenly suffocated. You may accustom yourself to other periodical evacuations, because should you omit them, Nature can supply the omission; but Nature cannot open a vein to blood you."—"I do not like to take an emetick, (said Taylor,) for fear of breaking some small vessels."—"Poh! (said Johnson,) if you have so many things that will break, you had better break your neck at once, and there's an end on't. You will break no small vessels:" (blowing with high derision.)

I mentioned to Dr. Johnson, that David Hume's persisting in his infidelity, when he was dying, shocked me much. JOHNSON: "Why should it shock you, Sir? Hume owned he had never read the New Testament with attention. Here then was a man who had been at no pains to enquire into the truth of religion, and had continually turned his mind the other way. It was not to be expected that the prospect of death would alter his way of thinking unless God should send an angel to set him right." I said, I had reason to believe that the thought of annihilation gave Hume no pain. JOHNSON: "It was not so, Sir. He had a vanity in being thought easy. It is more probable that he should assume an appearance of ease, than so very improbable a thing should be, as a man not afraid of going (as, in spite of his delusive theory, he cannot be sure but he may go), into an unknown state, and not being uneasy at leaving all he knew. And you are to consider, that upon his own principle of annihilation he had no motive to speak the truth." The horrour of death, which I had always observed in Dr. Johnson, appeared strong to-night. I ventured to tell him, that I had been, for moments in my life, not afraid of death; therefore I could suppose another man in that state of mind for a considerable space of time. He said, "he never had a moment in which death was not terrible to him." He added, that it had been observed, that scarce any man dies in publick, but with apparent resolution; from that desire of praise which never quits us.

On Wednesday, September 17, Dr. Butter, physician at Derby, drank tea with us; and it was settled that Dr. Johnson and I should go on Friday and dine with him. Johnson said, "I'm glad of this." He seemed weary of the uniformity of life at Dr. Taylor's.

Talking of biography, I said, in writing a life, a man's peculiarities should be mentioned, because they mark his character. JOHNSON: "Sir, there is no doubt as to peculiarities: the question is, whether a man's vices should be mentioned; for instance, whether it should be mentioned that Addison and Parnell drank too freely; for people will probably more easily indulge in drinking from knowing this; so that more ill may be done by the example, than good by telling the whole truth." Here was an instance of his varying from himself in talk; for when Lord Hailes and he sat one morning calmly conversing in my house at Edinburgh, I well remember that Dr. Johnson maintained, that "If a man is to write *A Panegyrick*, he may keep vices out of sight: but if he professes to write *A Life*, he must represent it really as it was;" and when I objected to the danger of telling that Parnell drank to excess, he said, that "it would produce an instructive caution to avoid drinking, when it was seen, that even the learning and genius of Parnell could be debased by it."

He had this evening, partly, I suppose, from the spirit of contradiction to his Whig friend, a violent argument with Dr. Taylor, as to the inclinations of the people of England at this time towards the Royal Family of Stuart. He grew so outrageous as to say, "that, if England were fairly polled, the present King would be sent away to-night, and his adherents hanged to-morrow." Taylor, who was as violent a Whig as Johnson was a Tory, was roused by this to a pitch of bellowing. He denied, loudly, what Johnson said; and maintained, that there was an abhorrence against the Stuart family, though he admitted that the people were not much attached to the present King. JOHNSON: "Sir, the state of the country is this: the people knowing it to be agreed on all hands that this King has not the hereditary right to the crown, and there being no hope that he who has it can be restored, have grown cold and indifferent upon the subject of loyalty, and have no warm attachment to any King. They would not, therefore, risk any thing to restore the exiled family. They would not give twenty shillings a piece to bring it about. But if a mere vote could do it, there would be twenty to one;

at least, there would be a very great majority of voices for it. For, Sir, you are to consider, that all those who think a King has a right to his crown, as a man has to his estate, which is the just opinion, would be for restoring the King who certainly has the hereditary right, could he be trusted with it; in which there would be no danger now, when laws and every thing else are so much advanced: and every King will govern by the laws. And you must also consider, Sir, that there is nothing on the other side to oppose to this: for it is not alledged by any one that the present family has any inherent right: so that the Whigs could not have a contest between two rights."

Dr. Taylor said something of the slight foundation of the hereditary right of the house of Stuart. "Sir, (said Johnson,) the house of Stuart succeeded to the full right of both the houses of York and Lancaster, whose common source had the undisputed right. A right to a throne is like a right to any thing else. Possession is sufficient, where no better right can be shown. This was the case with the Royal Family of England, as it is now with the King of France: for as to the first beginning of the right we are in the dark."

Thursday, September 18. Last night Dr. Johnson had proposed that the crystal lustre, or chandelier, in Dr. Taylor's large room, should be lighted up some time or other. Taylor said, it should be lighted up next night. "That will do very well, (said I,) for it is Dr. Johnson's birth-day." When we were in the Isle of Sky, Johnson had desired me not to mention his birth-day. He did not seem pleased at this time that I mentioned it, and said (somewhat sternly,) "he would *not* have the lustre lighted the next day."

Some ladies, who had been present yesterday, when I mentioned his birth-day, came to dinner to-day, and plagued him unintentionally, by wishing him joy. I know not why he disliked having his birth-day mentioned, unless it were that it reminded him of his approaching nearer to death, of which he had a constant dread.

He observed, that a gentleman of eminence on literature had got into a bad style of Poetry of late. "He puts (said he) a very common thing in a strange dress till he does not know it himself, and thinks other people do not know it." BOSWELL: "That is owing to his being so much versant in old English poetry." JOHNSON: "What is that to the purpose, Sir? If I say a man is drunk, and you tell me it is owing to his taking much drink, the matter is not mended. No, Sir, —— has taken to an odd mode. For example; he'd write thus:

> " ' Hermit hoar, in solemn cell,
>   Wearing out life's evening gray.'

Gray evening is common enough; but *evening gray* he'd think fine.— Stay;—we'll make out the stanza:

> " ' Hermit hoar, in solemn cell,
>   Wearing out life's evening gray:
>   Smite thy bosom, sage, and tell,
>   What is bliss? and which the way? ' "

BOSWELL: "But why smite his bosom, Sir?" JOHNSON: "Why to shew he was in earnest," (smiling).—He at an after period added the following stanza:

> " Thus I spoke; and speaking sigh'd;
>   —Scarce repress'd the starting tear;—
>   When the smiling sage reply'd—
>   —Come, my lad, and drink some beer."

Friday, September 19, after breakfast, Dr. Johnson and I set out in Dr. Taylor's chaise to go to Derby.

In our way, Johnson strongly expressed his love of driving fast in a post-chaise. "If (said he) I had no duties, and no reference to futurity, I would spend my life in driving briskly in a post-chaise with a pretty woman; but she should be one who could understand me, and would add something to the conversation." I observed, that we were this day to stop just where the Highland army did in 1745. JOHNSON: "It was a noble attempt." BOSWELL: "I wish we could have an authentick history of it." JOHNSON: "If you were not an idle dog you might write it, by collecting from every body what they can tell, and putting down your authorities." BOSWELL: "But I could not have the advantage of it in my life-time." JOHNSON: "You might have the satisfaction of its fame, by printing it in Holland; and as to profit, consider how long it was before writing came to be considered in a pecuniary view. Baretti says, he is the first man that ever received copy-money in Italy."

We dined with Dr. Butter, whose lady is daughter of my cousin Sir John Douglas, whose grandson is now presumptive heir of the noble family of Queensberry. Johnson and he had a good deal of medical conversation. Johnson said, he had somewhere or other given an account of Dr. Nichols's discourse "*De anima Medica.*"

182

He told us "that whatever a man's distemper was, Dr. Nicols would not attend him as a physician, if his mind was not at ease; for he believed that no medicines would have any influence. He once attended a man in trade, upon whom he found none of the medicines he prescribed had any effect; he asked the man's wife privately whether his affairs were not in a bad way? She said no. He continued his attendance some time, still without success. At length the man's wife told him she had discovered that her husband's affairs *were* in a bad way. When Goldsmith was dying, Dr. Turton said to him, 'Your pulse is in greater disorder than it should be, from the degree of fever which you have: is your mind at ease?' Goldsmith answered it was not."

He said, "Goldsmith was a plant that flowered late. There appeared nothing remarkable about him when he was young; though when he had got high in fame, one of his friends began to recollect something of his being distinguished at College. Goldsmith in the same manner recollected more of that friend's early years, as he grew a greater man."

I mentioned that Lord Monboddo told me, he awaked every morning at four, and then for his health got up and walked in his room naked, with the window open, which he called taking *an air bath*; after which he went to bed again, and slept two hours more. Johnson, who was always ready to beat down any thing that seemed to be exhibited with disproportionate importance, thus observed: "I suppose, Sir, there is no more in it than this, he wakes at four, and cannot sleep till he chills himself, and makes the warmth of the bed a grateful sensation."

I talked of the difficulty of rising in the morning. Dr. Johnson told me, "that the learned Mrs. Carter, at that period when she was eager in study, did not awake as early as she wished, and she therefore had a contrivance, that, at a certain hour, her chamber-light should burn a string to which a heavy weight was suspended, which then fell with a strong sudden noise: this roused her from sleep, and then she had no difficulty in getting up."

As we drove back to Ashbourne, Dr. Johnson recommended to me, as he had often done, to drink water only: "For (said he) you are then sure not to get drunk; whereas, if you drink wine, you are never sure." I said, drinking wine was a pleasure I was unwilling to give up. "Why, Sir (said he,) there is no doubt that not to drink wine is a great deduction from life: but it may be necessary." He however owned, that in his opinion a free use of wine did not shorten life; and said, he would not give less for the life of a certain Scotch Lord (whom he named) celebrated for hard drinking, than for that of a sober man. "But stay (said he, with his usual intelligence, and accuracy of enquiry,) does it take much wine to make him drunk?" I answered, "a great deal either of wine or strong punch."—"Then (said he) that is the worse."

On Saturday, September 20, after breakfast, when Taylor was gone out to his farm, Dr. Johnson and I had a serious conversation by ourselves on melancholy and madness; which he was, I always thought, erroneously inclined to confound together.

Johnson said, "A madman loves to be with people whom he fears; not as a dog fears the lash: but of whom he stands in awe."

He added, "Madmen are all sensual in the lower stages of the distemper. They are eager for gratifications to sooth their minds, and divert their attention from the misery which they suffer: but when they grow very ill, pleasure is too weak for them, and they seek for pain. Employment, Sir, and hardships, prevent melancholy. I suppose in all our army in America, there was not one man who went mad."

I suggested a doubt, that if I were to reside in London, the exquisite zest with which I relished it in occasional visits might go off, and I might grow tired of it. JOHNSON: "Why, Sir, you find no man, at all intellectual, who is willing to leave London. No, Sir, when a man is tired of London, he is tired of life; for there is in London all that life can afford."

We talked of employment being absolutely necessary to preserve the mind from wearying and growing fretful, especially in those who have a tendency to melancholy; and I mentioned to him a saying which somebody had related of an American savage, who, when an European was expatiating on all the advantages of money, put this question: "Will it purchase *occupation*?" JOHNSON: "Depend upon it, Sir, this saying is too refined for a savage. And, Sir, money *will* purchase occupation; it will purchase all the conveniences of life; it will purchase variety of company; it will purchase all sorts of entertainment."

I shall present my readers with a series of what I gathered this evening from the Johnsonian garden.

"Did we not hear so much said of Jack Wilkes, we should think more highly of his conversation. Jack has a great variety of talk, Jack is a scholar, and Jack has the manners of a gentleman. But after hearing his name sounded from pole to pole, as the phœnix of convivial felicity, we are disappointed in his company. He has always been *at me*: but I would do Jack a kindness, rather than not. The contest is now over."

"Colley Cibber once consulted me as to one of his birthday Odes, a long time before it was wanted. I objected very freely to several passages. Cibber lost patience, and would not read his Ode to an end. When we had done with criticism, we walked over to Richardson's, the authour of *Clarissa*, and I wondered to find Richardson displeased that I 'did not treat Cibber with more *respect*.' Now, Sir, to talk of *respect* for a *player*!" (smiling disdainfully.) BOSWELL: "There, Sir, you are always heretical: you never will allow merit to a player." JOHNSON: "Merit, Sir, what merit? Do you respect a rope-dancer, or a ballad-singer?" BOSWELL: "No, Sir; but we respect a great player, as a man who can conceive lofty sentiments, and can express them gracefully." JOHNSON: "What, Sir, a fellow who claps a hump on his back, and a lump on his leg, and cries, '*I am Richard the Third*'? Nay, Sir, a ballad-singer is a higher man, for he does two things; he repeats and he sings: there is both recitation and musick in his performance: the player only recites." BOSWELL: "My dear Sir! you may turn any thing into ridicule. I allow, that a player of farce is not entitled to respect; he does a little thing: but he who can represent exalted characters, and touch the noblest passions, has very respectable powers; and mankind have agreed in admiring great talents for the stage. We must consider, too, that a great player does what very few are capable to do: his art is a very rare faculty. *Who* can repeat Hamlet's soliloquy, 'To be, or not to be,' as Garrick does it?" JOHNSON: "Any body may. Jemmy, there (a boy about eight years old, who was in the room) will do it as well in a week." BOSWELL: "No, no, Sir: and as a proof of the merit of great acting, and of the value which mankind set upon it, Garrick has got a hundred thousand pounds." JOHNSON: "Is getting a hundred thousand pounds a proof of excellence? That has been done by a scoundrel commissary."

On Monday, September 22, when at breakfast, I unguardedly said to Dr. Johnson, "I wish I saw you and Mrs. Macaulay together." He grew very angry; and, after a pause, while a cloud gathered on his brow, he burst out, "No, Sir; you would not see us quarrel, to make you sport. Don't you know that it is very uncivil to *pit* two people against one another?" Then, checking himself, and wishing to be more gentle, he added, "I do not say

185

you should be hanged or drowned for this; but it *is* very uncivil."
Dr. Taylor thought him in the wrong, and spoke to him privately
of it; but I afterwards acknowledged to Johnson that I was to
blame, for I candidly owned, that I meant to express a desire to
see a contest between Mrs. Macaulay and him; but then I knew
how the contest would end; so that I was to see him triumph.
JOHNSON: "Sir, you cannot be sure how a contest will end; and no
man has a right to engage two people in a dispute by which their
passions may be enflamed, and they may part with bitter resentment
against each other. I would sooner keep company with a man from
whom I must guard my pockets, than with a man who contrives
to bring me into a dispute with somebody that he may hear it.
This is the great fault of ——, (naming one of our friends) endeavouring to introduce a subject upon which he knows two people
in the company differ." BOSWELL: "But he told me, Sir, he does
it for instruction." JOHNSON: "Whatever the motive be, Sir, the
man who does so, does very wrong. He has no more right to
instruct himself at such risk, than he has to make two people fight
a duel, that he may learn how to defend himself."

He had found great fault with a gentleman of our acquaintance
for keeping a bad table. "Sir, (said he,) when a man is invited to
dinner, he is disappointed if he does not get something good. I
advised Mrs. Thrale, who has no card-parties at her house, to give
sweet-meats, and such good things, in an evening, as are not
commonly given, and she would find company enough come to
her; for every body loves to have things which please the palate put
in their way, without trouble or preparation." Such was his
attention to the *minutiæ* of life and manners.

He thus characterised the Duke of Devonshire, grandfather of
the present representative of that very respectable family: "He
was not a man of superior abilities, but he was a man strictly
faithful to his word. If for instance, he had promised you an
acorn, and none had grown that year in his woods, he would not
have contented himself with that excuse: he would have sent to
Denmark for it. So unconditional was he in keeping his word:
so high as to the point of honour." This was a liberal testimony
from the Tory Johnson to the virtue of a great Whig nobleman.

Talking of Dr. Johnson's unwillingness to believe extraordinary
things I ventured to say, "Sir, you come near Hume's argument
against miracles, 'That it is more probable witnesses should lie,
or be mistaken, than that they should happen.'" JOHNSON: "Why,

Sir, Hume, taking the proposition simply, is right. But the Christian revelation is not proved by the miracles alone, but as connected with prophecies, and with the doctrines in confirmation of which the miracles were wrought."

He repeated his observation, that the differences among Christians are really of no consequence. "For instance, (said he,) if a Protestant objects to a Papist, 'You worship images;' the Papist can answer, 'I do not insist on your doing it; you may be a very good Papist without it: I do it only as a help to my devotion.'" I said, the great article of Christianity is the revelation of immortality. Johnson admitted it was.

In the evening, a gentleman-farmer, who was on a visit at Dr. Taylor's, attempted to dispute with Johnson in favour of Mungo Campbell, who shot Alexander, Earl of Eglintoune, upon his having fallen, when retreating from his Lordship, who he believed was about to seize his gun, as he had threatened to do. He said, he should have done just as Campbell did. JOHNSON: "Whoever would do as Campbell did, deserves to be hanged; not that I could, as a juryman, have found him legally guilty of murder; but I am glad they found means to convict him." The gentleman-farmer said, "A poor man has as much honour as a rich man; and Campbell had *that* to defend." Johnson exclaimed, "A poor man has no honour." The English yeoman, not dismayed, proceeded: "Lord Eglintoune was a damned fool to run on upon Campbell, after being warned that Campbell would shoot him if he did." Johnson, who could not bear anything like swearing, angrily replied, "He was *not a damned* fool: he only thought too well of Campbell. He did not believe Campbell would be such a *damned* scoundrel, as to do so *damned* a thing." His emphasis on *damned*, accompanied with frowning looks, reproved his opponent's want of decorum in *his* presence.

During this interview at Ashbourne, Johnson seemed to be more uniformly social, cheerful, and alert, than I had almost ever seen him. He was prompt on great occasions and on small. Taylor, who praised every thing of his own to excess, in short, "whose geese were all swans," as the proverb says, expatiated on the excellence of his bull-dog, which he told us, was "perfectly well shaped." Johnson, after examining the animal attentively, thus repressed the vain-glory of our host:—"No, Sir, he is *not* well shaped; for there is not the quick transition from the thickness of the fore-part, to the *tenuity*—the thin part—behind,—which a bulldog ought to have." This *tenuity* was the only *hard word* that I heard him use during this interview, and it will be observed, he instantly put another expression in its place. Taylor said, a small bull-dog was as good as a large one. JOHNSON: "No, Sir; for, in proportion to his size, he has strength: and your argument would prove, that a good bull-dog may be as small as a mouse."

This evening, (Sept. 23rd.) while some of the tunes of ordinary composition were played with no great skill, my frame was agitated, and I was conscious of a generous attachment to Dr. Johnson, as my preceptor and friend, mixed with an affectionate regret that he was an old man, whom I should probably lose in a short time. I thought I could defend him at the point of my sword. My reverence and affection for him were in full glow. I said to him, "My dear Sir, we must meet every year, if you don't quarrel with me." JOHNSON: "Nay, Sir, you are more likely to quarrel with me, than I with you. My regard for you is greater almost than I have words to express; but I do not chuse to be always repeating it; write it down in the first leaf of your pocket-book, and never doubt of it again."

I talked to him of misery being "the doom of man," in this life, as displayed in his *Vanity of Human Wishes*. Yet I observed that things were done upon the supposition of happiness; grand houses were built, fine gardens were made, splendid places of publick amusement were contrived, and crowded with company. JOHNSON: "Alas, Sir, these are all only struggles for happiness. When I first entered Ranelagh, it gave an expansion and gay sensation to my mind, such as I never experienced any where else. But, as Xerxes wept when he viewed his immense army, and considered that not one of that great multitude would be alive a hundred year afterwards, so it went to my heart to consider that there was not one in all that brilliant circle, that was not afraid to go home and think; but that the thoughts of each individual there, would be distressing when alone."

I suggested, that being in love, and flattered with hopes of success; or having some favourite scheme in view for the next day, might prevent that wretchedness of which we had been talking. JOHNSON: "Why, Sir, it may sometimes be so as you suppose; but my conclusion is in general but too true."

While Johnson and I stood in calm conference by ourselves in Dr. Taylor's garden, at a pretty late hour in a serene autumn night, looking up to the heavens, I directed the discourse to the subject of a future state. My friend was in a placid and most benignant frame of mind. "Sir, (said he,) I do not imagine that all things will be made clear to us immediately after death, but that the ways of Providence will be explained to us very gradually." I ventured to ask him whether, although the words of some texts of Scripture seemed strong in support of the dreadful doctrine of an eternity of punishment, we might not hope that the denunciation was figurative, and would not literally be executed. JOHNSON: "Sir, you are to consider the intention of punishment in a future state. We have no reason to be sure that we shall then be no longer liable to offend against God. We do not know that even the angels are quite in a state of security; nay, we know that some of them have fallen. It may therefore, perhaps, be necessary, in order to preserve both men and angels in a state of rectitude, that they should have continually before them the punishment of those who have deviated from it: but we may hope that by some other means a fall from rectitude may be prevented. Some of the texts of Scripture upon this subject, are, as you observe, indeed strong; but they may admit of a mitigated interpretation." He talked to me upon this awful and delicate question in a gentle tone, and as if afraid to be decisive.

I departed on September 24.

CHAPTER IX

In Seventeen Seventy-eight

ON WEDNESDAY, March 18, [1778], I arrived in London, and was informed by good Mr. Francis, that his master was better and was gone to Mr. Thrale's at Streatham, to which place I wrote to him, begging to know when he would be in town. He was not expected for some time; but next day having called on Dr. Taylor, in Dean's-yard, Westminster, I found him there, and was told he had come to town for a few hours. He met me with his usual kindness, but instantly returned to the writing of something on which he was employed when I came in, and on which he seemed much intent. Finding him thus engaged, I made my visit very short, and had no more of his conversation, except his expressing a serious regret that a friend of ours was living at too much expence, considering how poor an appearance he made: "If (said he) a man has splendour from his expence, if he spends his money in pride or in pleasure, he has value: but if he lets others spend it for him, which is most commonly the case, he has no advantage from it."

On Friday, March 20, I found him at his own house.

Tom Davies soon after joined us. He had now unfortunately failed in his circumstances, and was much indebted to Dr. Johnson's kindness for obtaining for him many alleviations of his distress. After he went away, Johnson blamed his folly in quitting the stage, by which he and his wife got five hundred pounds a year. I said, I believed it was owing to Churchill's attack upon him,

' He mouths a sentence, as curs mouth a bone.'

JOHNSON: "I believe so, too, Sir. But what a man is he, who is to be driven from the stage by a line? Another line would have driven him from his shop."

I told him that I was engaged as Counsel at the bar of the House of Commons to oppose a road-bill in the county of Stirling, and asked him what mode he would advise me to follow in addressing such an audience. JOHNSON: "Why, Sir, you must provide yourself with a good deal of extraneous matter, which you are to

190

produce occasionally, so as to fill up the time; for you must consider, that they do not listen much. If you begin with the strength of your cause, it may be lost before they begin to listen. When you catch a moment of attention, press the merits of the question upon them." He said, as to one point of the merits, that he thought "it would be a wrong thing to deprive the small landholders of the privilege of assessing themselves for making and repairing the high roads; *it was destroying a certain portion of liberty, without a good reason, which was always a bad thing.*" When I mentioned this observation next day to Mr. Wilkes, he pleasantly said, "What! does *he* talk of liberty? *Liberty* is as ridiculous in *his* mouth as *Religion* in *mine.*" Mr. Wilkes's advice as to the best mode of speaking at the bar of the House of Commons, was not more respectful towards the senate, than that of Dr. Johnson. "Be as impudent as you can, as merry as you can, and say whatever comes uppermost. Jack Lee is the best heard there of any Counsel; and he is the most impudent dog, and always abusing us."

He returned next day to Streatham, to Mr. Thrale's; I went to Streatham on Monday, March 30.

Next morning, while we were at breakfast, Johnson gave a very earnest recommendation of what he himself practised with the utmost conscientiousness: I mean a strict attention to truth, even in the most minute particulars. "Accustom your children (said he) constantly to this; if a thing happened at one window, and they, when relating it, say that it happened at another, do not let it pass, but instantly check them; you do not know where deviation from truth will end." BOSWELL: "It may come to the door: and when once an account is at all varied in one circumstance, it may by degrees be varied, so as to be totally different from what really happened." Our lively hostess, whose fancy was impatient of the rein, fidgeted at this, and ventured to say, "Nay, this is too much. If Mr. Johnson should forbid me to drink tea, I would comply, as I should feel the restraint only twice a day; but little variations in narrative must happen a thousand times a day, if one is not perpetually watching." JOHNSON: "Well, Madam, and you *ought* to be perpetually watching. It is more from carelessness about truth than from intentional lying, that there is so much falsehood in the world."

Talking of ghosts, he said, "It is wonderful that five thousand years have now elapsed since the creation of the world, and still it is undecided whether or not there has ever been an instance of the spirit of any person appearing after death. All argument is against it; but all belief is for it."

He said, "John Wesley's conversation is good, but he is never at leisure. He is always obliged to go at a certain hour. This is very disagreeable to a man who loves to fold his legs and have out his talk, as I do."

On Friday, April 3, I dined with him in London, in a company where were present several eminent men, whom I shall not name, but distinguish their parts in the conversation by different letters.

F. "I have been looking at this famous antique marble dog of Mr. Jennings, valued at a thousand guineas, said to be Alcibiades's dog." JOHNSON: "His tail then must be docked. That was the mark of Alcibiades's dog." E: "A thousand guineas! The representation of no animal whatever is worth so much. At this rate a dead dog would indeed be better than a living lion." JOHNSON: "Sir, it is not the worth of the thing, but of the skill in forming it which is so highly estimated. Every thing that enlarges the sphere of human powers, that shews man he can do what he thought he could not do, is valuable. The first man who balanced a straw upon his nose; Johnson who rode upon three horses at a time; in short, all such men deserved the applause of mankind, not on account of the use of what they did, but of the dexterity which they exhibited." BOSWELL: "Yet a misapplication of time, and assiduity is not to be encouraged. Addison, in one of his *Spectators*, commends the judgement of a King, who as a suitable reward to a man that by long perseverance had attained to the art of throwing a barley-corn through the eye of a needle, gave him a bushel of barley." JOHNSON: "He must have been a King of Scotland, where barley is scarce." F: "One of the most remarkable antique figures of an animal is the boar at Florence." JOHNSON: "The first boar that is well made in marble, should be preserved as a wonder. When men arrive at a facility of making boars well, then the workmanship is not of such value, but they should however be preserved as examples, and as a greater security for the restoration of the art, should it be lost."

E: "We hear prodigious complaints at present of emigration. I am convinced that emigration makes a country more populous." J: "That sounds very much like a paradox." E: "Exportation of men, like exportation of all other commodities, makes more be produced." JOHNSON: "But there would be more people were there not emigration, provided there were food for more." E: "No;

leave a few breeders, and you'll have more people than if there were no emigration." JOHNSON: "Nay, Sir, it is plain there will be more people, if there are more breeders. Thirty cows in good pasture will produce more calves than ten cows, provided they have good bulls." E: "There are bulls enough in Ireland." JOHNSON: (smiling,) "So, Sir, I should think from your argument." BOSWELL: "You said, exportation of men, like exportation of other commodities, makes more be produced. But a bounty is given to encourage the exportation of corn, and no bounty is given for the exportation of men; though, indeed, those who go gain by it." R: "But the bounty on the exportation of corn is paid at home." E: "That is the same thing." JOHNSON: "No, Sir." R: "A man who stays at home, gains nothing by his neighbour's emigrating." BOSWELL: "I can understand that emigration may be the cause that more people may be produced in a country; but the country will not therefore be the more populous; for the people issue from it. It can only be said that there is a flow of people. It is an encouragement to have children, to know that they can get a living by emigration." R: "Yes, if there were an emigration of children under six years of age. But they don't emigrate till they could earn their livelihood in some way at home." C: "It is remarkable that the most unhealthy countries, where there are the most destructive diseases, such as Egypt and Bengal, are the most populous." JOHNSON: "Countries which are the most populous have the most destructive diseases. *That* is the true state of the proposition." C: "Holland is very unhealthy, yet it exceedingly populous." JOHNSON: "I know not that Holland is unhealthy. But its populousness is owing to an influx of people from all other countries. Disease cannot be the cause of populousness, for it not only carries off a great proportion of the people; but those who are left are weakened, and unfit for the purposes of increase."

R: "Mr. E., I don't mean to flatter, but when posterity reads one of your speeches in Parliament, it will be difficult to believe that you took so much pains, knowing with certainty that it could produce no effect, that not one vote would be gained by it." E: "Waiving your compliment to me, I shall say in general, that it is very well worth while for a man to take pains to speak well in parliament. A man, who has vanity, speaks to display his talents; and if a man speaks well, he gradually establishes a certain reputation and consequence in the general opinion, which sooner or later will have its political reward. Besides, though not one vote is gained, a good speech has its effect. Though an act which has been ably opposed passes into a law, yet in its progress it is modelled, it is softened in such a manner that we see plainly the Minister has been told, that the members attached to him are so sensible of its injustice or absurdity from what they have heard, that it must be altered." JOHNSON: "And, Sir, there is a gratification of pride. Though we cannot out-vote them we will out-argue them. They shall not do wrong without its being shown both to themselves and to the world." E: "The House of Commons is a mixed body. (I except the minority, which I hold to be pure, [smiling] but I take the whole House.) It is a mass by no means pure; but neither is it wholly corrupt, though there is a large proportion of corruption in it. There are many members who generally go with the Minister, who will not go all lengths. There are many honest well-meaning country gentlemen who are in parliament only to keep up the consequence of their families. Upon most of these a good speech will have influence." JOHNSON: "We are all more or less governed by interest. But interest will not make us do every thing. In a case which admits of doubt, we try to think on the side which is for our interest, and generally bring ourselves to act accordingly. But the subject must admit of diversity of colouring; it must receive a colour on that side. In the House of Commons there are members enough who will not vote what is grossly unjust or absurd. No, Sir, there must always be right enough, or appearance of right, to keep wrong in countenance." BOSWELL: "There is surely always a majority in parliament who have places, or who want to have them, and who therefore will be generally ready to support government without requiring any pretext." E: "True, Sir; that majority will always follow

' Quo clamor vocat et turba faventium'." [1]

BOSWELL: "Well, now, let us take the common phrase, Place-hunters. I thought they had hunted without regard to any thing, just as their huntsman, the Minister, leads, looking only to the prey." J: "But taking your metaphor, you know that in hunting there are few so desperately keen as to follow without reserve. Some do not choose to leap ditches and hedges and risk their necks, or gallop over steeps, or even to dirty themselves in bogs and mire." BOSWELL: "I am glad there are some good, quiet, moderate political hunters." E: "I believe in any body of men in England

[1] Where clamour and the crowd of partisans call.

194

I should have been in the Minority; I have always been in the Minority." P: "The House of Commons resembles a private company. How seldom is any man convinced by another's argument; passion and pride rise against it." R: "What would be the consequence, if a Minister, sure of a majority in the House of Commons, should resolve that there should be no speaking at all upon his side?" E: "He must soon go out. That has been tried; but it was found it would not do."——

E: "From the experience which I have had,—and I have had a great deal,—I have learnt to think *better* of mankind." JOHNSON: "From my experience I have found them worse in commercial dealings, more disposed to cheat than I had any notion of; but more disposed to do one another good than I had conceived." J: "Less just and more beneficent." JOHNSON: "And really it is wonderful, considering how much attention is necessary for men to take care of themselves, and ward off immediate evils which press upon them, it is wonderful how much they do for others. As it is said of the greatest liar, that he tells more truth than falsehood; so it may be said of the worst man, that he does more good than evil." BOSWELL: "Perhaps from experience man may be found *happier* than we suppose." JOHNSON: "No, Sir; the more we enquire we shall find men the less happy." P: "As to thinking better or worse of mankind from experience, some cunning people will not be satisfied unless they have put men to the test, as they think. There is a very good story told of Sir Godfrey Kneller, in his character of a justice of the peace. A gentleman brought his servant before him, upon an accusation of having stolen some money from him; but it having come out that he had laid it purposely in the servant's way, in order to try his honesty, Sir Godfrey sent the master to prison." JOHNSON: "To resist temptation once, is not a sufficient proof of honesty. If a servant, indeed, were to resist the continued temptation of silver lying in a window, as some people let it lye, when he is sure his master does not know how much there is of it, he would give a strong proof of honesty. But this is a proof to which you have no right to put a man. You know, humanly speaking, there is a certain degree of temptation, which will overcome any virtue. Now, in so far as you approach temptation to man, you do him an injury; and, if he is overcome, you share his guilt." P: "And, when once overcome, it is easier for him to be got the better of again." BOSWELL: "Yes, you are his seducer; you have debauched him. I have known a man resolve to put friendship to the test, by asking a man to lend him money, merely with that view, when he did not want it." JOHNSON: "That is very wrong, Sir. Your friend may be a narrow man, and yet have many good qualities: narrowness may be his only fault. Now you are trying his general character as a friend, by one particular singly, in which he happens to be defective, when, in truth, his character is composed of many particulars."

E: "I understand the hogshead of claret, which this society was favoured with by our friend the Dean, is nearly out; I think he should be written to, to send another of the same kind. Let the request be made with a happy ambiguity of expression, so that we may have the chance of his sending *it* also as a present." JOHNSON: "I am willing to offer my services as secretary on this occasion." P: "As many as are for Dr. Johnson being secretary hold up your hands.—Carried unanimously." BOSWELL: "He will be our Dictator." JOHNSON: "No, the company is to dictate to me. I am only to write for wine; and I am quite disinterested, as I drink none; I shall not be suspected of having forged the application. I am no more than humble *scribe*." E: "Then you shall *pre*scribe." BOSWELL: "Very well. The first play of words to-day." J: "No, no; the *bulls* in Ireland." JOHNSON: "Were I your Dictator, you should have no wine. It would be my business *cavere ne quid detrimenti Respublica caperet*,[1] and wine is dangerous. Rome was ruined by luxury," (smiling.) E: "If you allow no wine as Dictator, you shall not have me for your master of horse."

On Saturday, April 4, I drank tea with Johnson at Dr. Taylors, where he had dined. He entertained us with an account of a tragedy written by a Dr. Kennedy, (not the Lisbon physician.) "The catastrophe of it (said he) was, that a King, who was jealous of his Queen with his prime-minister, castrated himself. This tragedy was actually shewn about in manuscript to several people, and, amongst others, to Mr. Fitzherbert, who repeated to me two lines of the Prologue:

> ' Our hero's fate we have but gently touch'd;
> The fair might blame us, if it were less couch'd.'

It is hardly to be believed what absurd and indecent images men will introduce into their writings, without being sensible of the absurdity and indencency. I remember Lord Orrery told me, that there was a pamphlet written against Sir Robert Walpole, the

---

[1] To see that the State suffered no harm.

whole of which was an allegory on the PHALLICK OBSCENITY. The Duchess of Buckingham asked Lord Orrery *who* this person was? He answered he did not know. She said, she would send to Mr. Pulteney, who, she supposed, could inform her. So then, to prevent her from making herself ridiculous, Lord Orrery sent her Grace a note, in which he gave her to understand what was meant."

He was very silent this evening; and read in a variety of books; suddenly throwing down one, and taking up another.

He talked of going to Streatham that night. TAYLOR: "You'll be robbed, if you do: or you must shoot a highwayman. Now I would rather be robbed than do that; I would not shoot a highwayman." JOHNSON: "But I would rather shoot him in the instant when he is attempting to rob me, than afterwards swear against him at the Old Bailey, to take away his life, after he has robbed me. I am surer I am right in the one case, than in the other. I may be mistaken as to the man when I swear: I cannot be mistaken, if I shoot him in the act. Besides, we feel less reluctance to take away a man's life, when we are heated by the injury, than to do it at a distance of time by an oath, after we have cooled." BOSWELL: "So, Sir, you would rather act from the motive of private passion, than that of publick advantage." JOHNSON: "Nay, Sir, when I shoot the highwayman, I act from both." BOSWELL: "Very well, very well.—There is no catching him." JOHNSON: "At the same time, one does not know what to say. For perhaps one may, a year after, hang himself from uneasiness for having shot a highwayman. Few minds are fit to be trusted with so great a thing." BOSWELL: "Then, Sir, you would not shoot him?" JOHNSON: "But I might be vexed afterwards for that too."

Thrale's carriage not having come for him, as he expected, I accompanied him some part of the way home to his own house. I told him, that I had talked of him to Mr. Dunning a few days before, and had said, that in his company we did not so much interchange conversation, as listen to him; and that Dunning observed, upon this, "One is always willing to listen to Dr. Johnson;" to which I answered, "That is a great deal from you, Sir."—"Yes, Sir, (said Johnson,) a great deal indeed. Here is a man willing to listen, to whom the world is listening all the rest of the year." BOSWELL: "I think, Sir, it is right to tell one man of such a handsome thing, which has been said of him by another. It tends to increase benevolence." JOHNSON: "Undoubtedly it is right, Sir."

On Tuesday, April 7, I breakfasted with him at his house. He said, "nobody was content." I mentioned to him a respectable person in Scotland whom he knew; and asserted, that I really believed he was always content. JOHNSON: "No, Sir, he is not content with the present; he has always some new scheme, some new plantation, something which is future. You know he was not content as a widower; for he married again." BOSWELL: "But he is not restless." JOHNSON: "Sir, he is only locally at rest. A chymist is locally at rest; but his mind is hard at work. This gentleman has done with external exertions. It is too late for him to engage in distant projects." BOSWELL: "He seems to amuse himself quite well; to have his attention fixed, and his tranquillity preserved by very small matters. I have tried this; but it would not do with me." JOHNSON: (laughing,) "No, Sir; it must be born with a man to be contented to take up with little things. Women have a great advantage that they may take up with little things, without disgracing themselves: a man cannot, except with fiddling. Had I learnt to fiddle, I should have done nothing else." BOSWELL: "Pray, Sir, did you ever play on any musical instrument?" JOHNSON: "No, Sir. I once bought me a flagelet; but I never made out a tune." BOSWELL: "A flagelet, Sir!—so small an instrument? I should have liked to hear you play on the violoncello. *That* should have been *your* instrument." JOHNSON: "Sir, I might as well have played on the violoncello as another; but I should have done nothing else. No, Sir; a man would never undertake great things, could he be amused with small. I once tried knotting. Dempster's sister undertook to teach me; but I could not learn it. BOSWELL: So, Sir, it will be related in pompous narrative, 'Once for his amusement he tried knotting; nor did this Hercules disdain the distaff.'" JOHNSON: "Knitting of stockings is a good amusement. As a freeman of Aberdeen I should be a knitter of stockings." He asked me to go down with him and dine at Mr. Thrale's at Streatham, to which I agreed. I had lent him *An Account of Scotland, in* 1702, written by a man of various enquiry, an English chaplain to a regiment stationed there. JOHNSON: "It is sad stuff, Sir, miserably written, as books in general then were. There is now an elegance of style universally diffused. No man now writes so ill as Martin's Account of the Hebrides is written. A man could not write so ill, if he should try. Set a merchant's clerk now to write, and he'll do better."

He talked to me with serious concern of a certain female friend's "laxity of narration, and inattention to truth."—"I am as much vexed (said he) at the ease with which she hears it mentioned to her, as at the thing itself. I told her, 'Madam, you are contented to hear every day said to you, what the highest of mankind have died for, rather than bear.'—You know, Sir, the highest of mankind have died rather than bear to be told they had uttered a falsehood. Do talk to her of it: I am weary."

Talking of drinking wine, he said, "I did not leave off wine, because I could not bear it; I have drunk three bottles of port without being the worse for it. University College has witnessed this." BOSWELL: "Why, then, Sir, did you leave it off?" JOHNSON: "Why, Sir, because it is so much better for a man to be sure that he is never to be intoxicated, never to lose the power over himself. I shall not begin to drink wine again till I grow old, and want it." BOSWELL: "I think, Sir, you once said to me, that not to drink wine was a great deduction from life." JOHNSON: "It is a diminution of pleasure, to be sure; but I do not say a diminution of happiness. There is more happiness in being rational." BOSWELL: "But if we could have pleasure always, should not we be happy? The greatest part of men would compound for pleasure." JOHNSON: "Supposing we could have pleasure always, an intellectual man would not compound for it. The greatest part of men would compound, because the greatest part of men are gross." BOSWELL: "I allow there may be greater pleasure than from wine. I have had more pleasure from your conversation. I have indeed; I assure you I have." JOHNSON: "When we talk of pleasure, we mean sensual pleasure. When a man says, he had pleasure with a woman, he does not mean conversation, but something of a very different nature. Philosophers tell you, that pleasure is *contrary* to happiness. Gross men prefer animal pleasure. So there are men who have preferred living among savages. Now what a wretch must he be, who is content with such conversation as can be had among savages! You may remember, an officer at Fort Augustus, who had served in America, told us of a woman whom they were obliged to *bind*, in order to get her back from savage life." BOSWELL: "She must have been an animal, a beast." JOHNSON: "Sir, she was a speaking cat."

I mentioned to him that I had become very weary in a company where I heard not a single intellectual sentence, except that "a man who had been settled ten years in Minorca was become a much inferiour man to what he was in London, because a man's mind grows narrow in a narrow place." JOHNSON: "A man's mind grows narrow in a narrow place, whose mind is enlarged only because he has lived in a large place: but what is got by books and thinking is preserved in a narrow place as well as in a large place. A man cannot know modes of life as well in Minorca as in London; but he may study mathematics as well in Minorca." BOSWELL: "I don't know, Sir: if you had remained ten years in the Isle of Col, you would not have been the man that you now are." JOHNSON: "Yes, Sir, if I had been there from fifteen to twenty-five; but not if from twenty-five to thirty-five." BOSWELL: "I own, Sir, the spirits which I have in London make me do every thing with more readiness and vigour. I can talk twice as much in London as any where else."

At dinner, Mrs. Thrale expressed a wish to go and see Scotland. JOHNSON: "Seeing Scotland, Madam, is only seeing a worse England. It is seeing the flower gradually fade away to the naked stalk. Seeing the Hebrides, indeed, is seeing quite a different scene."

He and I returned to town in the evening. Upon the road, I endeavoured to maintain, in argument, that a landed gentleman is not under any obligation to reside upon his estate; and that by living in London he does no injury to his country. JOHNSON: "Why, Sir, he does no injury to his country in general, because the money which he draws from it gets back again in circulation; but to his particular district, his particular parish, he does an injury. All that he has to give away is not given to those who have the first claim to it. And though I have said that the money circulates back, it is a long time before that happens. Then, Sir, a man of family and estate ought to consider himself as having the charge of a district, over which he is to diffuse civility and happiness."

On Thursday, April 9, I dined with him at Sir Joshua Reynolds's, with the Bishop of St. Asaph, (Dr. Shipley,) Mr. Allan Ramsay, Mr. Gibbon, Mr. Cambridge, and Mr. Langton.

Goldsmith being mentioned, Johnson observed, that it was long before his merit came to be acknowledged: that he once complained to him, in ludicrous terms of distress, "Whenever I write any thing, the publick *make a point* to know nothing about it:" but that his *Traveller* brought him into high reputation. LANGTON: "There is not one bad line in that poem; not one of Dryden's careless verses." SIR JOSHUA: "I was glad to hear Charles Fox say, it was one of the finest poems in the English language." LANGTON: "Why were you glad? You surely had no doubt of this before." JOHNSON: "No;

the merit of *The Traveller* is so well established, that Mr. Fox's praise cannot augment it, nor his censure diminish it." SIR JOSHUA: "But his friends may suspect they had too great a partiality for him." JOHNSON: "Nay, Sir, the partiality of his friends was always against him. It was with difficulty we could give him a hearing. Goldsmith had no settled notions upon any subject; so he talked always at random. It seemed to be his intention to blurt out whatever was in his mind, and see what would become of it. He was angry, too, when catched in an absurdity; but it did not prevent him from falling into another the next minute. I remember Chamier, after talking with him some time, said 'Well, I do believe he wrote this poem himself: and, let me tell you, that is believing a great deal.' Chamier once asked him, what he meant by *slow* the last word in the first line of *The Traveller*,

'Remote, unfriended, melancholy, slow,'—

Did he mean tardiness of locomotion? Goldsmith, who would say something without consideration, answered, 'Yes.' I was sitting by, and said, 'No, Sir, you do not mean tardiness of locomotion; you mean, that sluggishness of mind which comes upon a man in solitude.' Chamier believed then that I had written the line, as much as if he had seen me write it. Goldsmith, however, was a man, who, whatever he wrote, did it better than any other man could do. He deserved a place in Westminster-Abbey; and every year he lived, would have deserved it bĕtter. He had, indeed, been at no pains to fill his mind with knowledge. He transplanted it from one place to another; and it did not settle in his mind; so he could not tell what was in his own books."

We talked of living in the country. JOHNSON: "No wise man will go to live in the country, unless he has some thing to do which can be better done in the country. For instance; if he is to shut himself up for a year to study a science, it is better to look out to the fields, than to an opposite wall. Then, if a man walks out in the country, there is nobody to keep him from walking in again; but if a man walks out in London, he is not sure when he shall walk in again. A great city is, to be sure, the school for studying life; and 'The proper study of mankind is man,' as Pope observes." BOSWELL: "I fancy, London is the best place for society; though I have heard that the very first society of Paris is still beyond any thing that we have here." JOHNSON: "Sir, I question if in Paris, such a company as is sitting round this table could be got together in less than half a year. They talk in France of the felicity of men and women living together: the truth is, that there the men are not higher than the women, they know no more than the women do, and they are not held down in their conversation by the presence of women." RAMSAY: "Literature is upon the growth, it is in its spring in France: here it is rather *passée*." JOHNSON: "Literature was in France long before we had it. Paris was the second city for the revival of letters: Italy had it first, to be sure. What have we done for literature, equal to what was done by the Stephani and others in France? Our literature came to us through France. Caxton printed only two books, Chaucer, and Gower, that were not translations from the French; and Chaucer, we know, took much from the Italians. No, Sir, if literature be in its spring in France, it is a second spring; it is after a winter. We are now before the French in literature; but we had it long after them. In England, any man who wears a sword and a powdered wig, is ashamed to be illiterate. I believe it is not so in France. Yet there is, probably, a great deal of learning in France, because they have such a number of religious establishments; so many men who have nothing else to do but study. I do not know this; but I take it upon the common principles of chance. Where there are many shooters, some will hit."

We talked of old age. Johnson (now in his seventieth year) said, "It is a man's own fault, it is from want of use, if his mind grows torpid in old age." The Bishop asked, if an old man does not lose faster than he gets. JOHNSON: "I think not, my Lord, if he exerts himself." One of the company rashly observed, that he thought it was happy for an old man that insensibility comes upon him. JOHNSON: (with a noble elevation and disdain,) "No, Sir, I should never be happy by being less rational." BISHOP OF ST. ASAPH: "Your wish then, Sir, is γηράσκειν διδασκόμενος.[1] JOHNSON: "Yes, my Lord." His Lordship mentioned a charitable establishment in Wales, where people were maintained, and supplied with everything, upon the condition of their contributing the weekly produce of their labour; and he said, they grew quite torpid for want of property. JOHNSON: "They have no object for hope. Their condition cannot be better. It is rowing without a port."

This season, there was a whimsical fashion in the news papers of applying Shakspeare's words to describe living persons well known in the world; which was done under the title of *Modern Characters from Shakspeare*; many of which were admirably

[1] To grow old while learning.

adapted. The fancy took so much, that they were afterwards collected
into a pamphlet. Somebody said to Johnson, across the table, that
he had not been in those characters. "Yes (said he) I have. I should
have been sorry to be left out." He then repeated what had been
applied to him,

> ' You must borrow me GARGANTUA's mouth.'

Miss Reynolds not perceiving at once the meaning of this, he
was obliged to explain it to her, which had something of an
aukward and ludicrous effect. "Why, Madam, it has a reference
to me, as using big words, which require the mouth of a giant to
pronounce them. Gargantua is the name of a giant in Rabelais."
BOSWELL: "But, Sir, there is another amongst them for you:

> " He would not flatter Neptune for his trident,
> Or Jove for his power to thunder.' "

JOHNSON: "There is nothing marked in that. No, Sir, Gargantua
is the best." Notwithstanding this ease and good humour, when I,
a little afterwards, repeated his sarcasm on Kenrick, which was
received with applause, he asked, "*Who* said that?" and on my
suddenly answering,—*Gargantua*, looked serious, which was a
sufficient indication that he did not wish it to be kept up.

After wandering about in a kind of pleasing distraction for some
time, I got into a corner, with Johnson, Garrick, and Harris.
GARRICK: (to Harris.) "Pray, Sir, have you read Potter's Æschylus?"
HARRIS: "Yes; and think it pretty." GARRICK: (to Johnson.) "And
what think you, Sir, of it?" JOHNSON: "I thought what I read of
it *verbiage*: but upon Mr. Harris's recommendation, I will read a
play. (To Mr. Harris.) Don't prescribe two." Mr. Harris suggested
one, I do not remember which. JOHNSON: "We must try its effect
as an English poem; that is the way to judge of the merit of a
translation. Translations are, in general, for people who cannot
read the original." I mentioned the vulgar saying, that Pope's
Homer was not a good representation of the original. JOHNSON:
"Sir, it is the greatest work of the kind that has ever been produced."
BOSWELL: "The truth is, it is impossible perfectly to translate
poetry. In a different language it may be the same tune, but it
has not the same tone. Homer plays it on a bassoon; Pope on a
flagelet." HARRIS: "I think, heroick poetry is best in blank verse;
yet it appears that rhyme is essential to English poetry, from our
deficiency in metrical quantities. In my opinion, the chief excellence of our language is numerous prose." JOHNSON: "Sir

203

William Temple was the first writer who gave cadence to English prose. Before this time they were careless of arrangement, and did not mind whether a sentence ended with an important word or an insignificant word, or with what part of speech it was concluded." Mr. Langton, who now had joined us, commended Clarendon. JOHNSON: "He is objected to for his parentheses, his involved clauses, and his want of harmony. But he is supported by his matter. It is, indeed, owing to a plethora of matter that his style is so faulty: every *substance*, (smiling to Mr. Harris,) has so many *accidents*.—To be distinct, we must talk *analytically*. If we analyse language, we must speak of it grammatically; if we analyse argument, we must speak of it logically." GARRICK: "Of all the translations that ever were attempted, I think Elphinstone's Martial the most extraordinary. He consulted me upon it, who am a little of an epigrammatist myself, you know. I told him freely, 'You don't seem to have that turn.' I asked him if he was serious; and finding he was, I advised him against publishing. Why, his translation is more difficult to understand than the original. I thought him a man of some talents; but he seems crazy in this." JOHNSON: "Sir, you have done what I had not courage to do. But he did not ask my advice, and I did not force it upon him, to make him angry with me." GARRICK: "But as a friend, Sir——" JOHNSON: "Why, such a friend as I am with him—no." GARRICK: "But if you see a friend going to tumble over a precipice?" JOHNSON: "That is an extravagant case, Sir. You are sure a friend will thank you for hindering him from tumbling over a precipice: but, in the other case, I should hurt his vanity, and do him no good. He would not take my advice. His brother-in-law, Strahan, sent him a subscription of fifty pounds, and said he would send him fifty more, if he would not publish." GARRICK: "What! eh! is Strahan a good judge of an Epigram? Is not he rather an *obtuse* man, eh?" JOHNSON: "Why, Sir, he may not be a judge of an Epigram: but you see he is a judge of what is *not* an Epigram." BOSWELL: "It is easy for you, Mr. Garrick, to talk to an authour as you talked to Elphinstone; you, who have been so long the manager of a theatre, rejecting the plays of poor authours. You are an old Judge, who have often pronounced sentence of death. You are a practised surgeon, who have often amputated limbs; and though this may have been for the good of your patients, they cannot like you. Those who have undergone a dreadful operation are not very fond of seeing the operator again." GARRICK: "Yes, I know enough of that. There was a reverend gentleman, (Mr. Hawkins,) who wrote a tragedy, the SIEGE of something, which I refused." HARRIS: "So, the siege was raised." JOHNSON: "Ay, he came to me and complained; and told me, that Garrick said his play was wrong in the *concoction*. Now, what is the concoction of a play?" (Here Garrick started, and twisted himself, and seemed sorely vexed; for Johnson told me, he believed the story was true.) GARRICK: "I—I—I—said, *first* concoction." JOHNSON: (smiling.) "Well, he left out *first*. And Rich, he said, refused him *in false English*: he could show it under his hand." GARRICK: "He wrote to me in violent wrath, for having refused his play: 'Sir, this is growing a very serious and terrible affair. I am resolved to publish my play. I will appeal to the world; and how will your judgement appear?' I answered, 'Sir, notwithstanding all the seriousness, and all the terrours, I have no objection to your publishing your play; and as you live at a great distance, (Devonshire, I believe) if you will send it to me, I will convey it to the press.' I never heard more of it, ha! ha! ha!"

On Friday, April 10, I found Johnson at home in the morning. We resumed the conversation of yesterday.

I said to him, "You were yesterday, Sir, in remarkably good humour; but there was nothing to offend you, nothing to produce irritation or violence. There was no bold offender. There was not one capital conviction. It was a maiden assize. You had on your white gloves."

He found fault with our friend Langton for having been too silent. "Sir, (said I,) you will recollect that he very properly took up Sir Joshua for being glad that Charles Fox had praised Goldsmith's *Traveller*, and you joined him. JOHNSON: "Yes, Sir, I knocked Fox on the head, without ceremony. Reynolds is too much under Fox and Burke at present. He is under the *Fox star*, and the *Irish constellation*. He is always under some planet." BOSWELL: "They say, indeed, a fox and a dog are the same animal."

I reminded him of a gentleman, who, Mrs. Cholmondeley said, was first talkative from affectation, and then silent from the same cause; that he first thought, "I shall be celebrated as the liveliest man in every company;" and then, all at once, "O! it is much more respectable to be grave and look wise." "He has reversed the Pythagorean discipline, by being first talkative, and then silent. He reverses the course of Nature too; he was first the gay butterfly, and then the creeping worm." Johnson laughed loud and long at this expansion and illustration of what he himself had told me.

We dined together with Mr. Scott (now Sir William Scott, his Majesty's Advocate General), at his chambers in the Temple, nobody else there. The company being small, Johnson was not in such spirits as he had been the preceding day, and for a considerable time little was said. At last he burst forth: "Subordination is sadly broken down in this age. No man, now, has the same authority which his father had,—except a gaoler. No master has it over his servants: it is diminished in our colleges; nay, in our grammar-schools." BOSWELL: "What is the cause of this, Sir?" JOHNSON: "Why, the coming in of the Scotch," (laughing sarcastically.) BOSWELL: "That is to say, things have been turned topsy-turvy.—But your serious cause." JOHNSON: "Why, Sir, there are many causes, the chief of which is, I think, the great increase of money. No man now depends upon the Lord of the Manour, when he can send to another country, and fetch provisions. The shoe-black at the entry of my court does not depend on me. I can deprive him but of a penny a day, which he hopes somebody else will bring him; and that penny I must carry to another shoe-black, so the trade suffers nothing. I have explained, in my *Journey to the Hebrides*, how gold and silver destroy feudal subordination. But, besides, there is a general relaxation of reverence. No son now depends upon his father, as in former times. Paternity used to be considered as of itself a great thing, which had a right to many claims. That is, in general, reduced to very small bounds. My hope is that as anarchy produces tyranny, this extreme relaxation will produce *freni strictio*."[1]

Talking of fame, for which there is so great a desire, I observed, how little there is of it in reality, compared with the other objects of human attention. "Let every man recollect, and he will be sensible how small a part of his time is employed in talking or thinking of Shakspeare, Voltaire, or any of the most celebrated men that have ever lived, or are now supposed to occupy the attention and admiration of the world. Let this be extracted and compressed; into what a narrow space will it go!" I then slily introduced Mr. Garrick's fame, and his assuming the airs of a great man. JOHNSON: "Sir, it is wonderful how *little* Garrick assumes. No, Sir, Garrick *fortunam reverenter habet.*[2] Consider, Sir; celebrated men, such as you have mentioned, have had their applause at a distance; but Garrick had it dashed in his face, sounded in his ears, and went home every night with the plaudits of a thousand in his *cranium*.

[1] Tightening of the reins.   [2] Carries his luck respectfully.

Then, Sir, Garrick did not *find*, but *made* his way to the tables, the levees, and amongst the bed chambers of the great. Then, Sir, Garrick had under him a numerous body of people; who, from fear of his power, and hopes of his favour, and admiration of his talents, were constantly submissive to him. And here is a man who has advanced the dignity of his profession. Garrick has made a player a higher character." SCOTT: "And he is a very sprightly writer too." JOHNSON: "Yes, Sir; and all this supported by great wealth of his own acquisition. If all this had happened to me, I should have had a couple of fellows with long poles walking before me, to knock down every body that stood in the way. Consider, if all this had happened to Cibber or Quin, they'd have jumped over the moon.—Yet Garrick speaks to *us*" (smiling.) BOSWELL: "And Garrick is a very good man, a charitable man." JOHNSON: "Sir, a liberal man. He has given away more money than any man in England. There may be a little vanity mixed; but he has shewn, that money is not his first object." BOSWELL: "Yet Foote used to say of him, that he walked out with an intention to do a generous action; but turning the corner of a street, he met with the ghost of a halfpenny, which frightened him." JOHNSON: "Why, Sir, that is very true, too; for I never knew a man of whom it could be said with less certainty to-day, what he will do to-morrow, than Garrick; it depends so much on his humour at the time." SCOTT: "I am glad to hear of his liberality. He has been represented as very saving." JOHNSON: "With his domestick saving we have nothing to do. I remember drinking tea with him long ago, when Peg Woffington made it, and he grumbled at her for making it too strong. He had then begun to feel money in his purse, and did not know when he should have enough of it."

On the subject of wealth, the proper use of it, and the effects of that art which is called economy, he observed, "It is wonderful to think how men of very large estates not only spend their yearly incomes, but are often actually in want of money. It is clear they have not value for what they spend. Lord Shelburne told me, that a man of high rank, who looks into his own affairs, may have all that he ought to have, all that can be of any use, or appear with any advantage, for five thousand pounds a year. Therefore a great proportion must go in waste; and, indeed, this is the case with most people, whatever their fortune is." BOSWELL: "I have no doubt, Sir, of this. But how is it? What is waste?" JOHNSON: "Why, Sir, breaking bottles, and a thousand other things. Waste

207

cannot be accurately told, though we are sensible how destructive it is. Economy on the one hand, by which a certain income is made to maintain a man genteely, and waste on the other, by which, on the same income, another man lives shabbily, cannot be defined. It is a very nice thing; as one man wears his coat out much sooner than another, we cannot tell how."

We talked of war. JOHNSON: "Every man thinks meanly of himself, for not having been a soldier, or not having been at sea." BOSWELL: "Lord Mansfield does not." JOHNSON: "Sir, if Lord Mansfield were in a company of General Officers and Admirals who have been in service, he would shrink; he'd wish to creep under the table." BOSWELL: "No; he'd think he could *try* them all." JOHNSON: "Yes, if he could catch them: but they'd try him much sooner. No, Sir: were Socrates and Charles the Twelfth of Sweden both present in any company, and Socrates to say, 'Follow me, and hear a lecture in philosophy;' and Charles, laying his hand on his sword, to say, 'Follow me, and dethrone the Czar;' a man would be ashamed to follow Socrates. Sir, the impression is universal: yet it is strange. As to the sailor, when you look down from the quarter-deck to the space below, you see the utmost extremity of human misery: such crowding, such filth, such stench!" BOSWELL: "Yet sailors are happy." JOHNSON: "They are happy as brutes are happy, with a piece of fresh meat,—with the grossest sensuality. But, Sir, the profession of soldiers and sailors has the dignity of danger. Mankind reverence those who have got over fear, which is so general a weakness." SCOTT: "But is not courage, mechanical, and to be acquired?" JOHNSON: "Why yes, Sir, in a collective sense. Soldiers consider themselves only as part of a great machine." SCOTT: "We find people fond of being sailors." JOHNSON: "I cannot account for that, any more than I can account for other strange perversions of imagination."

He sometimes could not bear being teazed with questions. I was once present when a gentleman asked so many, as "What did you do, Sir?" "What did you say, Sir?" that he at last grew enraged, and said, "I will not be put to the *question*. Don't you consider, Sir, that these are not the manners of a gentleman? I will not be baited with *what* and *why*; what is this? what is that? why is a cow's tail long? why is a fox's tail bushy?" The gentleman, who was a good deal out of countenance, said, "Why, Sir, you are so good, that I venture to trouble you." JOHNSON: "Sir, my being so *good* is no reason why you should be so *ill*."

He talked with an uncommon animation of travelling into distant countries; that the mind was enlarged by it, and that an acquisition of dignity of character was derived from it. He expressed a particular enthusiasm with respect to visiting the wall of China. I catched it for the moment, and said I really believed I should go and see the wall of China had I not children, of whom it was my duty to take care. "Sir, (said he,) by doing so, you would do what would be of importance in raising your children to eminence. There would be a lustre reflected upon them from your spirit and curiosity. They would be at all times regarded as the children of a man who had gone to visit the wall of China. I am serious, Sir."

On Sunday, April 12, he and I, and Mrs. Williams, went to dine with the Reverend Dr. Percy. Talking of Goldsmith, Johnson said, he was very envious. I defended him, by observing that he owned it frankly upon all occasions. JOHNSON: "Sir, you are enforcing the charge. He had so much envy, that he could not conceal it. He was so full of it, that he overflowed. He talked of it to be sure often enough. Now, Sir, what a man avows, he is not ashamed to think; though many a man thinks what he is ashamed to avow. We are all envious naturally; but by checking envy, we get the better of it. So we are all thieves naturally; a child always tries to get at what it wants the nearest way, by good instruction and good habits this is cured, till a man has not even an inclination to seize what is another's; has no struggle with himself about it."

And here I shall record a scene of too much heat between Dr. Johnson and Dr. Percy, which I should have suppressed, were it not that it gave occasion to display the truly tender and benevolent heart of Johnson, who as soon as he found a friend was at all hurt by any thing which he had "said in his wrath," was not only prompt and desirous to be reconciled, but exerted himself to make ample reparation.

Books of Travels having been mentioned, Johnson praised Pennant very highly, as he did at Dunvegan, in the Isle of Skye. Dr. Percy knowing himself to be the heir male of the ancient Percies, and having the warmest and most dutiful attachment to the noble House of Northumberland, could not sit quietly and hear a man praised, who had spoken disrespectfully of Alnwick-Castle and the Duke's pleasure-grounds, especially as he thought meanly of his travels. He therefore opposed Johnson eagerly. JOHNSON: "Pennant, in what he has said of Alnwick, has done what he intended; he has made you very angry." PERCY: "He has said the garden is trim, which is representing it like a citizen's parterre, when the truth is, there is a very large extent of fine turf and gravel walks." JOHNSON: "According to your own account, Sir, Pennant is right. It *is* trim. Here is grass cut close, and gravel rolled smooth. Is not that trim? The extent is nothing against that; a mile may be as trim as a square yard. Your extent puts me in mind of the citizen's enlarged dinner, two pieces of roast-beef, and two puddings. There is no variety, no mind exerted in laying out the ground, no trees." PERCY: "He pretends to give the natural history of Northumberland, and yet takes no notice of the immense number of trees planted there of late." JOHNSON: "That, Sir, has nothing to do with the *natural* history; that is *civil* history. A man who gives the natural history of the oak, is not to tell how many oaks have been planted in this place or that. A man who gives the natural history of the cow, is not to tell how many cows are milked at Islington. The animal is the same, whether milked in the Park or at Islington." PERCY: "Pennant does not describe well; a carrier who goes along the side of Lochlomond would describe it better." JOHNSON: "I think he describes very well." PERCY: "I travelled after him." JOHNSON: "And *I* travelled after him." PERCY: "But, my good friend, you are short-sighted, and do not see so well as I do." I wondered at Dr. Percy's venturing thus. Dr. Johnson said nothing at the time: but inflammable particles were collecting for a cloud to burst. In a little while Dr. Percy said something more in disparagement of Pennant. JOHNSON: (pointedly) "This is the resentment of a narrow mind, because he did not find every thing in Northumberland." PERCY: (feeling the stroke) "Sir, you may be as rude as you please." JOHNSON: "Hold, Sir! don't talk of rudeness; remember, Sir, you told me, (puffing hard with passion struggling for a vent) I was short-sighted. We have done with civility. We are to be as rude as we please." PERCY: "Upon my honour, Sir, I did not mean to be uncivil." JOHNSON: "I cannot say so, Sir; for I *did* mean to be uncivil, thinking *you* had been uncivil." Dr. Percy rose, ran up to him, and taking him by the hand, assured him affectionately that his meaning had been misunderstood; upon which a reconciliation instantly took place. JOHNSON: "My dear Sir, I am willing you shall *hang* Pennant." PERCY: (resuming the former subject) "Pennant complains that the helmet is not hung out to invite to the hall of hospitality. Now I never heard that it was a custom to hang out a *helmet*." JOHNSON: "Hang him up, hang him up." BOSWELL: (humouring the joke) "Hang out his skull instead of a helmet, and you may drink ale out of it in your hall of Odin, as he is your enemy; that will be truly ancient. *There* will be *Northern Antiquities*." JOHNSON: "He's a *Whig*, Sir; a *sad dog*, (smiling at his own violent expressions, merely for *political* difference of opinion.) But he's the best traveller I ever read; he observes more things than any one else does."

We had a calm after the storm, staid the evening and supped, and were pleasant and gay. But Dr. Percy told me he was very uneasy at what had passed; for there was a gentleman there who was well acquainted with the Northumberland family, to whom he hoped to have appeared more respectable, by shewing how intimate he was with Dr. Johnson, and who might now, on the contrary, go away with an opinion to his disadvantage. He begged I would mention this to Dr. Johnson, which I afterwards did. His observation upon it was, "This comes of *stratagem*; had he told me that he wished to appear to advantage before that gentleman, he should have been at the top of the house all the time." He spoke of Dr. Percy in the handsomest manner. "Then, Sir, (said I) may I be allowed to suggest a mode by which you may effectually counteract any unfavourable report of what passed. I will write a letter to you upon the subject of the unlucky contest of that day, and you will be kind enough to put in writing as an answer to that letter, what you have now said, and as Lord Percy is to dine with us at General Paoli's soon, I will take an opportunity to read the correspondence in his Lordship's presence." This friendly scheme was accordingly carried into execution without Dr. Percy's knowledge. Johnson's letter placed Dr. Percy's unquestionable merit in the fairest point of view; and I contrived that Lord Percy should hear the correspondence, by introducing it at General Paoli's, as an instance of Dr. Johnson's kind disposition towards one in whom his Lordship was interested. Thus every unfavourable impression was obviated that could possibly have been made on those by whom he wished most to be regarded.

On Monday, April 13, I dined with Johnson at Mr. Langton's, where were Dr. Porteus, then Bishop of Chester, now of London, and Dr. Stinton. He was at first in a very silent mood. Before dinner he said nothing but "Pretty baby," to one of the children. Langton said very well to me afterwards, that he could repeat Johnson's conversation before dinner, as Johnson had said that he could repeat a complete chapter of *The Natural History of Iceland*, from the Danish of *Horrebow*, the whole of which was exactly thus:

"CHAP. LXXII. *Concerning Snakes.*

"There are no snakes to be met with throughout the whole island."

Mr. Topham Beauclerk came in the evening, and he and Dr. Johnson and I staid to supper. It was mentioned that Dr. Dodd had once wished to be a member of the LITERARY CLUB. JOHNSON: "I should be sorry if any of our Club were hanged. I will not say but some of them deserve it." BEAUCLERK: (supposing this to be aimed at persons for whom he had at that time a wonderful fancy, which, however, did not last long,) was irritated, and eagerly said, "You, Sir, have a friend (naming him) who deserves to be hanged; for he speaks behind their backs against those with whom he lives on the best terms, and attacks them in the news-papers. *He* certainly ought to be *kicked.*" JOHNSON: "Sir, we all do this in some degree: '*Veniam petimus damusque vicissim.*'[1] To be sure it may be done so much, that a man may deserve to be kicked." BEAUCLERK: "He is very malignant." JOHNSON: "No, Sir; he is not malignant. He is mischievous, if you will. He would do no man an essential injury; he may, indeed, love to make sport of people by vexing their vanity. I, however, once knew an old gentleman who was absolutely malignant. He really wished evil to others, and rejoiced at it." BOSWELL: "The gentleman, Mr. Beauclerk, against whom you are so violent, is, I know, a man of good principles." BEAUCLERK: "Then he does not wear them out in practice."

On Tuesday, April 14, I dined with him at General Oglethorpe's, with General Paoli and Mr. Langton. General Oglethorpe declaimed against luxury. JOHNSON: "Depend upon it, Sir, every state of society is as luxurious as it can be. Men always take the best they can get." OGLETHORPE: "But the best depends much upon ourselves; and if we can be as well satisfied with plain things, we are in the wrong to accustom our palates to what is high-seasoned and expensive. What says Addison on his *Cato,* speaking of the Numidian?

> ' Coarse are his meals, the fortune of the chace,
> Amid the running stream he slakes his thirst,
> Toils all the day, and at the approach of night,
> On the first friendly bank he throws him down,
> Or rests his head upon a rock till morn;
> And if the following day he chance to find
> A new repast, or an untasted spring,
> Blesses his stars, and thinks it luxury.'

[1] We ask and give forgiveness in turn.

"Let us have *that* kind of luxury, Sir, if you will." JOHNSON: "But hold, Sir; to be merely satisfied is not enough. It is in refinement and elegance that the civilized man differs from the savage. A great part of our industry, and all our ingenuity is exercised in procuring pleasure; and, Sir, a hungry man has not the same pleasure in eating a plain dinner, that a hungry man has in eating a luxurious dinner. You see I put the case fairly. A hungry man may have as much, nay, more pleasure in eating a plain dinner, than a man grown fastidious has in eating a luxurious dinner. But I suppose the man who decides between the two dinners, to be equally a hungry man."

Talking of different governments,—JOHNSON: "The more contracted power is, the more easily it is destroyed. A country governed by a despot is an inverted cone. Government there cannot be so firm, as when it rests upon a broad basis gradually contracted, as the government of Great Britain, which is founded on the parliament, then is in the privy-council, then in the King."

At Mr. Dilly's next day were Mrs. Knowles, the ingenious Quaker lady, Miss Seward, the poetess of Lichfield, the Reverend Dr. Mayo, and the Rev. Mr. Beresford, Tutor to the Duke of Bedford. Before dinner Dr. Johnson seized upon Mr. Charles Sheridan's *Account of the late Revolution in Sweden*, and seemed to read it ravenously, as if he devoured it, which was to all appearance his method of studying. "He knows how to read better than any one (said Mrs. Knowles); he gets at the substance of a book directly; he tears out the heart of it." He kept it wrapt up in the table-cloth in his lap during the time of dinner, from an avidity to have one entertainment in readiness, when he should have finished another; resembling (if I may use so coarse a simile) a dog who holds a bone in his paws in reserve, while he eats something else which has been thrown to him.

The subject of cookery having been very naturally introduced at a table where Johnson, who boasted of the niceness of his palate, owned that "he always found a good dinner," he said "I could write a better book of cookery than has ever yet been written; it should be a book upon philosophical principles. Pharmacy is now made much more simple. Cookery may be made so too. A prescription which is now compounded of five ingredients, had formerly fifty in it. So in cookery, if the nature of the ingredients be well known, much fewer will do. Then, as you cannot make bad meat good, I would tell what is the best butcher's meat, the best

213

beef, the best pieces; how to choose young fowls; the proper seasons of different vegetables; and then how to roast and boil and compound." DILLY: "Mrs. Glasse's *Cookery*, which is the best, was written by Dr. Hill. Half the *trade* know this." JOHNSON: "Well, Sir. This shews how much better the subject of Cookery may be treated by a philosopher. I doubt if the book be written by Dr. Hill; for, in Mrs. Glasse's *Cookery*, which I have looked into, salt-petre and sal-prunella are spoken of as different substances, whereas sal-prunella is only salt-petre burnt on charcoal; and Hill could not be ignorant of this. However, as the greatest part of such a book is made by transcription, this mistake may have been carelessly adopted. But you shall see what a Book of Cookery I shall make! I shall agree with Mr. Dilly for the copy-right." MISS SEWARD: "That would be Hercules with the distaff indeed." JOHNSON: "No, Madam. Women can spin very well; but they cannot make a good book of Cookery."

JOHNSON: "O! Mr. Dilly—you must know that an English Benedictine Monk at Paris has translated *The Duke of Berwick's Memoirs*, from the original French, and has sent them to me to sell. I offered them to Strahan, who sent them back with this answer:— 'That the first book he had published was the Duke of Berwick's Life, by which he had lost: and he hated the name:'—Now I honestly tell you, that Strahan has refused them; but I also honestly tell you, that he did it upon no principle, for he never looked into them." DILLY: "Are they well translated, Sir?" JOHNSON: "Why, Sir, very well—in a style very current and very clear. I have written to the Benedictine to give me an answer upon two points;—What evidence is there that the letters are authentick? (for if they are not authentick, they are nothing;)—And how long will it be before the original French is published? For if the French edition is not to appear for a considerable time, the translation will be almost as valuable as an original book. They will make two volumes in octavo; and I have undertaken to correct every sheet as it comes from the press." Mr. Dilly desired to see them, and said he would send for them. He asked Dr. Johnson, if he would write a Preface to them. JOHNSON: "No, Sir. The Benedictines were very kind to me, and I'll do what I undertook to do; but I will not mingle my name with them. I am to gain nothing by them. I'll turn them loose upon the world, and let them take their chance." DR. MAYO: "Pray, Sir, are Ganganelli's letters authentick?" JOHNSON: "No, Sir. Voltaire put the same question to the editor of them, that I did to Macpherson—Where are the originals?"

Mrs. Knowles affected to complain that men had much more liberty allowed them than women. JOHNSON: "Why, Madam, women have all the liberty they should wish to have. We have all the labour and the danger, and the women all the advantage. We go to sea, we build houses, we do every thing, in short, to pay our court to the women." MRS. KNOWLES: "The Doctor reasons very wittily, but not convincingly. Now, take the instance of building; the mason's wife, if she is ever seen in liquor, is ruined; the mason may get himself drunk as often as he pleases, with little loss of character; nay, may let his wife and children starve." JOHNSON: "Madam, you must consider, if the mason does get himself drunk, and let his wife and children starve, the parish will oblige him to find security for their maintenance. We have different modes of restraining evil. Stocks for the men, a ducking-stool for women, and a pound for beasts. If we require more perfection from women than from ourselves, it is doing them honour. And women have not the same temptations that we have; they may always live in virtuous company; men must live in the world indiscriminately. If a woman has no inclination to do what is wrong, being secure from it is no restraint to her. I am at liberty to walk into the Thames; but if I were to try it, my friends would restrain me in Bedlam, and I should be obliged to them." MRS. KNOWLES: "Still, Doctor, I cannot help thinking it a hardship that more indulgence is allowed to men than to women. It gives a superiority to men, to which I do not see how they are entitled." JOHNSON: "It is plain, Madam, one or other must have the superiority. As Shakspeare says, 'If two men ride on a horse, one must ride behind.'" DILLY: "I suppose, Sir, Mrs. Knowles would have them ride in panniers, one on each side." JOHNSON: "Then, Sir, the horse would throw them both." MRS. KNOWLES: "Well, I hope that in another world the sexes will be equal." BOSWELL: "That is being too ambitious, Madam. *We* might as well desire to be equal with the angels. We shall all, I hope, be happy in a future state, but we must not expect to be all happy in the same degree. It is enough, if we be happy according to our several capacities. A worthy carman will get to heaven as well as Sir Isaac Newton. Yet, though equally good, they will not have the same degrees of happiness." JOHNSON: "Probably not."

Dr. Mayo having asked Johnson's opinion of Soame Jenyns's

215

View of the Internal Evidence of the Christian Religion;—JOHNSON:
"I think it a pretty book; not very theological indeed; and there
seems to be an affectation of ease and carelessness, as if it were not
suitable to his character to be very serious about the matter."
BOSWELL: "He may have intended this to introduce his book the
better among genteel people, who might be unwilling to read
too grave a treatise. There is a general levity in the age. We have
physicians now with bag-wigs; may we not have airy divines, at
least somewhat less solemn in their appearance than they used
to be?" JOHNSON: "Jenyns might mean as you say." BOSWELL:
"*You* should like his book, Mrs. Knowles, as it maintains, as your
friends do, that courage is not a Christian virtue." MRS. KNOWLES:
"Yes, indeed, I like him there; but I cannot agree with him, that
friendship is not a Christian virtue." JOHNSON: "Why, Madam,
strictly speaking, he is right. All friendship is preferring the interest
of a friend, to the neglect, or, perhaps, against the interests of
others; so that an old Greek said, 'He that has *friends* has *no friend*.'
Now Christianity recommends universal benevolence,—to consider
all men as our brethren; which is contrary to the virtue of friendship, as described by the ancient philosophers. Surely, Madam, your
sect must approve of this; for, you call all men *friends*." MRS.
KNOWLES: "We are commanded to do good to all men, 'but
especially to them who are of the household of Faith.'" JOHNSON:
"Well, Madam. The household of Faith is wide enough." MRS.
KNOWLES: "But, Doctor, our Saviour had twelve Apostles, yet
there was *one* whom he *loved*. John was called 'the disciple whom
JESUS loved.'" JOHNSON: (with eyes sparkling benignantly) "Very
well, indeed, Madam. You have said very well." BOSWELL: "A
fine application. Pray, Sir, had you ever thought of it?" JOHNSON:
"I had not, Sir."

From this pleasing subject, he I know not how or why, made
a sudden transition to one upon which he was a violent aggressor;
for he said, "I am willing to love all mankind, *except an American*:"
and his inflammable corruption bursting into horrid fire, he
"breathed out threatenings and slaughter;" calling them, "Rascals
—Robbers—Pirates;" and exclaiming, he'd "burn and destroy
them." Miss Seward, looking to him with mild but steady astonishment, said, "Sir, this is an instance that we are always most
violent against those whom we have injured."—He was irritated
still more by this delicate and keen reproach; and roared out another
tremendous volley which one might fancy could be heard across

the Atlantick. During this tempest I sat in great uneasiness, lamenting his heat of temper; till, by degrees, I diverted his attention to other topicks.

DR. MAYO, (to Dr. Johnson.) "Pray, Sir, have you read Edwards, of New England, on Grace?" JOHNSON: "No, Sir." BOSWELL: "It puzzles me so much as to the freedom of the human will, by stating, with wonderful acute ingenuity, our being actuated by a series of motives which we cannot resist, that the only relief I had was to forget it." MAYO: "But he makes the proper distinction between moral and physical necessity." BOSWELL: "Alas, Sir, they come both to the same thing. You may be bound as hard by chains when covered by leather, as when the iron appears. The argument for the moral necessity of human actions is always, I observe, fortified by supposing universal prescience to be one of the attributes of the Deity." JOHNSON: "You are surer that you are free, than you are of prescience; you are surer that you can lift up your finger or not as you please, than you are of any conclusion from a deduction of reasoning. But let us consider a little the objection from prescience. It is certain I am either to go home to-night or not; that does not prevent my freedom." BOSWELL: "That it is certain you are *either* to go home or not, does not prevent your freedom: because the liberty of choice between the two is compatible with that certainty. But if *one* of these events be certain *now*, you have no *future* power of volition. If it be certain you are to go home to-night, you *must* go home." JOHNSON: "If I am well acquainted with a man, I can judge with great probability how he will act in any case, without his being restrained by my judging. God may have this probability increased to certainty." BOSWELL: "When it is increased to *certainty*, freedom ceases, because that cannot be certainly foreknown, which is not certain at the time; but if it be certain at the time, it is a contradiction in terms to maintain that there can be afterwards any *contingency* dependent upon the exercise of will or any thing else." JOHNSON: "All theory is against the freedom of the will; all experience for it."

He, as usual, defended luxury: "You cannot spend money in luxury without doing good to the poor. Nay you do more good to them by spending it in luxury, you make them exert industry, whereas by giving it, you keep them idle. I own, indeed, there may be more virtue in giving it immediately in charity, than in spending it in luxury; though there may be pride in that too." Miss Seward asked, if this was not Mandeville's doctrine of "private vices publick benefits." JOHNSON: "The fallacy of that book is, that Mandeville defines neither vices nor benefits. He reckons among vices every thing that gives pleasure. He takes the narrowest system of morality, monastick morality, which holds pleasure itself to be a vice, such as eating salt with our fish, because it makes it eat better; and he reckons wealth as a publick benefit, which is by no means always true. Pleasure of itself is not a vice. Having a garden, which we all know to be perfectly innocent, is a great pleasure. At the same time, in this state of being there are many pleasures vices, which however are so immediately agreeable that we can hardly abstain from them. The happiness of Heaven will be, that pleasure and virtue will be perfectly consistent. Mandeville puts the case of a man who gets drunk at an alehouse; and says it is a publick benefit, because so much money is got by it to the publick. But it must be considered, that all the good gained by this, through the gradation of alehouse-keeper, brewer, maltster, and farmer is overbalanced by the evil caused to the man and his family by his getting drunk. This is the way to try what is vicious, by ascertaining whether more evil than good is produced upon the whole, which is the case in all vice. It may happen that good is produced by vice, but not as vice; for instance, a robber may take money from its owner, and give it to one who will make a better use of it. Here is good produced: but not by the robbery as robbery, but as translation of property. I read Mandeville forty, or, I believe fifty years ago. He did not puzzle me; he opened my views into real life very much. No, it is clear that the happiness of society depends on virtue. In Sparta, theft was allowed by general consent; theft, therefore, was *there* not a crime, but then there was no security; and what a life must they have had when there was no security! Without truth there must be a dissolution of society. As it is, there is so little truth, that we are almost afraid to trust our ears; but how should we be, if falsehood were multiplied ten times! Society is held together by communication and information; and I remember this remark of Sir Thomas Brown's, "Do the devils lie? No; for then Hell could not subsist."

Somebody mentioned the Reverend Mr. Mason's prosecution of Mr. Murray, the bookseller, for having inserted in a collection of *Gray's Poems*, only fifty lines, of which Mr. Mason had still the exclusive property, under the statute of Queen Anne; and that Mr. Mason had persevered, notwithstanding his being requested to name his own terms of compensation. Johnson signified his displeasure at Mr. Mason's conduct very strongly; but added, by way of shewing that he was not surprized at it, "Mason's a Whig." MRS. KNOWLES, (not hearing distinctly:) "What! a Prig, Sir?" JOHNSON: "Worse, Madam; a Whig! But he is both!"[1]

I expressed a horrour at the thought of death. MRS. KNOWLES: "Nay, thou should'st not have a horrour for what is the gate of life." JOHNSON: (standing upon the hearth rolling about, with a serious, solemn, and somewhat gloomy air:) "No rational man can die without uneasy apprehension." MRS. KNOWLES: "The Scriptures tell us, 'The righteous shall have *hope* in his death.'" JOHNSON: "Yes, Madam; that is, he shall not have despair. But, consider, his hope of salvation must be founded on the terms on which it is promised that the mediation of our SAVIOUR shall be applied to us,— namely, obedience; and where obedience has failed, then, as suppletory to it, repentance. But what man can say that his obedience has been such, as he would approve of in another, or even in himself upon close examination, or that his repentance has not been such as to require being repented of? No man can be sure that his obedience and repentance will obtain salvation." MRS. KNOWLES: "But divine intimation of acceptance may be made to the soul." JOHNSON: "Madam, it may; but I should not think the better of a man who should tell me on his death-bed, he was sure of salvation. A man cannot be sure himself that he has divine intimation of acceptance; much less can he make others sure that he has it." BOSWELL: "Then, Sir, we must be contented to acknow-ledge that death is a terrible thing." JOHNSON: "Yes, Sir, I have made no approaches to a state which can look on it as not terrible." MRS. KNOWLES: (seeming to enjoy a pleasing serenity in the per-suasion of benignant divine light:) "Does not St. Paul say, 'I have fought the good fight of faith, I have finished my course; henceforth is laid up for me a crown of life'?" JOHNSON: "Yes, Madam; but here was a man inspired, a man who had been con-verted by supernatural interposition." BOSWELL: "In prospect death is dreadful; but in fact we find that people die easy." JOHNSON: "Why, Sir, most people have not *thought* much of the matter, so cannot *say* much, and it is supposed they die easy. Few believe it certain they are then to die; and those who do, set themselves to behave with resolution, as a man does who is going to be hanged: —he is not the less unwilling to be hanged." MISS SEWARD: "There is one mode of the fear of death, which is certainly absurd: and that

[1] 'Prig' in 18th Century slang meant 'thief.'

is the dread of annihilation, which is only a pleasing sleep without a dream." JOHNSON: "It is neither pleasing, nor sleep; it is nothing. Now mere existence is so much better than nothing, that one would rather exist even in pain, than not exist." BOSWELL: "If annihilation be nothing, then existing in pain is not a comparative state, but is a positive evil, which I cannot think we should choose. I must be allowed to differ here, and it would lessen the hope of a future state founded on the argument, that the Supreme Being, who is good as He is great, will here after compensate for our present sufferings in this life. For if existence, such as we have it here, be comparatively a good, we have no reason to complain, though no more of it should be given to us. But if our only state of existence were in this world then we might with some reason complain that we are so dissatisfied with our enjoyments compared with our desires." JOHNSON: "The lady confounds annihilation, which is nothing, with the apprehension of it, which is dreadful. It is in the apprehension of it that the horrour of annihilation consists."

Of John Wesley, he said, "He can talk well on any subject." BOSWELL: "Pray, Sir, what has he made of his story of a ghost?" JOHNSON: "Why, Sir, he believes it; but not on sufficient authority. He did not take time enough to examine the girl. It was at Newcastle, where the ghost was said to have appeared to a young woman several times, mentioning something about the right to an old house, advising application to be made to an attorney, which was done; and, at the same time, saying the attorney would do nothing, which proved to be the fact. 'This (says John) is a proof that the ghost knows our thoughts.' Now (laughing) it is not necessary to know our thoughts, to tell that an attorney will sometimes do nothing. Charles Wesley, who is a more stationary man, does not believe the story. I am sorry that John did not take more pains to enquire into the evidence for it." MISS SEWARD, (with an incredulous smile:) "What, Sir! about a ghost?" JOHNSON: (with solemn vehemence:) "Yes, Madam: this is a question, which, after five thousand years, is yet undecided; a question, whether in theology or philosophy, one of the most important that can come before the human understanding."

Mrs. Knowles mentioned, as a proselyte to Quakerism, Miss ———, a young lady well known to Dr. Johnson, for whom he had shewn much affection; while she ever had, and still retained, a great respect for him. Mrs. Knowles at the same time took an opportunity of letting him know "that the amiable young creature was sorry at finding that he was offended at her leaving the Church of England, and embracing a simpler faith;" and, in the gentlest and most persuasive manner, solicited his kind indulgence for what was sincerely a matter of conscience. JOHNSON: (frowning very angrily,) "Madam, she is an odious wench. She could not have any proper conviction that it was her duty to change her religion, which is the most important of all subjects, and should be studied with all care and with all the helps we can get. She knew no more of the Church which she left, and that which she embraced, than she did of the difference between the Copernican and Ptolemaick systems." MRS. KNOWLES: "She had the New Testament before her." JOHNSON: "Madam, she could not understand the New Testament, the most difficult book in the world, for which the study of a life is required." MRS. KNOWLES: "It is clear as to essentials." JOHNSON: "But not as to controversial points. The heathen were easily converted, because they had nothing to give up; but we ought not, without very strong conviction indeed, to desert the religion in which we have been educated. That is the religion given you, the religion in which it may be said Providence has placed you. If you live conscientiously in that religion, you may be safe. But errour is dangerous indeed, if you err when you choose a religion for yourself." MRS. KNOWLES: "Must we then go by implicit faith?" JOHNSON: "Why, Madam, the greatest part of our knowledge is implicit faith; and as to religion, have we heard all that a disciple of Confucius, all that a Mahometan, can say for himself?" He then rose again into passion, and attacked the young proselyte in the severest terms of reproach, so that both ladies seemed to be much shocked.

April 17, being Good-Friday, I waited on Johnson, as usual.

I expressed some inclination to publish an account of my *Travels* upon the continent of Europe, for which I had a variety of materials collected. JOHNSON: "I do not say, Sir, you may not publish your travels; but I give you my opinion, that you would lessen yourself by it. What can you tell of countries so well known as those upon the continent of Europe, which you have visited?" BOSWELL: "But I can give an entertaining narrative, with many incidents, anecdotes, *jeux d'esprit*, and remarks, so as to make very pleasant reading." JOHNSON: "Why, Sir, most modern travellers in Europe who have published their travels, have been laughed at: I would not have you added to the number. The world is now not contented to be merely entertained by a traveller's narrative; they want to learn something. Now some of my friends asked me, why I did not give some account of my travels in France. The reason is plain; intelligent readers had seen more of France than I had. *You* might have liked my travels in France, and THE CLUB might have liked them; but, upon the whole, there would have been more ridicule than good produced by them." BOSWELL: "I cannot agree with you, Sir. People would like to read what you say of anything. Suppose a face has been painted by fifty painters before; still we love to see it done by Sir Joshua." JOHNSON: "True, Sir, but Sir Joshua cannot paint a face when he has not time to look on it." BOSWELL: "Sir, a sketch of any sort by him is valuable. And, Sir, to talk to you in your own style (raising my voice, and shaking my head,) you *should* have given us your travels in France. I am *sure* I am right, and *there's an end on't.*"

I said to him that it was certainly true, as my friend Dempster had observed in his letter to me upon the subject, that a great part of what was in his *Journey to the Western Islands of Scotland*, had been in his mind before he left London. JOHNSON: "Why yes, Sir, the topicks were; and books of travels will be good in proportion to what a man has previously in his mind; his knowing what to observe; his power of contrasting one mode of life with another. As the Spanish proverb says, 'He, who would bring home the wealth of the Indies, must carry the wealth of the Indies with him.' So it is in travelling; a man must carry knowledge with him, if he would bring home knowledge." BOSWELL: "The proverb, I suppose, Sir, means, he must carry a large stock with him to trade with." JOHNSON: "Yes, Sir."

It was a delightful day: as we walked to St. Clement's church, I again remarked that Fleet-street was the most cheerful scene in the world. "Fleet-street (said I,) is in my mind more delightful than Tempé." JOHNSON: "Ay, Sir; but let it be compared with Mull."

And now I am to give a pretty full account of one of the most curious incidents in Johnson's life, of which he himself has made the following minute on this day: "In my return from church, I was accosted by Edwards, an old fellow-collegian, who had not seen me since 1729. He knew me, and asked if I remembered one Edwards; I did not at first recollect the name, but gradually as we walked along, recovered it, and told him a conversation that had passed at an alehouse between us. My purpose is to continue our acquaintance."

It was in Butcher-row that this meeting happened. Mr. Edwards, who was a decent-looking elderly man in grey clothes, and a wig of many curls, accosted Johnson with familiar confidence, knowing who he was, while Johnson returned his salutation with a courteous formality, as to a stranger. But as soon as Edwards had brought to his recollection their having been at Pembroke-College together nine-and-forty years ago, he seemed much pleased, asked where he lived, and said he should be glad to see him in Bolt-court. EDWARDS: "Ah, Sir! we are old men now." JOHNSON: (who never liked to think of being old:) "Don't let us discourage one another." EDWARDS: "Why, Doctor, you look stout and hearty, I am happy to see you so; for the newspapers told us you were very ill." JOHNSON: "Ay, Sir, they are always telling lies of *us old fellows*."

Wishing to be present at more of so singular a conversation as that between two fellow-collegians, who had lived forty years in London without ever having chanced to meet, I whispered to Mr. Edwards that Dr. Johnson was going home, and that he had better accompany him now. So Edwards walked along with us, I eagerly assisting to keep up the conversation. Mr. Edwards informed Dr. Johnson that he had practised long as a solicitor in Chancery, but that he now lived in the country upon a little farm, about sixty acres, just by Stevenage, in Hertfordshire, and that he came to London (to Barnard's Inn, No. 6,) generally twice a week.

When we got to Dr. Johnson's house, and were seated in his library, the dialogue went on admirably. EDWARDS: "Sir, I remember you would not let us say *prodigious* at College. For even then, Sir, (turning to me,) he was delicate in language, and we all feared him." JOHNSON: (to Edwards), "From your having practised the law long, Sir, I presume you must be rich." EDWARDS: "No, Sir; I got a good deal of money; but I had a number of poor relations to whom I gave a great part of it." JOHNSON: "Sir, you have been rich in the most valuable sense of the word." EDWARDS: "But I shall not die rich." JOHNSON: "Nay, sure, Sir, it is better to *live* rich, than to *die* rich." EDWARDS: "I wish I had continued at College." JOHNSON: "Why do you wish that, Sir?" EDWARDS: "Because I think I should have had a much easier life than mine has been. I should have been a parson, and had a good living, like Bloxham and several others, and lived comfortably." JOHNSON: "Sir, the life of a parson, of a conscientious clergyman, is not easy. I have always considered a clergyman as the father of a larger family than he is able to maintain. I would rather have Chancery suits upon my hands than the cure of souls. No, Sir, I do not envy a clergyman's life as an easy life, nor do I envy the clergyman who makes it an easy life."—Here taking himself up all of a sudden, he exclaimed, "O! Mr. Edwards! I'll convince you that I recollect you. Do you remember our drinking together at an alehouse near Pembroke gate? At that time, you told me of the Eton boy, who, when verses on our SAVIOUR'S turning water into wine were prescribed as an exercise, brought up a single line, which was highly admired:

> ' Vidit et erubuit lympha pudica DEUM.'[1]

and I told you of another fine line in *Camden's Remains*, an eulogy upon one of our Kings, who was succeeded by his son, a prince of equal merit:

> ' Mira cano, Sol occubuit, nox nulla secuta est.' "[2]

EDWARDS: "You are a philosopher, Dr. Johnson. I have tried too in my time to be a philosopher; but, I don't know how, cheerfulness was always breaking in." EDWARDS: "I have been twice married, Doctor. You, I suppose, have never known what it was to have a wife." JOHNSON: "Sir, I have known what it was to have a wife, and (in solemn tender faultering tone) I have known what it was to *lose a wife.*—It had almost broke my heart."

EDWARDS: "How do you live, Sir? For my part, I must have my regular meals, and a glass of good wine. I find I require it." JOHNSON: "I now drink no wine, Sir. Early in life I drank wine: for many years I drank none. I then for some years drank a great deal." EDWARDS: "Some hogsheads, I warrant you." JOHNSON: "I then had a severe illness, and left it off, and I have never begun it again. I never felt any difference upon myself from eating one thing rather than another, nor from one kind of weather rather than another. There are people, I believe, who feel a difference; but I am not one of them. And as to regular meals, I have fasted from the Sunday's dinner to the Tuesday's dinner, without any inconvenience. I believe it is best to eat just as one is hungry: but a man who is in business, or a man who has a family, must have stated meals. I am a straggler. I may leave this town and go to Grand Cairo, without being missed here or observed there." EDWARDS: "Don't you eat supper, Sir?" JOHNSON: "No, Sir." EDWARDS: "For my part, now, I consider supper as a turn-pike through which one must pass, in order to get to bed."

[1] The bashful water saw GOD and blushed.
[2] I tell a wonder: the sun set and no night followed.

JOHNSON: "You are a lawyer, Mr. Edwards. Lawyers know life practically. A bookish man should always have them to converse with. They have what he wants." EDWARDS: "I am grown old: I am sixty-five." JOHNSON: "I shall be sixty-eight next birthday. Come, Sir, drink water, and put in for a hundred."

Mr. Edwards mentioned a gentleman who had left his whole fortune to Pembroke College. JOHNSON: "Whether to leave one's whole fortune to a College be right, must depend upon circumstances. I would leave the interest of the fortune I bequeathed to a college to my relations or my friends, for their lives. It is the same thing to a College, which is a permanent society, whether it gets the money now or twenty years hence; and I would wish to make my relations or friends feel the benefit of it."

This interview confirmed my opinion of Johnson's most humane and benevolent heart. His cordial and placid behaviour to an old fellow collegian, a man so different from himself; and his telling him that he would go down to his farm and visit him, shewed a kindness of disposition very rare at an advanced age. He observed, "how wonderful it was that they had both been in London forty years, without having ever once met, and both walkers in the street too!" Mr. Edwards, when going away, again recurred to his consciousness of senility, and looking full in Johnson's face, said to him, "You'll find in Dr. Young,

O my coevals! remnants of yourselves."

Johnson did not relish this at all; but shook his head with impatience. Edwards walked off seemingly highly-pleased with the honour of having been thus noticed by Dr. Johnson. When he was gone, I said to Johnson, I thought him but a weak man. JOHNSON: "Why, yes, Sir. Here is a man who has passed through life without experience: yet I would rather have him with me than a more sensible man who will not talk readily. This man is always willing to say what he has to say." Yet Dr. Johnson had himself by no means that willingness which he praised so much, and I think so justly; for who has not felt the painful effect of the dreary void, when there is a total silence in a company, for any length of time; or, which is as bad, or perhaps worse, when the conversation is with difficulty kept up by a perpetual effort?

Johnson once observed to me, "Tom Tyers described me the best: 'Sir, (said he,) you are like a ghost; you never speak till you are spoken to.'"

Mr. Edwards had said to me aside, that Dr. Johnson should have been of a profession. I repeated the remark to Johnson that I might have his own thoughts on the subject. JOHNSON: "Sir, it *would* have been better that I had been of a profession. I ought to have been a lawyer." BOSWELL: "I do not think, Sir, it would have been better, for we should not have had the *English Dictionary*." JOHNSON: "But you would have had *Reports*." BOSWELL: "Aye; but there would not have been another, who could have written the *Dictionary*. There have been very many good Judges. Suppose you had been Lord Chancellor; you would have delivered opinions with more extent of mind, and in a more ornamented manner, than perhaps any Chancellor ever did, or ever will do. But, I believe, causes have been as judiciously decided as you could have done." JOHNSON: "Yes, Sir. Property has been as well settled."

Johnson, however, had a noble ambition floating in his mind, and had, undoubtedly, often speculated on the possibility of his supereminent powers being rewarded in this great and liberal country by the highest honours of the State. Sir William Scott informs me, that upon the death of the late Lord Lichfield, who was Chancellor of the University of Oxford, he said to Johnson, "What a pity it is, Sir, that you did not follow the profession of the law. You might have been Lord Chancellor of Great Britain, and attained to the dignity of the peerage; and now that the title of Lichfield, your native city, is extinct, you might have had it." Johnson, upon this, seemed much agitated; and, in an angry tone, exclaimed, "Why will you vex me by suggesting this, when it is too late?"

But he did not repine at the prosperity of others. The late Dr. Thomas Leland told Mr. Courtenay, that when Mr. Edmund Burke shewed Johnson his fine house and lands near Beaconsfield, Johnson coolly said, "*Non equidem invideo, miror magis.*"[1]

Goldsmith, in his diverting simplicity, complained one day, in a mixed company, of Lord Camden. "I met him (said he) at Lord Clare's house in the country, and he took no more notice of me than if I had been an ordinary man." The company having laughed heartily, Johnson stood forth in defence of his friend. "Nay, Gentlemen, (said he,) Dr. Goldsmith is in the right. A nobleman ought to have made up to such a man as Goldsmith; and I think it is much against Lord Camden that he neglected him."

[1] I do not envy; rather, I admire.

Nor could he patiently endure to hear, that such respect as he thought due only to higher intellectual qualities, should be bestowed on men of slighter, though perhaps more amusing, talents. I told him, that one morning, when I went to breakfast with Garrick, who was very vain in his intimacy with Lord Camden, he accosted me thus:—"Pray now, did you—did you meet a little lawyer turning the corner, eh?"—"No, Sir, (said I.) Pray what do you mean by the question?"—"Why, (replied Garrick, with an affected indifference, yet as if standing on tip-toe,) Lord Camden has this moment left me. We had had a long walk together." JOHNSON: "Well, Sir, Garrick talked very properly. Lord Camden *was a little lawyer* to be associating so familiarly with a player."

Sir Joshua Reynolds observed, with great truth, that Johnson considered Garrick to be as it were his *property*. He would allow no man either to blame or to praise Garrick in his presence, without contradicting him.

Having fallen into a very serious frame of mind, in which mutual expressions of kindness passed between us, such as would be thought too vain in me to repeat, I talked with regret of the sad inevitable certainty that one of us must survive the other. JOHNSON: "Yes, Sir, that is an affecting consideration. I remembering Swift, in one of his letters to Pope, says, 'I intend to come over, that we may meet once more; and when we must part, it is what happens to all human beings.'" BOSWELL: "The hope that we shall see our departed friends again must support the mind." JOHNSON: "Why, yes, Sir." BOSWELL: "There is a strange unwillingness to part with life, independent of serious fears as to futurity. A reverend friend of ours (naming him) tells me, that he feels an uneasiness at the thoughts of leaving his house, his study, his books." JOHNSON: "This is foolish in *****. A man need not be uneasy on these grounds; for, as he will retain his consciousness, he may say with the philosopher, *Omnia mea mecum porto.*"[1] BOSWELL: "True Sir; we may carry our books in our heads; but still there is something painful in the thought of leaving for ever what has given us pleasure. I remember, many years ago, when my imagination was warm, and I happened to be in a melancholy mood, it distressed me to think of going into a state of being in which Shakespeare's poetry did not exist. A lady whom I then much admired, a very amiable woman, humoured my fancy, and relieved me by saying, 'The first thing you will meet in the other world, will be an elegant copy of

[1] All my property I carry with me.

Shakspeare's works presented to you.'" Dr. Johnson smiled benignantly at this, and did not appear to disapprove of the notion.

On Saturday, April 18 I drank tea with him.

Talking of a recent seditious delinquent, he said, "They should set him in the pillory, that he may be punished in a way that would disgrace him." I observed, that the pillory does not always disgrace. And I mentioned an instance of a gentleman, who I thought was not dishonoured by it. JOHNSON: "Ay, but he was, Sir. He could not mouth and strut as he used to do, after having been there. People are not willing to ask a man to their tables, who has stood in the pillory."

The gentleman who had dined with us at Dr. Percy's came in. Johnson attacked the Americans with intemperate vehemence of abuse. I said something in their favour; and added, that I was always sorry, when he talked on that subject. This, it seems, exasperated him; though he said nothing at the time. The cloud was charged with sulphureous vapour, which was afterwards to burst in thunder. —We talked of a gentleman who was running out his fortune in London; and I said, "We must get him out of it. All his friends must quarrel with him, and that will soon drive him away." JOHNSON: "Nay, Sir, we'll send *you* to him. If your company does not drive a man out of his house, nothing will." This was a horrible shock, for which there was no visible cause. I afterwards asked him, why he had said so harsh a thing. JOHNSON: "Because, Sir, you make me angry about the Americans." BOSWELL: "But why did you not take your revenge directly?" JOHNSON: (smiling,) "Because, Sir, I had nothing ready. A man cannot strike till he has his weapons." This was a candid and pleasant confession.

We talked of the numbers of people that sometimes have composed the households of great families. I mentioned that there were a hundred in the family of the present Earl of Eglintoune's father. Dr. Johnson seeming to doubt it, I began to enumerate. "Let us see: my Lord and my Lady two." JOHNSON: "Nay, Sir, if you are to count by twos, you may be long enough." BOSWELL: "Well, but now I add two sons and seven daughters, and a servant for each, that will make twenty; so we have the fifth part already." JOHNSON: "Very true. You get at twenty pretty readily; but you will not so easily get further on. We grow to five feet pretty readily; but it is not so easy to grow to seven."

On Sunday, April 19, being Easter day, after the solemnities of the festival in St. Paul's Church, I visited him, but could not stay to dinner. I expressed a wish to have the arguments for Christianity always in readiness, that my religious faith might be as firm and clear as any proposition whatever, so that I need not be under the least uneasiness, when it should be attacked. JOHNSON: "Sir, you cannot answer all objections. You have demonstration for a First Cause: you see he must be good as well as powerful, because there is nothing to make him otherwise, and goodness of itself is preferable. Yet you have against this, what is very certain, the unhappiness of human life. This, however, gives us reason to hope for a future state of compensation, that there may be a perfect system. But of that we were not sure, till we had a positive revelation."

On Monday, April 20, I found him at home in the morning. We talked of a gentleman who we apprehended was gradually involving his circumstances by bad management. JOHNSON: "Wasting a fortune is evaporation by a thousand imperceptible means. If it were a stream, they'd stop it. You must speak to him. It is really miserable. Were he a gamester, it could be said he had hopes of winning. Were he a bankrupt in trade, he might have grown rich; but he has neither spirit to spend, nor resolution to spare. He does not spend fast enough to have pleasure from it. He has the crime of prodigality, and the wretchedness of parsimony. If a man is killed in a duel, he is killed as many a one has been killed; but it is a sad thing for a man to lie down and die; to bleed to death, because he has not fortitude enough to sear the wound, or even to stitch it up."

On Saturday, April 25, I dined with him at Sir Joshua Reynolds's, with the learned Dr. Musgrave, Counsellor Leland of Ireland, son to the historian, Mrs. Cholmondeley, and some more ladies. "The Project," a new poem, was read to the company by Dr. Musgrave. JOHNSON: "Sir, it has no power. Were it not for the well-known names with which it is filled, it would be nothing: the names carry the poet, not the poet the names." MUSGRAVE: "A temporary poem always entertains us." JOHNSON: "So does an account of the criminals hanged yesterday entertain us."

He proceeded:—"Demosthenes Taylor, as he was called, (that is, the Editor of Demosthenes,) was the most silent man, the merest statue of a man that I have ever seen. I once dined in company with him, and all he said during the whole time was no more than *Richard*. How a man should say only Richard, it is not easy to imagine. But it was thus: Dr. Douglas was talking of Dr. Zachary

Grey, and ascribing to him something that was written by Dr. Richard Grey. So, to correct him, Taylor said, (imitating his affected sententious emphasis and nod) '*Richard.*'"

I happened, I know not how, to say that a pamphlet meant a prose piece. JOHNSON: "No, Sir, A few sheets of poetry unbound are a pamphlet, as much as a few sheets of prose." MUSGRAVE: "A pamphlet may be understood to mean a poetical piece in Westminster-Hall, that is, in formal language; but in common language it is understood to mean prose." JOHNSON: (and here was one of the many instances of his knowing clearly and telling exactly how a thing is,) "A pamphlet is understood in common language to mean prose, only from this, that there is so much more prose written than poetry; as when we say a *book*, prose is understood for the same reason though a book may as well be in poetry as in prose. We understand what is most general, and we name what is less frequent."

We talked of a lady's verses on Ireland. MISS REYNOLDS: "Have you seen them, Sir?" JOHNSON: "No, Madam, I have seen a translation from Horace, by one of her daughters. She shewed it me." MISS REYNOLDS: "And how was it, Sir?" JOHNSON: "Why, very well for a young Miss's verses;—that is to say, compared with excellence, nothing; but, very well for the person who wrote them. I am vexed at being shewn verses in that manner." MISS REYNOLDS: "But if they should be good, why not give them hearty praise?" JOHNSON: "Why, Madam, because I have not then got the better of my bad humour from having been shewn them. You must consider, Madam; before-hand they may be bad as well as good. Nobody has a right to put another under such a difficulty, that he must either hurt the person by telling the truth, or hurt himself by telling what is not true." BOSWELL: "A man often shews his writings to people of eminence, to obtain from them, either from their good-nature, or from their not being able to tell the truth firmly, a commendation, of which he may afterwards avail himself." JOHNSON: "Very true, Sir. Therefore, the man, who is asked by an authour what he thinks of his work, is put to the torture, and is not obliged to speak the truth; so that what he says is not considered as his opinion; yet he has said it, and cannot retract it; and this authour, when mankind are hunting him with a cannister at his tail, can say, 'I would not have published, had not Johnson, or Reynolds, or Musgrave, or some other good judge commended the work.' Yet I consider it as a very difficult question in conscience, whether one should advise a man not to publish a work, if profit be his object; for the man may say, 'Had it not been for you, I should have had the money.' Now you cannot be sure; for you have only your own opinion, and the publick may think very differently." SIR JOSHUA REYNOLDS: "You must upon such an occasion have two judgements; one as to the real value of the work, the other as to what may please the general taste at the time." JOHNSON: "But you can be *sure* of neither; and therefore I should scruple much to give a suppressive vote. Both Goldsmith's comedies were once refused; his first by Garrick, his second by Colman, who was prevailed on at last by much solicitation, nay, a kind of force, to bring it on. His *Vicar of Wakefield* I myself did not think would have had much success. It was written and sold to a bookseller, before his *Traveller*; but published after; so little expectation had the bookseller from it. Had it been sold after the *Traveller*, he might have had twice as much money for it, though sixty guineas was no mean price. The bookseller had the advantage of Goldsmith's reputation from *The Traveller* in the sale, though Goldsmith had it not in selling the copy."

His friend, Edward Cave, having been mentioned, he told us, "Cave used to sell ten thousand of *The Gentleman's Magazine*; yet such was then his minute attention and anxiety that the sale should not suffer the smallest decrease, that he would name a particular person who he heard had talked of leaving off the *Magazine*, and would say, 'Let us have something good next month.'"

It was observed, that avarice was inherent in some dispositions. JOHNSON: "No man was born a miser, because no man was born to possession. Every man is born *cupidus*—desirous of getting; but not *avarus*—desirous of keeping." BOSWELL: "I have heard old Mr. Sheridan maintain, with much ingenuity, that a complete miser is a happy man; a miser who gives himself wholly to the one passion of saving." JOHNSON: "That is flying in the face of all the world, who have called an avaricious man a *miser*, because he is miserable. No, Sir, a man who both spends and saves money is the happiest man, because he has both enjoyments."

He observed, "A man cannot with propriety speak of himself, except he relates simple facts; as, 'I was at Richmond:' or what depends on mensuration; as, 'I am six feet high.' He is sure he has been at Richmond; he is sure he is six feet high: but he cannot be sure he is wise, or that he has any other excellence. Then, all censure of a man's self is oblique praise. It is in order to shew how much he can spare. It has all the invidiousness of self-praise, and all the reproach of falsehood. BOSWELL: "Sometimes it may proceed from a man's strong consciousness of his faults being observed. He knows that others would throw him down, and therefore he had better lie down softly of his own accord."

On Tuesday, April 28, he was engaged to dine at General Paoli's.

At General Paoli's were Sir Joshua Reynolds, Mr. Langton, Marchese Gherardi of Lombardy, and Mr. John Spottiswoode the younger, of Spottiswoode, the solicitor. At this time fears of an invasion were circulated; to obviate which, Mr. Spottiswoode observed, that Mr. Fraser the engineer, who had lately come from Dunkirk, said, that the French had the same fears of us. JOHNSON: "It is thus that mutual cowardice keeps us in peace. Were one-half of mankind brave, and one-half cowards, the brave would be always beating the cowards. Were all brave, they would lead a very uneasy life; all would be continually fighting: but being all cowards, we go on very well."

We talked of drinking wine. JOHNSON: "I require wine, only when I am alone. I have then often wished for it, and often taken it." SPOTTISWOODE: "What, by way of a companion, Sir?" JOHNSON: "To get rid of myself, to send myself away. Wine gives great pleasure; and every pleasure is of itself a good. It is a good, unless counterbalanced by evil. A man may have a strong reason not to drink wine; and that may be greater than the pleasure. Wine makes a man better pleased with himself. I do not say that it makes him more pleasing to others. Sometimes it does. But the danger is, that while a man grows better pleased with himself, he may be growing less pleasing to others. Wine gives a man nothing. It neither gives him knowledge nor wit; it only animates a man, and enables him to bring out what a dread of the company has repressed. It only puts in motion what has been locked up in frost. But this may be good, or it may be bad." SPOTTISWOODE: "So, Sir, wine is a key which opens a box; but this box may be either full or empty?" JOHNSON: "Nay, Sir, conversation is the key: wine is a pick-lock, which forces open the box, and injures it. A man should cultivate his mind so as to have that confidence and readiness without wine, which wine gives." BOSWELL: "The great difficulty of resisting wine is from benevolence. For instance, a good worthy man asks you to taste his wine, which he has had twenty years in his cellar."

JOHNSON: "Sir, all this notion about benevolence arises from a man's imagining himself to be of more importance to others, than he really is. They don't care a farthing whether he drinks wine or not." SIR JOSHUA REYNOLDS: "Yes, they do for the time." JOHNSON: "For the time!—if they care this minute, they forget it the next. And as for the good worthy man; how do you know he is good and worthy? No good and worthy man will insist upon another man's drinking wine. As to the wine twenty years in the cellar,—of ten men, three say this, merely because they must say something; three are telling a lie, when they say they have had the wine twenty years;—three would rather save the wine;—one, perhaps, cares. I allow it is something to please one's company; and people are always pleased with those who partake pleasure with them. But after a man has brought himself to relinquish the great personal pleasure which arises from drinking wine, any other consideration is a trifle. To please others by drinking wine, is something only, if there be nothing against it. I should, however, be sorry to offend worthy men:

'Curst be the verse, how well so e'er it flow,
    That tends to make one worthy man my foe.'"

BOSWELL: "Curst be the *spring*, the *water*." JOHNSON: "But let us consider what a sad thing it would be, if we were obliged to drink or do any thing else that may happen to be agreeable to the company where we are." LANGTON: "By the same rule you must join with a gang of cut-purses." JOHNSON: "Yes, Sir: but yet we must do justice to wine; we must allow it the power it possesses. To make a man pleased with himself, let me tell you, is doing a very great thing;

Si patriae volumus, si NOBIS vivere cari."[1]

I was at this time myself a water-drinker, upon trial, by Johnson's recommendation. JOHNSON: "Boswell is a bolder combatant than Sir Joshua: he argues for wine without the help of wine; but Sir Joshua with it." SIR JOSHUA REYNOLDS: "But to please one's company is a strong motive." JOHNSON: (who, from drinking only water, supposed every body who drank wine to be elevated,) "I won't argue any more with you, Sir. You are too far gone." SIR JOSHUA: "I should have thought so indeed, Sir, had I made such a speech as you have now done." JOHNSON: (drawing himself in, and, I really thought blushing,) "Nay, don't be angry. I did not mean

[1] If we wish to be dear to our country, to ourselves.

233

to offend you." SIR JOSHUA: "At first the taste of wine was disagreeable to me; but I brought myself to drink it, that I might be like other people. The pleasure of drinking wine is so connected with pleasing your company, that altogether there is something of social goodness in it." JOHNSON: "Sir, this is only saying the same thing over again." SIR JOSHUA: "No, this is new." JOHNSON: "You put it in new words, but it is an old thought. This is one of the disadvantages of wine, it makes a man mistake words for thoughts." BOSWELL: "I think it is a new thought; at least, it is in a new *attitude*." JOHNSON: "Nay, Sir, it is only in a new coat; or an old coat with a new facing. (Then laughing heartily.) It is the old dog in a new doublet.—An extraordinary instance, however, may occur where a man's patron will do nothing for him, unless he will drink: *there* may be a good reason for drinking."

I mentioned a nobleman, who I believed was really uneasy, if his company would not drink hard. JOHNSON: "That is from having had people about him whom he has been accustomed to command." BOSWELL: "Supposing I should be *tête-à-tête* with him at table." JOHNSON: "Sir, there is no more reason for you drinking with *him*, than his being sober with *you*." BOSWELL: "Why, that is true; for it would do him less hurt to be sober, than it would do me to get drunk." JOHNSON: "Yes, Sir; and from what I have heard of him, one would not wish to sacrifice himself to such a man. If he must always have somebody to drink with him, he should buy a slave, and then he would be sure to have it. They who submit to drink as another pleases, make themselves his slaves." BOSWELL: "But, Sir, you will surely make allowance for the duty of hospitality. A gentleman who loves drinking, comes to visit me." JOHNSON: "Sir, a man knows whom he visits; he comes to the table of a sober man." BOSWELL: "But, Sir, you and I should not have been so well received in the Highlands and Hebrides, if I had not drunk with our worthy friends. Had I drunk water only as you did, they would not have been so cordial." JOHNSON: "Sir William Temple mentions, that in his travels through the Netherlands he had two or three gentlemen with him; and when a bumper was necessary, he put it on *them*. Were I to travel again through the islands, I would have Sir Joshua with me to take the bumpers." BOSWELL: "But, Sir, let me put a case. Suppose Sir Joshua should take a jaunt into Scotland; he does me the honour to pay me a visit at my house in the country; I am overjoyed at seeing him; we are quite by ourselves; shall I unsociably and churlishly let him sit drinking by himself? No, no, my dear Sir Joshua, you shall not be treated so, I *will* take a bottle with you."

On Wednesday, April 29, I dined with him at Mr. Allan Ramsay's, where were Lord Binning, Dr. Robertson the historian, Sir Joshua Reynolds, and the Honourable Mrs. Boscawen, widow of the Admiral, and mother of the present Viscount Falmouth.

RAMSAY: "I am old enough to have been a contemporary of Pope. His poetry was highly admired in his life-time, more a great deal than after his death." JOHNSON: "Sir, it has not been less admired since his death; no authours ever had so much fame in their own life-time as Pope and Voltaire; and Pope's poetry has been as much admired since his death as during his life; it has only not been as much talked of, but that is owing to its being now more distant, and people having other writings to talk of. Virgil is less talked of than Pope, and Homer is less talked of than Virgil; but they are not less admired. We must read what the world reads at the moment. It has been maintained that this superfetation, this teeming of the press in modern times, is prejudicial to good literature, because it obliges us to read so much of what is of inferiour value, in order to be in the fashion; so that better works are neglected for want of time, because a man will have more gratification of his vanity in conversation, from having read modern books, than from having read the best works of antiquity. But it must be considered that we have now more knowledge generally diffused; all our ladies read now, which is a great extension. Modern writers are the moons of literature; they shine with reflected light, with light borrowed from the ancients. Greece appears to me to be the fountain of knowledge; Rome of elegance." RAMSAY: "I suppose Homer's *Iliad* to be a collection of pieces which had been written before his time. I should like to see a translation of it in poetical prose, like the book of Ruth or Job." ROBERTSON: "Would you, Dr. Johnson, who are master of the English language, but try your hand upon a part of it." JOHNSON: "Sir, you could not read it without the pleasure of verse."

Dr. Robertson expatiated on the character of a certain nobleman; that he was one of the strongest-minded men that ever lived; that he would sit in company quite sluggish, while there was nothing to call forth his intellectual vigour; but the moment that any important subject was started, for instance, how this country is to be defended against a French invasion, he would rouse himself, and shew his extraordinary talents with the most powerful ability and animation. JOHNSON: "Yet this man cut his own throat. The true strong and sound mind is the mind that can embrace equally great things and small. Now I am told the King of Prussia will say to a servant, 'Bring me a bottle of such a wine, which came in such a year; it lies in such a corner of the cellars.' I would have a man great in great things, and elegant in little things." He said to me afterwards, when we were by ourselves, "Robertson was in a mighty romantick humour, he talked of one he did not know; but I *downed* him with the King of Prussia."—"Yes, Sir, (said I,) you threw a *bottle* at his head."

An ingenious gentleman was mentioned, concerning whom both Robertson and Ramsay agreed that he had a constant firmness of mind; for after a laborious day, and amidst a multiplicity of cares and anxieties, he would sit down with his sisters and be quite cheerful and good-humoured. Such a disposition, it was observed, was a happy gift of nature. JOHNSON: "I do not think so; a man has from nature a certain portion of mind; the use he makes of it depends upon his own free will. That a man has always the same firmness of mind, I do not say; because every man feels his mind less firm at one time than another; but I think, a man's being in a good or bad humour depends upon his will."

Johnson harangued against drinking wine. "A man (said he,) may choose whether he will have abstemiousness and knowledge, or claret and ignorance." Dr. Robertson, (who is very companionable,) was beginning to dissent as to the proscription of claret. JOHNSON: (with a placid smile,) "Nay, Sir, you shall not differ with me; as I have said that the man is most perfect who takes in the most things, I am for knowledge and claret." ROBERTSON: (holding a glass of generous claret in his hand,) "Sir, I can only drink your health." JOHNSON: "Sir, I should be sorry if *you* should be ever in such a state as to be able to do nothing more." ROBERTSON: "Dr. Johnson, allow me to say, that in one respect I have the advantage of you; when you were in Scotland you would not come to hear any of our preachers, whereas, when I am here, I attend your publick worship without scruple, and indeed with great satisfaction." JOHNSON: "Why, Sir, that is not so extraordinary: the King of Siam sent ambassadors to Louis the Fourteenth; but Louis the Fourteenth sent none to the King of Siam."

Here my friend for once discovered a want of knowledge or forgetfulness; for Louis the Fourteenth did send an embassy to the

King of Siam, and the Abbé Choisi, who was employed in it, published an account of it in two volumes.

Next day, Thursday, April 30, I found him at home by himself. JOHNSON: "Well, Sir, Ramsay gave us a splendid dinner. I love Ramsay. You will not find a man in whose conversation there is more instruction, more information, and more elegance, than in Ramsay's." BOSWELL: "What I admire in Ramsay, in his continuing to be so young." JOHNSON: "Why, yes, Sir; it is to be admired. I value myself upon this, that there is nothing of the old man in my conversation. I am now sixty-eight, and I have no more of it than at twenty-eight." BOSWELL: "But, Sir, would not you wish to know old age? He who is never an old man, does not know the whole of human life; for old age is one of the divisions of it." JOHNSON: "Nay, Sir, what talk is this?" BOSWELL: "I mean, Sir, the Sphinx's description of it;—morning, noon, and night. I would know night, as well as morning and noon." JOHNSON: "What, Sir, would you know what it is to feel the evils of old age? Would you have the gout? Would you have decrepitude?"

JOHNSON: "Mrs. Thrale's mother said of me what flattered me much. A clergyman was complaining of want of society in the country where he lived; and said, 'They talk of *runts*;' (that is, young cows.) 'Sir, (said Mrs. Salusbury,) Mr. Johnson would learn to talk of runts;' meaning that I was a man who would make the most of my situation, whatever it was." He added, "I think myself a very polite man."

On Saturday, May 2, I dined with him at Sir Joshua Reynolds's, where there was a very large company and a great deal of conversation; but owing to some circumstances which I cannot now recollect, I have no record of any part of it, except that there were several people there by no means of the Johnsonian school; so that less attention was paid to him than usual, which put him out of humour; and upon some imaginary offence from me, he attacked me with such rudeness, that I was vexed and angry, because it gave those persons an opportunity of enlarging upon his supposed ferocity, and ill-treatment of his best friends. I was so much hurt, and had my pride so much roused, that I kept away from him for a week; and perhaps, might have kept away much longer, nay, gone to Scotland without seeing him again, had not we fortunately met and been reconciled. To such unhappy chances are human friendships liable.

On Friday, May 8, I dined with him at Mr. Langton's. I was

237

reserved and silent, which I suppose he perceived, and might recollect the cause. After dinner, when Mr. Langton was called out of
the room, and we were by ourselves, he drew his chair near to mine,
and said in a tone of conciliating courtesy, "Well, how have you
done?" BOSWELL: "Sir, you have made me very uneasy by your
behaviour to me when we last were at Sir Joshua Reynolds's.
You know, my dear Sir, no man has a greater respect and affection
for you, or would sooner go to the end of the world to serve you.
Now to treat me so———" He insisted that I had interrupted
him, which I assured him was not the case; and proceeded—"But
why treat me so before people who neither love you nor me?"
JOHNSON: "Well, I am sorry for it. I'll make it up to you twenty
different ways, as you please." BOSWELL: "I said to-day to Sir
Joshua, when he observed that you *tossed* me sometimes—I don't
care how often, or how high he tosses me, when only friends are
present, for then I fall upon soft ground: but I do not like falling
on stones, which is the case when enemies are present.—I think this
a pretty good image, Sir." JOHNSON: "Sir, it is one of the happiest
I have ever heard."

When Mr. Langton returned to us, the "flow of talk" went on.
An eminent authour being mentioned;—JOHNSON: "He is not a
pleasant man. His conversation is neither instructive nor brilliant.
He does not talk as if impelled by any fulness of knowledge or
vivacity of imagination. His conversation is like that of any other
sensible man. He talks with no wish either to inform or to hear,
but only because he thinks it does not become —— —— to sit in a
company and say nothing."

Mr. Langton having repeated the anecdote of Addison having
distinguished between his powers in conversation and in writing,
by saying, "I have only nine-pence in my pocket; but I can draw
for a thousand pounds;"—JOHNSON: "He had not that retort
ready, Sir; he had prepared it beforehand." LANGTON: (turning
to me,) "A fine surmise. Set a thief to catch a thief."

Johnson called the East-Indians barbarians. BOSWELL: "You will
except the Chinese, Sir?" JOHNSON: "No, Sir." BOSWELL: "Have
they not arts?" JOHNSON: "They have pottery." BOSWELL: "What
do you say to the written characters of their language?" JOHNSON:
"Sir, they have not an alphabet. They have not been able to form
what all other nations have formed." BOSWELL: "There is more
learning in their language than in any other, from the immense
number of their characters." JOHNSON: "It is only more difficult

238

from its rudeness; as there is more labour in hewing down a tree with a stone than with an axe."

On Saturday, May 9, we dined by ourselves at the Mitre, according to old custom. There was, on these occasions, a little circumstance of kind attention to Mrs. Williams, which must not be omitted. Before coming out, and leaving her to dine alone, he gave her her choice of a chicken, a sweetbread, or any other little nice thing, which was carefully sent to her from the tavern ready-drest.

Our conversation to-day, I know not how, turned, I think, for the only time at any length, during our long acquaintance, upon the sensual intercourse between the sexes, the delight of which he ascribed chiefly to imagination. "Were it not for imagination, Sir, (said he,) a man would be as happy in the arms of a Chambermaid as of a Duchess. But such is the adventitious charm of fancy, that we find men who have violated the best principles of society, and ruined their fame and their fortune, that they might possess a woman of rank." It would not be proper to record the particulars of such a conversation in moments of unreserved frankness, when nobody was present on whom it could have any hurtful effect.

"From grave to gay, from lively to severe,"—we were soon engaged in very different speculation; humbly and reverently considering and wondering at the universal mystery of all things, as our imperfect faculties can now judge of them. "There are (said he) innumerable questions to which the inquisitive mind can in this state receive no answer: Why do you and I exist? Why was this world created? Since it was to be created, why was it not created sooner?"

On May the 13th, at Mrs. Thrale's, at Streatham, talking of divorces, I asked if Othello's doctrine was not plausible:

"He that is robb'd, not wanting what is stolen,
    Let him not know't, and he's not robbed at all."

Dr. Johnson and Mrs. Thrale joined against this. JOHNSON: "Ask any man if he'd wish not to know of such an injury." BOSWELL: "Would you tell your friend to make him unhappy?" JOHNSON: "Perhaps, Sir, I should not; but that would be from prudence on my own account. A man would tell his father." BOSWELL: "Yes; because he would not have spurious children to get any share of the family inheritance." MRS. THRALE: "Or he would tell his brother." BOSWELL: "Certainly, his *elder* brother." JOHNSON: "You would tell your friend of a woman's infamy, to prevent his marrying a whore: there is the same reason to tell him of his wife's infidelity when he is married, to prevent the consequences of imposition. It is a breach of confidence not to tell a friend." BOSWELL: "Would you tell Mr.——?" (naming a gentleman who assuredly was not in the least danger of such a miserable disgrace, though married to a fine woman.) JOHNSON: "No, Sir; because it would do no good; he is so sluggish, he'd never go to parliament and get through a divorce."

He said of one of our friends, "He is ruining himself without pleasure. A man who loses at play, or who runs out his fortune at court, makes his estate less, in hopes of making it bigger: (I am sure of this word, which was often used by him:) but it is a sad thing to pass through the quagmire of parsimony, to the gulph of ruin. To pass over the flowery path of extravagance, is very well."

Amongst the numerous prints pasted on the walls of the dining-room at Streatham, was Hogarth's "Modern Midnight Conversation." I asked him what he knew of Parson Ford, who makes a conspicuous figure in the riotous group. JOHNSON: "Sir, he was my acquaintance and relation, my mother's nephew. He had purchased a living in the country, but not simoniacally. I never saw him but in the country. I have been told he was a man of great parts; very profligate, but I never heard he was impious." BOSWELL: "Was there not a story of his ghost having appeared?" JOHNSON: "Sir, it was believed. A waiter at the Hummums, in which house Ford died, had been absent for some time, and returned, not knowing that Ford was dead. Going down to the cellar, according to the story, he met him; going down again, he met him a second time. When he came up he asked some of the people of the house what Ford could be doing there. They told him Ford was dead. The waiter took a fever, in which he lay for some time. When he recovered, he said he had a message to deliver to some women from Ford; but he was not to tell what, or to whom. He walked out; he was followed; but somewhere about St. Paul's they lost him. He came back, and said he had delivered the message, and the women exclaimed, 'Then we are all undone!' Dr. Pellet, who was not a credulous man, inquired into the truth of this story, and he said, the evidence was irresistible. My wife went to the Hummums; (it is a place where people get themselves cupped.) I believe she went with intention to hear about this story of Ford. At first they were unwilling to tell her; but, after they had talked to her, she came away satisfied that it was true. To be sure, the man had a fever; and this vision may have been the beginning of it. But if the message to the women, and their behaviour upon it, were true as related, there was something supernatural. That rests upon his word; and there it remains."

After Mrs. Thrale was gone to bed, Johnson and I sat up late. We resumed Sir Joshua Reynolds's argument on the preceding Sunday, that a man would be virtuous, though he had no other motive than to preserve his character. JOHNSON: "Sir, it is not true; for as to this world, vice does not hurt a man's character." BOSWELL: "Yes, Sir, debauching a friend's wife will." JOHNSON: "No, Sir. Who thinks the worse of —— for it?" BOSWELL: "Lord —— was not his friend." JOHNSON: "That is only a circumstance, Sir; a slight distinction. He could not get into the house but by Lord ——. A man is chosen Knight of the shire, not the less for having debauched ladies." BOSWELL: "What, Sir, if he debauched the ladies of gentlemen in the county, will not there be a general resentment against him?" JOHNSON: "No, Sir. He will lose those particular gentlemen; but the rest will not trouble their heads about it," (warmly). BOSWELL: "Well, Sir, I cannot think so." JOHNSON: "Nay, Sir, there is no talking with a man who will dispute what every body knows, (angrily.) Don't you know this?" BOSWELL: "No, Sir; and I wish to think better of your country than you represent it. I knew in Scotland a gentleman obliged to leave it for debauching a lady; and in one of our counties an Earl's brother lost his election, because he had debauched the lady of another Earl in that county, and destroyed the peace of a noble family."

Still he would not yield, He proceeded: "Will you not allow, Sir, that vice does not hurt a man's character so as to obstruct his prosperity in life, when you know that —— was loaded with wealth and honours; a man who had acquired his fortune by such crimes, that his consciousness of them impelled him to cut his own throat?" BOSWELL: "You will recollect, Sir, that Dr. Robertson said, he cut his throat because he was weary of still life; little things not being sufficient to move his great mind." JOHNSON: (very angry,) "Nay, Sir, what stuff is this? You had no more this opinion after Robertson said it, than before. I know nothing more offensive than repeating what one knows to be foolish things, by way of continuing a dispute, to see what a man will answer,—to make him your butt!" (angrier still.) BOSWELL: "My dear Sir, I had no such intention as you seem to suspect; I had not indeed. Might not this nobleman have felt every thing 'weary, stale, flat, and unprofitable,' as Hamlet says?" JOHNSON: "Nay, if you are to bring in gabble, I'll talk no more. I will not, upon my honour."—My readers will decide upon this dispute.

I staid all next day with him at Streatham. He talked a great deal in very good humour.

Looking at Messrs. Dilly's splendid edition of Lord Chesterfield's miscellaneous works, he laughed, and said, "Here are now two speeches ascribed to him, both of which were written by me: and the best of it is, they have found out that one of them is like Demosthenes, and the other like Cicero."

He censured Lord Kames's *Sketches of the History of Man*, for misrepresenting Clarendon's account of the appearance of Sir George Villiers's ghost, as if Clarendon were weakly credulous; when the truth is, that Clarendon only says, that the story was upon a better foundation of credit, than usually such discourses are founded upon; nay, speaks thus of the person who was reported to have seen the vision, "the poor man, *if he had been at all waking;*" which Lord Kames has omitted. He added, "in this book it is maintained that virtue is natural to man, and, that if we would but consult our own hearts, we should be virtuous. Now after consulting our own hearts all we can, and with all the helps we have, we find how few of us are virtuous. This is saying a thing which all mankind know not to be true." BOSWELL: "Is not modesty natural?" JOHNSON: "I cannot say, Sir, as we find no people quite in a state of nature; but I think the more they are taught, the more modest they are. The French are a gross, ill-bred, untaught people; a lady there will spit on the floor and rub it with her foot. What I gained by being in France was, learning to be better satisfied with my own country. Time may be employed to more advantage from nineteen to twenty-four, almost in any way than in travelling; when you set travelling against mere negation, against doing nothing, it is better to be sure; but how much more would a young man improve were he to study during those years. Indeed, if a young man is wild, and must run after women and bad company, it is better this should be done abroad, as, on his return, he can break off such connections, and begin at home a new man, with a character to form, and acquaintances to make. How little does travelling supply to the conversation of any man who has travelled; how little to Beauclerk?" BOSWELL: "What say you to Lord ——?" JOHNSON: "I never but once heard him talk of what he had seen, and that was of a large serpent in one of the Pyramids of Egypt." BOSWELL: "Well, I happened to hear him tell the same thing, which made me mention him."

I talked of a country life.—JOHNSON: "Were I to live in the country, I would not devote myself to the acquisition of popularity; I would live in a much better way, much more happily. I would have my time at my own command." BOSWELL: "But, Sir, is it not a sad thing to be at a distance from all our literary friends?" JOHNSON: "Sir, you will by and by have enough of this conversation, which now delights you so much."

As he was a zealous friend of subordination, he was at all times watchful to suppress the vulgar cant against the manners of the great; "High people, Sir, (said he,) are the best; take a hundred ladies of quality, you'll find them better wives, better mothers, more willing to sacrifice their own pleasures to their children, than a hundred other women. Tradeswomen (I mean the wives of tradesmen) in the city, who are worth from ten to fifteen thousand pounds, are the worst creatures upon the earth, grossly ignorant, and thinking viciousness fashionable. Farmers, I think, are often worthless fellows. Few lords will cheat; and, if they do, they'll be ashamed of it: farmers cheat and are not ashamed of it: they have all the sensual vices too of the nobility, with cheating into the bargain. There is as much fornication and adultery amongst farmers as amongst noblemen." BOSWELL: "The notion of the world, Sir, however, is, that the morals of women of quality are worse than those in lower stations." JOHNSON: "Yes, Sir, the licentiousness of one woman of quality makes more noise than that of a number of women in lower stations; then, Sir, you are to consider the malignity of women in the city against women of quality, which will make them believe any thing of them, such as that they call their coachmen to bed. No, Sir, so far as I have observed, the higher in rank, the richer ladies are, they are the better instructed, and the more virtuous."

On Sunday, May 17, I presented to him Mr. Fullarton, of Fullarton.

He said, "Lord Chatham was a Dictator; he possessed the power of putting the State in motion; now there is no power all order is relaxed." BOSWELL: "Is there no hope of a change to the better?" JOHNSON: "Why, yes, Sir, when we are weary of this relaxation. So the City of London will appoint its Mayors again by seniority." BOSWELL: "But is not that taking a mere chance for having a good or a bad Mayor?" JOHNSON: "Yes, Sir; but the evil of competition is greater than that of the worst Mayor that can come; besides, there is no more reason to suppose that the choice of a rabble will be right, than that chance will be right."

On Tuesday, May 19, I was to set out for Scotland in the evening. He was engaged to dine with me at Mr. Dilly's; I waited upon him to remind him of his appointment and attend him thither; he gave me some salutary counsel, and recommended vigorous resolution against any deviation from moral duty. BOSWELL: "But you would not have me to bind myself by a solemn obligation?" JOHNSON: (much agitated,) "What! a vow—O, no, Sir, a vow is a horrible thing, it is a snare for sin. The man who cannot go to heaven without a vow—may go——" Here, standing erect, in the middle of his library, and rolling grand, his pause was truly a curious compound of the solemn and the ludicrous; he half-whistled in his usual way, when pleasant, and he paused, as if checked by religious awe.—Methought he would have added—to Hell—but was restrained. I humoured the dilemma. "What! Sir, (said I,) 'In cælum jusseris ibit?'[1]" alluding to his imitation of it,

> ' And bid him go to Hell, to Hell he goes.'

My illustrious friend and I parted with assurances of affectionate regard.

[1] He will go to the sky if you order him to.

CHAPTER X

In Seventeen Seventy-nine

I ARRIVED in London on Monday, March 15, 1779, and next morning at a late hour, found Dr. Johnson sitting over his tea, attended by Mrs. Desmoulins, Mr. Levett, and a clergyman, who had come to submit some poetical pieces to his revision. It is wonderful what a number and variety of writers, some of them even unknown to him, prevailed on his good-nature to look over their works, and suggest corrections and improvements. My arrival interrupted for a little while the important business of this true representative of Bayes; upon its being resumed, I found that the subject under immediate consideration was a translation, yet in manuscript, of the *Carmen Seculare* of Horace, which had this year been set to musick, and performed as a publick entertainment in London, for the joint benefit of Monsieur Philidor and Signor Baretti. When Johnson had done reading, the authour asked him bluntly, "If upon the whole it was a good translation?" Johnson, whose regard for truth was uncommonly strict, seemed to be puzzled for a moment, what answer to make; as he certainly could not honestly commend the performance: with exquisite address he evaded the question thus, "Sir, I do not say that it may not be made a very good translation." Here nothing whatever in favour of the performance was affirmed, and yet the writer was not shocked. A printed "Ode to the Warlike Genius of Britain" came next in review; the bard was a lank bony figure, with short black hair; he was writhing himself in agitation, while Johnson read, and shewing his teeth in a grin of earnestness, exclaimed in broken sentences, and in a keen sharp tone, "Is that poetry, Sir?—Is it Pindar?" JOHNSON: "Why, Sir, there is here a great deal of what is called poetry." Then turning to me the poet cried "My muse has not been long upon the town, and (pointing to the Ode) it trembles under the hand of the great critick." Johnson, in a tone of displeasure asked him, "Why do you praise Anson?" I did not trouble him by asking his reason for this question. He proceeded, "Here is an errour, Sir; you have made Genius feminine."—"Palpable, Sir;

(cried the enthusiast) I know it. But (in a lower tone) it was to pay a compliment to the Duchess of Devonshire, with which her Grace was pleased. She is walking across Coxheath, in the military uniform, and I suppose her to be the Genius of Britain." JOHNSON: "Sir, you are giving a reason for it; but that will not make it right. You may have a reason why two and two should make five; but they will still make but four."

Although I was several times with him in the course of the following days, such it seems were my occupations, or such my negligence, that I have preserved no memorial of his conversation till Friday, March 26, when I visited him. He said he expected to be attacked on account of his *Lives of the Poets*, "However (said he) I would rather be attacked than unnoticed. For the worst thing you can do to an authour is to be silent as to his works. An assault upon a town is a bad thing; but starving it is still worse; an assault may be unsuccessful, you may have more men killed than you kill; but if you starve the town, you are sure of victory."

Talking of a friend of ours associating with persons of very discordant principles and characters; I said he was a very universal man, quite a man of the world. JOHNSON: "Yes, Sir; but one may be so much a man of the world, as to be nothing in the world. I remember a passage in Goldsmith's *Vicar of Wakefield*, which he was afterwards fool enough to expunge: 'I do not love a man who is zealous for nothing.'" BOSWELL: "That was a fine passage." JOHNSON: "Yes, Sir: there was another fine passage too, which he struck out: 'When I was a young man, being anxious to distinguish myself, I was perpetually starting new propositions. But I soon gave this over; for, I found that generally what was new was false.'" I said I did not like to sit with people of whom I had not a good opinion. JOHNSON: "But you must not indulge your delicacy too much; or you will be a *tête-à-tête* man all your life."

During my stay in London this spring, I find I was unaccountably negligent in preserving Johnson's sayings, more so than at any time when I was happy enough to have an opportunity of hearing his wisdom and wit. I, therefore, in some instances, can only exhibit a few detached fragments.

Talking of the wonderful concealment of the authour of the celebrated letters signed *Junius*, he said, "I should have believed Burke to be Junius, because I know no man but Burke who is capable of writing these letters; but Burke spontaneously denied it to me. The case would have been different, had I asked him if he

246

was the authour; a man so questioned, as to an anonymous publication, may think he has a right to deny it."

On Saturday, April 3, I visited him at night, and found him sitting in Mrs. Williams's room, with her, and one whom he afterwards told me was a natural son of the second Lord Southwell. The table had a singular appearance, being covered with a heterogeneous assemblage of oysters and porter for his company, and tea for himself. I mentioned my having heard an eminent physician, who was himself a Christian, argue in favour of universal toleration, and maintain, that no man could be hurt by another man's differing from him in opinion. JOHNSON: "Sir, you are to a certain degree hurt by knowing that even one man does not believe."

On Wednesday, April 7, I dined with him at Sir Joshua Reynolds's. I have not marked what company was there. Johnson harangued upon the qualities of different liquors; and spoke with great contempt of claret, as so weak, that "a man would be drowned by it before it made him drunk." He was persuaded to drink one glass of it, that he might judge, not from recollection, which might be dim, but from immediate sensation. He shook his head, and said, "Poor stuff! No, Sir, claret is the liquor for boys; port for men; but he who aspires to be a hero (smiling) must drink brandy. In the first place, the flavour of brandy is most grateful to the palate; and then brandy will do soonest for a man what drinking *can* do for him. There are, indeed, few who are able to drink brandy. That is a power rather to be wished for than attained. And yet, (proceeded he) as in all pleasure hope is a considerable part, I know not but fruition comes too quick by brandy. Florence wine I think the worst; it is wine only to the eye; it is wine neither while you are drinking it, nor after you have drunk it; it neither pleases the taste, nor exhilarates the spirits." I reminded him how heartily he and I used to drink wine together, when we were first acquainted; and how I used to have a head-ache after sitting up with him. He did not like to have this recalled, or, perhaps, thinking that I boasted improperly, resolved to have a witty stroke at me: "Nay, Sir, it was not the *wine* that made your head ache, but the *sense* that I put into it." BOSWELL: "What, Sir! will sense make the head ache?" JOHNSON: "Yes, Sir, (with a smile) when it is not used to it."

On Thursday, April 8, I dined with him at Mr. Allan Ramsay's, with Lord Graham, and some other company. We talked of Shakespeare's witches. JOHNSON: "They are beings of his own creation; they are a compound of malignity and meanness, without any abilities: and are quite different from the Italian magicians. King James says in his *Dæmonology* 'Magicians command the devils: witches are their servants.' The Italian magicians are elegant beings." RAMSAY: "Opera witches, not Drury-lane witches." —Johnson observed, that abilities might be employed in a narrow sphere, as in getting money, which he said he believed no man could do, without vigorous parts, though concentrated to a point. RAMSAY: "Yes, like a strong horse in a mill; he pulls better."

Lord Graham, while he praised the beauty of Loch-lomond, on the banks of which is his family seat, complained of the climate, and said he could not bear it. JOHNSON: "Nay, my Lord, don't talk so: you may bear it well enough. Your ancestors have borne it more years than I can tell."

Lord Graham commended Dr. Drummond at Naples as a man of extraordinary talents; and added, that he had a great love of liberty. JOHNSON: "He is *young*, my Lord; (looking at his Lordship with an arch smile) all *boys* love liberty, till experience convinces them they are not so fit to govern themselves as they imagined. We are all agreed as to our own liberty; we would have as much of it as we can get, but we are not agreed as to the liberty of others: for in proportion as we take, others must lose. I believe we hardly wish that the mob should have liberty to govern us. When that was the case some time ago, no man was at liberty not to have candles in his windows." RAMSAY: "The result is, that order is better than confusion." JOHNSON: "The result is, that order cannot be had but by subordination."

On Friday, April 16, I had been present at the trial of the unfortunate Mr. Hackman, who, in a fit of frantick jealous love, had shot Miss Ray, the favourite of a nobleman.

This day a violent altercation arose between Johnson and Beauclerk, which having made much noise at the time, I think it proper, in order to prevent any future misrepresentation, to give a minute account of it.

In talking of Hackman, Johnson argued, as Judge Blackstone had done, that his being furnished with two pistols was a proof that he meant to shoot two persons. Mr. Beauclerk said, "No; for that every wise man who intended to shoot himself, took two pistols, that he might be sure of doing it at once. Lord ——'s cook shot himself with one pistol, and lived ten days in great agony. Mr. ——, who loved buttered muffins, but durst not eat them because they disagreed with his stomach, resolved to shoot himself; and then he eat three buttered muffins for breakfast, before shooting himself, knowing that he should not be troubled with indigestion; *he* had two charged pistols; one was found lying charged upon the table by him, after he had shot himself with the other."—"Well, (said Johnson, with an air of triumph,) you see here one pistol was sufficient." Beauclerk replied smartly, "Because it happened to kill him." And either then or a very little afterwards, being piqued at Johnson's triumphant remark, added, "This is what you don't know, and I do." There was then a cessation of the dispute; and some minutes intervened, during which, dinner and the glass went on cheerfully; when Johnson suddenly and abruptly exclaimed, "Mr. Beauclerk, how came you to talk so petulantly to me, as 'This is what you don't know, but what I know?' One thing *I* know, which *you* don't seem to know, that you are very uncivil." BEAUCLERK: "Because *you* began by being uncivil, (which you always are.)" The words in parentheses were, I believe, not heard by Dr. Johnson. Here again there was a cessation of arms. Johnson told me, that the reason why he waited at first some time without taking any notice of what Mr. Beauclerk said, was because he was thinking whether he should resent it. But when he considered that there were present a young Lord and an eminent traveller, two men of the world with whom he had never dined before, he was apprehensive that they might think they had a right to take such liberties with him as Beauclerk did, and therefore resolved he would not let it pass; adding, "that he would not appear a coward." A little while after this, the conversation turned on the violence of Hackman's temper. Johnson then said, "It was his business to *command* his temper, as my friend, Mr. Beauclerk, should have done some time ago." BEAUCLERK: "I should learn of *you*, Sir." JOHNSON: "Sir, you have given *me* opportunities enough of learning, when I have been in *your* company. No man loves to be treated with contempt." BEAUCLERK: (with a polite inclination towards Johnson:) "Sir, you have known me twenty years, and however I may have treated others, you may be sure I could never treat you with contempt." JOHNSON: "Sir, you have said more than was necessary." Thus it ended; and Beauclerk's coach not having come for him till very late, Dr. Johnson and another gentleman sat with him a long time after the rest of the company were gone; and he and I dined at Beauclerk's on the Saturday se'nnight following.

After this tempest had subsided, I recollect the following particulars of his conversation:

"I am always for getting a boy forward in his learning; for that is a sure good. I would let him at first read *any* English book which happens to engage his attention; because you have done a great deal, when you have brought him to have entertainment from a book. He'll get better books afterwards."

"Mallet, I believe, never wrote a single line of his projected life of the Duke of Marlborough. He groped for materials; and thought of it, till he had exhausted his mind. Thus it sometimes happens that men entangle themselves in their own schemes."

"To be contradicted, in order to force you to talk is mighty unpleasing. You *shine*, indeed; but it is by being *ground*."

Of a gentleman who made some figure among the *Literati* of his time (Mr. Fitzherbert,) he said, "What eminence he had was by a felicity of manner: he had no more learning than what he could not help."

On Saturday, April 24, I dined with him at Mr. Beauclerk's, with Sir Joshua Reynolds, Mr. Jones (afterwards Sir William,) Mr. Langton, Mr. Stevens, Mr. Paradise, and Dr. Higgins. I mentioned that Mr. Wilkes had attacked Garrick to me, as a man who had no friend. JOHNSON: "I believe he is right, Sir. Οἱ φίλοι, οὐ φίλος—He had friends, but no friend. Garrick was so diffused, he had no man to whom he wished to unbosom himself. He found people always ready to applaud him, and that always for the same thing: so he saw life with great uniformity." I took upon me, for once, to fight with Goliath's weapons, and play the sophist.— "Garrick did not need a friend, as he got from every body all he wanted. What is a friend? One who supports you and comforts you, while others do not. Friendship, you know, Sir, is the cordial drop, 'to make the nauseous draught of life go down:' but if the draught be not nauseous, if it be all sweet, there is no occasion for that drop." JOHNSON: "Many men would not be content to live so. I hope I should not. They would wish to have an intimate friend, with whom they might compare minds, and cherish private virtues." One of the company mentioned Lord Chesterfield, as a man who had no friend. JOHNSON: "There were more materials to make friendship in Garrick, had he not been so diffused." BOSWELL: "Garrick was pure gold, but beat out to thin leaf. Lord Chesterfield was tinsel." JOHNSON: "Garrick was a very good man, the cheerfulest man of his age; a decent liver in a profession which is supposed to give indulgence to licentiousness; and a man who gave away freely, money acquired by himself. He began the world with a great hunger for money; the son of a half-pay officer, bred in a family whose study was to make four-pence do as much as others made four-pence halfpenny do. But, when he had got money, he was very liberal." I presumed to animadvert on his eulogy on Garrick, in his *Lives of the Poets*. "You say, Sir, his death eclipsed the gaiety of nations." JOHNSON: "I could not have said more nor less. It is the truth; *eclipsed*, not *extinguished*; and his death *did* eclipse; it was like a storm." BOSWELL: "But why nations? Did his gaiety extend further than his own nation?" JOHNSON: "Why, Sir, some exaggeration must be allowed. Besides, nations may be said—if we allow the Scotch to be a nation, and to have gaiety,— which they have not. *You* are an exception, though. Come, gentle-men, let us candidly admit that there is one Scotchman who is cheerful." BEAUCLERK: "But he is a very unnatural Scotchman." I, however, continued to think the compliment to Garrick hyper-bolically untrue. His acting had ceased sometime before his death; at any rate he had acted in Ireland, but a short time, at an early period of his life, and never in Scotland. I objected also to what appears an anticlimax of praise, when contrasted with the preceding panegyrick,—"and diminished the publick stock of harmless pleasure!"—"Is not *harmless pleasure* very tame?" JOHNSON: "Nay, Sir, harmless pleasure is the highest praise. Pleasure is a word of dubious import; pleasure is in general dangerous, and pernicious to virtue; to be able therefore to furnish pleasure that is harmless, pleasure pure and unalloyed, is as great a power as man can possess." This was, perhaps, as ingenious a defence as could be made; still, however, I was not satisfied.

A celebrated wit being mentioned, he said, "One may say of him as was said of a French wit, *il n'a de l'esprit que contre Dieu*. I have been several times in company with him, but never perceived any strong power of wit. He produces a general effect by various means; he has a cheerful countenance and a gay voice. Besides, his trade is wit. It would be as wild in him to come into company without merriment, as for a highwayman to take the road without his pistols."

Talking of the effects of drinking, he said, "Drinking may be practised with great prudence; a man who exposes himself when he is intoxicated, has not the art of getting drunk; a sober man who happens occasionally to get drunk, readily enough goes into a new company, which a man who has been drinking should never do. Such a man will undertake any thing; he is without skill in inebriation. I used to slink home when I had drunk too much. A man accustomed to self-examination will be conscious when he is drunk, though an habitual drunkard will not be conscious of it. I knew a physician, who for twenty years was not sober; yet in a pamphlet, which he wrote upon fevers, he appealed to Garrick and me for his vindication from a charge of drunkenness. A bookseller (naming him) who got a large fortune by trade, was so habitually and equably drunk, that his most intimate friends never perceived that he was more sober at one time than another."

Talking of celebrated and successful irregular practisers in physick, he said, "Taylor was the most ignorant man I ever knew, but sprightly: Ward, the dullest. Taylor challenged me once to talk Latin with him; (laughing.) I quoted some of Horace, which he took to be a part of my own speech. He said a few words well enough." BEAUCLERK: "I remember, Sir, you said, that Taylor was an instance how far impudence could carry ignorance."— Mr. Beauclerk was very entertaining this day, and told us a number of short stories in a lively elegant manner, and with that air of *the world* which has I know not what impressive effect, as if there were something more than is expressed, or than perhaps we could perfectly understand. As Johnson and I accompanied Sir Joshua Reynolds in his coach, Johnson said, "There is in Beauclerk a predominance over his company, that one does not like. But he is a man who has lived so much in the world, that he has a short story on every occasion; he is always ready to talk, and is never exhausted."

On May 3rd I set out for Scotland.

CHAPTER XI

Further Conversations in Seventeen Seventy-nine

On MONDAY, October 4, 1779, I called at his house before he was up. He sent for me to his bedside, and expressed his satisfaction at this incidental meeting with as much vivacity as if he had been in the gaiety of youth. He called briskly, "Frank, go and get coffee, and let us breakfast *in splendour.*"

On Sunday, October 10, we dined together at Mr. Strahan's. The conversation having turned on the prevailing practice of going to the East-Indies in quest of wealth;—JOHNSON: "A man had better have ten thousand pounds at the end of ten years passed in England, than twenty thousand pounds at the end of ten years passed in India, because you must compute what you *give* for money; and a man who has lived ten years in India, has given up ten years of social comfort and all those advantages which arise from living in England. The ingenious Mr. Brown, distinguished by the name of *Capability Brown,* told me, that he was once at the seat of Lord Clive, who had returned from India with great wealth; and that he shewed him at the door of his bed-chamber a large chest, which he said he had once had full of gold; upon which Brown observed, 'I am glad you can bear it so near your bed-chamber.'"

We talked of the state of the poor in London.—JOHNSON: "Saunders Welch, the Justice, who was once High-Constable of Holborn, and had the best opportunities of knowing the state of the poor, told me that I under-rated the number, when I computed that twenty a week, that is, above a thousand a year, died of hunger; not absolutely of immediate hunger; but of the wasting and other diseases which are the consequences of hunger. This happens only in so large a place as London, where people are not known. What we are told about the great sums got by begging, is not true: the trade is overstocked. And, you may depend upon it, there are many who cannot get work. A particular kind of manufacture fails: those who have been used to work at it, can for some time, work at nothing else. You meet a man begging; you charge him with idleness: he says, 'I am willing to labour. Will you give me work?'

—'I cannot.'—'Why then you have no right to charge me with idleness.'"

I went home with him, and we had a long quiet conversation.

BOSWELL: "Why, Sir, do people play this trick which I observe now, when I look at your grate, putting the shovel against it to make the fire burn?" JOHNSON: "They play the trick, but it does not make the fire burn. *There* is a better; (setting the poker perpendicularly up at right angles with the grate.) In days of superstition they thought, as it made a cross with the bars, it would drive away the witch."

BOSWELL: "By associating with you, Sir, I am always getting an accession of wisdom. But perhaps a man, after knowing his own character—the limited strength of his own mind, should not be desirous of having too much wisdom, considering, *quid valeant humeri*, how little he can carry." JOHNSON: "Sir, be as wise as you can; let a man be *aliis lætus, sapiens sibi*:[1]

> 'Though pleas'd to see the dolphins play,
> I mind my compass and my way.'

You may be wise in your study in the morning, and gay in company at a tavern in the evening. Every man is to take care of his own wisdom and his own virtue, without minding too much what others think."

I mentioned to him a dispute between a friend of mine and his lady, concerning conjugal infidelity, which my friend had maintained was by no means so bad in the husband, as in the wife.

JOHNSON: "Your friend was in the right, Sir. Between a man and his Maker it is a different question; but between a man and his wife, a husband's infidelity is nothing. They are connected by children, by fortune, by serious considerations of community. Wise married women don't trouble themselves about infidelity in their husbands; they detest a mistress, but don't mind a whore. My wife told me I might lye with as many women as I pleased, provided I *loved* her alone."

BOSWELL: "She was not in earnest."

JOHNSON: "But she was; consider, Sir, how gross it is in a wife to complain of her husband's going to other women, merely as women; it is that she has not enough of what she would be ashamed to avow."

BOSWELL: "And was Mrs. Johnson then so liberal, Sir? To be sure there is a great difference between the offence of infidelity in a man and his wife."

[1] Cheerful to others, to himself wise.

JOHNSON: "The difference is boundless."

BOSWELL: "Yes, boundless as to property and honours."

JOHNSON: "The man imposes no bastards upon his wife."

BOSWELL: "Suppose, Sir, a woman be of a very cold constitution, has she any right to complain of her husband's infidelity?"

JOHNSON: "Sir, if she refuses, she has no right to complain."

BOSWELL: "Then, Sir, according to your doctrine, upon every such occasion a man may make a note in his pocket-book, and do as he pleases with a safe conscience."

JOHNSON: "Nay, Sir, this is wild indeed (smiling); you must consider that fornication is a crime in a single man; and you cannot have more liberty by being married."

He this evening expressed himself strongly against the Roman Catholicks; observing, "In every thing in which they differ from us, they are wrong." He was even against the invocation of saints; in short, he was in the humour of opposition.

On Tuesday, October 12, I dined with him at Mr. Ramsay's, with Lord Newhaven, and some other company.

Lord Newhaven and Johnson carried on an argument for some time, concerning the Middlesex election. Johnson said, "Parliament may be considered as bound by law, as a man is bound where there is nobody to tie the knot. As it is clear that the House of Commons may expel, and expel again and again, why not allow of the power to incapacitate for that parliament rather than have a perpetual contest kept up between parliament and the people." Lord Newhaven took the opposite side; but respectfully said, "I speak with great deference to you, Dr. Johnson; I speak to be instructed." This had its full effect on my friend. He bowed his head almost as low as the table, to a complimenting nobleman; and called out, "My Lord, my Lord, I do not desire all this ceremony; let us tell our minds to one another quietly." After the debate was over, he said, "I have got lights on the subject to-day, which I had not before." This was a great deal from him, especially as he had written a pamphlet upon it.

He observed, "The House of Commons was originally not a privilege of the people, but a check, for the Crown, on the House of Lords. I remember, Henry the Eighth wanted them to do something; they hesitated in the morning, but did it in the afternoon. He told them, 'It is well you did; or half your heads should have been upon Temple-bar.' But the House of Commons is now no longer under the power of the Crown, and therefore must be bribed." He added, "I have no delight in talking of publick affairs."

255

Of his fellow-collegian, the celebrated Mr. George Whitefield, he said, "Whitefield never drew as much attention as a mountebank does; he did not draw attention by doing better than others, but by doing what was strange. Were Astley to preach a sermon standing upon his head on a horse's back, he would collect a multitude to hear him; but no wise man would say he had made a better sermon for that. I never treated Whitefield's ministry with contempt. I believe he did good. He had devoted himself to the lower classes of mankind, and among them he was of use. But when familiarity and noise claim the praise due to knowledge, art, and elegance, we must beat down such pretensions."

What I have preserved of his conversation during the remainder of my stay in London at this time, is only what follows: I told him that when I objected to keeping company with a notorious infidel, a celebrated friend of ours said to me, "I do not think that men who live laxly in the world, as you and I do, can with propriety assume such an authority: Dr. Johnson may, who is uniformly exemplary in his conduct. But it is not very consistent to shun an infidel to-day and get drunk to-morrow." JOHNSON: "Nay, Sir, this is sad reasoning. Because a man cannot be right in all things, is he to be right in nothing? Because a man sometimes gets drunk, is he therefore to steal? This doctrine would very soon bring a man to the gallows."

He, I know not why, shewed upon all occasions an aversion to go to Ireland, where I proposed to him that we should make a tour. JOHNSON: "It is the last place where I should wish to travel." BOSWELL: "Should you not like to see Dublin, Sir?" JOHNSON: "No, Sir; Dublin is only a worse capital." BOSWELL: "Is not the Giant's-causeway worth seeing?" JOHNSON: "Worth seeing? yes; but not worth going to see."

Yet he had a kindness for the Irish nation, and thus generously expressed himself to a gentleman from that country, on the subject of an UNION which artful Politicians have often had in view—"Do not make an union with us, Sir. We should unite with you only to rob you. We should have robbed the Scotch, if they had had any thing of which we could have robbed them."[1]

I left London on Monday, October 18.

[1] Boswell quotes about this period the following anecdote reported by Mr. Langton:

"A gentleman who introduced his brother to Dr. Johnson, was earnest to recommend him to the Doctor's notice, which he did by saying, 'When we have sat together some time, you'll find my brother grow very entertaining.'—'Sir, (said Johnson,) I can wait.'"

CHAPTER XII

In Seventeen Eighty-one

On Monday, March 19, 1781, I arrived in London, and on Tuesday, the 20th, met him in Fleet-street, walking, or rather indeed moving along; for his peculiar march is thus described in a very just and picturesque manner, in a short *Life* of him published very soon after his death:—"When he walked the streets, what with the constant roll of his head, and the concomitant motion of his body, he appeared to make his way by that motion, independent of his feet." That he was often much stared at while he advanced in this manner, may easily be believed; but it was not safe to make sport of one so robust as he was. Mr. Langton saw him one day, in a fit of absence, by a sudden start, drive the load off a porter's back, and walk forward briskly, without being conscious of what he had done. The porter was very angry, but stood still, and eyed the huge figure with much earnestness, till he was satisfied that his wisest course was to be quiet, and take up his burthen again.

Our accidental meeting in the street after a long separation, was a pleasing surprize to us both. He stepped aside with me into Falcon-court, and made kind enquiries about my family, and as we were in a hurry going different ways, I promised to call on him next day; he said he was engaged to go out in the morning. "Early, Sir?" said I. JOHNSON: "Why, Sir, a London morning does not go with the sun."

I found on visiting his friend, Mr. Thrale, that he was now very ill, and had removed, I suppose by the solicitation of Mrs. Thrale, to a house in Grosvenor-square. I was sorry to see him sadly changed in his appearance.

He told me I might now have the pleasure to see Dr. Johnson drink wine again, for he had lately returned to it. When I mentioned this to Johnson, he said, "I drink it now sometimes, but not socially." The first evening that I was with him at Thrale's, I observed he poured a large quantity of it into a glass, and swallowed it greedily. Every thing about his character and manners was forcible and violent; there never was any moderation; many a day did he fast, many a year did he refrain from wine; but when he did eat, it was voraciously; when he did drink wine, it was copiously. He could practise abstinence, but not temperance.

Johnson's profound reverence for the Hierarchy made him expect from Bishops the highest degree of decorum; he was offended even at their going to taverns; "A bishop (said he) has nothing to do at a tippling-house. It is not indeed immoral in him to go to a tavern; neither would it be immoral in him to whip a top in Grosvenor-square: but, if he did, I hope the boys would fall upon him, and apply the whip to *him*. There are gradations in conduct; there is morality,—decency,—propriety. None of these should be violated by a bishop. A bishop should not go to a house where he may meet a young fellow leading out a wench." BOSWELL: "But, Sir, every tavern does not admit women." JOHNSON: "Depend upon it, Sir, any tavern will admit a well-drest man and a well-drest woman; they will not perhaps admit a woman whom they see every night walking by their door, in the street. But a well-drest man may lead in a well-drest woman to any tavern in London. Taverns sell meat and drink, and will sell them to any body who can eat and can drink. You may as well say, that a mercer will not sell silks to a woman of the town."

Johnson, and his friend, Beauclerk, were once together in company with several clergymen, who thought that they should appear to advantage, by assuming the lax jollity of *men of the world*; which, as it may be observed in similar cases, they carried to noisy excess. Johnson, who they expected would be *entertained*, sat grave and silent for some time; at last, turning to Beauclerk, he said, by no means in a whisper, "This merriment of parsons is mighty offensive."

On Friday, March 30, I dined with him at Sir Joshua Reynolds's, with the Earl of Charlemont, Sir Annesley Stewart, Mr. Eliot, of Port-Eliot, Mr. Burke, Dean Marlay, Mr. Langton; a most agreeable day, of which I regret that every circumstance is not preserved; but it is unreasonable to require such a multiplication of felicity.

Mr. Eliot, with whom Dr. Walter Harte had travelled, talked to us of his *History of Gustavus Adolphus*, which he said was a very good book in the German translation. JOHNSON: "Harte was excessively vain. He put copies of his book in manuscript into the hands of Lord Chesterfield and Lord Granville, that they might revise it. Now how absurd was it to suppose that two such noblemen would revise so big a manuscript. Poor man! he left London the day of the publication of his book, that he might be out of the way of the great praise he was to receive; and he was ashamed to return, when he found how ill his book had succeeded. It was unlucky in coming out on the same day with Robertson's *History of Scotland*. His husbandry, however, is good." BOSWELL: "So he was fitter for that than for heroick history: he did well, when he turned his sword into a plough-share."

Mr. Eliot mentioned a curious liquor peculiar to his country, which the Cornish fishermen drink. They call it *Mahogany*; and it is made of two parts gin, and one part treacle, well beaten together. I begged to have some of it made, which was done with proper skill by Mr. Eliot. I thought it very good liquor; and said it was a counterpart of what is called *Athol Porridge* in the Highlands of Scotland, which is a mixture of whisky and honey. Johnson said, "that must be a better liquor than the Cornish, for both its component parts are better." He also observed, "*Mahogany* must be a modern name; for it is not long since the wood called mahogany was known in this country." I mentioned his scale of liquors:— claret for boys,—port for men,—brandy for heroes. "Then (said Mr. Burke) let me have claret: I love to be a boy; to have the careless gaiety of boyish days." JOHNSON: "I should drink claret too, if it would give me that; but it does not: it neither makes boys men, nor men boys. You'll be drowned by it, before it has any effect upon you."

I ventured to mention a ludicrous paragraph in the newspapers, that Dr. Johnson was learning to dance of Vestris. Lord Charlemont, wishing to excite him to talk, proposed in a whisper, that he should be asked, whether it was true. "Shall I ask him?" said his Lordship. We were, by a great majority, clear for the experiment. Upon which his Lordship very gravely, and with a courteous air said, "Pray, Sir, is it true that you are taking lessons of Vestris?" This was risking a good deal, and required the boldness of a General of Irish Volunteers to make the attempt. Johnson was at first startled, and in some heat answered, "How can your Lordship ask so simple a question?" But immediately recovering himself, whether from unwillingness to be deceived, or to appear deceived, or whether from real good humour, he kept up the joke: "Nay, but if any body were to answer the paragraph, and contradict it, I'd have a reply, and would say, that he who contradicted it was no friend either to Vestris or me. For why should not Dr. Johnson add to his other powers a little corporeal agility? Socrates learnt to dance at an advanced age, and Cato learnt Greek at an advanced age. Then it might proceed to say, that this Johnson, not content with dancing on the ground, might dance on the rope; and they might introduce the elephant dancing on the rope. A nobleman[1] wrote a play, called *Love in a Hollow Tree*. He found out that it was a bad one, and therefore wished to buy up all the copies, and burn them. The Duchess of Marlborough had kept one; and when he was against her at an election, she had a new edition of it printed, and prefixed to it, as a frontispiece, an elephant dancing on a rope; to shew, that his Lordship's writing comedy was as aukward as an elephant dancing on a rope."

On Sunday, April 1, I dined with him at Mr. Thrale's, with Sir Philip Jennings Clerk and Mr. Perkins, who had the superintendence of Mr. Thrale's brewery, with a salary of five hundred pounds a year. Sir Philip had the appearance of a gentleman of ancient family, well advanced in life. He wore his own white hair in a bag of goodly size, a black velvet coat, with an embroidered waistcoat, and very rich laced ruffles; which Mrs. Thrale said were old fashioned, but which, for that reason, I thought the more respectable, more like a Tory; yet Sir Philip was then in Opposition in Parliament. "Ah, Sir, (said Johnson,) ancient ruffles and modern principles do not agree." Sir Philip defended the Opposition to the American war ably and with temper, and I joined him. He said the majority of the nation was against the ministry. JOHNSON: "*I*, Sir, am against the ministry; but it is for having too little of that, of which Opposition thinks they have too much. Were I minister, if any man wagged his finger against me, he should be turned out; for that which it is in the power of government to give at pleasure to one or to another, should be given to the supporters of Government. If you will not oppose at the expence of losing your place, your opposition will not be honest, you will feel no serious grievance; and the present opposition is only a contest to get what others have. Sir Robert Walpole acted as I would do. As to the American war, the *sense* of the nation is *with* the ministry. The majority of those who can *understand* is with it; the majority of those who can only *hear* is against it; and as those who can only hear are more numerous than those who can understand, and Opposition is always loudest, a majority of the rabble will be for Opposition."

Mrs. Thrale gave high praise to Mr. Dudley Long, (now North.) JOHNSON: "Nay, my dear lady, don't talk so. Mr. Long's character

[1] William, the first Viscount Grimston.

is very *short*. It is nothing. He fills a chair. He is a man of genteel appearance, and that is all. I know nobody who blasts by praise as you do: for whenever there is exaggerated praise, every body is set against a character. They are provoked to attack it. Now there is Pepys; you praised that man with such disproportion, that I was incited to lessen him, perhaps more than he deserves. His blood is upon your head. By the same principles, your malice defeats itself; for your censure is too violent. And yet (looking to her with a leering smile) she is the first woman in the world, could she but restrain that wicked tongue of hers;—she would be the only woman, could she but command that little whirligig."

Upon the subject of exaggerated praise I took the liberty to say, that I thought there might be very high praise given to a known character which deserved it, and therefore it would not be exaggerated. Thus, one might say of Mr. Edmund Burke, he is a very wonderful man. JOHNSON: "No, Sir, you would not be safe, if another man had a mind perversely to contradict. He might answer, 'Where is all the wonder? Burke is, to be sure, a man of uncommon abilities, with a great quantity of matter in his mind, and a great fluency of language in his mouth. But we are not to be stunned and astonished by him.' So you see, Sir, even Burke would suffer, not from any fault of his own, but from your folly."

Mr. Thrale appeared very lethargick to-day. I saw him again on Monday evening, at which time he was not thought to be in immediate danger; but early in the morning of Wednesday the 4th, he expired.

On Saturday, April 7, I dined with Johnson at Mr. Hoole's with Governor Bouchier and Captain Orme, both of whom had been long in the East-Indies; and being men of good sense and observation, were very entertaining. Johnson defended the oriental regulation of different *casts* of men, which was objected to as totally destructive of the hopes of rising in society by personal merit. He shewed that there was a *principle* in it sufficiently plausible by analogy. "We see (said he) in metals that there are different species; and so likewise in animals, though one species may not differ very widely from another, as in the species of dogs,—the cur, the spaniel, the mastiff. The Bramins are the mastiffs of mankind."

On Thursday, April 12, I dined with him at a Bishop's, where were Sir Joshua Reynolds, Mr. Berenger, and some more company. He had dined the day before at another Bishop's. I have unfortunately recorded none of his conversation at the Bishop's where we dined together: but I have preserved the ingenious defence of his dining twice abroad in Passion-week. "Why, Sir, a Bishop's calling company together in this week, is, to use the vulgar phrase, not *the thing*. But you must consider laxity is a bad thing; but preciseness is also a bad thing; and your general character may be more hurt by preciseness than by dining with a Bishop in Passion-week. There might be a handle for reflection. It might be said, 'He refuses to dine with a Bishop in Passion-week, but was three Sundays absent from church.'" BOSWELL: "Very true, Sir. But suppose a man to be uniformly of good conduct, would it not be better that he should refuse to dine with a Bishop in this week, and so not encourage a bad practice by his example?" JOHNSON: "Why, Sir, you are to consider whether you might not do more harm by lessening the influence of a Bishop's character by your disapprobation in refusing him, than by going to him."

On Friday, April 13, being Good-Friday, I went to St. Clement's church with him as usual. There I saw again his old fellow-collegian, Edwards, to whom I said, "I think, Sir, Dr. Johnson and you meet only at Church." "Sir, (said he,) it is the best place we can meet in, except Heaven, and I hope we shall meet there too." Dr. Johnson told me, that there was very little communication between Edwards and him, after their unexpected renewal of acquaintance. "But (said he, smiling) he met me once, and said, 'I am told you have written a very pretty book called *The Rambler*.' I was unwilling that he should leave the world in total darkness, and sent him a set."

Mr. Berenger visited him to-day, and was very pleasing. We talked of an evening society for conversation at a house in town, of which we were all members, but of which Johnson said, "It will never do, Sir. There is nothing served about there, neither tea, nor coffee, nor lemonade, nor any thing whatever; and depend upon it, Sir, a man does not love to go to a place from whence he comes out exactly as he went in." I endeavoured for argument's sake, to maintain that men of learning and talents might have very good intellectual society, without the aid of any little gratifications of the senses. Berenger joined with Johnson, and said, that without these any meeting would be dull and insipid. He would therefore have all the slight refreshments; nay, it would not be amiss to have some cold meat, and a bottle of wine upon a sideboard. "Sir, (said Johnson to me, with an air of triumph,) Mr. Berenger knows the world. Every body loves to have good things furnished to them without any trouble. I told Mrs. Thrale once, that as she did not choose to have card-tables, she should have a profusion of the best sweetmeats, and she would be sure to have company enough come to her."

On Sunday, April 15, being Easter-day, after solemn worship in St. Paul's church, I found him alone; Dr. Scott of the Commons, came in.

We talked of the difference between the mode of education at Oxford, and that in those Colleges where instruction is chiefly conveyed by lectures. JOHNSON: "Lectures were once useful; but now, when all can read, and books are so numerous, lectures are unnecessary. If your attention fails, and you miss a part of the lecture, it is lost; you cannot go back as you do upon a book." Dr. Scott agreed with him. "But yet (said I), Dr. Scott, you yourself gave lectures at Oxford." He smiled. "You laughed then (said I) at those who came to you."

Dr. Scott left us, and soon afterwards we went to dinner. Our company consisted of Mrs. Williams, Mrs. Desmoulins, Mr. Levett, Mr. Allen, the printer, (Mr. Macbean,) and Mrs. Hall, sister of the Reverend Mr. John Wesley, and resembling him, as I thought, both in figure and manner. Johnson produced now, for the first time, some handsome silver salvers, which he told me he had bought fourteen years ago; so it was a great day. I was not a little amused by observing Allen perpetually struggling to talk in the manner of Johnson, like the little frog in the fable blowing himself up to resemble the stately ox.

I mentioned a kind of religious Robinhood Society, which met every Sunday evening at Coachmakers'-hall, for free debate; and that the subject for this night was, the text which relates, with other miracles which happened at our SAVIOUR's death, "And the graves were opened, and many bodies of the saints which slept arose, and came out of the graves after his resurrection, and went into the holy city, and appeared unto many." Mrs. Hall said it was a very curious subject, and she should like to hear it discussed. JOHNSON: (somewhat warmly:) "One would not go to such a place to hear it,— one would not be seen in such a place—to give countenance to such a meeting." I, however, resolved that I would go. "But, Sir, (said she to Johnson,) I should like to hear *you* discuss it." He seemed reluctant to engage in it. She talked of the resurrection of the human race in general, and maintained that we shall be raised with the same bodies. JOHNSON: "Nay, Madam, we see that it is not to be the same body; for the Scripture uses the illustration of grain sown, and we know that the grain which grows is not the

263

same with what is sown. You cannot suppose that we shall rise with a diseased body; it is enough if there be such a sameness as to distinguish identity of person." She seemed desirous of knowing more, but he left the question in obscurity.

Of apparitions, he observed, "A total disbelief of them is adverse to the opinion of the existence of the soul between death and the last day; the question simply is, whether departed spirits ever have the power of making themselves perceptible to us: a man who thinks he has seen an apparition, can only be convinced himself; his authority will not convince another; and his conviction, if rational, must be founded on being told something which cannot be known but by supernatural means."

He mentioned a thing as not unfrequent, of which I had never heard before,—being *called*, that is, hearing one's name pronounced by the voice of a known person at a great distance, far beyond the possibility of being reached by any sound uttered by human organs. "An acquaintance, on whose veracity I can depend, told me, that walking home one evening to Kilmarnock, he heard himself called from a wood, by the voice of a brother who had gone to America; and the next packet brought accounts of that brother's death." Macbean asserted that this inexplicable *calling* was a thing very well known. Dr. Johnson said, that one day at Oxford, as he was turning the key of his chamber, he heard his mother distinctly call—*Sam*. She was then at Lichfield; but nothing ensued.

On Friday, April 20, I spent with him one of the happiest days that I remember to have enjoyed in the whole course of my life. Mrs. Garrick, whose grief for the loss of her husband was, I believe, as sincere as wounded affection and admiration could produce, had this day, for the first time since his death, a select party of his friends to dine with her. The company was, Miss Hannah More, who lived with her, and whom she called her Chaplain; Mrs. Boscawen, Mrs. Elizabeth Carter, Sir Joshua Reynolds, Dr. Burney, Dr. Johnson, and myself. We found ourselves very elegantly entertained at her house in the Adelphi, where I have passed many a pleasing hour with him "who gladdened life."

The general effect of this day dwells upon my mind in fond remembrance, but I do not find much conversation recorded. What I have preserved shall be faithfully given.

One of the company mentioned Mr. Thomas Hollis, the strenuous Whig, who used to send over Europe presents of democratical books, with their boards stamped with daggers and caps of liberty. Mrs. Carter said, "He was a bad man: he used to talk uncharitably." JOHNSON: "Poh! poh! Madam; who is the worse for being talked of uncharitably? Besides, he was a dull poor creature as ever lived: and I believe he would not have done harm to a man whom he knew to be of very opposite principles to his own. I remember once at the Society of Arts, when an advertisement was to be drawn up, he pointed me out as the man who could do it best. This, you will observe, was kindness to me. I however slipt away and escaped it."

Mrs. Carter having said of the same person, "I doubt he was an Atheist." JOHNSON: "I don't know that. He might perhaps have become one, if he had had time to ripen, (smiling.) He might have *exuberated* into an Atheist."

In the evening we had a large company in the drawing-room; several ladies, the Bishop of Killaloe, Dr. Percy, Mr. Chamberlayne, of the Treasury, &c. &c. Somebody said, the life of a mere literary man could not be very entertaining. JOHNSON: "But it certainly may. This is a remark which has been made, and repeated, without justice; why should the life of a literary man be less entertaining than the life of any other man? Are there not as interesting varieties in such a life? As *a literary life* it may be very entertaining." BOSWELL: "But it must be better surely, when it is diversified with a little active variety—such as his having gone to Jamaica:—or—his having gone to the Hebrides." Johnson was not displeased at this.

Talking of a very respectable authour, he told us a curious circumstance in his life, which was, that he had married a printer's devil. REYNOLDS: "A Printer's devil, Sir! Why, I thought a printer's devil was a creature with a black face and in rags." JOHNSON: "Yes, Sir. But I suppose he had her face washed, and put clean clothes on her. (Then looking very serious, and very earnest.) And she did not disgrace him;—the woman had a bottom of good sense." The word *bottom* thus introduced, was so ludicrous when contrasted with his gravity, that most of us could not forbear tittering and laughing; though I recollect that the Bishop of Killaloe kept his countenance with perfect steadiness, while Miss Hannah More slyly hid her face behind a lady's back who sat on the same settee with her. His pride could not bear that any expression of his should excite ridicule, when he did not intend it; he therefore resolved to assume and exercise despotick power, glanced sternly around, and called out in a strong tone, "Where's the merriment?" Then collecting himself, and looking awful, to make us feel how he could impose restraint, and as it were searching his mind for a still more ludicrous word, he slowly pronounced, "I say the *woman* was *fundamentally* sensible;" as if he had said, hear this now, and laugh if you dare. We all sat composed as at a funeral.

On Tuesday, May 8, I had the pleasure of again dining with him and Mr. Wilkes, at Mr. Dilly's. No *negociation* was now required to bring them together; for Johnson was so well satisfied with the former interview, that he was very glad to meet Wilkes again, who was this day seated between Dr. Beattie and Dr. Johnson; (between *Truth* and *Reason*, as General Paoli said, when I told him of it.) WILKES: "I have been thinking, Dr. Johnson, that there should be a bill brought into parliament that the controverted elections for Scotland should be tried in that country, at their own Abbey of Holy-Rood House, and not here; for the consequence of trying them here is, that we have an inundation of Scotchmen, who come up and never go back again. Now here is Boswell, who is come upon the election for his own county, which will not last a fortnight." JOHNSON: "Nay, Sir, I see no reason why they should be tried at all; for, you know, one Scotchman is as good as another." WILKES: "Pray, Boswell, how much may be got in a year by an Advocate at the Scotch bar?" BOSWELL: "I believe, two thousand pounds." WILKES: "How can it be possible to spend that money in Scotland?" JOHNSON: "Why, Sir, the money may be spent in England; but there is a harder question. If one man in Scotland gets possession of two thousand pounds, what remains for all the rest of the nation?" WILKES: "You know, in the last war, the immense booty which Thurot carried off by the complete plunder of seven Scotch isles; he re-embarked with *three and six-pence*."

The subject of quotation being introduced, Mr. Wilkes censured it as pedantry. JOHNSON: "No, Sir, it is a good thing; there is a community of mind in it. Classical quotation is the *parole* of literary men all over the world." WILKES: "Upon the continent they all quote the vulgate Bible. Shakspeare is chiefly quoted here; and we quote also Pope, Prior, Butler, Waller, and sometimes Cowley."

We talked of Letter-writing. JOHNSON: "It is now become so much the fashion to publish letters, that, in order to avoid it, I put as little into mine as I can." BOSWELL: "Do what you will, Sir, you cannot avoid it. Should you even write as ill as you can, your letters would be published as curiosities:

      'Behold a miracle! instead of wit,
        See two dull lines with Stanhope's pencil writ.'"

He gave us an entertaining account of *Bet Flint*, a woman of the town, who, with some eccentrick talents and much effrontery, forced herself upon his acquaintance. "Bet (said he) wrote her own *Life* in verse, which she brought to me, wishing that I would furnish her with a Preface to it. (Laughing.) I used to say of her, that she was generally slut and drunkard;—occasionally, whore and thief. She had, however, genteel lodgings, a spinnet on which she played, and a boy that walked before her chair. Poor Bet was taken up on a charge of stealing a counterpane, and tried at the Old Bailey. Chief Justice——, who loved a wench, summed up favourably, and she was acquitted. After which, Bet said, with a gay and satisfied air, 'Now that the counterpane is *my own*, I shall make a petticoat of it.'"

Talking of oratory, Mr. Wilkes described it as accompanied with all the charms of poetical expression. JOHNSON: "No, Sir; oratory is the power of beating down your adversary's arguments, and putting better in their place." WILKES: "But this does not move the passions." JOHNSON: "He must be a weak man, who is to be so moved." WILKES: (naming a celebrated orator:) "Amidst all the brilliancy of ——'s imagination, and the exuberance of his wit, there is a strange want of *taste*. It was observed of Apelles's Venus, that her flesh seemed as if she had been nourished by roses: his oratory would sometimes make one suspect that he eats potatoes and drinks whisky."

Mr. Wilkes observed, how tenacious we are of forms in this country; and gave as an instance, the vote of the House of Commons for remitting money to pay the army in America *in Portugal pieces*, when, in reality, the remittance is made not in Portugal money, but in our specie. JOHNSON: "Is there not a law, Sir, against exporting the current coin of the realm?" WILKES: "Yes, Sir; but might not the House of Commons, in case of real evident necessity order our own current coin to be sent into our own colonies?"—Here Johnson, with that quickness of recollection which distinguished him so eminently, gave the *Middlesex Patriot* an admirable retort upon his own ground. "Sure, Sir, *you* don't think a *resolution of the House of Commons* equal to the *law of the land*." WILKES: (at once perceiving the application:) "God forbid, Sir."

Mr. Beauclerk's great library was this season sold in London by auction. Mr. Wilkes said, he wondered to find in it such a numerous collection of sermons: seeming to think it strange that a gentleman of Mr. Beauclerk's character in the gay world, should have chosen to have many compositions of that kind. JOHNSON: "Why, Sir, you are to consider that sermons make a considerable branch of English literature; so that a library must be very imperfect if it has not a numerous collection of sermons: and in all collections, Sir, the desire of augmenting them grows stronger in proportion to the advance in acquisition; as motion is accelerated by the continuance of the *impetus*. Besides, Sir, (looking at Mr. Wilkes with a placid but significant smile,) a man may collect sermons with intention of making himself better by them. I hope Mr. Beauclerk intended that some time or other that should be the case with him."

Mr. Wilkes said to me, loud enough for Dr. Johnson to hear, "Dr. Johnson should make me a present of his *Lives of the Poets*, as I am a poor patriot, who cannot afford to buy them." Johnson seemed to take no notice of this hint; but in a little while, he called to Mr. Dilly, "Pray, Sir, be so good as to send a set of my *Lives* to Mr. Wilkes, with my compliments." This was accordingly done; and Mr. Wilkes paid Dr. Johnson a visit, was courteously received, and sat with him a long time.

The company gradually dropped away. Mr. Dilly himself was called down stairs upon business; I left the room for some time; when I returned, I was struck with observing Dr. Samuel Johnson and John Wilkes, Esq. literally *tête-à-tête*; for they were reclined upon their chairs, with their heads leaning almost close to each other, and talking earnestly, in a kind of confidential whisper, of the personal quarrel between George the Second and the King of Prussia. Such a scene of perfectly easy sociality between two such opponents in the war of political controversy, as that which I now beheld, would have been an excellent subject for a picture. It presented to my mind the happy days which are foretold in Scripture, when the lion shall lie down with the kid.

While I remained in London this year, Johnson and I dined together at several places. I recollect a placid day at Dr. Butler's, who had now removed from Derby to Lower Grosvenor-street, London; but of his conversation on that and other occasions during this period, I neglected to keep any regular record, and shall therefore insert here some miscellaneous articles which I find in my Johnsonian notes.

His disorderly habits, when "making provision for the day that was passing over him," appear from the following anecdote, communicated to me by Mr. John Nichols:—"In the year 1763, a young bookseller, who was an apprentice to Mr. Whiston, waited on him with a subscription to his *Shakspeare*: and observing that
268

the Doctor made no entry in any book of the subscriber's name, ventured diffidently to ask, whether he would please to have the gentleman's address, that it might be properly inserted in the printed list of subscribers.—'*I shall print no List of Subscribers,*' said Johnson, with great abruptness: but almost immediately recollecting himself, added, very complacently, 'Sir, I have two very cogent reasons for not printing any list of subscribers;—one, that I have lost all the names,—the other, that I have spent all the money.'"

Johnson could not brook appearing to be worsted in argument, even when he had taken the wrong side, to shew the force and dexterity of his talents. When, therefore, he perceived that his opponent gained ground, he had recourse to some sudden mode of robust sophistry. Once when I was pressing upon him with visible advantage, he stopped me thus:—"My dear Boswell, let's have no more of this; you'll make nothing of it. I'd rather have you whistle a Scotch tune."

Care, however, must be taken to distinguish between Johnson when he "talked for victory," and Johnson when he had no desire but to inform and illustrate.—"One of Johnson's principal talents (says an eminent friend of his) was shewn in maintaining the wrong side of an argument, and in a splendid perversion of the truth.— If you could contrive to have his fair opinion on a subject, and without any bias from personal prejudice, or from a wish to be victorious in argument, it was wisdom itself, not only convincing, but overpowering."

Johnson had called twice on the Bishop of Killaloe before his Lordship set out for Ireland, having missed him the first time. He said, "It would have hung heavy on my heart if I had not seen him. No man ever paid more attention to another than he has done to me; and I have neglected him, not wilfully, but from being otherwise occupied. Always Sir, set a high value on spontaneous kindness. He whose inclination prompts him to cultivate your friendship of his own accord, will love you more than one whom you have been at pains to attach to you."

Johnson told me, that he was once much pleased to find that a carpenter, who lived near him, was very ready to shew him some things in his business which he wished to see: "It was paying (said he) respect to literature."

I asked him, if he was not dissatisfied with having so small a share of wealth, and none of those distinctions in the state which are the objects of ambition. He had only a pension of three hundred a year. Why was he not in such circumstances as to keep his coach? Why had he not some considerable office? JOHNSON: "Sir, I have never complained of the world; nor do I think that I have reason to complain. It is rather to be wondered at that I have so much. My pension is more out of the usual course of things than any instance that I have known. Here, Sir, was a man avowedly no friend to Government at the time, who got a pension without asking for it. I never courted the great; they sent for me; but I think they now give me up. They are satisfied: they have seen enough of me." Upon my observing that I could not believe this; for they must certainly be highly pleased by his conversation; conscious of his own superiority, he answered, "No, Sir; great Lords and great Ladies don't love to have their mouths stopped." This was very expressive of the effect which the force of his understanding and brilliancy of his fancy could not but produce; and, to be sure, they must have found themselves strangely diminished in his company. When I warmly declared how happy I was at all times to hear him;—"Yes, Sir, (said he); but if you were Lord Chancellor, it would not be so; you would then consider your own dignity."

On Saturday, June 2, I set out for Scotland, and had promised to pay a visit, in my way, as I sometimes did, at Southill, in Bedfordshire, at the hospitable mansion of 'Squire Dilly, the elder brother of my worthy friends, the booksellers, in the Poultry. Dr. Johnson agreed to be of the party this year, with Mr. Charles Dilly and me, and to go and see Lord Bute's seat at Luton Hoe.

Upon the road we talked of the uncertainty of profit with which authours and booksellers engage in the publication of literary works. JOHNSON: "My judgement I have found is no certain rule as to the sale of a book." BOSWELL: "Pray, Sir, have you been much plagued with authours sending you their works to revise?" JOHNSON: "No, Sir; I have been thought a sour surly fellow." BOSWELL: "Very lucky for you, Sir,—in that respect." I must however, observe, that notwithstanding what he now said, which he no doubt imagined at the time to be the fact, there was, perhaps, no man who more frequently yielded to the solicitations even of very obscure authours, to read their manuscripts, or more liberally assisted them with advice and correction.

At Shefford I had another affectionate parting from my revered friend.

CHAPTER XIII

In Seventeen Eighty-three

O N FRIDAY, March 21, 1783, having arrived in London the night before, I was glad to find him at Mrs. Thrale's house, in Argyll-street, appearances of friendship between them being still kept up. I was shewn into his room, and after the first salutation he said, "I am glad you are come: I am very ill." He looked pale, and was distressed with a difficulty of breathing: but after the common enquiries he assumed his usual strong animated style of conversation. Seeing me now for the first time as a *Laird*, or proprietor of land, he began thus: "Sir, the superiority of a country gentleman over the people upon his estate is very agreeable: and he who says he does not feel it to be agreeable, lies; for it must be agreeable to have a casual superiority over those who are by nature equal with us." BOSWELL: "Yet, Sir, we see great proprietors of land who prefer living in London." JOHNSON: "Why, Sir, the pleasure of living in London, the intellectual superiority that is enjoyed there may counterbalance the other. Besides, Sir, a man may prefer the state of the country-gentleman upon the whole, and yet there may never be a moment when he is willing to make the change to quit London for it." He said, "It is better to have five *per cent.* out of land, than out of money, because it is more secure; but the readiness of transfer, and promptness of interest, make many people rather choose the funds. Nay, there is another disadvantage belonging to land, compared with money. A man is not so much afraid of being a hard creditor, as of being a hard landlord." BOSWELL: "Because there is a sort of kindly connection between a landlord and his tenants." JOHNSON: "No, Sir, many landlords with us never see their tenants. It is because if a landlord drives away his tenants he may not get others; whereas the demand for money is so great, it may always be lent."

He talked with regret and indignation of the factious opposition to Government at this time, and imputed it in a great measure to the Revolution, "Sir, (said he, in a low voice, having come nearer to me, while his old prejudices seemed to be fermenting in his mind,) this Hanoverian family is *isolée* here. They have no friends. Now the Stuarts had friends who stuck by them so late as 1745. When the right of the King is not reverenced, there will not be reverence for those appointed by the King."

He sent a message to acquaint Mrs. Thrale that I was arrived. I had not seen her since her husband's death. She soon appeared, and favoured me with an invitation to stay to dinner, which I accepted. There was no other company but herself and three of her daughters, Dr. Johnson and I.

Talking of conversation, he said, "There must, in the first place, be knowledge, there must be materials;—in the second place, there must be a command of words;—in the third place, there must be imagination, to place things in such views as they are not commonly seen in;—and in the fourth place, there must be presence of mind, and a resolution that is not to be overcome by failures; this last is an essential requisite; for want of it many people do not excel in conversation. Now *I* want it; I throw up the game upon losing a trick." I wondered to hear him talk thus of himself, and said, "I don't know, Sir, how this may be; but I am sure you beat other people's cards out of their hands." I doubt whether he heard this remark.

It has been observed and wondered at, that Mr. Charles Fox never talked with any freedom in the presence of Dr. Johnson; though it is well known, and I myself can witness, that his conversation is various, fluent, and exceedingly agreeable. Johnson's own experience, however, of that gentleman's reserve was a sufficient reason for his going on thus: "Fox never talks in private company; not from any determination not to talk, but because he has not the first motion. A man who is used to the applause of the House of Commons, has no wish for that of a private company. A man accustomed to throw for a thousand pounds, if set down to throw for sixpence, would not be at the pains to count his dice. Burke's talk is the ebullition of his mind; he does not talk from a desire of distinction, but because his mind is full."

After musing for some time, he said, "I wonder how I should have any enemies; for I do harm to nobody." BOSWELL: "In the first place, Sir, you will be pleased to recollect, that you set out with attacking the Scotch; so you got a whole nation for your enemies." JOHNSON: "Why, I own, that by my definition of *oats* I meant to vex them." BOSWELL: "Pray, Sir, can you trace the cause of your antipathy to the Scotch?" JOHNSON: "I cannot, Sir." BOSWELL:

272

"Old Mr. Sheridan says, it was because they sold Charles the First." JOHNSON: "Then, Sir, old Mr. Sheridan has found out a very good reason."

On Sunday, March 23, I breakfasted with Dr. Johnson, who seemed much relieved, having taken opium the night before. He however protested against it, as a remedy that should be given with the utmost reluctance, and only in extreme necessity. I mentioned how commonly it was used in Turkey, and that therefore it could not be so pernicious as he apprehended. He grew warm, and said, "Turks take opium, and Christians take opium; but Russell, in his account of Aleppo, tells us, that it is as disgraceful in Turkey to take too much opium, as it is with us to get drunk. Sir, it is amazing how things are exaggerated. A gentleman was lately telling in a company where I was present, that in France as soon as a man of fashion marries he takes an opera girl into keeping; and this he mentioned as a general custom. 'Pray, Sir, (said I,) how many opera girls may there be?' He answered, 'About four-score.' 'Well then, Sir, (said I,) you see there can be no more than fourscore men of fashion who can do this.'"

Mrs. Desmoulins made tea; and she and I talked before him upon a topick which he had once borne patiently from me when we were by ourselves,—his not complaining of the world, because he was not called to some great office, nor had attained to great wealth. He flew into a violent passion, I confess with some justice, and commanded us to have done. "Nobody, (said he) has a right to talk in this manner, to bring before a man his own character, and the events of his life, when he does not choose it should be done. I never have sought the world; the world was not to seek me. It is rather wonderful that so much has been done for me. All the complaints which are made of the world are unjust. I never knew a man of merit neglected: it was generally by his own fault that he failed of success. A man may hide his head in a hole: he may go into the country, and publish a book now and then which nobody reads, and then complain he is neglected. There is no reason why any person should exert himself for a man who has written a good book: he has not written it for any individual. I may as well make a present to the postman who brings me a letter. When patronage was limited, an authour expected to find a Mæcenas, and complained if he did not find one. Why should he complain? This Mæcenas has others as good as he, or others who have got the start of him." BOSWELL: "But surely, Sir, you will allow that there are men of merit at the bar, who never get practice." JOHNSON: "Sir, you are sure that practice is got from an opinion that the person employed deserves it best; so that if a man of merit at the bar does not get practice, it is from errour, not from injustice. He is not neglected. A horse that is brought to market may not be bought, though he is a very good horse: but that is from ignorance, not from intention."

On the subject of the right employment of wealth, Johnson observed, "A man cannot make a bad use of his money, so far as regards Society, if he does not hoard it; for if he either spends it or lends it out, Society has the benefit. It is in general better to spend money than to give it away; for industry is more promoted by spending money than by giving it away. A man who spends his money is sure he is doing good with it: he is not so sure when he gives it away. A man who spends ten thousand a year will do more good than a man who spends two thousand and gives away eight."

In the evening I came to him again.

He said, "Goldsmith's blundering speech to Lord Shelburne, which has been so often mentioned, and which he really did make to him, was only a blunder in emphasis: 'I wonder they should call your Lordship *Malagrida*, for Malagrida was a very good man;'—meant, I wonder they should use *Malagrida* as a term of reproach."

On Sunday, March 30, I found him at home in the evening, and had the pleasure to meet with Dr. Brocklesby, whose reading and knowledge of life, and good spirits, supply him with a never-failing source of conversation. He mentioned a respectable gentleman, who became extremely penurious near the close of his life. Johnson said there must have been a degree of madness about him. "Not at all, Sir, (said Dr. Bocklesby,) his judgement was entire." Unluckily, however, he mentioned that although he had a fortune of twenty-seven thousand pounds, he denied himself many comforts, from an apprehension that he could not afford them. "Nay, Sir, (cried Johnson,) when the judgement is so disturbed that a man cannot count, that is pretty well."

I shall here insert a few of Johnson's sayings, without the formality of dates, as they have no reference to any particular time or place.

"Raising the wages of day-labourers is wrong; for it does not make them live better, but only makes them idler, and idleness is a very bad thing for human nature."

"It is a very good custom to keep a journal for a man's own use; he may write upon a card a day all that is necessary to be written, after he has had experience of life. At first there is a great deal to be written, because there is a great deal of novelty; but when once a man has settled his opinions, there is seldom much to be set down."

I praised the accuracy of an account-book of a lady whom I mentioned. JOHNSON: "Keeping accounts, Sir, is of no use when a man is spending his own money, and has nobody to whom he is to account. You won't eat less beef to-day, because you have written down what it cost yesterday." I mentioned another lady who thought as he did, so that her husband could not get her to keep an account of the expence of the family, as she thought it enough that she never exceeded the sum allowed her. JOHNSON: "Sir, it is fit she should keep an account because her husband wishes it; but I do not see its use." I maintained that keeping an account has this advantage, that it satisfies a man that his money has not been lost or stolen, which he might sometimes be apt to imagine, were there no written state of his expence; and besides, a calculation of economy so as not to exceed one's income, cannot be made without a view of the different articles in figures, that one may see how to retrench in some particulars less necessary than others. This he did not attempt to answer.

Talking of an acquaintance of ours, whose narratives, which abounded in curious and interesting topicks, were unhappily found to be very fabulous; I mentioned Lord Mansfield's having said to me, "Suppose we believe one *half* of what he tells." JOHNSON: "Ay; but we don't know *which* half to believe. By his lying we lose not only our reverence for him, but all comfort in his conversation." BOSWELL: "May we not take it as amusing fiction?" JOHNSON: "Sir, the misfortune is, that you will insensibly believe as much of it as you incline to believe."

As a small proof of his kindliness and delicacy of feeling, the following circumstance may be mentioned: One evening when we were in the street together, and I told him I was going to sup at Mr. Beauclerk's, he said, "I'll go with you." After having walked part of the way, seeming to recollect something, he suddenly stopped, and said, "I cannot go,—but *I do not love Beauclerk the less.*"

He said, "How few of his friends' houses would a man choose to be at, when he is sick!" He mentioned one or two. I recollect only Thrale's.

He observed, "There is a wicked inclination in most people to suppose an old man decayed in his intellects. If a young or middle-aged man, when leaving a company, does not recollect where he laid his hat, it is nothing; but if the same inattention is discovered in an old man, people will shrug up their shoulders, and say, 'His memory is going.'"

Johnson's dexterity in retort, when he seemed to be driven to an extremity by his adversary, was very remarkable. Of his power in this respect, our common friend, Mr. Windham, of Norfolk, has been pleased to furnish me with an eminent instance. However unfavourable to Scotland, he uniformly gave liberal praise to George Buchanan, as a writer. In a conversation concerning the literary merits of the two countries, in which Buchanan was introduced, a Scotchman, imagining that on this ground he should have an undoubted triumph over him, exclaimed, "Ah, Dr. Johnson, what would you have said of Buchanan, had he been an Englishman?"—"Why, Sir, (said Johnson, after a little pause,) I should *not* have said of Buchanan, had he been an *Englishman*, what I will now say of him as a *Scotchman*,—that he was the only man of genius his country ever produced."

Though his usual phrase for conversation was *talk*, yet he made a distinction; for when he once told me that he dined the day before at a friend's house, with "a very pretty company;" and I asked him if there was good conversation, he answered, "No, Sir; we had *talk* enough, but no *conversation*; there was nothing *discussed*."

Talking of the success of the Scotch in London, he imputed it in a considerable degree to their spirit of nationality. "You know, Sir, (said he,) that no Scotchman publishes a book, or has a play brought upon the stage, but there are five hundred people ready to applaud him."

Mr. Hoole told him, he was born in Moorfields, and had received part of his early instruction in Grub-street. "Sir, (said Johnson, smiling,) you have been *regularly* educated." Having asked who was his instructor, and Mr. Hoole having answered, "My uncle, Sir, who was a taylor;" Johnson, recollecting himself, said, "Sir, I knew him; we called him the *metaphysical taylor*. He was of a club in Old-street, with me and George Psalmanazar, and some others: but pray, Sir, was he a good taylor?" Mr. Hoole having answered that he believed he was too mathematical, and used to draw squares and triangles on his shop-board, so that he did not excel in the cut of a coat;—"I am sorry for it, (said Johnson,) for I would have every man to be master of his own business."

He said to Sir William Scott, "The age is running mad after innovation; and all the business of the world is to be done in a new way; men are to be hanged in a new way; Tyburn itself is not safe from the fury of innovation." It having been argued that this was an improvement.—"No, Sir, (said he, eagerly,) it is *not* an improvement; they object, that the old method drew together a number of spectators. Sir, executions are intended to draw spectators. If they do not draw spectators, they don't answer their purpose. The old method was most satisfactory to all parties; the publick was gratified by a procession; the criminal was supported by it. Why is all this to be swept away?"

Of Dr. Hurd, Bishop of Worcester, Johnson said to a friend,— "Hurd, Sir, is one of a set of men who account for every thing systematically; for instance, it has been a fashion to wear scarlet breeches; these men would tell you, that according to causes and effects, no other wear could at that time have been chosen." He, however, said of him at another time to the same gentleman, "Hurd, Sir, is a man whose acquaintance is a valuable acquisition."

That learned and ingenious Prelate it is well known published at one period of his life *Moral and Political Dialogues*, with a woefully whiggish cast. Afterwards, his Lordship having thought better, came to see his errour, and republished the work with a more constitutional spirit. Johnson, however, was unwilling to allow him full credit for his political conversion. I remember when his Lordship declined the honour of being Archbishop of Canterbury, Johnson said, "I am glad he did not go to Lambeth; for, after all, I fear he is a Whig in his heart."

The heterogeneous composition of human nature was remarkably exemplified in Johnson. His liberality in giving his money to persons in distress was extraordinary. Yet there lurked about him a prospensity to paltry saving. One day I owned to him, that "I was occasionally troubled with a fit of *narrowness*." "Why, Sir, (said he,) so am I. *But I do not tell it.*" He has now and then borrowed a shilling of me; and when I asked him for it again, seemed to be rather out of humour. A droll little circumstance once occurred: As if he meant to reprimand my minute exactness as a creditor, he thus addressed me:—"Boswell, *lend* me sixpence—*not to be repaid.*"

Though a stern *true-born Englishman*, and fully prejudiced against all other nations, he had discernment enough to see, and candour enough to censure, the cold reserve too common among Englishmen towards strangers: "Sir, (said he,) two men of any other nation who are shewn into a room together, at a house where they are both visitors, will immediately find some conversation. But two Englishmen will probably go each to a different window, and remain in obstinate silence. Sir, we as yet do not enough understand the common rights of humanity."

Maurice Morgann, Esq. authour of the very ingenious *Essay on the character of Falstaff*, and he had a dispute pretty late at night, in which Johnson would not give up, though he had the wrong side; and in short, both kept the field. Next morning, when they met in the breakfasting-room, Dr. Johnson accosted Mr. Morgann thus: "Sir, I have been thinking on our dispute last night;—*You were in the right.*"

Johnson, for sport perhaps, or from the spirit of contradiction, eagerly maintained that Derrick had merit as a writer. Mr. Morgann argued with him directly, in vain. At length he had recourse to this device. "Pray, Sir, (said he,) whether do you reckon Derrick or Smart the best poet?" Johnson at once felt himself roused; and answered, "Sir, there is no settling the point of precedency between a louse and a flea."

Once, when checking my boasting too frequently of myself in company, he said to me, "Boswell, you often vaunt so much as to provoke ridicule. You put me in mind of a man who was standing in the kitchen of an inn with his back to the fire, and thus accosted the person next him 'Do you know, Sir, who I am?' 'No, Sir, (said the other,) I have not that advantage.' 'Sir, (said he,) I am the *great* TWALMLEY, who invented the New Floodgate Iron.'"

His acute observation of human life made him remark, "Sir, there is nothing by which a man exasperates most people more, than by displaying a superior ability of brilliancy in conversation. They seem pleased at the time; but their envy makes them curse him at their hearts."

Johnson's love of little children, which he discovered upon all occasions, calling them "pretty dears," and giving them sweet-meats, was an undoubted proof of the real humanity and gentleness of his disposition.

278

Nor would it be just under his head, to omit the fondness which he shewed for animals which he had taken under his protection. I never shall forget the indulgence with which he treated Hodge, his cat; for whom he himself used to go out and buy oysters, lest the servants, having that trouble, should take a dislike to the poor creature. I am, unluckily, one of those who have an antipathy to a cat, so that I am uneasy when in the room with one; and I own, I frequently suffered a good deal from the presence of this same Hodge. I recollect him one day scrambling up Dr. Johnson's breast, apparently with much satisfaction, while my friend smiling and half-whistling, rubbed down his back, and pulled him by the tail; and when I observed he was a fine cat, saying, "why, yes, Sir, but I have had cats whom I liked better than this;" and then as if perceiving Hodge to be out of countenance, adding, "but he is a very fine cat, a very fine cat indeed."

This reminds me of the ludicrous account which he gave Mr. Langton, of the despicable state of a young gentleman of good family. "Sir, when I heard of him last, he was running about town shooting cats." And then in a sort of kindly reverie, he bethought himself of his own favourite cat, and said, "But Hodge shan't be shot: no, no, Hodge shall not be shot."

On Thursday, April 10, I introduced to him, at his house in Bolt-court, the Honourable and Reverend William Stuart, son of the Earl of Bute; a gentleman truly worthy of being known to Johnson; being, with all the advantages of high birth, learning, travel, and elegant manners, an exemplary parish-priest in every respect.

After some compliments on both sides, the tour which Johnson and I had made to the Hebrides was mentioned.—JOHNSON: "I got an acquisition of more ideas by it than by any thing that I remember. I saw quite a different system of life." BOSWELL: "You would not like to make the same journey again?" JOHNSON: "Why, no, Sir; not the same: it is a tale told. Gravina, an Italian critick, observes, that every man desires to see that of which he has read; but no man desires to read an account of what he has seen: so much does description fall short of reality. Description only excites curiosity: seeing satisfies it. Other people may go and see the Hebrides." BOSWELL: "I should wish to go and see some country totally different from what I have been used to; such as Turkey, where religion and every thing else are different." JOHNSON: "Yes, Sir; there are two objects of curiosity,—the Christian world, and the Mahometan world. All the rest may be considered as barbarous."

BOSWELL: "This has been a very factious reign, owing to the too great indulgence of Government." JOHNSON: "*I* think so, Sir. What at first was lenity, grew timidity. Yet this is reasoning *à posteriori*, and may not be just. Supposing a few had at first been punished, I believe faction would have been crushed; but it might have been said, that it was a sanguinary reign. A man cannot tell *à priori* what will be best for government to do. This reign has been very unfortunate. We have had an unsuccessful war; but that does not prove that we have been ill governed. One side or other must prevail in war, as one or other must win at play. When we beat Louis, we were not better governed; nor were the French better governed, when Louis beat us."

On Saturday, April 12, I visited him, in company with Mr. Windham, of Norfolk, whom, though a Whig, he highly valued. One of the best things he ever said was to this gentleman; who, before he set out for Ireland as Secretary to Lord Northington, when Lord Lieutenant, expressed to the Sage some modest and virtuous doubts, whether he could bring himself to practise those arts which it is supposed a person in that situation has occasion to employ. "Don't be afraid, Sir, (said Johnson, with a pleasant smile,) you will soon make a very pretty rascal."

On April 18, (being Good-Friday,) I found him at breakfast, in his usual manner upon that day, drinking tea without milk, and eating a cross bun to prevent faintness; we went to St. Clement's church, as formerly. When we came home from church, he placed himself on one of the stone-seats at his garden-door, and I took the other, and thus in the open air, and in a placid frame of mind, he talked away very easily. JOHNSON: "Were I a country gentleman, I should not be very hospitable, I should not have crowds in my house." BOSWELL: "Sir Alexander Dick tells me, that he remembers having a thousand people in a year to dine at his house; that is, reckoning each person as one, each time that he dined there." JOHNSON: "That, Sir, is about three a day." BOSWELL: "How your statement lessens the idea." JOHNSON: "That, Sir, is the good of counting. It brings every thing to a certainty, which before floated in the mind indefinitely." BOSWELL: "But *Omne ignotum pro magnifico est*: one is sorry to have this diminished." JOHNSON: "Sir, you should not allow yourself to be delighted with errour." BOSWELL: "Three a day seem but few." JOHNSON: "Nay, Sir, he who entertains three a day, does very liberally. And if there is a large family, the poor entertain those three, for they eat what the poor would get: there must be superfluous meat; it must be given to the poor, or thrown out." BOSWELL: "I observe in London, that the poor go about and gather bones, which I understand are manufactured." JOHNSON: "Yes, Sir; they boil them, and extract a grease from them for greasing wheels and other purposes. Of the best pieces they make a mock ivory, which is used for hafts to knives, and various other things; the coarser pieces they burn, and pound, and sell the ashes." BOSWELL: "For what purpose, Sir?" JOHNSON: "Why, Sir, for making a furnace for the chemist for melting iron. A paste made of burnt bones will stand a stronger heat than any thing else. Consider, Sir; if you are to melt iron, you cannot line your pot with brass, because it is softer than iron, and would melt sooner; nor with iron, for though malleable iron is harder than cast iron, yet it would not do; but a paste of burnt-bones will not melt." BOSWELL: "Do you know, Sir, I have discovered a manu-facture to a great extent, of what you only piddle at,—scraping and drying the peel of oranges. At a place in Newgate-street, there is a prodigious quantity prepared, which they sell to the distillers." JOHNSON: "Sir, I believe they make a higher thing out of them than a spirit; they make what is called orange-butter, the oil of the orange inspissated, which they mix perhaps with common pomatum, and make it fragrant. The oil does not fly off in the drying."

BOSWELL: "I wish to have a good walled garden." JOHNSON: "I don't think it would be worth the expence to you. We compute, in England, a park-wall at a thousand pounds a mile; now a garden-wall must cost at least as much. You intend your trees should grow higher than a deer will leap. Now let us see;—for a hundred pounds, you could only have forty-four square yards, which is very little; for two hundred pounds, you may have eighty-four square yards, which is very well. But when will you get the value of two hundred pounds of walls, in fruit, in your climate? No, Sir, such contention with Nature is not worth while. I would plant an orchard, and have plenty of such fruit as ripen well in your country. My friend, Dr. Madden, of Ireland, said, that 'in an orchard there should be enough to eat, enough to lay up, enough to be stolen, and enough to rot upon the ground.' Cherries are an early fruit, you may have them; and you may have the early apples and pears." BOSWELL: "We cannot have nonpareils." JOHNSON: "Sir, you can no more have nonpareils, than you can have grapes." BOSWELL: "We have them, Sir; but they are very bad." JOHNSON: "Nay, Sir, never try to have a thing, merely to shew that you *cannot* have it. From ground that would let for forty shillings you may have a large orchard; and you see it costs you only forty shillings. Nay, you may graze the ground, when the trees are grown up; you cannot, while they are young." BOSWELL: "Is not a good garden a very common thing in England, Sir?" JOHNSON: "Not so common, Sir, as you imagine. In Lincolnshire there is hardly an orchard; in Staffordshire very little fruit." BOSWELL: "Has Langton no orchard?" JOHNSON: "No, Sir." BOSWELL: "How so, Sir?" JOHNSON: "Why, Sir, from the general negligence of the county. He has it not, because nobody else has it." BOSWELL: "A hothouse is a certain thing: I may have that." JOHNSON: "A hot-house is pretty certain; but you must first build it, then you must keep fires in it, and you must have a gardener to take care of it." BOSWELL: "But if I have a gardener at any rate?——" JOHNSON: "Why, yes." BOSWELL: "I'd have it near my house; there is no need to have it in the orchard." JOHNSON: "Yes, I'd have it near my house.—I would plant a great many currants; the fruit is good, and they make a pretty sweetmeat."

Mr. Walker, the celebrated master of elocution, came in, and then we went up stairs into the study. I asked him if he had taught many clergymen. JOHNSON: "I hope not." WALKER: "I have taught only one, and he is the best reader I ever heard, not by my teaching, but by his own natural talents." JOHNSON: "Were he the best reader in the world, I would not have it told that he was taught." Here was one of his peculiar prejudices. Could it be any disadvantage to the clergyman to have it known that he was taught an easy and graceful delivery? BOSWELL: "Will you not allow, Sir, that a man may be taught to read well?" JOHNSON: "Why, Sir, so far as to read better than he might do without being taught, yes. Formerly it was supposed that there was no difference in reading, but that one read as well as another." BOSWELL: "It is wonderful to see old Sheridan as enthusiastick about oratory as ever." WALKER: "His enthusiasm as to what oratory will do, may be too great: but he reads well." JOHNSON: "He reads well, but he reads low; and you know it is much easier to read low than to read high; for when you read high, you are much more limited, your loudest note can be but one, and so the variety is less in proportion to the loudness. Now some people have occasion to speak to an extensive audience, and must speak loud to be heard." WALKER: "The art is to read strong, though low."

Talking of the origin of language;—JOHNSON: "It must have

come by inspiration. A thousand, nay, a million of children could not invent a language. While the organs are pliable, there is not understanding enough to form a language; by the time that there is understanding enough, the organs are become stiff. We know that after a certain age we cannot learn to pronounce a new language. No foreigner, who comes to England when advanced in life, ever pronounces English tolerably well; at least such instances are very rare. When I maintain that language must have come by inspiration, I do not mean that inspiration is required for rhetorick, and all the beauties of language; for when once man has language, we can conceive that he may gradually form modifications of it. I mean only that inspiration seems to me to be necessary to give man the faculty of speech; to inform him that he may have speech; which I think he could no more find out without inspiration, than cows or hogs would think of such a faculty." WALKER: "Do you think, Sir, that there are any perfect synonimes in any language?" JOHNSON: "Originally there were not; but by using words negligently, or in poetry, one word comes to be confounded with another."

Mrs. Burney, wife of his friend Dr. Burney, came in, and he seemed to be entertained with her conversation.

Garrick's funeral was talked of as extravagantly expensive. Johnson, from his dislike to exaggeration, would not allow that it was distinguished by any extraordinary pomp. "Were there not six horses to each coach?" said Mrs. Burney. JOHNSON: "Madam, there were no more six horses than six phœnixes."

Mrs. Burney wondered that some very beautiful new buildings should be erected in Moorfields, in so shocking a situation as between Bedlam and St. Luke's Hospital; and said she could not live there. JOHNSON: "Nay, Madam, you see nothing there to hurt you. You no more think of madness by having windows that look to Bedlam, than you think of death by having windows that look to a church-yard." MRS. BURNEY: "We may look to a church-yard, Sir; for it is right that we should be kept in mind of death." JOHNSON: "Nay, Madam, if you go to that, it is right that we should be kept in mind of madness, which is occasioned by too much indulgence of imagination. I think a very moral use may be made of these new buildings: I would have those who have heated imaginations live there, and take warning." MRS. BURNEY: "But, Sir, many of the poor people that are mad, have become so from disease, or from distressing events. It is therefore, not their fault, but their misfortune; and, therefore, to think of them, is a melancholy consideration."

On Sunday, April 20, being Easter-day, after attending solemn service at St. Paul's, I came to Dr. Johnson, and found Mr. Lowe, the painter, sitting with him. Mr. Lowe mentioned the great number of new buildings of late in London, yet that Dr. Johnson had observed, that the number of inhabitants was not increased. JOHNSON: "Why, Sir, the bills of mortality prove that no more people die now than formerly; so it is plain no more live. The register of births proves nothing, for not one-tenth of the people of London are born there." BOSWELL: "I believe, Sir, a great many of the children born in London die early." JOHNSON: "Why, yes, Sir." BOSWELL: "But those who do live, are as stout and strong people as any: Dr. Price says, they must be naturally strong to get through." JOHNSON: "That is system, Sir. A great traveller observes, that it is said there are no weak or deformed people among the Indians; but he with much sagacity assigns the reason of this, which is, that the hardship of their lives as hunters and fishers, does not allow weak or diseased children to grow up. Now had I been an Indian, I must have died early; my eyes would not have served me to get food. I indeed now could fish, give me English tackle; but had I been an Indian, I must have starved, or they would have knocked me on the head, when they saw I could do nothing." BOSWELL: "Perhaps they would have taken care of you; we are told they are fond of oratory—you would have talked to them." JOHNSON: "Nay, Sir, I should not have lived long enough to be fit to talk; I should have been dead before I was ten years old. Depend upon it, Sir, a savage, when he is hungry, will not carry about with him a looby of nine years old, who cannot help himself. They have no affection, Sir." BOSWELL: "I believe natural affection, of which we hear so much, is very small." JOHNSON: "Sir, natural affection is nothing: but affection from principle and established duty, is sometimes wonderfully strong." LOWE: "A hen, Sir, will feed her chickens in preference to herself." JOHNSON: "But we don't know that the hen is hungry; let the hen be fairly hungry, and I'll warrant she'll peck the corn herself. A cock, I believe, will feed hens instead of himself; but we don't know that the cock is hungry." BOSWELL: "And that, Sir, is not from affection but gallantry. But some of the Indians have affection." JOHNSON: "Sir, that they help some of their children is plain; for some of them live, which they could not do without being helped."

Having next day gone to Mr. Burke's seat in the country, from whence I was recalled by an express, that a near relation of mine had killed his antagonist in a duel, and was himself dangerously wounded, I saw little of Dr. Johnson till Monday, April 28, when I spent a considerable part of the day with him, and introduced the subject, which then chiefly occupied my mind. JOHNSON: "I do not see, Sir, that fighting is absolutely forbidden in Scripture; I see revenge forbidden, but not self-defence." BOSWELL: "The Quakers say it is; 'Unto him that smiteth thee on one cheek, offer him also the other.'" JOHNSON: "But stay, Sir; the text is meant only to have the effect of moderating passion; it is plain that we are not to take it in a literal sense. We see this from the context, where there are other recommendations, which I warrant you the Quaker will not take literally; as, for instance, 'From him that would borrow of thee, turn thou not away.' Let a man whose credit is bad, come to a Quaker, and say, 'Well, Sir, lend me a hundred pounds;' he'll find him as unwilling as any other man. No, Sir, a man may shoot the man who invades his character, as he may shoot him who attempts to break into his house. So in 1745, my friend, Tom Cumming the Quaker, said he would not fight, but he would drive an ammunition cart; and we know that the Quakers have sent flannel waistcoats to our soldiers, to enable them to fight better." BOSWELL: "When a man is the aggressor, and by ill-usage forces on a duel in which he is killed, have we not little ground to hope that he is gone to a state of happiness?" JOHNSON: "Sir, we are not to judge determinately of the state in which a man leaves this life. He may in a moment have repented effectually, and it is possible may have been accepted of God. There is in *Camden's Remains*, an epitaph upon a very wicked man, who was killed by a fall from his horse, in which he is supposed to say

' Between the stirrup and the ground,
  I mercy ask'd, I mercy found.' "

BOSWELL: "Is not the expression in the Burial-service,—'in the *sure* and *certain* hope of a blessed resurrection,'—too strong to be used indiscriminately, and, indeed, sometimes when those over whose bodies it is said, have been notoriously profane?" JOHNSON: "It is sure and certain *hope*, Sir, not *belief*." I did not insist further; but cannot help thinking that less positive words would be more proper.

Talking of a man who was growing very fat, so as to be incommoded with corpulency; he said, "He eats too much Sir."

BOSWELL: "I don't know, Sir; you will see one man fat, who eats moderately, and another lean, who eats a great deal." JOHNSON: "Nay, Sir, whatever may be the quantity that a man eats, it is plain that if he is too fat, he has eaten more than he should have done. One man may have a digestion that consumes food better than common; but it is certain that solidity is increased by putting something to it." BOSWELL: "But may not solids swell and be distended?" JOHNSON: "Yes, Sir, they may swell and be distended; but that is not fat."

We talked of the accusation against a gentleman for supposed delinquencies in India. JOHNSON: "What foundation there is for accusation I know not, but they will not get at him. Where bad actions are committed at so great a distance, a delinquent can obscure the evidence till the scent becomes cold; there is a cloud between, which cannot be penetrated: therefore all distant power is bad. I am clear that the best plan for the government of India is a despotick governour; for if he be a good man, it is evidently the best government; and supposing him to be a bad man, it is better to have one plunderer than many. A governour, whose power is checked, lets others plunder, that he himself may be allowed to plunder; but if despotick, he sees that the more he lets others plunder, the less there will be for himself, so he restrains them and though he himself plunders, the country is a gainer, compared with being plundered by numbers."

On Monday, April 28, I found him at home in the morning, and Mr. Seward with him. Horace having been mentioned;— BOSWELL: "There is a great deal of thinking in his works. One finds there almost everything but religion." SEWARD: "He speaks of his returning to it, in his Ode *Parcus Deorum cultor et infrequens*." JOHNSON: "Sir, he was not in earnest; this was merely poetical." BOSWELL: "There are, I am afraid, many people who have no religion at all." SEWARD: "And sensible people too." JOHNSON: "Why, Sir, not sensible in that respect. There must be either a natural or a moral stupidity, if one lives in a total neglect of so very important a concern." SEWARD: "I wonder that there should be people without religion." JOHNSON: "Sir, you need not wonder at this, when you consider how large a proportion of almost every man's life is passed without thinking of it. I myself was for some years totally regardless of religion. It had dropped out of my mind. It was at an early part of my life. Sickness brought it back, and I hope I have never lost it since." BOSWELL: "My dear Sir, what a man must you have been without religion! Why you must have gone on drinking, and swearing, and——" JOHNSON: (with a smile:) "I drank enough and swore enough to be sure." SEWARD: "One should think that sickness, and the view of death would make more men religious." JOHNSON: "Sir, they do not know how to go about it: they have not the first notion. A man who has never had religion before, no more grows religious when he is sick, than a man who has never learnt figures can count, when he has need of calculation."

I mentioned a worthy friend of ours whom we valued much, but observed that he was too ready to introduce religious discourse upon all occasions. JOHNSON: "Why, yes, Sir, he will introduce religious discourse without seeing whether it will end in instruction and improvement, or produce some profane jest. He would introduce it in the company of Wilkes, and twenty more such."

I mentioned Dr. Johnson's excellent distinction between liberty of conscience and liberty of teaching. JOHNSON: "Consider, Sir; if you have children whom you wish to educate in the principles of the Church of England, and there comes a Quaker who tries to pervert them to his principles, you would drive away the Quaker. You would not trust to the predomination of right, which you believe is in your opinions; you will keep wrong out of their heads. Now the vulgar are the children of the State. If any one attempts to teach them doctrines contrary to what the State approves, the magistrate may and ought to restrain him." SEWARD: "Would you restrain private conversation, Sir?" JOHNSON: "Why, Sir, it is difficult to say where private conversation begins, and where it ends. If we three should discuss even the great question concerning the existence of a Supreme Being by ourselves, we should not be restrained; for that would be to put an end to all improvement. But if we should discuss it in the presence of ten boarding-school girls, and as many boys, I think the magistrate would do well to put us in the stocks, to finish the debate there."

On Thursday, May 1, I visited him in the evening along with young Mr. Burke. He said, "It is strange that there should be so little reading in the world, and so much writing. People in general do not willingly read, if they can have any thing else to amuse them. There must be an external impulse; emulation, or vanity, or avarice. The progress which the understanding makes through a book, has more pain than pleasure in it. Language is scanty, and inadequate to express the nice gradations and mixtures of our feelings. No man reads a book of science from pure inclination. The books that we do read with pleasure are light compositions which contain a quick succession of events. However, I have this year read all Virgil through. I read a book of the Æneid every night, so it was done in twelve nights, and I had a great delight in it. The Georgicks did not give me so much pleasure, except the fourth book. The Eclogues I have almost all by heart. I do not think the story of the Æneid interesting. I like the story of the Odyssey much better; and this not on account of the wonderful things which it contains; for there are wonderful things enough in the Æneid;— the ships of the Trojans turned to sea-nymphs,—The tree at Polydorus's tomb dropping blood. The story of the Odyssey is interesting, as a great part of it is domestick.—It has been said, there is pleasure in writing, particularly in writing verses. I allow, you may have pleasure from writing, after it is over, if you have written well; but you don't go willingly to it again. I know when I have been writing verses, I have run my finger down the margin, to see how many I had made, and how few I had to make."

He seemed to be in a very placid humour, and although I have no note of the particulars of young Mr. Burke's conversation, it is but justice to mention in general, that it was such that Dr. Johnson said to me afterwards, "He did very well indeed; I have a mind to tell his father."

I have no minute of any interview with Johnson till Thursday, May 15th, when I find what follows: BOSWELL: "I wish much to be in Parliament, Sir." JOHNSON: "Why, Sir, unless you come resolved to support any administration, you would be the worse for being in Parliament, because you would be obliged to live more expensively."—BOSWELL: "Perhaps, Sir, I should be the less happy for being in Parliament. I never would sell my vote, and I should be vexed if things went wrong." JOHNSON: "That's cant, Sir. It would not vex you more in the house than in the gallery: publick affairs vex no man." BOSWELL: "Have not they vexed yourself a little, Sir? Have not you been vexed by all the turbulence of this reign, and by that absurd vote of the House of Commons, 'That the influence of the Crown has increased, is increasing, and ought to be diminished'?" JOHNSON: "Sir, I have never slept an hour less, nor eat an ounce less meat. I would have knocked the factious dogs on the head, to be sure; but I was not *vexed*." BOSWELL: "I declare, Sir, upon my honour, I did imagine I was vexed, and took a pride in it; but it *was* perhaps, cant; for I own I neither eat less, nor slept less." JOHNSON: "My dear friend, clear your
288

mind of cant. You may *talk* as other people do: you may say to a man, 'Sir, I am your most humble servant.' You are *not* his most humble servant. You may say, 'These are bad times; it is a melancholy thing to be reserved to such times.' You don't mind the times. You tell a man, 'I am sorry you had such bad weather the last day of your journey, and were so much wet.' You don't care six-pence whether he is wet or dry. You may *talk* in this manner; it is a mode of talking in Society: but don't *think* foolishly."

I talked of living in the country. JOHNSON: "Don't set up for what is called hospitality: it is a waste of time, and a waste of money; you are eaten up, and not the more respected for your liberality. If your house be like an inn, nobody cares for you. A man who stays a week with another, makes him a slave for a week." BOSWELL: "But there are people, Sir, who make their houses a home to their guests, and are themselves quite easy." JOHNSON: "Then, Sir, home must be the same to the guests, and they need not come."

Here he discovered a notion common enough in persons not much accustomed to entertain company, that there must be a degree of elaborate attention, otherwise company will think themselves neglected; and such attention is no doubt very fatiguing. He proceeded: "I would not, however, be a stranger in my own country; I would visit my neighbours, and receive their visits; but I would not be in haste to return visits. If a gentleman comes to see me, I tell him he does me a great deal of honour. I do not go to see him perhaps for ten weeks; then we are very complaisant to each other. No, Sir, you will have much more influence by giving or lending money where it is wanted, than by hospitality."

On Saturday, May 17, I saw him for a short time. Having mentioned that I had that morning been with old Mr. Sheridan, he remembered their former intimacy with a cordial warmth, and said to me, "Tell Mr. Sheridan, I shall be glad to see him, and shake hands with him." BOSWELL: "It is to me very wonderful that resentment should be kept up so long." JOHNSON: "Why, Sir, it is not altogether resentment that he does not visit me; it is partly falling out of the habit,—partly disgust, such as one has at a drug that has made him sick. Besides, he knows that I laugh at his oratory."

Another day I spoke of one of our friends, of whom he, as well as I, had a very high opinion. He expatiated in his praise; but added, "Sir, he is a cursed Whig, a *bottomless* Whig, as they all are now."

I mentioned my expectations from the interest of an eminent person then in power; adding, "but I have no claim but the claim of friendship; however, some people will go a great way from that motive." JOHNSON: "Sir, they will go all the way from that motive." A gentleman talked of retiring. "Never think of that," said Johnson. The gentleman urged, "I should then do no ill." JOHNSON: "Nor no good either. Sir, it would be a civil suicide."

On Monday, May 26, I found him at tea, and the celebrated Miss Burney, the authour of *Evelina* and *Cecilia*, with him. I asked, if there would be any speakers in Parliament, if there were no places to be obtained. JOHNSON: "Yes, Sir. Why do you speak here? Either to instruct and entertain, which is a benevolent motive; or for distinction, which is a selfish motive." I mentioned *Cecilia*. JOHNSON: (with an air of animated satisfaction) "Sir, if you talk of *Cecilia*, talk on."

I asked, whether a man naturally virtuous, or one who has overcome wicked inclinations, is the best. JOHNSON: "Sir, to *you*, the man who has overcome wicked inclinations, is not the best. He has more merit to *himself*: I would rather trust my money to a man who has no hands, and so a physical impossibility to steal, than to a man of the most honest principles. There is a witty satirical story of Foote. He had a small bust of Garrick placed upon his bureau. 'You may be surprised (said he) that I allow him to be so near my gold;—but you will observe, he has no hands.'"

On Friday, May 29, being to set out for Scotland next morning, I passed a part of the day with him in more than usual earnestness; as his health was in a more precarious state than at any time when I had parted from him. He, however, was quick and lively, and critical, as usual. I mentioned one who was a very learned man. JOHNSON: "Yes, Sir, he has a great deal of learning; but it never lies straight. There is never one idea by the side of another: 'tis all entangled: and then he drives it so aukwardly upon conversation!"

I stated to him an anxious thought, by which a sincere Christian might be disturbed, even when conscious of having lived a good life, so far as is consistent with human infirmity; he might fear that he should afterwards fall away, and be guilty of such crimes as would render all his former religion vain. Could there be, upon this awful subject, such a thing as balancing of accounts? Suppose a man who has led a good life for seven years, commits an act of wickedness, and instantly dies; will his former good life have any effect in his favour? JOHNSON: "Sir, if a man has led a good life for seven years, and then is hurried by passion to do what is wrong, and is suddenly carried off, depend upon it he will have the reward of his seven years' good life: God will not take a catch of him. Upon this principle Richard Baxter believes that a Suicide may be saved. 'If (says he) it should be objected that what I maintain may encourage suicide, I answer, I am not to tell a lie to prevent it.'" BOSWELL: "But does not the text say, 'As the tree falls, so it must lie?'" JOHNSON: "Yes, Sir; as the tree falls: but,—(after a little pause) that is meant as to the general state of the tree, not what is the effect of a sudden blast." In short, he interpreted the expression as referring to condition, not to position.

He said, "Get as much force of mind as you can. Live within your income. Always have something saved at the end of the year. Let your imports be more than your exports, and you'll never go far wrong."

I assured him, that in the extensive and various range of his acquaintance there never had been any one who had a more sincere respect and affection for him than I had. He said, "I believe it, Sir. Were I in distress, there is no man to whom I should sooner come than to you. I should like to come and have a cottage in your park, toddle about, live mostly on milk, and be taken care of by Mrs. Boswell. She and I are good friends now; are we not?"

Talking of devotion, he said, "Though it be true that 'God dwelleth not in Temples made with hands,' yet in this state of being, our minds are more piously affected in places appropriated to divine worship, than in others. Some people have a particular room in their houses, where they say their prayers; of which I do not disapprove, as it may animate their devotion."

He embraced me, and gave me his blessing, as usual when I was leaving him for any length of time. I walked from his door to-day, with a fearful apprehension of what might happen before I returned.

CHAPTER XIV

In Seventeen Eighty-four

ON SATURDAY, May 15, 1784, I dined with Johnson at Dr. Brocklesby's, where were Colonel Vallancy, Mr. Murphy, and that ever-cheerful companion Mr. Devaynes, apothecary to his Majesty. Of these days, and others on which I saw him, I have no memorials, except the general recollection of his being able and animated in conversation, and appearing to relish society as much as the youngest man. I find only these three small particulars:— When a person was mentioned, who said, "I have lived fifty-one years in this world, without having had ten minutes of uneasiness;" he exclaimed, "The man who says so, lies: he attempts to impose on human credulity." One of the company provoked him greatly by doing what he could least of all bear, which was quoting something of his own writing, against what he then maintained. "What, Sir, (cried the gentleman,) do you say to

> ' The busy day, the peaceful night,
> Unfelt, uncounted, glided by? ' "

Johnson finding himself thus presented as giving an instance of a man who had lived without uneasiness, was much offended, for he looked upon such a quotation as unfair, his anger burst out in an unjustifiable retort, insinuating that the gentleman's remark was a sally of ebriety; "Sir, there is one passion I would advise you to command: when you have drunk out that glass, don't drink another." Here was exemplified what Goldsmith said of him, with the aid of a very witty image from one of Cibber's Comedies: "There is no arguing with Johnson: for if his pistol misses fire, he knocks you down with the butt end of it."

Another was this: when a gentleman of eminence in the literary world was violently censured for attacking people by anonymous paragraphs in newspapers; he, from the spirit of contradiction as I thought, took up his defence and said, "Come, come, this is not so terrible a crime; he means only to vex them a little. I do not say that I should do it; but there is a great difference between him and me; what is fit for Hephæstion is not fit for Alexander."—Another, when I told him that a young and handsome Countess had said to me, "I should think that to be praised by Dr. Johnson would make one a fool all one's life;" and that I answered, "Madam, I shall make him a fool to-day, by repeating this to him;" he said, "I am too old to be made a fool; but if you say I am made a fool I shall not deny it. I am much pleased with a compliment, especially from a pretty woman."

On the evening of Saturday, May 15, he was in fine spirits at our Essex-Head Club. He told us, "I dined yesterday at Mrs. Garrick's with Mrs. Carter, Miss Hannah More, and Miss Fanny Burney. Three such women are not to be found: I know not where I could find a fourth, except Mrs. Lennox, who is superiour to them all." BOSWELL: "What! had you them all to yourself, Sir?" JOHNSON: "I had them all, as much as they were had; but it might have been better had there been more company there." BOSWELL: "Might not Mrs. Montagu have been a fourth?" JOHNSON: "Sir, Mrs. Montagu does not make a trade of her wit; but Mrs. Montagu is a very extraordinary woman: she has a constant stream of conversation, and it is always impregnated; it has always meaning." BOSWELL: "Mr. Burke has a constant stream of conversation." JOHNSON: "Yes, Sir; if a man were to go by chance at the same time with Burke under a shed, to shun a shower, he would say—'this is an extraordinary man.' If Burke should go into a stable to see his horse drest, the ostler would say—'we have had an extraordinary man here.'" BOSWELL: "Foote was a man who never failed in conversation. If he had gone into a stable——" JOHNSON: "Sir, if he had gone into the stable, the ostler would have said, here has been a comical fellow: but he would not have respected him." BOSWELL: "And, Sir, the ostler would have answered him, would have given him as good as he brought, as the common saying is." JOHNSON: "Yes, Sir; and Foote would have answered the ostler.— When Burke does not descend to be merry, his conversation is very superiour indeed. There is no proportion between the powers which he shews in serious talk and in jocularity. When he lets himself down to that, he is in the kennel." Mr. Windham now said low to me, that he differed from our great friend in this observation; for that Mr. Burke was often very happy in his merriment. It would not have been right for either of us to have contradicted Johnson at this time, in a Society all of whom did not know and value Mr. Burke as much as we did. It might have occasioned something

293

more rough, and at any rate would probably have checked the flow of Johnson's good-humour. He called to us with a sudden air of exultation, as the thought started into his mind, "O! gentlemen, I must tell you a very great thing. The Empress of Russia has ordered the *Rambler* to be translated into the Russian language: so I shall be read on the banks of the Wolga. Horace boasts that his fame would extend as far as the banks of the Rhone; now the Wolga is farther from me than the Rhone was from Horace." BOSWELL: "You must certainly be pleased with this, Sir." JOHNSON: "I am pleased, Sir, to be sure. A man is pleased to find he has succeeded in that which he has endeavoured to do."

One of the company mentioned his having seen a noble person driving in his carriage, and looking exceedingly well, notwithstanding his great age. JOHNSON: "Ah, Sir; that is nothing. Bacon observes, that a stout healthy old man is like a tower undermined."

On Sunday, May 16, I found him alone; he talked of Mrs. Thrale with much concern, saying, "Sir, she has done every thing wrong since Thrale's bridle was off her neck."

Johnson, talking of the fear of death, said, "Some people are not afraid, because they look upon salvation as the effect of an absolute decree, and think they feel in themselves the marks of sanctification. Others, and those the most rational in my opinion, look upon salvation as conditional; and as they never can be sure that they have complied with the conditions, they are afraid."

On Wednesday, May 19, I sat a part of the evening with him, by ourselves. I observed, that the death of our friends might be a consolation against the fear of our own dissolution, because we might have more friends in the other world than in this. He perhaps felt this a reflection upon his apprehension as to death; and said, with heat, "How can a man know *where* his departed friends are, or whether they will be his friends in the other world? How many friendships have you known formed upon principles of virtue? Most friendships are formed by caprice or by chance, mere confederacies in vice or leagues in folly."

We talked of our worthy friend Mr. Langton. He said, "I know not who will go to Heaven if Langton does not. Sir, I could almost say, *Sit anima mea cum Langtono.*"[1] I mentioned a very eminent friend as a virtuous man. JOHNSON: "Yes, Sir; but —— has not the evangelical virtue of Langton. ——, I am afraid, would not scruple to pick up a wench."

[1] May my soul be with Langton.

He however charged Mr. Langton with what he thought want of judgement upon an interesting occasion. "When I was ill, (said he) I desired he would tell me sincerely in what he thought my life was faulty. Sir, he brought me a sheet of paper, on which he had written down several texts of Scripture, recommending christian charity. And when I questioned him what occasion I had given for such an animadversion, all that he could say amounted to this,— that I sometimes contradicted people in conversation. Now what harm does it do to any man to be contradicted?" BOSWELL: "I suppose he meant the *manner* of doing it; roughly,—and harshly." JOHNSON: "And who is the worse for that?" BOSWELL: "It hurts people of weaker nerves." JOHNSON: "I know no such weak-nerved people." Mr. Burke, to whom I related this conference, said, "It is well, if when a man comes to die, he has nothing heavier upon his conscience than having been a little rough in conversation."

Johnson, at the time when the paper was presented to him, though at first pleased with the attention of his friend, whom he thanked in an earnest manner, soon exclaimed in a loud and angry tone, "What is your drift, Sir?" Sir Joshua Reynolds pleasantly observed, that it was a scene for a comedy, to see a penitent get into a violent passion and belabour his confessor.

I have preserved no more of his conversation at the times when I saw him during the rest of this month, till Sunday, the 30th of May, when I met him in the evening at Mr. Hoole's, where there was a large company both of ladies and gentlemen. Sir James Johnston happened to say that he paid no regard to the arguments of counsel at the bar of the House of Commons, because they were paid for speaking. JOHNSON: "Nay, Sir, argument is argument. You cannot help paying regard to their arguments, if they are good. If it were testimony, you might disregard it, if you knew that it were purchased. There is a beautiful image in Bacon, upon this subject: testimony is like an arrow shot from a long bow; the force of it depends on the strength of the hand that draws it. Argument is like an arrow from a cross-bow, which has equal force though shot by a child."

He had now a great desire to go to Oxford, as his first jaunt after his illness; we talked of it for some days, and I had promised to accompany him.

On Thursday, June 3, the Oxford post-coach took us up in the morning at Bolt-court. The other two passengers were Mrs. Beresford and her daughter, two very agreeable ladies from

America; they were going to Worcestershire, where they then resided. I found from the way-bill that Dr. Johnson had made our names be put down. Mrs. Beresford, who had read it, whispered me, "Is this the great Dr. Johnson?" I told her it was; so she was then prepared to listen.

I was surprized at his talking without reserve in the publick post-coach of the state of his affairs; "I have (said he) about the world I think above a thousand pounds, which I intend shall afford Frank an annuity of seventy pounds a-year." Indeed his openness with people at a first interview was remarkable. He said once to Mr. Langton, "I think I am like Squire Richard in *The Journey to London*, '*I'm never strange in a strange place.*'" He was truly *social*. He strongly censured what is much too common in England among persons of condition,—maintaining an absolute silence, when unknown to each other; as for instance, when occasionally brought together in a room before the master or mistress of the house has appeared. "Sir, that is being so uncivilized as not to understand the common rights of humanity."

At the inn where we stopped he was exceedingly dissatisfied with some roast mutton which he had for dinner. The ladies, I saw, wondered to see the great philosopher whose wisdom and wit they had been admiring all the way, get into ill humour from such a cause. He scolded the waiter saying, "It is as bad as bad can be: it is ill-fed, ill-killed, ill-kept, and ill-drest."

He bore the journey very well, and seemed to feel himself elevated as he approached Oxford, that magnificent and venerable seat of Learning, Orthodoxy, and Toryism. We were received with the most polite hospitality at the house of his old friend Dr. Adams, Master of Pembroke College, who had given us a kind invitation. Before we were set down, I communicated to Johnson, my having engaged to return to London directly, but that I would hasten back to him again. He was pleased that I had made this journey merely to keep him company. He was easy and placid, with Dr. Adams, Mrs. and Miss Adams, and Mrs. Kennicot, widow of the learned Hebræan, who was here on a visit. He soon dispatched the enquiries which were made about his illness and recovery, by a short and distinct narrative; and then assuming a gay air, repeated from Swift,

" Nor think on our approaching ills,
And talk of spectacles and pills."

Dr. Newman, the Bishop of Bristol, having been mentioned, Johnson, recollecting the manner in which he had been censured by that Prelate, thus retaliated:—"Tom knew he should be dead before what he has said of me would appear. He durst not have printed it while he was alive." DR. ADAMS: "I believe his *Dissertations on the Prophecies* is his great work." JOHNSON: "Why, Sir, it is *Tom's* great work; but how far it is great, or how much of it is Tom's, are other questions. I fancy a considerable part of it was borrowed." DR. ADAMS: "He was a very successful man." JOHNSON: "I don't think so, Sir.—He did not get very high. He was late in getting what he did get; and he did not get it by the best means. I believe he was a gross flatterer."

I fulfilled my intention by going to London, and returned to Oxford on Wednesday, the 9th of June, when I was happy to find myself again in the same agreeable circle at Pembroke College, with the comfortable prospect of making some stay. Johnson welcomed my return with more than ordinary glee.

Next morning at breakfast, he pointed out a passage in Savage's *Wanderer*, saying "These are fine verses."—"If (said he) I had written with hostility of Warburton in my Shakspeare, I should have quoted this couplet:

> ' Here Learning, blinded first, and then beguil'd,
> Looks dark as Ignorance, as Frenzy wild.'

You see they'd have fitted him to a *T*" (smiling.) DR. ADAMS: "But you did not write against Warburton." JOHNSON: "No, Sir, I treated him with great respect both in my preface and in my Notes."

Mrs. Kennicot spoke of her brother, the Reverend Mr. Chamberlayne, who had given up great prospects in the Church of England on his conversion to the Roman Catholick faith. Johnson, who warmly admired every man who acted from a conscientious regard to principle, erroneous or not, exclaimed fervently, "God bless him."

Mrs. Kennicot, in confirmation of Dr. Johnson's opinion, that the present was not worse than former ages, mentioned that her brother assured her, there was now less infidelity on the Continent than there had been; Voltaire and Rousseau were less read. I asserted, from good authority, that Hume's infidelity was certainly less read. JOHNSON: "All infidel writers drop into oblivion, when personal connections and the floridness of novelty are gone; though now and then a foolish fellow, who thinks he can be witty upon them, may bring them again into notice. There will some-times start up a College joker, who does not consider that what is a joke in a College will not do in the world. To such defenders of Religion I would apply a stanza of a poem which I remember to have seen in some old collection:

> ' Henceforth be quiet and agree,
> Each kiss his empty brother;
> Religion scorns a foe like thee,
> But dreads a friend like t'other.'

The point is well, though the expression is not correct; *one*, not *thee*, should be opposed to *t'other*."

On the Roman Catholick religion he said, "If you join the Papists externally, they will not interrogate you strictly as to your belief in their tenets. No reasoning Papist believes every article of their faith. There is one side on which a good man might be persuaded to embrace it. A good man of a timorous disposition, in great doubt of his acceptance with God, and pretty credulous, may be glad to be of a church where there are so many helps to get to heaven. I would be a Papist if I could. I have fear enough; but an obstinate rationality prevents me. I shall never be a Papist, unless on the near approach of death, of which I have a very great terrour. I wonder that women are not all Papists." BOSWELL: "They are not more afraid of death than men are." JOHNSON: "Because they are less wicked." DR. ADAMS: "They are more pious." JOHNSON: "No, hang 'em, they are not more pious. A wicked fellow is the most pious when he takes to it. He'll beat you all at piety."

He argued in defence of some of the peculiar tenets of the Church of Rome. As to the giving the bread only to the laity, he said, "They may think, that in what is merely ritual, deviations from the primitive mode may be admitted on the ground of convenience; and I think they are as well warranted to make this alteration, as we are to substitute sprinkling in the room of the ancient baptism." As to the invocation of saints, he said, "Though I do not think it authorised, it appears to me, that 'the communion of saints' in the Creed means the communion with the saints in Heaven, as connected with 'The holy Catholick church.'" He admitted the influence of evil spirits upon our minds, and said, "Nobody who believes the New Testament can deny it."

After dinner, when one of us talked of there being a great enmity between Whig and Tory;—JOHNSON: "Why, not so much, I think, unless when they come into competition with each other. There is none when they are only common acquaintance, none when they are of different sexes. A Tory will marry into a Whig family, and a Whig into a Tory family, without any reluctance. But, indeed, in a matter of much more concern than political tenets, and that is religion, men and women do not concern themselves much about difference of opinion; and ladies set no value on the moral character of men who pay their addresses to them; the greatest profligate will be as well received as the man of the greatest virtue, and this by a very good woman, by a woman who says her prayers three times a day." Our ladies endeavoured to defend their sex from this charge; but he roared them down! "No, no, a lady will take Jonathan Wild as readily as St. Austin, if he has threepence more; and, what is worse, her parents will give her to him. Women have a perpetual envy of our vices; they are less vicious than we, not from choice, but because we restrict them; they are the slaves of order and fashion; their virtue is of more consequence to us than our own, so far as concerns this world."

Miss Adams mentioned a gentleman of licentious character, and said, "Suppose I had a mind to marry that gentleman, would my parents consent?" JOHNSON: "Yes, they'd consent, and you'd go. You'd go, though they did not consent." MISS ADAMS: "Perhaps their opposing might make me go." JOHNSON: "O, very well; you'd take one whom you think a bad man, to have the pleasure of vexing your parents. You put me in mind of Dr. Barrowby, the physician, who was very fond of swine's flesh. One day, when he was eating it, he said, 'I wish I was a Jew.'—'Why so? (said somebody,) the Jews are not allowed to eat your favourite meat.'— 'Because (said he,) I should then have the gust of eating it, with the pleasure of sinning.'"—Johnson then proceeded in his declamation.

Miss Adams soon afterwards made an observation that I do not recollect, which pleased him much; he said with a good-humoured smile, "That there should be so much excellence united with so much *depravity*, is strange."

Indeed, this lady's good qualities, merit, and accomplishments, and her constant attention to Dr. Johnson, were not lost upon him. She happened to tell him that a little coffee-pot, in which she had made him coffee, was the only thing she could call her own. He turned to her with a complacent gallantry, "Don't say so, my dear; I hope you don't reckon my heart as nothing."

I asked him if it was true as reported, that he had said lately, "I am for the King against Fox; but I am for Fox against Pitt."

JOHNSON: "Yes, Sir; the King is my master; but I do not know Pitt; and Fox is my friend."

"Fox, (added he,) is a most extraordinary man; here is a man (describing him in strong terms of objection in some respects according as he apprehended, but which exalted his abilities the more,) who has divided the Kingdom with Cæsar; so that it was a doubt whether the nation should be ruled by the sceptre of George the Third, or the tongue of Fox."

Dr. Wall, physician at Oxford, drank tea with us. Johnson had in general a peculiar pleasure in the company of physicians, which was certainly not abated by the conversation of this learned, ingenious, and pleasing gentleman. Johnson said, "It is wonderful how little good Radcliffe's travelling fellowships have done. I know nothing that has been imported by them; yet many additions to our medical knowledge might be got in foreign countries. Inoculation, for instance, has saved more lives than war destroys: and the cures performed by the Peruvian-bark are innumerable. But it is in vain to send our travelling physicians to France, and Italy, and Germany, for all that is known there is known here: I'd send them out of Christendom; I'd send them among barbarous nations."

On Friday, June 11, we talked at breakfast, of forms of prayer. JOHNSON: "I know of no good prayers but those in the 'Book of Common Prayer.'" DR. ADAMS: (in a very earnest manner,) "I wish, Sir, you would compose some family prayers." JOHNSON: "I will not compose prayers for you, Sir, because you can do it for yourself. But I have thought of getting together all the books of prayers which I could, selecting those which should appear to me the best, putting out some, inserting others, adding some prayers of my own, and prefixing a discourse on prayer." We all now gathered about him, and two or three of us at a time joined in pressing him to execute this plan. He seemed to be a little displeased at the manner of our importunity, and in great agitation called out, "Do not talk thus of what is so awful. I know not what time God will allow me in this world. There are many things which I wish to do." Some of us persisted, and Dr. Adams said, "I never was more serious about any thing in my life." JOHNSON: "Let me alone, let me alone; I am over powered." And then he put his hands before his face, and reclined for some time upon the table.

I mentioned Jeremy Taylor's using, in his forms of prayer, "I am the chief of sinners," and other such self-condemning

300

expressions. "Now, (said I) this cannot be said with truth by every man, and therefore is improper for a general printed form. I myself cannot say that I am the worst of men; I *will* not say so." JOHNSON: "A man may know, that physically, that is, in the real state of things, he is not the worst man; but that morally he may be so. Law observes, 'that every man knows something worse of himself, than he is sure of in others.' You may not have committed such crimes as some men have done; but you do not know against what degree of light they have sinned. Besides, Sir, 'the chief of sinners' is a mode of expression for 'I am a great sinner.' So St. Paul, speaking of our SAVIOUR's having died to save sinners, says, 'of whom I am the chief;' yet he certainly did not think himself so bad as Judas Iscariot." BOSWELL: "But, Sir, Taylor means it literally, for he founds a conceit upon it. When praying for the conversion of sinners, and of himself in particular, he says, 'Lord, thou wilt not leave thy *chief* work undone.'" JOHNSON: "I do not approve of figurative expressions in addressing the Supreme Being; and I never use them. Taylor gives a very good advice: 'Never lie in your prayers; never confess more than you really believe; never promise more than you mean to perform.'"

Dr. Johnson and I went in Dr. Adams's coach to dine with Mr. Nowell, Principal of St. Mary Hall, at his beautiful villa at Iffley, on the banks of the Isis, about two miles from Oxford. While we were upon the road, I had the resolution to ask Johnson whether he thought that the roughness of his manner had been an advantage or not, and if he would not have done more good if he had been more gentle. I proceeded to answer myself thus: "Perhaps it has been of advantage, as it has given weight to what you said: you could not, perhaps, have talked with such authority without it." JOHNSON: "No, Sir; I have done more good as I am. Obscenity and Impiety have always been repressed in my company." BOSWELL: "True, Sir; and that is more than can be said of every Bishop. Greater liberties have been taken in the presence of a Bishop, though a very good man, from his being milder, and therefore not commanding such awe. Yet, Sir, many people who might have been benefited by your conversation, have been frightened away. A worthy friend of ours has told me, that he has often been afraid to talk to you." JOHNSON: "Sir, he need not have been afraid, if he had any thing rational to say. If he had not, it was better he did not talk."

We were well entertained and very happy at Dr. Nowell's, where was a very agreeable company; and we drank "Church and King," after dinner, with true Tory cordiality.

We talked of a certain clergyman of extraordinary character, who, by exerting his talents in writing on temporary topicks, and displaying uncommon intrepidity, had raised himself to affluence. I maintained that we ought not to be indignant at his success; for merit of every sort was entitled to reward. JOHNSON: "Sir, I will not allow this man to have merit. No, Sir; what he has is rather the contrary; I will, indeed, allow him courage, and on this account we so far give him credit. We have more respect for a man who robs boldly on the highway, than for a fellow who jumps out of a ditch and knocks you down behind your back. Courage is a quality so necessary for maintaining virtue, that it is always respected, even when it is associated with vice."

I censured the coarse invectives which were become fashionable in the House of Commons, and said, that if members of parliament must attack each other personally in the heat of debate, it should be done more genteely. JOHNSON: "No, Sir; that would be much worse. Abuse is not so dangerous when there is no vehicle of wit or delicacy, no subtle conveyance. The difference between coarse and refined abuse is as the difference between being bruised by a club, and wounded by a poisoned arrow."

On Saturday, June 12, there drank tea with us at Dr. Adams's, Mr. John Henderson, student of Pembroke College, celebrated for his wonderful acquirements in Alchymy, Judicial Astrology, and other abstruse and curious learning; and the Reverend Herbert Croft, who, I am afraid, was somewhat mortified by Dr. Johnson's not being highly pleased with some *Family Discourses*, which he had printed; they were in too familiar a style to be approved of by so manly a mind. I have no note of this evening's conversation, except a single fragment. When I mentioned Thomas Lord Lyttelton's vision, the prediction of the time of his death, and its exact fulfilment;—JOHNSON: "It is the most extraordinary thing that has happened in my day. I heard it with my own ears from his uncle, Lord Westcote. I am so glad to have every evidence of the spiritual world, that I am willing to believe it." DR. ADAMS: "You have evidence enough; good evidence, which needs not such support." JOHNSON: "I like to have more."

Mr. Henderson, with whom I had sauntered in the venerable walks of Merton-College, and found him a very learned and pious man, supped with us. Dr. Johnson surprized him not a little by

302

acknowledging with a look of horrour, that he was much oppressed by the fear of death. The amiable Dr. Adams suggested that God was infinitely good. JOHNSON: "That he is infinitely good, as far as the perfection of his nature will allow, I certainly believe; but it is necessary for good upon the whole, that individuals should be punished. As to an *individual*, therefore, he is not infinitely good; and as I cannot be *sure* that I have fulfilled the conditions on which salvation is granted, I am afraid I may be one of those who shall be damned" (looking dismally.) DR. ADAMS: "What do you mean by damned?" JOHNSON: (passionately and loudly) "Sent to Hell, Sir, and punished everlastingly." DR. ADAMS: "I don't believe that doctrine." JOHNSON: "Hold, Sir, do you believe that some will be punished at all?" DR. ADAMS: "Being excluded from Heaven will be a punishment; yet there may be no great positive suffering." JOHNSON: "Well, Sir; but, if you admit any degree of punishment, there is an end of your argument for infinite goodness simply considered; for, infinite goodness would inflict no punishment whatever. There is no infinite goodness physically considered; morally there is." BOSWELL: "But may not a man attain to such a degree of hope as not to be uneasy from the fear of death?" JOHNSON: "A man may have such a degree of hope as to keep him quiet. You see I am not quiet, from the vehemence with which I talk; but I do not despair." MRS. ADAMS: "You seem, Sir, to forget the merits of our Redeemer." JOHNSON: "Madam, I do not forget the merits of my Redeemer; but my Redeemer has said that he will set some on his right hand and some on his left."— He was in gloomy agitation, and said, "I'll have no more on't."

It was observed to Dr. Johnson, that it seemed strange that he, who has so often delighted his company by his lively and brilliant conversation, should say he was miserable. JOHNSON: "Alas! it is all outside; I may be cracking my joke, and cursing the sun. *Sun, how I hate thy beams!*"

On Sunday, June 13, our philosopher was calm at breakfast. There was something exceedingly pleasing in our leading a College life, without restraint, and with superior elegance, in consequence of our living in the Master's House, and having the company of ladies. Mrs. Kennicot related, in his presence, a lively saying of Dr. Johnson's to Miss Hannah More, who had expressed a wonder that the poet who had written "Paradise Lost," should write such poor Sonnets:—"Milton, Madam, was a genius that could cut a

303

Colossus from a rock, but could not carve heads upon cherry-stones."

We talked of the casuistical question, "Whether it was allowable at any time to depart from *Truth?*" JOHNSON: "The general rule is, that Truth should never be violated, because it is of the utmost importance to the comfort of life, that we should have a full security by mutual faith; and occasional inconveniences should be willingly suffered, that we may preserve it. There must, however, be some exceptions. If, for instance, a murderer should ask you which way a man is gone, you may tell him what is not true, because you are under a previous obligation not to betray a man to a murderer." BOSWELL: "Supposing the person who wrote *Junius* were asked whether he was the authour, might he deny it?" JOHNSON: "I don't know what to say to this. If you were *sure* that he wrote *Junius*, would you, if he denied it, think as well of him afterwards? Yet it may be urged, that what a man has no right to ask, you may refuse to communicate; and there is no other effectual mode of preserving a secret and an important secret, the discovery of which may be very hurtful to you, but a flat denial; for if you are silent, or hesitate, or evade, it will be held equivalent to a confession. But stay, Sir, here is another case. Supposing the authour had told me confidentially that he had written *Junius*, and I were asked if he had, I should hold myself at liberty to deny it, as being under a previous promise, express, or implied, to conceal it. Now what I ought to do for the authour, may I not do for myself? But I deny the lawfulness of telling a lie to a sick man, for fear of alarming him. You have no business with consequences; you are to tell the truth. Besides, you are not sure, what effect your telling him he is in danger may have. It may bring his distemper to a crisis, and that may cure him. Of all lying, I have the greatest abhorrence of this, because I believe it has been frequently practised on myself."

On Monday, June 14, and Tuesday, 15, Dr. Johnson and I dined, on one of them, I forget which, with Mr. Mickle, translator of the *Lusiad*, at Wheatley, a very pretty country place a few miles from Oxford; and on the other with Dr. Wetherell, Master of University-College. From Dr. Wetherell's he went to visit Mr. Sackville Parker, the bookseller; and when he returned to us, gave the following account of his visit, saying, "I have been to see my old friend, Sack. Parker; I find he has married his maid; he has done right. She had lived with him many years in great confidence, and they had mingled minds; I do not think he could have found any wife that would have made him so happy. The woman was very attentive and civil to me; she pressed me to fix a day for dining with them, and to say what I liked, and she would be sure to get it for me. Poor Sack! He is very ill, indeed. We parted as never to meet again. It has quite broke me down."

In the morning of Tuesday, June 15, while we sat at Dr. Adams's, we talked of a printed letter from the reverend Herbert Croft, to a young gentleman who had been his pupil, in which he advised him to read to the end of whatever books he should begin to read. JOHNSON: "This is surely a strange advice; you may as well resolve that whatever men you happen to get acquainted with, you are to keep to them for life. A book may be good for nothing; or there may be only one thing in it worth knowing; are we to read it all through? These *Voyages*, (pointing to the three large volumes of *Voyages to the South Sea*, which were just come out) *who* will read them through? A man had better work his way before the mast, than read them through; they will be eaten by rats and mice, before they are read through. There can be little entertainment in such books; one set of Savages is like another." BOSWELL: "I do not think the people of Otaheite can be reckoned Savages." JOHNSON: "Don't cant in defence of Savages." BOSWELL: "They have the art of navigation." JOHNSON: "A dog or a cat can swim." BOSWELL: "They carve very ingeniously." JOHNSON: "A cat can scratch, and a child with a nail can scratch." I perceived this was none of the *mollia tempora fandi*;[1] so desisted.

Upon his mentioning that when he came to College he wrote his first exercise twice over, but never did so afterwards; MISS ADAMS: "I suppose, Sir, you could not make them better?" JOHNSON: "Yes, Madam, to be sure I could make them better. Thought is better than no thought." MISS ADAMS: "So you think, Sir, you could make your *Ramblers* better?" JOHNSON: "Certainly I could." BOSWELL: "I'll lay a bet, Sir, you cannot." JOHNSON: "But I will, Sir, if I choose. I shall make the best of them you shall pick out, better."—BOSWELL: "But you may add to them. I will not allow of that." JOHNSON: "Nay, Sir, there are three ways of making them better;—putting out,—adding,—or correcting."

During our visit at Oxford, the following conversation passed between him and me on the subject of my trying my fortune

[1] Gentle times of speaking.

at the English bar. Having asked, whether a very extensive acquaintance in London, which was very valuable, and of great advantage to a man at large, might not be prejudicial to a lawyer, by preventing him from giving sufficient attention to his business?—JOHNSON: "Sir, you will attend to business, as business lays hold of you. When not actually employed, you may see your friends as much as you do now. You may dine at a Club every day, and sup with one of the members every night; and you may be as much at publick places as one who has seen them all would wish to be. But you must take care to attend constantly in Westminster Hall; both to mind your business, as it is almost all learnt there, (for nobody reads now,) and to shew that you want to have business. And you must not be too often seen at publick places, that competitors may not have it to say, 'He is always at the Playhouse or at Ranelagh, and never to be found at his chambers.' And, Sir, there must be a kind of solemnity in the manner of a professional man. I have nothing particular to say to you on the subject. All this I should say to any one; I should have said it to Lord Thurlow twenty years ago."

On Wednesday, June 16, Dr. Johnson and I returned to London; he was not well to-day, and said very little, employing himself chiefly in reading Euripides.

It having been mentioned to Dr. Johnson that a gentleman who had a son whom he imagined to have an extreme degree of timidity, resolved to send him to a publick school, that he might acquire confidence; "Sir, (said Johnson,) this is a preposterous expedient for removing his infirmity; such a disposition should be cultivated in the shade. Placing him at a publick school is forcing an owl upon day."

Speaking of a gentleman whose house was much frequented by low company; "Rags, Sir, (said he,) will always make their appearance where they have a right to do it."

Of the same gentleman's mode of living, he said, "Sir, the servants, instead of doing what they are bid, stand round the table in idle clusters, gaping upon the guests; and seem as unfit to attend a company, as to steer a man of war."

A dull country magistrate gave Johnson a long, tedious account of his exercising his criminal jurisdiction, the result of which was his having sentenced four convicts to transportation. Johnson, in an agony of impatience to get rid of such a companion, exclaimed, "I heartily wish, Sir, that I were a fifth."

Johnson was present when a tragedy was read, in which there occurred this line:

" Who rules o'er freemen should himself be free."

The company having admired it much, "I cannot agree with you (said Johnson:) It might as well be said,

' Who drives fat oxen should himself be fat.' "

Johnson having argued for some time with a pertinacious gentleman; his opponent, who had talked in a very puzzling manner, happened to say, "I don't understand you, Sir;" upon which Johnson observed, "Sir, I have found you an argument; but I am not obliged to find you an understanding."

He disapproved of Lord Hailes, for having modernised the language of the ever-memorable John Hales of Eton, in an edition which his Lordship published of that writer's works. "An authour's language, Sir, (said he,) is a characteristical part of his composition, and is also characteristical of the age in which he writes. Besides, Sir, when the language is changed we are not sure that the sense is the same. No, Sir; I am sorry Lord Hailes has done this."

Here it may be observed, that his frequent use of the expression, *No, Sir*, was not always to intimate contradiction; for he would say so when he was about to enforce an affirmative proposition which had not been denied, as in the instance last mentioned. I used to consider it as a kind of flag of defiance: as if he had said, "Any argument you may offer against this, is not just. No, Sir, it is not." It was like Falstaff's "I deny your Major."

Sir Joshua Reynolds having said that he took the altitude of a man's taste by his stories and his wit, and of his understanding by the remarks which he repeated; being always sure that he must be a weak man, who quotes common things with an emphasis as if they were oracles;—Johnson agreed with him; and Sir Joshua having also observed that the real character of a man was found out by his amusements;—Johnson added, "Yes, Sir; no man is a hypocrite in his pleasures."

Had Johnson treated at large *de Claris Oratoribus*,[1] he might have given us an admirable work. When the Duke of Bedford attacked the ministry as vehemently as he could, for having taken upon them to extend the time for the importation of corn, Lord Chatham, in his first speech in the House of Lords, boldly avowed himself to

[1] About famous speakers.

be an adviser of that measure. "My colleagues, (said he,) as I was confined by indisposition, did me the signal honour of coming to the bedside of a sick man, to ask his opinion. But, had they not thus condescended, I should have *taken up my bed and walked*, in order to have delivered that opinion at the Council-Board." Mr. Langton, who was present, mentioned this to Johnson, who observed, "Now, Sir, we see that he took these words as he found them; without considering, that though the expression in Scripture, *take up thy bed and walk*, strictly suited the instance of the sick man restored to health and strength, who would of course be supposed to carry his bed with him, it could not be proper in the case of a man who was lying in a state of feebleness, and who certainly would not add to the difficulty of moving at all, that of carrying his bed."

When I pointed out to him in the news-paper one of Mr. Grattan's animated and glowing speeches, in favour of the freedom of Ireland, in which this expression occurred (I know not if accurately taken): "We will persevere, till there is not one link of the English chain left to clank upon the rags of the meanest beggar in Ireland;"—"Nay, Sir, (said Johnson,) don't you perceive that *one* link cannot clank?"

An authour of most anxious and restless vanity being mentioned, "Sir, (said he,) there is not a young sapling upon Parnassus more severely blown about by every wind of criticism than that poor fellow."

The difference, he observed, between a well-bred and an ill-bred man is this: "One immediately attracts your liking, the other your aversion. You love the one till you find reason to hate him; you hate the other till you find reason to love him."

The wife of one of his acquaintance had fraudulently made a purse for herself out of her husband's fortune. Feeling a proper compunction in her last moments, she confessed how much she had secreted; but before she could tell where it was placed, she was seized with a convulsive fit and expired. Her husband said, he was more hurt by her want of confidence in him, than by the loss of his money. "I told him, (said Johnson,) that he should console himself: for *perhaps* the money might be *found*, and he was *sure* that his wife was *gone*."

A foppish physician once reminded Johnson of his having been in company with him on a former occasion, "I do not remember it, Sir." The physician still insisted; adding that he that day wore so fine a coat that it must have attracted his notice. "Sir, (said Johnson,) had you been dipt in Pactolus, I should not have noticed you."

He seemed to take pleasure in speaking in his own style; for when he had carelessly missed it, he would repeat the thought translated into it. Talking of the Comedy of "The Rehearsal," he said, "It has not wit enough to keep it sweet." This was easy;—he therefore caught himself, and pronounced a more round sentence; "It has not vitality enough to preserve it from putrefaction."

He censured a writer of entertaining Travels for assuming a feigned character, saying, (in his sense of the word,) "He carries out one lye; we know not how many he brings back." At another time, talking of the same person, he observed, "Sir, your assent to a man whom you have never known to falsify, is a debt: but after you have known a man to falsify, your assent to him then is a favour."

No man was more ready to make an apology when he had censured unjustly, than Johnson. When a proof-sheet of one of his works was brought to him, he found fault with the mode in which a part of it was arranged, refused to read it, and in a passion desired that the compositor might be sent to him. The compositor was Mr. Manning, a decent sensible man, who had composed about one half of his *Dictionary*, when in Mr. Strahan's printing-house; and a great part of his *Lives of the Poets*, when in that of Mr. Nichols; and who (in his seventy-seventh year) when in Mr. Baldwin's printing-house, composed a part of the first edition of this work concerning him. By producing the manuscript, he at once satisfied Dr. Johnson that he was not to blame. Upon which Johnson candidly and earnestly said to him, "Mr. Compositor, I ask your pardon; Mr. Compositor, I ask your pardon, again and again."

He once in his life was known to have uttered what is called a *bull*: Sir Joshua Reynolds, when they were riding together in Devonshire, complained that he had a very bad horse, for that even when going down hill he moved slowly step by step. "Ay (said Johnson,) and when he *goes* up hill, he *stands still*."

He had a great aversion to gesticulating in company. He called once to a gentleman who offended him in that point, "Don't *attitudenise*." And when another gentleman thought he was giving additional force to what he uttered, by expressive movements of his hands, Johnson fairly seized them, and held them down.

An authour of considerable eminence having engrossed a good

share of the conversation in the company of Johnson, and having said nothing but what was trifling and insignificant; Johnson when he was gone, observed to us, "It is wonderful what a difference there sometimes is between a man's powers of writing and of talking. ****** writes with great spirit, but is a poor talker; had he held his tongue, we might have supposed him to have been restrained by modesty; but he has spoken a great deal to-day; and you have heard what stuff it was."

A gentleman having said that a *congé d'elire* has not, perhaps, the force of a command, but may be considered only as a strong recommendation;—"Sir, (replied Johnson, who overheard him,) it is such a recommendation, as if I should throw you out of a two pair of stairs window, and recommend to you to fall soft."

On Sunday, June 27, I found him rather better. I mentioned to him a young man who was going to Jamaica with his wife and children, in expectation of being provided for by two of her brothers settled in that island, one a clergyman, and the other a physician. JOHNSON: "It is a wild scheme, Sir, unless he has a positive and deliberate invitation. There was a poor girl, who used to come about me, who had a cousin in Barbadoes, that, in a letter to her, expressed a wish she should come out to that Island, and expatiated on the comforts and happiness of her situation. The poor girl went out: her cousin was much surprized, and asked her how she could think of coming. 'Because, (said she,) you invited me.'—'Not I,' answered the cousin. The letter was then produced. 'I see it is true, (said she,) that I did invite you: but I did not think you would come.' They lodged her in an outhouse, where she passed her time miserably; and as soon as she had an opportunity she returned to England. Always tell this, when you hear of people going abroad to relations, upon a notion of being well received. In the case which you mention, it is probable the clergyman spends all he gets, and the physician does not know how much he is to get."

We this day dined at Sir Joshua Reynolds's, with General Paoli, Lord Eliot, (formerly Mr. Eliot, of Port Eliot,) Dr. Beattie and some other company. Talking of Lord Chesterfield;—JOHNSON: "His manner was exquisitely elegant, and he had more knowledge than I expected." BOSWELL: "Did you find, Sir, his conversation to be of a superiour style?" JOHNSON: "Sir, in the conversation which I had with him I had the best right to superiority, for it was upon philology and literature." Lord Eliot, who had travelled at the same time with Mr. Stanhope, Lord Chesterfield's natural son, justly observed, that it was strange that a man who shewed he had so much affection for his son as Lord Chesterfield did, by writing so many long and anxious letters to him, almost all of them when he was Secretary of State, which certainly was a proof of great goodness of disposition, should endeavour to make his son a rascal. His Lordship told us, that Foote had intended to bring on the stage a father who had thus tutored his son, and to shew the son an honest man to every one else, but practising his father's maxims upon him, and cheating him. JOHNSON: "I am much pleased with this design; but I think there was no occasion to make the son honest at all. No; he should be a consummate rogue: the contrast between honesty and knavery would be the stronger. It should be contrived so that the father should be the only sufferer by the son's villany, and thus there would be poetical justice."

An addition to our company came after we went up to the drawing-room; Dr. Johnson seemed to rise in spirits as his audience increased. He said, "He wished Lord Orford's pictures, and Sir Ashton Lever's Museum, might be purchased by the publick, because both the money, and the pictures, and the curiosities would remain in the country; whereas if they were sold into another kingdom, the nation would indeed get some money, but would lose the pictures and curiosities, which it would be desirable we should have, for improvement in taste and natural history. The only question was, as the nation was much in want of money, whether it would not be better to take a large price from a foreign State?"

He entered upon a curious discussion of the difference between intuition and sagacity; one being immediate in its effect, the other requiring a circuitous process; one he observed was the *eye* of the mind, the other the *nose* of the mind.

A young gentleman present took up the argument against him, and maintained that no man ever thinks of the *nose of the mind*, not adverting that though that figurative sense seems strange to us, as very unusual, it is truly not more forced than Hamlet's "In my *mind's eye*, Horatio." He persisted much too long, and appeared to Johnson as putting himself forward as his antagonist with too much presumption: upon which he called to him in a loud tone, "What is it you are contending for if you *be* contending?"—And afterwards imagining that the gentleman retorted upon him with a kind of smart drollery, he said, " Mr. ***** it does not become you to talk so to me. Besides, ridicule is not your talent; you have *there* neither intuition nor sagacity."—The gentleman protested that he had intended no improper freedom, but had the greatest respect for Dr. Johnson. After a short pause, during which we were somewhat uneasy.—JOHNSON: "Give me your hand, Sir. You were too tedious, and I was too short." Mr. *****, "Sir, I am honoured by your attention in any way." JOHNSON: "Come, Sir, let's have no more of it. We offended one another by our contention; let us not offend the company by our compliments."

[Boswell left London on July 1st.]

CHAPTER XV

Dr. John's Last Days

In 1784 he visited Lichfield, his native city, for the last time.

To Mr. Henry White, a young clergyman, with whom he now formed an intimacy, so as to talk to him with great freedom, he mentioned that he could not in general accuse himself of having been an undutiful son. "Once, indeed, (said he,) I was disobedient; I refused to attend my father to Uttoxeter-market. Pride was the source of that refusal, and the remembrance of it was painful. A few years ago I desired to atone for this fault. I went to Uttoxeter in very bad weather, and stood for a considerable time bareheaded in the rain, on the spot where my father's stall used to stand. In contrition I stood, and I hope the penance was expiatory."

"I told him (says Miss Seward) in one of my latest visits to him, of a wonderful learned pig, which I had seen at Nottingham; and which did all that we have observed exhibited by dogs and horses. The subject amused him. 'Then, (said he,) the pigs are a race unjustly calumniated. *Pig* has, it seems, not been wanting to *man*, but *man* to *pig*. We do not allow *time* for his education, we kill him at a year old.' Mr. Henry White, who was present, observed that if this instance had happened in or before Pope's time, he would not have been justified in instancing the swine as the lowest degree of grovelling instinct. Dr. Johnson seemed pleased with the observation, while the person who made it proceeded to remark, that great torture must have been employed, ere the indocility of the animal could have been subdued.—'Certainly, (said the Doctor;) but, (turning to me,) how old is your pig?' I told him, three years old. 'Then, (said he,) the pig has no cause to complain; he would have been killed the first year if he had not been *educated*, and protracted existence is a good recompence for very considerable degrees of torture.'"

Soon after Johnson's return to the metropolis, both the asthma and dropsy became more violent and distressful. He had for some time kept a journal in Latin of the state of his illness, and the remedies which he used, under the title of *Ægri Ephemeris*, which he began on the 6th of July, but continued it no longer than the 8th of November; finding, I suppose, that it was a mournful and unavailing register. It is in my possession; and is written with great care and accuracy.

During his last illness, Johnson experienced the steady and kind attachment of his numerous friends. Mr. Hoole has drawn up a narrative of what passed in the visits which he paid him during the time, from the 10th of November to the 13th of December, 1784, the day of his death, inclusive, and has favoured me with a perusal of it, with permission to make extracts, which I have done. Nobody was more attentive to him than Mr. Langton, to whom he tenderly said, *Te teneam moriens deficiente manu.*[1] And I think it highly to the honour of Mr. Windham, that his important occupations as an active statesman did not prevent him from paying assiduous respect to the dying Sage whom he revered. Mr. Langton informs me, that, "one day he found Mr. Burke and four or five more friends sitting with Johnson. Mr. Burke said to him, 'I am afraid Sir, such a number of us may be oppressive to you.'—'No, Sir, (said Johnson,) it is not so; and I must be in a wretched state, indeed, when your company would not be a delight to me.' Mr. Burke, in a tremulous voice, expressive of being very tenderly affected, replied, 'My dear Sir, you have always been too good to me.' Immediately afterwards he went away. This was the last circumstance in the acquaintance of these two eminent men."

The following particulars of his conversation within a few days of his death, I give on the authority of Mr. John Nichols:

"He said, that the Parliamentary Debates were the only part of his writings which then gave him any compunction: but that at the time he wrote them, he had no conception he was imposing upon the world, though they were frequently written from very slender materials, and often, from none at all,—the mere coinage of his own imagination. He never wrote any part of his works with equal velocity. Three columns of the *Magazine*, in an hour, was no uncommon effort, which was faster than most persons could have transcribed that quantity.

"Of his friend Cave, he always spoke with great affection. 'Yet, (said he,) Cave, (who never looked out of his window, but with a view to the *Gentleman's Magazine*,) was a penurious paymaster; he would contract for lines by the hundred, and expect

[1] When I die may I hold you with my weakening hand.

314

the long hundred; but he was a good man, and always delighted to have his friends at his table.'

"He said at another time, three or four days only before his death, speaking of the little fear he had of undergoing a chirurgical operation, 'I would give one of these legs for a year more of life, I mean of comfortable life, not such as that which I now suffer;'—and lamented much his inability to read during his hours of restlessness. 'I used formerly, (he added,) when sleepless in bed, *to read like a Turk.*'

"Whilst confined by his last illness, it was his regular practice to have the church-service read to him, by some attentive and friendly Divine. The Rev. Mr. Hoole performed this kind office in my presence for the last time, when, by his own desire, no more than the litany was read; in which his responses were in the deep and sonorous voice which Mr. Boswell has occasionally noticed, and with the most profound devotion that can be imagined. His hearing not being quite perfect, he more than once interrupted Mr. Hoole, with, 'Louder, my dear Sir, louder, I entreat you, or you pray in vain!'—and, when the service was ended, he, with great earnestness, turned round to an excellent lady who was present, saying, 'I thank you, Madam, very heartily, for your kindness in joining me in this solemn exercise. Live well, I conjure you; and you will not feel the compunction at the last, which I now feel.' So truly humble were the thoughts which this great and good man entertained of his own approaches to religious perfection."

Amidst the melancholy clouds which hung over the dying Johnson, his characteristical manner shewed itself on different occasions.

When Dr. Warren in the usual style, hoped that he was better; his answer was, "No, Sir; you cannot conceive with what acceleration I advance towards death."

A man whom he had never seen before was employed one night to sit up with him. Being asked next morning how he liked his attendant, his answer was, "Not at all, Sir: the fellow's an idiot; he is aukward as a turn-spit when first put into the wheel, and as sleepy as a dormouse."

Mr. Windham having placed a pillow conveniently to support him, he thanked him for his kindness, and said, "That will do,—all that a pillow can do."

Johnson, with that native fortitude, which, amidst all his bodily

315

distress and mental sufferings, never forsook him, asked Dr. Brocklesby, as a man in whom he had confidence, to tell him plainly whether he could recover. "Give me (said he) a direct answer." The Doctor having first asked him if he could bear the whole truth, which way soever it might lead, and being answered that he could, declared that, in his opinion, he could not recover without a miracle. "Then, (said Johnson,) I will take no more physick, not even my opiates: for I have prayed that I may render up my soul to God unclouded." In that resolution he persevered, and, at the same time, used only the weakest kinds of sustenance. Being pressed by Mr. Windham to take somewhat more generous nourishment, lest too low a diet should have the very effect which he dreaded, by debilitating his mind, he said, "I will take any thing but inebriating sustenance."

Having made his will on the 8th and 9th of December, and settled all his worldly affairs, he languished till Monday, the 13th of that month, when he expired about seven o'clock in the evening, with so little apparent pain that his attendants hardly perceived when his dissolution took place.

Of his last moments, my brother, Thomas David, has furnished me with the following particulars:

"The Doctor, from the time that he was certain his death was near, appeared to be perfectly resigned; was seldom or never fretful or out of temper, and often said to his faithful servant, who gave me this account, 'Attend, Francis to the salvation of your soul which is the object of greatest importance:' he also explained to him passages in the scripture, and seemed to have pleasure in talking upon religious subjects.

"On Monday, the 13th of December, the day on which he died, a Miss Morris, daughter to a particular friend of his called, and said to Francis, that she begged to be permitted to see the Doctor, that she might earnestly request him to give her his blessing. Francis went into his room, followed by the young lady, and delivered the message. The Doctor turned himself in the bed, and said, 'God bless you, my dear!' These were the last words he spoke.—His difficulty of breathing increased till about seven o'clock in the evening, when Mr. Barber and Mrs. Desmoulins, who were sitting in the room, observing that the noise he made in breathing had ceased, went to the bed, and found he was dead."

Graham, Lord: 247, 248
Grainger, Dr: 144
Granville, John Carteret: 258
Grattan, Henry: 308
Gravina: 279
Gray, Sir James: 84
Gray, Thomas: 23, 114–5
Greece and the Greeks: 81, 82, 162, 235
Greek language: 40, 53, 130, 259
Grey, Sir Richard. 230
Grey, Dr Zachary: 229–30
Grief: 177, 178
Grotius: 39, 136
Gulliver's Travels: 112
Gwyn, Mr: 139, 140

Hackman, Rev: 248, 249
Hailes, Lord: 180, 307
Hale, Lord Chief Justice: 76
Hales, John: 307
Hall, Mrs: 263
Happiness: 32, 33, 34, 37, 46, 53, 77, 78, 79, 94, 97, 103, 122, 126, 135, 144, 150, 153, 188, 199, 215, 218, 285
Harris, Mr: 96, 203, 204, 205
Harte, Dr Walter: 258
Harwood, Dr: 164
Hawkesworth, Dr: 104, 153
Hawkins, Sir John: 143
Hawkins, Thomas: 205
Hay, Lord Charles: 154
Hector, Edmund: 145, 146, 147
Henderland, Lord: 154
Henderson, John: 302
Henry VIII: 255
Hermippus Redivivus: 26, 135
Hervey, Thomas: 118
Hicky, Thomas: 118
Higgins, Dr: 250
Hill, Dr John: 214
History and historians: 28, 57, 90, 101, 128, 157
History of Animated Nature: 157
History of Ireland: 109
History of Scotland: 51, 259
Hodge, Johnson's cat: 279
Holland: 43, 182, 193
Hollis, Thomas: 264
Home, John: 113, 175
Homer: 21, 203, 235
Honesty: 50, 166, 195
Hoole, John: 116, 163, 261, 276, 277, 295, 314, 315
Horace: 57, 126, 141, 230, 245, 252, 286
Horrebow: 211
Hospitality: 80, 95, 210, 234, 289
House of Commons: 77, 124, 190, 191, 194, 195, 255, 267, 272, 288, 295, 302
House of Lords: 32, 77, 82, 154, 169, 255, 307
Hudibras: 129, 163
Hume, David: 35, 41, 46, 51, 70, 101, 179, 186, 187, 297

Hunting: 194
Hurd, Dr, Bishop of Worcester: 277
Hypocrite, The: 113

Idleness: 30, 65, 80, 117, 217, 253–4, 275
Idler, The: 16
Iliad, The: 235
Imagination: 25, 27, 28, 239, 272
Immortality: 45, 126, 187
India and Indians: 90, 119, 253, 284, 296
Industry: 135, 168, 217, 274
Infidels and infidelity: 24, 45, 48, 58, 64, 106, 126, 142–3, 168, 179, 256, 297
Ireland and Irishmen: 66, 77, 103, 109, 193, 196, 256, 308
Irish language: 121
Italy and Italians: 73, 119, 162, 202

James II: 31, 119, 248
Jennings, Mr: 192
Jenyns, Soame: 167, 215, 216
Jews: 299
Johnston, Sir James: 295
Jonathan Wild: 299
Jones, Phil: 141
Jones, Sir William: 102, 250
Joseph Andrews: 83
Journals: 275
Journey to the Hebrides: 206
Journeys to the Western Islands of Scotland: 127, 222
Judges: 28, 50, 119–20, 123
Junius: 79, 246, 304

Kames, Lord: 51, 242
Kennedy, Dr: 196
Kennicot, Mrs: 296, 297, 303
Kenrick, Dr: 203
Ketch, Jack: 170
Killaloe, Bishop of: 265, 269
Kindness: 137, 169, 269
Kneller, Sir Godfrey: 195
Knowledge: 22, 26, 36, 39, 40, 82, 91, 104, 110, 125, 126, 128, 163, 222, 235, 236, 272
Knowles, Mrs: 176, 213, 215, 216, 219, 220, 221

Land: 67, 68, 120, 135, 136, 271
Landlords and tenants: 25, 67, 118, 271
Langton, Bennet: 53, 88, 98, 103, 109, 112, 117, 118, 121, 122, 144, 200, 204, 205, 211, 212, 232, 233, 237, 238, 250, 257, 258, 279, 282, 294–5, 296, 308, 314